MW00786925

Whom Gods Destroy

Whom Gods Destroy

ELEMENTS OF GREEK
AND TRAGIC MADNESS

Ruth Padel

PRINCETON UNIVERSITY PRESS

PRINCETON, NEW JERSEY

Copyright © 1995 by Princeton University Press
Published by Princeton University Press, 41 William Street,
Princeton, New Jersey 08540
In the United Kingdom: Princeton University Press, Chichester, West Sussex

All Rights Reserved

Library of Congress Cataloging-in-Publication Data

Padel, Ruth, 1946–
Whom Gods destroy : elements of Greek and tragic madness /
by Ruth Padel.
p. cm.
Includes bibliographical references and index.
ISBN 0-691-03360-9 (CL)
1. Greek drama (Tragedy)—History and criticism.   2. Literature
and mental illness—Greece.   3. Mythology, Greek, in literature.
4. Mentally ill in literature.   5. Gods, Greek, in literature.   I. Title.
PA3131.P23   1995   882'.0109—dc20   94-25529

This book has been composed in Galliard

Princeton University Press books are printed on acid-free paper
and meet the guidelines for permanence and durability of the
Committee on Production Guidelines for Book Longevity of the
Council on Library Resources

Printed in the United States of America

3   5   7   9   10   8   6   4   2

For Myles

Much love

CONTENTS

PREFACE AND ACKNOWLEDGMENTS

THIS IS A book of ingredients. Not of madness, but of how madness has been seen and represented. It argues that the grammar of Western responses to madness is basically both Greek and tragic. That elements of madness as tragedy represents it are still at work in us, though we use them differently. The societies that handed on the tradition changed things. After the Greeks, tragedy went on finding madness useful. The old images of madness continued, but their resonance and value changed.

The book is built round three images that dominate Greek representation of madness: darkness, wandering, and damage. It aims to lay out the elements of Greek tragic thoughts about madness, and also, in some cases, to follow these through: to mark how Greek tragic madness struck later ages, and how these other ages (especially the Renaissance and the nineteenth century) changed the Greek picture. I consider how the images in their changed form encourage us to misunderstand the Greeks and distort our reading of them. Towards the end (Chapter 21) I discuss what this might mean for psychoanalysts responding to the Greek material.

I have written for anyone generally interested in madness and the self, in tragedy, or in Greek culture. The work is based on the Greek tragedies. I translate and transliterate linguistic material, and make this as welcoming as possible to non-Greek readers. There *are* a lot of words. I've tried to make them go down easy. If you want to give language a miss, skip Chapters 2 and 3, the second, third, and fourth sections of Chapter 12, Chapter 16, and parts of Chapter 17.

But I have also written for specialists: historians of madness and ideas, classicists and students of Greek society, readers of tragedy from all epochs. Also for anthropologists and psychoanalysts interested in ways of reading madness from another culture and time.

Many thanks for questions answered to Natsu Hatton, Jane Haynes, Roy Porter, and Francois Rigolot. To people who read and commented on drafts long ago, including Anne Barton, Mary Lefkowitz, Godfrey Lienhardt, Geoffrey Lloyd, Hugh Lloyd-Jones, Charles Rycroft, Christiane Sourvinou-Inwood, and Tom Stinton. To the supervisors of my D.Phil. thesis long ago, E. R. Dodds and Hugh Lloyd-Jones, and its examiners, John Gould and Tony Long. Also to Edward Fitzgerald, who first put Foucault in my hands; my brothers Oliver and Felix; and especially my father, John Padel, who has read many drafts over many years and never fails to come up with new perceptions and new literary associations, as well as guiding me through his psychoanalytic library. Thanks also to the

Tyrone Guthrie Centre, Annaghmakerrig, where I finished several chapters. It gave me a lot of pleasure to work among the books of someone who gave his life to drama, whose productions made Greek tragedy live in new ways, and who left his home for people making new things. Thanks also to the Wingate Foundation, for assistance on another project that also helped to fund this one. To Jane Davies, for unfailing sympathetic help on computers, and for the Toshiba. To the Wellcome Institute, for inviting me to seminars on the history of madness and medicine that I much enjoyed. To Froma Zeitlin, who said *mega biblion mega kakon* at me and introduced me to Princeton University Press. And to my wonderful copy editor, Alice Falk.

Above all, to Myles Burnyeat. For encouragement, criticism, and rubbing my nose in philosophers; for help with child care, books, lucidity, and Plato. I couldn't have done this book without him.

I gratefully make acknowledgments to the following: *Granta*, for permission to reprint material from Ian Hamilton, *Gazza Agonistes*, © 1993 by Ian Hamilton; Christopher Logue, for permission to quote from *War Music*, © 1981 C. Logue; Penguin Books [Peters Fraser and Dunlop], for permission to reprint material from James Fenton, *Out of Danger*, © 1993 James Fenton, and Carter Dickson, *The Red Widow Murders*, © 1935 John Dickson Carr; Victor Gollanz [Henry Holt], for permission to reprint material from Hannah Green, *I Never Promised You a Rose Garden*, © 1964 Hannah Green; Bloodaxe Books, for permission to reprint material from Brendan Kennelly, *Breathing Spaces*, © 1993 Brendan Kennelly; and Faber [Farrar Straus Giroux] for permission to reprint material from Derek Walcott, *Omeros*, © 1990 Derek Walcott.

ABBREVIATIONS

THIS LIST contains abbreviations of periodicals, authors, and texts, but no editions. Fragments sometimes have their editor's name or initial after their number. "A. fr. 156N" means "Aeschylus," "fragment 156 in Nauck's edition." No commentaries are included either: these appear by editor's name on particular lines specified by *ad* or *ad loc*. Texts, lexicons, and editions are not normally included in the bibliography.

Homer, Hesiod, Aeschylus, Sophocles, and Euripides are abbreviated by title, not author (except fragments and the plays whose titles overlap, S. *El.*, E. *El.*, A. *Supp.*, E. *Supp.*). Where there is a Loeb volume of a Hippocratic work, I give its volume and page number in parentheses; the main references are to Littré's edition. Pre-Socratics are referred to by DK number, or number and page number in KRS or KR.

A. = Aeschylus
Ag. = A. *Agamemnon*
Aj. = S. *Ajax*
Alc. = E. *Alcestis*
Anaxag. = Anaxagoras
Andr. = E. *Andromache*
Ant. = S. *Antigone*
AP = *Anthologia Palatina*
Apollod. = Apollodorus
Ar. = Aristophanes:
  Ach. = *Acharnians*
  Av. = *Birds*
  Ecc. = *Ecclesiazousae*
  Eq. = *Knights*
  Lys. = *Lysistrata*
  Nub. = *Clouds*
  Pl. = *Plutus*
  Ran. = *Frogs*
  Thesm. = *Thesmophoriazousae*
  V. = *Wasps*
Archil. = Archilochus
Arist. = Aristotle:
  Cat. = *Categories*
  EE = *Eudemian Ethics*
  EN = *Nicomachean Ethics*

HA = *Historia animalium*
Met. = *Metaphysica*
PA = *De partibus animalium*
Poet. = *Poetics*
Pol. = *Politics*
Rh. = *Rhetoric*
Ba. = E. *Bacchae*
Bacc. = Bacchylides
BICS = *Bulletin of the Institute of Classical Studies*
Call. = Callimachus
Cho. = A. *Choephoroe*
Cic. = Cicero:
  TD = *Tusculan Disputations*
Cyc. = E. *Cyclops*
Dem. = Demosthenes
DK = H. Diels and W. Kranz, *Die Fragmente der Vorsokratiker*, 6th ed., 3
    vols. (Berlin 1951–52)
D.L. = Diogenes Laertius
E. = Euripides
El. = *Electra*
Emp. = Empedocles
Epich. = Epicharmus
Erg. = Hes. *Works and Days*
Eum. = A. *Eumenides*
H. = Homer
h. Dem. = H. *Hymn to Demeter*
h. Merc. = H. *Hymn to Hermes*
Hdt. = Herodotus
Hec. = E. *Hecuba*
Hel. = E. *Helen*
Heraclid. = E. *Heraclidae*
Hes. = Hesiod
HF = E. *Hercules Furens*
Hipp. = E. *Hippolytus*
Hp. = Hippocratic author:
  Anc. Med. = *On Ancient Medicine*
  Aph. = *Aphorisms*
  Arthr. = *Peri Arthrōn Embolēs*
  AWP = *Airs Waters Places*
  Coac. = *Koakai Prognoseis*
  DMS = *On the Sacred Disease*
  Epid. I = *Epidemics I*
  Epid. III = *Epidemics III*

Fract. = *On Fractures*
Hum. = *Humors*
Mul. = *On Women*
Nat. Hom. = *De natura hominis*
Nat. Mul. = *De natura mulierum*
Progn. = *Prognostic*
Prorrh. = *Prorrhētikon*
Reg. Acut. Dis. = *Regimen in Acute Diseases*
HSCP = *Harvard Studies in Classical Philology*
IA = E. *Iphigeneia at Aulis*
Il. = H. *Iliad*
Ion = E. *Ion*
IT = E. *Iphigeneia among the Taurians*
KR = G. Kirk and J. E. Raven, *The Presocratic Philosophers* (Cambridge
      1957)
KRS = G. Kirk, J. E. Raven, and M. Schofield, *The Presocratic Philoso-*
      phers, 2d ed. (Cambridge 1983)
Leg. Gort. = *Gortyn Lawcode*
LSJ = H. G. Liddell, R. Scott, and H. S. Jones, *Greek-English Lexicon*
      (Oxford 1961)
Med. = E. *Medea*
Men. = Menander
OC = S. *Oedipus at Colonus*
OCT = Oxford Classical Text
Od. = H. *Odyssey*
Or. = E. *Orestes*
OT = S. *Oedipus Rex*
Paus. = Pausanias
PCPS = *Proceedings of the Cambridge Philological Society*
Pers. = A. *The Persians*
Phil. = S. *Philoctetes*
Phoen. E. *Phoenician Women*
Pi. = Pindar:
  I. = *Isthmian Odes*
  N. = *Nemean Odes*
  O. = *Olympian Odes*
  P. = *Pythian Odes*
Pl. = Plato:
  Apol. = *Apology*
  Charm. = *Charmides*
  Crat. = *Cratylus*
  Euthyd. = *Euthydemus*
  Hipp. Min. = *Hippias Minor*

Legg. = *Laws*
Phd. = *Phaedo*
Phdr. = *Phaedrus*
Phlb. = *Philebus*
Rep. = *Republic*
Symp. = *Symposium*
Ti. = *Timaeus*
Plot. = Plotinus
Pliny *NH* = Pliny *Natural History*
Plu. = Plutarch:
  Art. = *Artaxerxes*
  Mor. = *Moralia*
PV = A. *Prometheus Bound*
S. = Sophocles
Schol. = Scholia
Sept. = A. *Seven against Thebes*
Supp. = *Suppliant Maidens*
TAPA = *Transactions of the American Philological Association*
Th. = Thucydides
Theoc. = Theocritus
Theog. = Hes. *Theogony*
Thgn. = Theognis
Thphr. = Theophrastus:
  Char. = *Characters*
  HP = *Historia plantarum*
Trach. = S. *Women of Trachis*
Trag. adesp. = *Tragica Adespota* ed. A. Nauck
Tro. = E. *Trojan Women*
V. = Virgil:
  Ec. = *Eclogues*
Xen. = Xenophon:
  An. = *Anabasis*
  Mem. = *Memorabilia*
  Symp. = *Symposium*
ZPE = *Zeitschrift für Papyrologie und Epigraphik*

Whom Gods Destroy

Chapter 1

INTRODUCTION: "HE FIRST MAKES MAD"

"Quem Deus Vult Perdere"

Quem deus vult perdere, dementat prius. "Whom God wishes to destroy, He first makes mad." Who first said that? And why?

It feels like a translation, a reworking of something Greek and tragic. Cicero maybe? Seneca? I think this is roughly right, but I do not think Romans had much to do with it, in spite of the Latin. That verb *dementare*, "make mad," is rare in Roman authors. Cicero and Seneca do not use it in their extant work.

The source was a puzzle even in Samuel Johnson's day. John Pitts wrote to Boswell discussing it. He mentioned "some gentlemen of Cambridge" who for a bet made a "long search" for the origin: "They found it among the fragments of Euripides, in what translation I do not recollect, where it is given as a translation of a Greek Iambic." No one knew at Oxford, either. Boswell and Johnson dined at University College in 1783. Boswell challenged the company to identify the source: "A pause. At last Dr Chandler said, in Horace. Another pause. Then Fisher remarked that he knew of no metre in Horace to which the words could be reduced: and Johnson said dictatorially, 'The young man is right.'" In his letter, Pitts produced a Greek version: *Hon theos thelei apolesai, prōt' apophrenai*, an exact rendering of the Latin. This Greek, he says, was found in the rooms of "Sir D. O., some years ago," after his suicide. Sir D. O. was "a man of classical acquirements: he left no other paper behind him."[1]

Was Sir D. O.'s Greek the source of the Latin tag? Unlikely that one British suicide had such influence. The Greek verb *apophrenai* is unknown even in late Greek. His Greek looks like a translation, perhaps by an Englishman, himself or someone else, of the Latin. So where does the *Latin* saying—which Pitts, incidentally, gives as *Quem Jupiter*, not *quem deus*—come from?

As far as I can track it in Britain, the Latin is a version of some different Greek lines. A version published in 1660 by an Englishman, James Duport, of a Greek fragment he attributes to Euripides. It is paraphrase rather than translation. A neutral translation of the Greek might run:

---

[1] See Birkbeck Hill 1888 4:181–82 n. 3; Birrell 1906 6:19–20, n. 1; Birkbeck Hill 1888 2:445 n. 1. Porter 1985 shows how deeply this line might have affected Johnson himself.

> When *daimōn* prepares evils for a man
> he first harms the *nous* [mind]
> of the man whom he advises.

Duport rendered this as *Quem Jupiter vult perdere, dementat prius*. Thirty-four years later, Joshua Barnes of Emmanuel College, in his 1694 edition of Euripides, borrowed Duport's Latin (substituting *deus* for "Jupiter"), and attributed the fragment to Euripides. You can find *Deus quos vult perdere, dementat prius* in his "Index Prior," under D.[2]

Where does this supposedly Euripidean fragment, on which the *dementat prius* is generally thought to be modelled, itself come from? Classical "fragments" do not float to us out of the blue. We meet them as quotations in other ancient authors. Why, for example, is it thought to be by Euripides?

It is quoted by an ancient commentator elucidating a passage in Sophocles' *Antigone*: part of the famous song on *atē*, "blind destructiveness." (We will meet *atē* extensively later.) Here are Sophocles' lines, on which this scholar comments:

> With wisdom some man
> spoke the famous saying
> that evil eventually seems good
> to the man whose *phrenes* [mind]
> *theos* [god] drives to *atē*.[3]

The ancient scholiast wants to explicate "the famous saying." He gives us our Greek fragment ("When *daimōn* . . .") to explain what Sophocles must mean here. In other words, he himself thinks this fragment is more ancient than *Antigone*, one of Sophocles' earlier extant plays. In his mind, at least, this fragment is actually earlier than Euripides.

Pitt's "gentlemen of Cambridge" may have amalgamated this fragment—which speaks not of destruction, but "preparing evils," not of madness, but damaging the *nous*—with Sir D. O.'s *apophrenai* line, which sounds, as I said, like a seventeenth-century Greek version of the Latin tag, familiar already by 1660.[4]

---

[2] *Trag. adesp.* 455N. See Duport 1660:282; King 1904:298.

[3] *Ant.* 620–25. *Phrenes, nous*: Padel 1992:20–23, 32–34. *Atē*: see below, Chapters 16, 17, Appendix.

[4] In France, the phrase appears in the pink pages of some editions of *Petit Larousse Illustré* and is traditionally attributed to Euripides as quoted by Athenagoras (*Hotan de daimōn* . . ."; Another Latin version is *At daemon homini quum struit aliquid malum / Pervertit illi primitus mentem suam*). There is no clue as to when the tag is first quoted in France: not from Erasmus's *Encomium Mori, Adagia*, nor the *Emblemata*, nor Montaigne's *Essays*, as far as I know. Racine does use similar expressions: cf. *Athalie*, 1.2, *in finem*. The tag was well-known by c. 1790. The hellenist Jean François Boissonade is credited with its use in scholarship.

But another iambic fragment is also involved. This one is quoted by a fourth-century B.C. Athenian orator, Lycurgus, who thinks it is very ancient, and clairvoyantly wise. The gods

> do nothing first but lead aside [*paragousi*] the understanding of bad human beings. Certain ancient poets seem to me to have left as it were oracles to those who came after, in these iambic lines:
>
> > When anger of *daimones* harms someone
> > it first does this: it takes away
> > the good *nous* from *phrenes*,
> > and turns it to the worse opinion,
> > that the man may know nothing
> > of errors he commits.[5]

There is here the same insistence on "firstness," but the epigrammatic pith and aggression, "wishes to destroy," is missing. These lines spell a lot out. They sound clumsy in translation; they do in Greek too. They are not exactly the *dementat prius*. But they work in the same area.

What this shows, I think, is that the urge to give to this thought a Greek iambic, specifically a Greek tragic source (Greek tragic dialogue is in iambic meter), has been going since the fourth century B.C., the century after the extant tragedies. The urge was given new impetus in the seventeenth century, and was widespread in the eighteenth.

It has been important to hear this thought expressed in an ancient language; as if it expressed something so horribly true that we *want* it to be ancient. Ancient, Greek, and tragic: the adjectives give it a pedigree.

Our consciousness of the *dementat prius* derives, therefore, from ancient comments on and consciousness of tragedy, going back to the fourth century, when tragedy was already felt to be clairvoyantly concerned with the damage gods do us: and do us "first" through the mind.

Christianity both sharpened and gentled things here. Sharpened by the shocking thought that the God of Love could "harden the heart" to allow sin, which He Himself will punish. This thought comes early in the Christian tradition, in the internal conflict of St. Paul over his new relationship to "my brethren, my kinsmen according to the flesh," the Jews. "I have," he says, "great heaviness and continual sorrow in my heart." He resolves it in two ways. First, human beings both are and are not what they seem. "They are not all Israel, which are of Israel." Second, God too is seen in an internally divided way which mirrors the writer's conflicted loyalties: "What shall we say then? Is there unrighteousness with God? God forbid. For He says to Moses, I will have mercy on whom I will have mercy and I

---

[5] Lycurgus *Contra Leocratem* 92 (= *Trag. adesp.* 296N).

will have compassion on whom I will have compassion. So it is not of him that wills, nor of him that runs, but of God that shows mercy. . . . He has mercy on whom He will have mercy, and whom He will He hardens."[6] "And whom He will He hardens." It is a devastating thing to say. Paul's following questions mark his *angst* on this point: "Has not the potter power over the clay, of the same lump to make one vessel unto honour, another unto dishonour?" He argues for divine justice and purpose: Israel stumbled. The Israelites did not attain righteousness, because they sought it by law not faith. But their fall may be "the riches of the world." They are the branches broken off a tree onto which Gentiles, like the Roman Christians to whom he is writing, are grafted. This is a pruning operation. God "concluded them all in unbelief, that He might have mercy upon all."[7]

Paul ends this self-conflicted passage by saying of God, "How unsearchable are His judgements, and His ways past finding out. For who has known the mind of the Lord? . . . of Him, and through Him, and to Him, are all things. . . ."[8] Here is the problem, conflict, and conclusion, in this most dramatic Christian questioning of the essential cause of self-destructiveness. The prayer "Lead us not into temptation [*peirasmon*, 'struggle, testing']" has real fear behind it. Leading into temptation is something God can do. Has done.[9]

The problem is knotted into legal and moral questions raised by madness well into the nineteenth century, and also in our own time. The first British acquittal on grounds of unsound mind is in 1505.[10] The first recorded instance of "psychiatric testimony" in British criminal courts is the trial of Earl Ferrers, in 1760. The earl defended himself on grounds of "occasional insanity." "My lords," said Dr. John Monro, superintendent of Bethlem, "in some sense, every crime proceeds from insanity. There were philosophers in ancient times who held this opinion." The Solicitor General addressed the jury on the subject of madness as exculpatory condition. But the defense was rejected. The earl was executed.[11]

The *dementat prius*, stressing divine responsibility for madness, is quoted particularly in the eighteenth century, which opened up the general possibility that madness was intellectual delusion.[12] Yet at the same time,

---

[6] Romans 9.3, 2, 6, 14–18. All New Testament citations are quoted from the English Authorized Version.

[7] Romans 9.21, 9.32, 11.12, 11.22, 11.32.

[8] Romans 11.33–36.

[9] Dodds 1951:63 (with n. 112).

[10] Walker 1968:26.

[11] Eigen 1985:37.

[12] Walker 1968 gives the legal question a historical perspective from the thirteenth century onwards. Eighteenth century: Foucault 1971:157; MacDonald 1981:230; Porter 1985:76–81; Porter 1987. See below, Chapter 19; see also Chapter 21, nn. 27, 31.

"the only belief-system within which people could *acknowledge themselves as mad* was a religious one." If someone else was mad, it was another story. "Within secular values, insanity . . . was wholly negative, meaningless; unreason betokened utter personal and social nothingness."[13] As the religious force of madness recedes from sane educated minds, the tag *quem vult perdere prius dementat*, with its unfathomed history, is constantly quoted. "Perhaps no scrap of Latin has been more quoted than this."[14]

The problem the words raise is an area of heat and complexity in the whole history of Christian legal, medical, and social institutions. But it goes back to Greek tragic thought. A steadfast element in Paul's conclusion to the terrifying idea that God might actually cause the emotional "hardness" that produces sin is that "all things are of God."

This answer too is shared with tragedy, and could be said to have been influenced, via the Hellenistic philosophers, by tragedy; though that does not make it less real for latecomers in the Greek tradition, like Paul. At the end of Sophocles' *Women of Trachis*, the chorus is told:

> You have seen huge, strange deaths,
> many miseries and weird suffering.
> And none of these is not Zeus.[15]

Zeus loved his son Heracles. But all this suffering, for Heracles and his family, "is" Zeus.

The idea that gods control all human affairs, not necessarily kindly or for our good, is basic Greek. "Apollo was these things," says Oedipus, newly self-blinded.[16] Expression of the thought is given particular edge in tragedy, and especially often in relation to madness. In later ages, madness is often linked with transgression of divine law. But Greek tragedy excels in the possibility, reflected even in Christian thought, that gods themselves can cause transgression.

Christianity, through redemption and divine purpose, can gentle the shock of this. By "hardening the heart," God creates a scenario in which He punishes the fallen part of human nature: the soul will find redemption through suffering, atoning for its crime. Greek tragedy faces the *dementat prius* unsoftened. Tragedy speaks in manifold ways to the divine cause of human destruction:

> God plants the cause in mortals
> when he wants to destroy a house entirely.

---

[13] Porter 1987:268.
[14] King 1904:298.
[15] *Trach.* 1276–79; see Easterling *ad loc.*
[16] *OT* 1329. See both Jebb and Easterling *ad. Trach.* 1278.

The "cause" is often identified with madness. In Homer, *atē* is "sent" or "given" by gods. In tragedy, "reckless *mania*" is *theothen*, "from god."[17]

In the *dementat prius* corridor of expressions about madness and divinity, there is a lot of looking back. We shall see how tragedy's own uses of madness looked back to the Homeric concept of *atē*.[18] Educated eighteenth-century men chatter and die with Christian-touched versions of these ancient comments on their lips. Faced with madness and self-destruction in their own life, they found the thought consoling that such violent lonely paths were trodden and explained in an ancient past. "Ancient poets seem as it were to have left oracles. . . ." The "suicide of fashion" left his last lines in an ancient language. There was, perhaps still is, a need to believe that divine causality behind human self-destruction in mind and life is an ancient, therefore authoritative, idea.

Each wave of poetry or theology is commenting on its own sense of a past. Past explanations of suffering come alive in you as you suffer yourself; and so they seem clairvoyant. In Boswell's day, *dementat prius* is a saying which everybody repeats, but nobody knows where to find. Continually mystified by the source of madness, Western culture attributes and reattributes it to tragedy or tragic verse.

All this reflects three things. The ongoing pain of the problem: what *is* the source of human self-destruction? A feeling that Greek tragedians made this question their business. And a feeling that madness is central to the ways they explored it.

A THEATER OF MAD GODS

Images of madness have played an important role in Greek tragedy's influence on Western imagination. Yet Greek assumptions about madness are very different from most around today in the Western world. They belong with a picture of emotion's relation to self, of the experience of emotion, that is alien to ours. Emotion is something coming at you from outside. When thought of physiologically, emotion is air and liquid bubbling within, swelling the entrails. Emotions do not belong to individuals. They are wandering, autonomous, daemonic, outside forces.[19]

This vision of emotion entails a chasm between understandings of madness available in fifth-century Athens and our own, which are based on ideas of the structure and dynamics of a personality, and are infused by a

---

[17] A. frr. 156N, 319N; *Il.* 19.88; *Od.* 4.261. *Atē* "sent" or given in Homer: below, pp. 173, 178.

[18] See Chapters 18, 19.

[19] Padel 1992:81–98, 114–61.

nineteenth-century notion of madness as a secret presence, latent and indi-vidual to the self.[20]

There are many further differences between our pictures of madness and theirs. Yet our picturings of madness are based on these Greek beginnings. So there is a paradox in our relationship to these Greek ideas. They helped to form ours. But, due to the millennia of change in between, ours now are extraordinarily different. This is why I spend time (see Chapters 16 and 17) on the background: on what came before tragedy itself.

This is a book by someone from one culture, about how madness was seen in another. That operation needs a lot of disentangling. I try to keep an anthropological strictness, as I conceive it, and place ideas of madness in the grain of the culture that produced them. But I also introduce new elements from the centuries between "us" and "them": new input from Church Fathers, the Renaissance, the seventeenth or nineteenth centuries. All of these added to and affected the presence of the Greek inheritance in us. This book is not only about antiquity and "us," but discusses, from time to time, elements in ideas of madness from the ages in between.

From doing this we learn more about the actual ideas (and the societies) than if we assume *our* ideas about sanity, madness and the self are natural, universal, godgiven. The "human nature hasn't changed" approach (see Chapter 21) takes our ideas of "human nature" for the thing itself, apply-ing them to an alien culture like silk-finish paint, which masks the textures specific to that culture. If we emulsioned Greek temples with our own paint, we would never know what was in the column drums. We would never learn the technology used to connect them, nor the crystal struc-tures, and hence the provenance, of the stone. The history of madness shows, in fact, how deeply wrought, through centuries, are "our own" ideas of these things: what a complex and often foreign artifact "our" idea of madness is. I shall go into this a little, after exploring Greek tragic madness in, as far as possible, its own terms.[21]

One vital difference between fifth-century Greeks and "us" (or the range of job-lot attitudes, which that word "us" represents) is that in their world seeing gods, coming into direct contact with divinity, was not evidence of madness. Or not in the way it is in ours. Our world generally tends to think seeing gods is evidence of madness because it is hallucinatory: be-cause gods do not exist. "He's been seeing things" means precisely the opposite. He has *not* been seeing things: not things that are really there. He has been making them up, "seeing" creations of his own disturbed imagination.

[20] Porter 1987:35.
[21] See Clarke 1975; MacDonald 1981; Showalter 1987; Porter 1987; below, Chapter 21.

But the plays that stake out the claims of madness on Western imagination were produced for the precinct of a "mad" god. A real god, really present in "his" theater. Dionysus's persona connected interior violence, the violence of the mind and distorted perception, with exterior violence: the violence of tragedy's action, its music, dances, and murders.[22] Seeing Dionysus was evidence of seeing Dionysus. That might well mean madness, not because Dionysus was not real, but because he was.

Tragedy's main daemonic icon was the Furies: embodiments of murderous madness, rising from relationships between people bound by promises, contracts, family blood. They are called up by blood spilled out on the ground. They are the murderousness with which people "see" when relations go wrong. They cause and punish madness and bloodshed. They are the spy in the mind. Seeing them is evidence of madness; again, not because they do not exist, but because they do. Like Dionysus, they are madness-makers, perceived as such by society, truly alive and at work in the world, in relationships, and in the mind.[23]

[22] Padel 1990b:336, 1992:175.
[23] Padel 1992:172–77.

PART 1

Language and Timing

Poetry is an opening of the doors of rooms that are never fully known.
>   —Brendan Kennelly, "Introduction" to *Breathing Spaces*

Chapter 2

TRAGIC MADNESS WORDS

NORMALITY

> For practical purposes, in my view, the history of mad-
> ness stands between histories of subjects such as plague
> or death and (on the other hand) histories of witchcraft.
> It must treat insanity, like heart-failure or buboes, as a
> physical fact; but it needs to interpret it, like witchcraft or
> possession, principally as a socially constructed fact.
> —Roy Porter, *Mind-Forg'd Manacles*

GREEK TRAGEDY represents normal consciousness as an inner and outer multiplicity. You experience feelings as you experience the nonhuman outside world: gods, animals, the weather coming at you, random and aggressive. Feelings are other in self.[1] Your own inwardness, the inner equipment with which you feel and think, is multiple too. This equipment, like your feelings, is in some sense divisible from you. In Homer, someone's *thumos*, spirit, "commands" them to act. You may act "willingly with an unwilling *thumos*." In tragedy too, innards can be differently impulsive from their owner. They may know more. They sing or prophesy. They move, tremble, knock against each other. "Heart kicks *phrēn*."[2]

These are the things that contain feeling. Feeling may be represented as mobile in two ways: as the movement of liquid and air inside, and as the movement of *daimōn* in you. Feelings move autonomously in you, darkening your innards. They stir in you, boil over, burn, destroy within.[3] This is tragedy's version of normal consciousness disturbed by passion: a background normality very different from ours. It would be odd if tragedy's ideas of madness were not very different too.

I shall start with basic madness words. Others will come in later. But here are the nouns and adjectives from which tragedy, and after it Western thought, builds its understanding of madness.

COMPOUND NOUNS

For us, Greek tragedies are made only of words. To understand their version of madness, we must begin with the medium through which they

---

[1] See Chapter 1, n. 19; Padel 1992:44–48, 114–17, 138–57.
[2] *Il.* 4.43; *PV* 881; Padel 1992:19–33, 68–74.
[3] Padel 1992:75–79, 81–88, 117–18, 129–32.

express it: the language. Studying madness in Greek tragedy is importantly different from studying madness in, say, the eighteenth century. The eighteenth century has a different order of evidence: contemporary documents describe mental institutions, theories, treatment. They include memoirs of the mad themselves.[4] For Greek tragedy, the starting point has to be the words of poets, presumed sane. We can set its madness in sociohistorical context only scrappily. Its study can never entirely leave the linguistic, literary plane. Vocabulary, even grammar, must come first.

English "madness" translates many Greek nouns. Some live on in technical English today. *Anoia* is absence of *nous* (mind, sense, intellect); *paranoia* is "movement aside of *nous*," a state in which *nous* is "aside," "astray."[5] *Aphrosunē* is loss of, absence of, *phrēn*: mind, organ of thought and feeling, "wit." The noun from which we get "schizo*phren*ia."[6]

Parakopē is a rarer, more colorful noun, centered on action done to an organ of mind, rather than the lost organ itself. *Parakopē* is a "striking aside," from *para*, "aside," a key word in madness language, and the verb *koptō*, "I strike" or "hit." Hitting, striking verbs are often used of emotion's effect on the mind.[7] In the *Oresteia*, *parakopē* is used first for the *prōtopēmōn* ("first-pain") madness of Agamemnon, when he kills his daughter: a madness that was *aischromētis*, "wicked-planning." At the end of the trilogy, *parakopē* appears again, describing the Erinyes' song: it is a punitive, inescapable "madness," maddening the mind of Agamemnon's son. Father's madness, son's madness. Madness initiating crime, madness punishing crime. Like *atē*, like the Erinyes, *parakopē* in the *Oresteia* links the first impulse to crime, initial crime, with subsequent suffering, and punishment of crime.[8]

These are all compound nouns. They appear especially in lyric song, "poetic," decorated passages. *Paranoia* "drives" people to commit terrible crimes. Sometimes there is a faint glaze of personification: *parakopē*, for example, is called "shame-planning beginner of miseries." But the personification is only light.

OISTROS AND IO

> Why should I mention Io? Why indeed?
> I know no reason why.
> —Housman, "A Fragment of Greek Tragedy"

---

[4] See Porter 1987; Ingram 1991.

[5] *Anoia*: e.g., *Sept.* 402; *PV* 1079; *Ant.* 603; *Andr.* 519; *Hipp.* 398. *Paranoia*: *Sept.* 756; *Or.* 824. *Nous*: Padel 1992:32–33.

[6] *OC* 1230 (plural); *Ba.* 387 (singular, used of Pentheus, in contrast to the *euphrosunai* of Dionysus: *Ba.* 377). *Phrēn*: Padel 1992:20–23.

[7] Emotion "hitting": Padel 1992:118; see Chapter 12, nn. 6–19, 22.

[8] *Ag.* 223; *Eum.* 329. *Atē*: see Chapters 16, 17. Causing and punishing crime: Padel 1992:166; see Chapter 18, nn. 26–34.

Oistros is quite different. The word means a fly that bites cows. And the itch of cows on heat. From it comes our word *oestrus*. In Homer, Athene drives the suitors like a herd of cows "whom darting *oistros* whirls along in spring." *Oistros* is female, bovine, mating-madness and its externalized cause: a tormenting fly. In mainland Greece, around Argos, it is deeply associated with Hera. Hera (or, in another version, Artemis) angrily inflicts the daughters of Proetus with madness and an itch. She also makes them repellent to men. (In several myths, skin disease plays a narrative role similar to madness.) They wander madly in the wild. A seer cures them, possibly with some kind of dance, of the itch, the wandering, and the madness.[9] This myth is set in territory central to Greek imaginings of Hera as cow: Hera the Cow-Eyed, Yoker (Zeuxidia), the Well-Cowed (Euboia). The mythic keeper of her shrine here was Io.

Housman chose Io as a beautifully irrelevant myth for his parody of a Greek tragic chorus. But we now know that myths in tragedy's choral odes matter more to their plays than they once seemed to do. "Why should I mention Io?" asks Housman's chorus. Well, as a Greek princess who founded a foreign dynasty, Io is a paradigm link in a theme that obsesses tragedy, the relation between Greek and foreign. She goes mad, wanders abroad, and her descendents return to Greece. She crystallizes the way that the relation of home and foreign (or self and other) overlaps Greek images of the relation between being "in" your mind, and being "out" of it. Inside is sane. Being "out" of home and all it stands for (mind, right place) is mad. Mad is outside, other, foreign.[10] Io embodies the connection between mad and abroad, home and sane. Maybe Housman, deeply tuned to Greek fantasy, chose her for, unconsciously, this reason.

Io is forced into wandering by madness externalized as *oistros*. In Aeschylus' *Suppliant Maidens*, her descendents return to Argos to escape Egyptian suitors:

> our clan says it came from here:
> from Zeus touching and breathing on
> the *oistros*-whirled cow.

This Argive "cow" is Io. They invoke her son Epaphos ("Touch"):

> calf sired by Zeus, born of his touch
> and his breathing on Io; son of
> our ancestress, the flower-grazing cow.

Here they are, where their "ancestress" first "grazed." To Greek eyes, they are strangely dressed,

[9] Hes. fr. 133; Löffler 1963; Burkert 1983:168–74; Dowden 1989:71–95, 117–37. See *Od.* 22.300; Padel 1992:120–21.

[10] See below Part 3. Tragedy's concern with home and foreign: Hall 1989. Hera's cow-titles: Farnell 1896–1909 1:181–82.

in un-Greek style, barbarian robes:
clothes not of Argive
or any Greek women.

But odd as they are, as "seed of a cow," of Io, they belong here. They and the Argive king meet in Io's story. Here, she was "key-holder" of Hera's shrine. Here, Zeus fell in love with her and Hera changed her to a cow. Zeus became bull: but Hera put a hundred-eyed guard to watch Io, and sent *oistros* to drive her out. Io came mad to Egypt, where Zeus got a son on her by touching her. Sharing this story with them, the king acknowledges their share in Argos.[11]

Io is "key-holder" in several senses. *Oistros* drove her from Greece to Egypt. As her descendents are driven fleeing sex with Egyptians, so Io was driven by madness, fleeing *oistros* and sex with Zeus:

pricked by the *oistros*, she fled, astray in mind:

. . . .

harassed by the winged herdsman's dart
she came to the snow-fed field,
and water of the Nile that no disease may touch,
mainomena [maddened] by dishonorable troubles,
and pains from Hera's goad.

As these foreign-looking women alarm the Argives back home, so Io alarmed the Egyptians:

The people who then lived there shook with pale terror,
seeing . . . a living mix, half-cow, half-woman—monstrous!

Io is between everything. Animal and human, Greek and foreign, mad and sane, Zeus and Hera, lust and fear. It is unclear if the pricks of *oistros* are punishment for arousing Zeus's lust, or the lust, the *oistros*, she feels as cow.

Zeus ends her impasse in Egypt:

Who was it who soothed far-wandering, miserable,
oistros-whirled Io? Zeus! . . . By his strong hand
and holy breathing, she found rest, let fall
her sorrow-shame with tears, conceived a child. . . .[12]

The end of *oistros* is the end of wandering. Out there on the far side of madness and the Nile, Io conceives "Touch": her half-beast, half-man son, link between Greece and Africa.

In *Suppliant Maidens*, this story signifies that the girls are related to the king. It is the token of their relation. In *Prometheus Bound*, the audience

---

[11] A. *Supp.* 15–17, 41–46, 234–37, 275, 291–312, 325.
[12] A. *Supp.* 540–64, 565–70, 574–80. Danaids, Io: Zeitlin 1992:227.

sees *oistros* in action. Wandering Io encounters Prometheus. *Oistros* attacks her:

> Where have I, unhappy, where have I wandered?
> Ah! Ah! E! E!—again it grazes me, some *oistros*. . . .
> . . . .
> It wastes and stings me with its goads—ah!—
> that make me wander—E! E!

She describes how it began: night visions said Zeus wanted her, ordered her into the fields to relieve Zeus's desire. Oracles told her father she must leave home and "wander to the farthest edges of earth." Leaving home, going "out," was when the madness, the *oistros*, came. She was transformed:

> At once my shape and mind were twisted.
> Horned, as you see me, stung by a sharp-mouthed fly,
> I rushed in mad leaps to the water . . . .
> . . . .
> *Oistros*-hit,
> I'm driven from land to land by god's goad.

Another bout of stinging madness takes her off-stage:

> Eleleu! Eleleu! Again,
> spasm and mind-blasting *maniai*
> burn me: the *oistros*'s flameless arrow.
> . . . .
> I'm carried off course by a *margos* [wild-greedy]
> blast of *lussa* [madness]. . . .[13]

Oistros is not confined to Io, and is not only a gadfly. In tragedy *oistros* is any frenzy, not only erotic. It is the madness of Phaedra, but also of maenads, birds, Orestes, and Heracles.[14]

LUSSA AND HERACLES

Oistros is insect torment: madness not so much personified as animalized. The noun tragedy personifies most thoroughly is *lussa*.

Before tragedy, *lussa* and *lussa*-related words are used especially of the *Iliad*'s two main war heroes, Hector and Achilles. Their *lussa* is violent,

---

[13] *PV* 565–99, 645–82, 877–84.
[14] *Hipp.* 1300; *Ba.* 665; *Ant.* 1002; *Or.* 791; *IA* 547; *HF* 862, 1144; Padel 1992:120–22.

wolfish "fighting rage."[15] After tragedy, prose writers also use it for "rabies," which underlines *lussa*'s early dog-feel. Lyssa is connected with hounds, mad dogs, wolves. "Go, hounds of Lyssa," cry the Asian maenads willing Pentheus to be slaughtered as the quarry of the Theban maenads. Lyssa is connected with Erinyes, "hounds," of Orestes' murdered mother. She appears in vase-paintings of tragic scenes (once with a dog's head over her hat), urging human beings or hounds to kill. She makes Lycurgus kill his wife and son, and Actaeon's hounds kill their master.[16]

For Lyssa comes into her own in tragedy. The frenzy of Io, Orestes, Pentheus, is *lussa*. Outside tragedy, *lussa* is also the madness of the Proetides, or of love. She had a speaking part in at least one tragedy of Aeschylus, maybe two.[17] And in one extant tragedy: Euripides' *Madness of Heracles*.

Up to Lyssa's entry in this play, the nastiness and manipulations are all human. A tyrant, a rescue. Now the elderly chorus celebrates Heracles, who has saved his family as he has "saved" all Greece. But divinity rips through the human fabric:

> Oh! Oh! Old men, do we all
> feel the same throb of fear?
> What do I see over the house?

"What they see" (and the audience sees too) rises from the roof of the stage building. The chorus prays to Apollo Healer to avert it. They want to run away. Half this vision is the messenger-god Iris. She calms them and explains her horrific companion:

> This that you see, old men, is Night's child, Lyssa.
> I am the gods' servant, Iris. We haven't come
> to harm your city. We're at war
> against the house of one man only.

Heracles was safe from Hera till he finished his labors. Now,

> Hera will fix the stain of kindred blood on him.
> She'll make him kill his children. And I want that too.

Lyssa is the only divinity who thinks this a bad idea. She wants justice between humans and gods. She urges Heracles' innocence and nobility. Iris, Hera's agent, stirs her into action:

[15] *Il.* 9.239, 395, 21.542 ("strong *lussa*" possesses Hector, he "has baneful *lussa*"; "strong *lussa*" holds Achilles' heart).

[16] Dog-Lyssa: Lincoln 1975; *Ba.* 977, cf. *Cho.* 1054; Padel 1992:125. Rabies: Xen. *An.* 5.7.26.

[17] *Xantriai, Toxotides.* See *PV* 883; *Cho.* 287; *Or.* 254; *Ba.* 851, 977. Cf. *Bacc.* 10.102; Ar. *Thesm.* 680; Pl. *Legg.* 839A. Cf. *lussēma*: e.g., *Or.* 270; Padel 1992:177. Lyssa's speaking parts: Padel 1992:163 n. 4.

Come! with your heart untouched by pity,

. . . .

drive *maniai* [madnesses] against the man,
send on him childkilling disturbances of mind,
chaotic wild-bounding feet! Prick him on. . . .

Lyssa calls Sun to witness that she does not wish to do this. Then she sets
to work, picturing her effect on Heracles:

Look! he already shakes his head at the starting-post!
In silence his eyeballs roll, his pupils distend
and swivel like a Gorgon's eyes. Now he's panting,
not sane, like a bull about to charge. Now he roars—
awful—calling on black Fates of Tartarus!
I'll make you dance! And more! I'll pipe to you
my terror-music! Iris—off! To Olympus
with your noble tread! I'll sink unseen
into the house of Heracles!

With exit lines whose sarcasm ("noble tread") foreshadows the play's issues of judgment and justice between gods and human beings, Lyssa
"sinks" into the home, "breast," mind of Heracles.[18] The chorus imagine
her at work in him. *This*—"Night's daughter, a Gorgon with a hundred
heads / hissing with snakes, glitter-eyed Madness"—has entered their savior king.[19]

In this play, Heracles is the human with two fathers, one human, one
divine. He will repudiate divinity's share in him. The play implies divine
parentage is no help: the only thing that helps is human friendship. Divinity's share in human action appears on stage as Iris, rainbow messenger of
destruction, and Lyssa's mad gargoyle ugliness.[20]

We cannot know how Lyssa looked on stage. Vase-painters of the time,
and in the next century, assimilate tragedy's Lyssa to Furies, who in Aeschylus look and behave like hounds. A hound's head appears above her
own on one vase, a snake winds round her arm on another. She has multiple snake hair like a Gorgon, carries goads in her hand like a Fury, and
wings as Gorgons and Furies mostly have.[21]

Lyssa sometimes appears in paintings of plays where we know she did
not have a speaking part. The painter is bringing out the madness in a play,
and also, maybe, showing that the scene *is* from a play. Lyssa indicates that

[18] *HF* 815–17, 822–25, 840–41, 833–37, 867–73.
[19] *HF* 882–83. See Chapter 12, n. 68.
[20] Two fathers: *HF* 1–3, 150, 339–40; repudiation of divinity's share: 1243, 1258–65;
gratitude for human friendship: 1350–51, 1402–404; 1234, 1340–46.
[21] See Padel 1992:118, 125, 131, 151, 157, 163. Hounds, snakes: Padel 1992:123–25.

this is a picture, not of a myth, but of a particular tragedy handling that myth. Like Furies, Lyssa becomes a visual signifier of the tragic stage. Appropriately: for painters also represent "Tragedy" as a maenad in Dionysus's train.[22]

We do not see Heracles in his madness. It is not "his." We see Madness herself before she enters him. Nothing could show more clearly that tragic madness is something external, invading, daemonic, autonomous. Like passion, as tragic language represents it: other in self, often personified, often multiple like Furies, the madness-senders. And, like Furies and Lyssa, it is mainly female.[23]

MANIA: A FIT OF MADNESS

The last noun is *mania*, commonest prose noun for madness. "The word denotes frenzy," says the great scholar of Greek religion, Walter Burkert, "as its etymological connection with *menos* would suggest, as an experience of intensified mental power."[24] *Menos* is angry force, violence. Some scholars have argued it "originally meant" blood. I do not think this "originally meant" approach is useful, though there is some close, unreachable Greek link between blood and *menos*. *Menos* is "force." It is fundamentally angry, but *not* fundamentally "mental"; except that when used of the mind, it conveys violence there too. Rivers and fire have *menos*.[25]

I would use the important association of *mania* with *menos* differently, pointing to the core violence of *mania*, resonant of the bloody force and flood of *menos*. *Mania* has the sudden violence of a "*fit* of madness." This violence is reflected, we shall see, in *mania*'s allied verb, *mainomai*.

Mania may have been personified sometimes in cult. On the road to Messene, Pausanias saw a shrine to "Maniai," Madnesses, plural of *mania*. Local tales connected them with Orestes:

> On the left of the road is a sanctuary of goddesses. They call these goddesses, and the land round the sanctuary, *Maniai*. In my view, this is a name for the Eumenides. People say that it was on this spot that Orestes went mad at murdering his mother. Not far off is a low earth mound, and on it a finger of stone. The mound's name is "Tomb of the Finger." Here, they say, Orestes went mad and bit off one of his fingers. Near this site is another, called Akē [Cures], because here Orestes was cured of his madness. The story is, that these goddesses appeared black to Orestes when they were going to madden him. When he'd bitten his finger off, they appeared white.

---

[22] Burkert 1985:185; Padel 1992:163. Erinys as tragedy's talismanic icon: Padel 1992:172; cf. Wilson and Taplin 1993:176.

[23] Padel 1992:116–31, 157–61.

[24] Burkert 1985:162.

[25] Padel 1992:24–26.

This story sounds pretty mad itself. Pausanias, and scholars after him, are content with an unverifiable identification: Maniai "are" the Eumenides, Furies before (black) and after (white), punishing Orestes.[26] I am interested in what the Erinyes (if these are they), and the land around, are called. "Madnesses": divinities personifying fits of *mania*.

Mania is not personified in tragedy. Tragic language treats it variously. As a divine tool, *mania* is Lyssa's weapon: she "sends child-killing *maniai* on Heracles." It is Dionysus's missile: he "sends" panic, a *mania*, on an army, as gods "send" passions and dangerous animals to human beings.[27] But the poets also treat *mania* topographically, as an area of experience. Anyone who denies a god is drawing "near *maniai*." Also, like passion and *menos*, *mania* can be a liquid swelling and trickling within. *Mania*'s "force" (*menos*) "drips away" after its climax.[28]

Paranoia, *anoia*, above all *oistros*, *lussa*, and *mania*, are tragedy's main madness nouns. Tragedy does not use *melancholia*. Writers sometimes use these words for erotic "frenzy" or clinical "delirium." In tragedy, they seem roughly interchangeable with each other. They are not different sorts of madness, but different words for the same thing. Someone who has *paranoia* has *mania*.[29]

ADJECTIVES

But when you think how much madness there is in tragedy, nouns for it are oddly rare. Poets prefer other parts of madness speech. The adjective *parakopos* ("struck out") is commoner than the noun *parakopē*.[30] But madness adjectives are not simple. There is not really any plain Greek adjective, "mad." There is a poetic word *margos*, but that is greedy, appetitive, "ravening." It is related to *margaō*, "I rage" (usually in battle), which has an appetitive tone and takes the genitive case of things it aims at: the grammatical case for something you aim at, grab, and hold. It signifies lust to possess or destroy, or both. Warring brothers "rage madly" to throw the spear at each other. In tragedy, *margos* has mostly the same destructive, greedy tone. The Egyptian race (exemplified by the men chasing Aeschylus's suppliant girls) is "*margos* and insatiable in battle." They are lust-

---

[26] Paus. 8.34.1; Farnell 1896–1909 5:442–43.

[27] *HF* 835; *Ba.* 305. Emotions or animals "sent" to punish and hurt: Padel 1992:146, 156.

[28] *Heraclid.* 904; *Ant.* 958. Cf. Ar. *Nub.* 832–33. *Menos* (also *cholos*) as liquid, or liquid passion: Padel 1992:23–26, 79–88.

[29] Ar. *Nub.* 845–46. "Delirium". Hp. *Progn.* 23 (*paranoia*); Hp. *Aph.* 7.5 (*mania*), 6.26 (*parakopē*). *Melancholia*: see Chapter 5.

[30] E.g., in tragedy *parakopē* is used twice (only in the *Oresteia*: see above, n. 8) while *parakopos* appears four times: *PV* 581; *Ba.* 33, 1000; also Timotheus *Persae* 77. The numbers are tiny. But for what they are worth, the adjective is twice as common.

ful, aggressive. Agamemnon killed Iphigeneia because Helen was *margē*, feminine of *margos*: "madly lustful."[31]

The "greedy-violent" sense of *margos* is present in some uses in the *Odyssey*. (Antinous is *margos*, plotting to kill Telemachus.) But not all. When Penelope hears Eurycleia say Odysseus has come and killed the suitors, she answers,

> Dear nurse, gods have made you *margē*.
> They can make anyone mad [*aphrōn*],
> however *epiphrōn* [sane] . . . .
>
> . . . .
> They've harmed you. Before,
> you were right in your *phrenes*.

Eurycleia (though rebuked for shouting with joy when she saw the corpses) is not accused of blood thirst. She is called *margē*, because she woke her lady with an impossible story. The word can be used ungreedily. Mad Io's "breath" is *margon*, and she is not bloodthirsty or lustful. But everywhere else in tragedy, *margos* suggests aggressive, greedy violence. Erinyes, eager for blood, are violent, ravening: *margai*.[32]

Apart from *margos*, tragic language has a jungle of adjectival alternatives. We look for a nice plain adjective, "mad," like ours. It is not there. Instead we find an amazingly rich, complicated range of words. First, there are a large number of relatively uncolored compounds. *Aphrōn*, *ekphrōn*, *paraphrōn*, *blapsiphrōn*, *anous*: "without *phrēn*," "out of *phrēn*" (or "with *phrēn* out"), "with *phrēn* astray," "with *phrēn* damaged," "without *nous*."[33]

Second, we find images: of wandering and twisting movement, of being "carried aside," "struck out" of one's mind. "Wanderer!" (meaning, "Madman!") shout the Ithacan suitors to the swineherd, when he offers the king's bow to a beggar. Citizens mock Clytemnestra for believing the beacon-signal. "I was made to seem *a wanderer*," she says. The "aside-ness" fundamental to Western perceptions of madness is articulated first in Greek epic and tragedy.[34]

Many of these images are not strictly adjectives but participles. At the heart of madness language is the verb.

---

[31] *Margos*: A. *Supp.* 741; E. *El.* 1027; *Sept.* 380; *HF* 1005 (with lust "to kill," *phonou*). Cf. *Hipp.* 1230 (*margōsai phrenas*). *Margaō*: *Phoen.* 1247. Genitive: e.g., *HF* 1005; cf. A. fr. 258.

[32] *Od.* 16.421, 23.11–14 (see *parex ereousa*), 22.406–15; *PV* 884; *Eum.* 67.

[33] *Eum.* 377 (cf. *Il.* 5.875); *Ant.* 99, 281; S. *El.* 473; *Hipp.* 232; *Sept.* 735 (cf. *phrenōlēs*, 757).

[34] *Od.* 21.363; *Ag.* 593. See Chapter 3, n. 30; Chapter 7, nn. 21, 38; Chapter 10, n. 31; Chapter 12, nn. 6–22, 47, 61–62, 67.

Chapter 3

GOD OF THE VERB

Madness Verbs and "God Of"

The Scythians blame the Greeks for *baccheuein*, for it is
not reasonable to set up a god who drives human beings
mad.
    —Herodotus

BASIC "I AM MAD" is *mainomai*, related to *mania*. It is almost exclusively a
"middle voice" verb. The middle voice is one of the riches of Greek syntax.
It represents, says Goodwin's *Greek Grammar*, "The subject as acting upon
himself, or in some manner which concerns himself."[1] It is what you *get
done for* yourself.

Formally, middle is very close to passive, what is done to you by an
outside agent. It differs from passive formally in only two tenses, future
and aorist. In the present tense, the forms of middle and passive are identi-
cal. Some verbs exist only in the middle. These are "deponent verbs." They
have no active form. There is no active *mainō*, "I madden." *Mainomai* is
more a deponent verb than not.

But there are two kinds of deponents in Greek, "middle" and "passive"
deponents, so called according to the form of their aorist. In the aorist you
can tell the difference between middle or passive voice. Some deponents
have a middle aorist, some passive. *Mainomai* has mainly a passive, though
the odd middle is found. Passive aorist suggests madness as something
"done to" you: there is some echo of a lost active form.

Though it is a deponent verb, *mainomai* does have active forms. These
are mostly unused.[2] They crop up only in past tenses. Judging the beauty
of those goddesses "maddened" Paris. A wife "maddened her husband
with drugs." When Xuthus greets Ion as his long-lost son, the boy thinks
gods have driven Xuthus mad.

> Stranger—are you in your right mind?
> Or has some divine damage made you mad?[3]

In many tenses, *mainomai*'s middle forms are the same as its passives. The
present, *mainomai*, "I am mad," could come over as middle, "I make my-

---

[1] Goodwin 1902:267, §1242.
[2] Cf. *aaomai*: see Chapter 16, nn. 12, 24–28.
[3] *IA* 580; Ar. *Thesm.* 561; *Ion* 520.

self mad," "get myself to be mad," or as passive, "I am *made* mad" by
something outside myself. The occasional appearance of the active suggests that *mainomai* could have a potentially passive, as well as middle, feel.
"I am mad" might convey "I rave (for myself)" *and* "I am made mad."

If so, the grammar holds, without separating, the two possibilities that
have perplexed the Western world since the Greeks. Does madness come
from within the self, or is it inflicted on it from outside? Middle? Or
passive?

What are the resonances of this central verb? Homer uses it of battle-
fury. As with *lussa*, so with *mainomai*: the Homeric history behind a tragic
word for craziness is lust to kill. The war god, the heroes, their hands and
spears: all "are mad" with desire to kill. These overtones continue in tragic
war contexts of *mainomai*.[4] The West's basic madness verb speaks of violence from the first. A physical, but not purely external, violence. Inner
organs do it too. The *ētor* (heart) "raves" or "rages" in the *phrenes*. *Phrenes*
and heart are "raving": the present participle, *mainomenoi*. The *prapis* (a
rare word for "mind") has "been made to rave."[5]

Mainomai has a vital Dionysian connection. Dionysus is mentioned only
three times in Homer. We cannot know what resonances have collected
round his name at this early point in his career, but in one Homeric line
he, like these inner organs, is glancingly called *mainomenos*. "Raving."
"Mad."

The context is the story of "man-killing" Lycurgus, who persecutes Dionysus's nurses. Infant Dionysus escapes to Thebes. The gods are angry
with Lycurgus. Zeus blinds him. He "did not live long, since he was hated
by all the gods."[6]

Aeschylus used this myth in a lost trilogy, the *Lycurgeia*, which linked
the deaths of Lycurgus and Orpheus: both punished by Dionysus, both
dying (like Pentheus in Euripides' *Bacchae*) on a mountain. Not Cithairon,
but Mount Pangaeum, in Thrace. Orpheus refused to honor Dionysus,
saying the Sun, Helios (whom he called Apollo), was the greatest god. He
rushed to see the sun rise from Mount Pangaeum, where deadly Dionysus,
dishonored, sent Thracian bacchants to tear him to pieces. Lycurgus,
Pentheus-like, a king-figure rather than visionary, insulted and expelled
Dionysus as he came West with his bacchants. The bacchants were imprisoned. Dionysus found asylum in the sea. The bacchants were freed.
Afterwards, Dionysus maddened Lycurgus as he was pruning a vine. He

---

[4] *Il.* 5.717, 16.245, 8.111, 16.75. Cf. *Ant.* 136: an attacker approaches Thebes with a
"raving rush" (*mainomēnāi hormāi*).

[5] *Il.* 8.413, 24.114; *Sept.* 781; *Med.* 432; *Ba.* 999. *Prapides* (singular *prapis* is rare): Padel
1992:19–20, 135.

[6] *Il.* 6.132 ("nurses of *mainomenoio Dionusoio*," "Dionysus being mad"; cf. "Heracles
Mainomenos"), 6.134, 139–40.

turned the axe from the vinestock to his own son, Dryas, lopping off
Dryas's head and extremities. Lycurgus recovered sanity, but the land was
barren and Dionysus let it be known things would recover if Lycurgus
died. The Edonians took him to Mount Pangaeum and tied him up, where
he died, destroyed by horses.

Aeschylus here used Thracian Dionysus-legends, the story-nexus that
surfaces in the *Iliad*. Theban Dionysus-legends gave him four or five other
plays.[7] The cross-fertilization of Thracian and Theban Dionysus horror-
stories is compacted into lines from a later Theban play, Sophocles' *Antigone*, which surround Lycurgus with elements of Orpheus's destruction,
stressing the music motif in it. Lycurgus "provoked" the "flute-loving
Muses."[8] In both Aeschylus and Sophocles, the Lycurgus-story, burdened
with Orpheus images, suggested music in its maddening, destructive, and
vulnerable role.[9] Dionysus's characterization as *mainomenos* in the *Iliad*
comes, therefore, from a story of violence and punishment involving mad
child killing, itself a hallmark of tragic madness.[10]

Homer's narrative balances this story by that of another man hated by
gods. Bellerophon,

> hated by all gods, wandered alone
> on the Aleian plain, eating his own *thumos*,
> avoiding the paths of human beings.

Homer does not say "mad" here, but the Aristotelian *Problem* 30 includes
Bellerophon in a list of people who went mad, and "eating his own
thumos" implies something like madness (see Chapter 19). One story of
madness and divine hatred is described in response to another. Homer is
mostly silent about madness. But this passage, which tosses like a time
bomb the image of "mad" Dionysus into Western imagination, has madness even in its story frame. The speakers exchange armor to show friendship. One exchanges gold for bronze: "Zeus stole his *phrenes*." Madness,
gods' hatred: and a mad exchange.[11]

The *Iliad* rarely mentions Dionysus. Calling him *mainomenos* must be

---

[7] Apollod. 3.5.1; Eratosthenes *Legends of the Constellations* 24.140 (Robert); A. frr. 23–
24A, 57–62 (Loeb 2:386, 398). See A. fr. 58, *enthousiāi de dōma, baccheuei stegē* (*Edoni*). The
Lycurgeia contained *Edoni, Bassarae*, and *Neanisci*: see Chapter 19, n. 56.

[8] *Ant.* 956–63. Jebb *ad loc.* cites a sarcophagus showing Lycurgus about to kill a nymph
surrounded by Furies, Dionysus, and Muses. But Sophocles' words must rest also on Aeschylus's trilogy, which linked Lycurgus and Orpheus. Theban legends: A. Loeb 2:378.

[9] See Padel 1992:65, 126–27.

[10] See Chapter 19, nn. 53–56.

[11] *Il.* 6.200–202, 234. *Kai keinos*, line 200, seems to secure the parallel with Lycurgus.
[Arist.] *Problem* 30.1: Klibansky, Panofsky, and Saxl 1964:16, 39; Simon 1978:232, 70;
see Chapter 6. "Eating" your *thumos*: cf. eating your children, below, Chapter 19, nn. 53–
54.

connected somehow to the fact that madness itself (not raging to kill, but delusional, distorting madness) is rare in Homer. Dionysus's art form, tragedy, foregrounds a madness almost absent from Homer's myths.

One critic suggests "the literary and narrative purposes of the poet did not require the portrayal of mad heroes."[12] This does not settle the question, just pushes it further back. *Why* did Homer's purposes not require this? They required so many other phenomena and experiences, from flies on milk pails to the genealogies of suffering families. Good poets don't let "purposes" boss them about. There must be better reasons for Homeric backgrounding of madness, and these reasons ought to explain also tragedy's foregrounding of it. I shall suggest an area of answer later (see Chapters 18 and 19).

That this first mention of Dionysus in Western literature calls him *mainomenos*, "raving mad," has mattered far outside classical studies. Dionysus has been a litmus test for every epoch's obsessions. Romantic Dionysus, the principle of life, replaced Renaissance Dionysus. Modern Dionysus is the principle of death and violence. He took shape in the 1870s, has run for over a hundred years, and shows little sign of letting up.[13]

Since the 1930s, though, he has been joined by a Dionysus of duality, a god of opposites, paradox, contradiction.[14] The image is too easy, I think, for in the Greek pantheon Dionysus does not have a monopoly on paradox and contradiction. All Greek gods were paradoxical. Each killed *and* helped, urged on *and* punished, loved *and* hated in that area of human experience they controlled, in which they found their "honors."[15] All, in their different spheres, were personae "of" contradiction. We, in a century dominated by warring claims of rationality and irrationality, tend to feel that opposition in this sphere is the essence of contradiction. "Euripides the Rationalist" was replaced by "Euripides the Irrationalist." Ideals of Greek reason were challenged by *The Greeks and the Irrational*. Dionysus, "mad" god, was central to these rethinkings.[16]

One answer to "why *mainomenos*?" lies in the violence of that verb. The epithet refers to the violence of Dionysiac worship, an important force in Dionysus-stories later than Homer. Violence is important to tragedy too.

[12] Simon 1978:66–68.

[13] Henrichs 1984:209–12 pinpoints differences between Romantic and modern Dionysus expressed in Kerenyi 1976; Detienne 1979. Violence is the key to Dionysus in Girard 1977; Burkert 1983 (both first published 1972).

[14] Madness through duality characterizes Otto's Dionysus. Otto 1965 [1933] began a god-of-paradox Dionysus, "the god who is mad": Otto 1965:121, 133–42, 127–29, and chs. 8–12 passim; see Segal 1982.

[15] See Padel 1992:7–8, 11, 166.

[16] Dodds ed. of *Ba.* came out in 1944. His Sather lectures (Dodds 1951) were given in 1949. His work, one foundation of modern reappraisals of Greek culture, had Dionysus at its heart. (Did this add to the extraordinary, Pentheus-like opposition to him at Oxford?)

But Dionysus's connection with wine is also early. Homer calls him a "joy to men": this suggests, though does not prove, a connection with wine.[17] There are strong Homeric connections between wine, damage done to and in the mind, and damage in the outside world. We shall meet them again:

> Wine damaged the centaur. . . .
>
> . . . .
>
> When wine damaged his *phrenes*
> he did terrible things
> through the house . . . *mainomenos*.

This inner and outer damage is the heart of the Homeric concept, *atē*.[18] It is also *mainomai*'s heart. And Dionysus, "god of" tragic theater: it is near the heart of his persona too.[19]

In tragedy, inward violence of mind parallels inward violence of the "house," where the murders mostly happen. Like Homeric *atē*, tragic madness is innard-damage, to mind, especially *phrenes*. Look at the images: "struck," "struck out," "harmed," "twisted aside." The idea that black bile caused madness, and that madness is "cured" with the poisonous root of hellebore, points to a similar violence expressed biologically rather than daemonically.[20]

People's *phrenes* vary. Odysseus has "stronger" ones than Ajax. But *phrenes* functioning normally in anyone are safe, sane. Mad is *aphrōn*, "*phrēn*-less"; or *ekphrōn*, out of "*phrēn*" (or, "with *phrēn* out"); or *paraphrōn*, with *phrēn* beside. Its opposite is *emphrōn*, "with *phrēn* in" (or "in the *phrēn*"). Or *sōphrōn*, "with a safe *phrēn*": core word for "prudent, self-controlled." In sanity, *phrēn* is safe. When it is hurt or lost, then it, or its owner, is mad.[21]

Dionysus specializes in unsafe mind-damage. In a way it is odd to call a Greek divinity "god of" anything. It is shorthand, with a distorting relation to Christian phrases like "God of" love. We make self-sense of alien people when we say "god of." Greek gods were "many-named": invested in many things at once. Artemis was "god of" childbirth, huntable animals, women's bloodshed, women's transitions, sometimes the moon.[22]

---

[17] *Il.* 14.325. Girard (1977:133) calls Dionysus as wine god (but "for no good reason," according to Henrichs 1984:233) a "later" palliation of the "god of violence." See Burkert 1985:161–67.

[18] *Od.* 21.295–98; see Chapter 16, nn. 10–12, and Chapter 17, nn. 2–8, 25, 32–33.

[19] Padel 1990b:336, 365 (cf. 1981:106, 128).

[20] See below, Chapter 7, n. 38, and Chapter 12, nn. 6–15; Padel 1992:116–20. Individual inwardness, tragic "house": Padel 1990b:343–46; 1992:74, 100, 112, 191. Black bile, hellebore, violence: see Chapter 5, nn. 7–12.

[21] Odysseus's "strong" *phrenes*: *Aj.* 445. *Aphrōn, sōphrōn*: Snell 1978:70–72, 76; Padel 1992:23. See Chapter 7, n. 42, and Chapter 12, n. 61.

[22] Padel 1992:7, 153.

We are stuck with "god of." It is part of us. So we might take it further and call Dionysus god of the verb in tragic madness. Especially of the first verb to label him in Western literature, *mainomai*. But other verbs speak of him even more acutely: like *bacchaō*, *baccheuō* ("I rave" or, causative, "I madden").

Herodotus uses *baccheuō* apparently technically ("I celebrate Bacchic rites") in the story of a barbarian king who copied everything Greek, including religion. The Scythians "blame the Greeks for *baccheuein*" because, says Herodotus, master of apparently artless irony, "it is not reasonable to set up a god who drives human beings mad." In the passive, in a fifth-century B.C. inscription from Cyme, *baccheuō* means "I am initiated into Dionysian cult." It is normally less technical: "I rave, am frenzied" (of, for instance, soldiers frenzied by Ares); or even "I stagger madly," of a poisoned dove.[23]

Bacchaō seems to have even wider force. A warrior possessed by Ares "raves towards battle." The Erinyes "madden" Orestes "with kindred blood." He is "frenzied by their madnesses." Amphitryon thinks Heracles "maddened" by his recent murder. In *Trojan Women*, Cassandra is *baccheuousa* ("raving"), *mainas*, a "madwoman." She "stands outside bacchic raving" enough to make a clear prophecy. *Apollo* "drove her," *exebaccheusen*, "out of her *phrenes*." Yet *Dionysus*'s verb is used, as if bacchic raving is the model for all others. Erinyes, Ares, Apollo: whatever they do to their victims' minds, Dionysus is in there, in the verb. *Mainas*, "maenad," Dionysus's celebrant, means "madwoman."[24]

There are other similar verbs. *Lussaō* (and *lussainō*), "I rave," suggests the activity of *lussa* in the mind, as *bacchaō* suggests that of Bacchus. When Oedipus learned who Jocasta was, "some *daimōn* showed him, *lussōnti* [raving]," where she was. Creon sees Ismene "*lussōsan*, not in control of her *phrenes*." He asks his son if he comes "raving against his father?"[25] A less specific verb, *daimonaō*, "I am mad," suggests an unknown *daimōn* acting on, or in, the mind. Oedipus's sons kill each other "*daimonōntes* in *atē*," "raving in destructive frenzy." Cadmus's family is "raving, daemon-ridden": mad-doomed—to ruin Thebes.[26]

Some of this borders on "possession," which I will not explore by itself in this book.[27] These verbs suggest madness as activity of *daimōn*, *lussa*,

---

[23] Hdt. 4.79; Schwyzer 1923:374, no. 792; *Ant.* 136 (which must echo *Sept.* 498: both refer to "mad" attackers on Thebes); *Ion* 1204.

[24] *Sept.* 498; *Or.* 411, 835; *HF* 966; *Tro.* 349–50, 367, 408. See also *sumbaccheuō*: e.g., *Ba.* 726. *Mainas*: below, nn. 28–29; Henrichs 1978.

[25] *OT* 1258; *Ant.* 492, 633; cf. Pl. *Rep.* 329C, 586C. *Lussōdēs*: *Ba.* 981. See Chapter 12, n. 68.

[26] *Sept.* 1007; *Phoen.* 888 (cf. *theomanēs*, *Sept.* 854); cf. Xen. *Mem.* 1.1.7–9.

[27] It has been argued (Smith 1965) there was no concept of possession in the fifth century. I don't agree (Padel 1983:12–14): see further Burkert 1985:301 n. 1, and below, Chapter 12, nn. 47–57.

above all Bacchus. In tragedy, his own art form, Dionysus connects inward damage with outer damage. Damage of mind, damage to fortune. You might say Dionysus becomes, in tragic codings of these myths, god of a sequence I shall discuss later: the Homeric "damage-chain" that stands behind tragedy. Dionysus and madness: both are rare in Homer, and found all over tragedy.

Late in the fifth century, madness verbs arose whose roots were not daemons but organic substances, bile and hellebore. We shall meet these later (see Chapter 5). They have an important bearing on our own responses to Greek images of madness. They do not appear in tragedy. But they were, again, verbs.

PARTICIPLES: THE PRE-EMINENCE OF THE VERB

In his early Homeric appearance, Dionysus's verb is a participle, *mainomenos*, "being mad." Madness, like Dionysus himself, belongs with action: with verbs.

This is clear even among the adjectives, which are so often verbal adjectives or participles. *Mainas* (a verbal adjective formed from the verb *mainomai*) is used as an adjective, "mad," qualifying *lussa*; more often it appears as a noun, "madwoman," used of Cassandra and even the Furies.[28] It is, as it were, intransitive, participle of a verb with no grammatical object: "raving."

But Furies are also mad*dening*. *Mainomai* can, we have seen, come over as the passive of an active and transitive verb, "I madden [someone]." *Mainas* too can work like this. Pindar uses it of the wryneck, a "maddening" bird used in erotic spells. There is a similar verbal adjective *lussas*, "raving, maddening."[29]

Euripides' Lyssa play is *Heracles Mainomenos*, "Heracles being Mad": the present participle again. There are multiple passive participles ("*having been* maddened, *having been* struck aside," "touched") plus active present ones ("wandering," "raving"). Images of the mad are marked by the temporary mobility of participles: by the fluid, on-the-wing nature of the verb.[30]

MADNESS IS TEMPORARY, AND KNOWN BY ITS APPEARANCE

I looked out in that dark hall, and saw a light in the door
of Alan's room. Alan was carrying a little electric lamp,

---

[28] As seeming adjective: of *lussa*, see S. fr. 941.4; of *bacchē*, *Ba.* 915. As noun, *Il.* 22. 460; *h. Dem.* 386; A. fr. 382; *OT* 212; *Tro.* 173. Cf. *lussas*, below n. 29. The femaleness of *maenas* is important: there is no male equivalent. See Padel 1983:11–17, 1992:106–13, 159–61.

[29] *Eum.* 500; Pi. *P.* 4.216 with Padel 1992:145. *Lussas*: Timotheus fr. 3; *HF* 1024 where it qualifies *moira*.

[30] See above, Chapter 2, n. 34; below, Chapter 10, nn. 27–31, and Chapter 12, nn. 6–11, 22.

the long cylindrical kind that miners use. The wire round
it made little shadows all over him. He looked twice as
big and broad as normal: he had on a black dressing-
gown with a red collar, and was peering round the hall. A
little of the light shone up on his face when he moved it: I
could see his freckles and his bull neck, and his red hair
damp with perspiration. But most of all, I could see his
eyeballs, a sort of horror like oysters, turning from side to
side. He was not smiling, though he looked as though he
meant to. And then I knew he was mad. . . .
  —Carter Dickson, *The Red Widow Murders*

What does tragedy's language tell us about how madness was conceived?
First, most basically, the reason why poets prefer verbs to other parts of
speech when speaking of madness is, I think, an overriding Greek sense
that madness is temporary.

In madness, innards are damaged but survive, like Prometheus's liver in
the myth. Inner damage lasts only while the madness is there.[31] Like emotion, madness comes in from outside: divine, malign, autonomous. It does
not belong to the person. It is itself. It comes, and it will go.[32] It is not a
long-term attribute, but temporary activity in which innards move,
change, wander, twist, are goaded and filled with blackness.[33] They "are
mad," in verbs (*bacchaō, lussaō, daimonaō*) coded with daemon.

How do other people know all this is going on inside? By watching; by
inference. The mad move differently. Their external appearance changes.
Observers infer inner changes they cannot see, from outer ones that they
can: a principle on which Greek medicine, a lot of philosophy, and tragic
performances were based. "Appearances," including the appearance of
people temporarily suffering invasion of daemon, "are sight of the obscure." Especially that most dark, obscure condition, madness.[34]

In later Europe too, up to the seventeenth century, madness was known
by its appearance. The idea that madness could be fearsomely latent was a
new development, from the characteristically nineteenth-century desire to
claim secret insight into long-hidden madness. Fifth-century observers

---

[31] Prometheus's liver as model for innards hurt by passion: Padel 1992:19, 120. Madness
as temporary: Padel 1981:108, 123.

[32] Padel 1992:80–83, 98, 116–32. Madness as extreme passion: below, Chapter 15. As
nonhuman: Chapter 13, nn. 53–64.

[33] "Blackness": Padel 1992:68–69, 73; below, Chapters 5, 6. Goaded, twisting, wandering mind: see Chapters 11, 12.

[34] Anaxag. fr. 21aDK; see Padel 1992:51, 55–57, 67–68; Padel 1990:336. Madness as
"black": below, Chapters 5, 6.

claimed insight *from* what was apparent: the nineteenth century *into* something hidden.[35]

In the Carter Dickson mystery quoted above, published in 1935, an elderly sister is accusing her brother of murder. (In fact, she has been hypnotized by the murderer to do so: another fin de siècle touch.) We haven't moved on much since. The passage would still ring persuasively in the tabloids, would still mirror popular notions. Of course latent madness "erupts." Our culture generally assumes madness is a long-term function of a personality. Madness may be not apparent, yet still "there." It "breaks out." We can even accept that behavior which seems sane may (when elucidated by an expert) express madness manifest in other activities or aspects of a person.

Carter Dickson is an impressionist, a master cook of the Gothic, using ingredients that go back beyond the nineteenth century, and the Renaissance, to Greek tragedy: to the tradition of tragic madness that fed European imagination. The red and the black, "shadows all over him," turning eyeballs, the more than normal size, the sense that murder is most aptly committed by the mad: Sophocles' *Ajax* is in there, and Euripides' *Heracles*.[36]

But Dickson has used these ingredients in a horizon of expectations about madness's relation to the self that are absolutely different from those of Greek tragedy. "And then I knew he was mad" is sudden insight into long-hidden madness. *He*'s the murderer! His acts came from a secret psychic den, from lurking mania. If someone in Greek tragedy said, "Then I knew X was mad," it would be because madness had suddenly attacked.[37] There would be no implications of a long-term condition. The words would simply refer to what had happened, a madness only present when apparent.

To understand Greek tragic madness in its own terms, we must tear out of ourselves, if we can, this nineteenth-century hold on our imagination. Historically, it is an oddity. It fits only the last hundred and fifty years of Western ideas about madness and leaves out many cultures and societies, including ancient Greece, which had and have deeply different views. Of course it is possible to use our terms, which assume long-term latent madness, in analyzing cultures who do not share this idea themselves. But I am exploring here how one society represented its own experience and perceptions. I want to find the meanings of madness in *its* terms.

[35] Porter 1987:35, 38. This coincides with the discovery that syphilis can lead, over a long period, to GPI: general paralysis of the insane. This link was documented and proved 1880–1906 (Quétel 1990:162–64), adding to ideas of latent madness.

[36] Shadow: see Chapter 7, nn. 12–19, 24, 26, 30. Twisting eyes: Chapter 7, nn. 38–40, 45. Heracles' eyes: *HF* 932; above, p. 19.

[37] Cf. *IT* 280–308: the watching herdsman knows when the stranger's madness begins and ends.

Compare the long-standing argument about the epidemic at Athens. What disease was it, really? Bubonic plague? Measles? The question throws up intriguing historical ironies, as well as reminders from within the medical community that even physical diseases mutate. The symptoms and nature of one disease differ in different climates and contexts. And identifying the disease tells us nothing about the people who lived and died in the epidemic, who wrote about and remembered it. How they experienced it; how they perceived and explained that experience; what difference it made to local images of self: these are the more serious questions. Analyzing alien experience in a closed cell of modern assumptions is an endgame on its own, not a responsible historical search.

It is very hard for psychoanalysts. Their practice depends on seeing other (the patient) in self's terms (of the trained analyst). The surface truth and expressed views of people to whom they listen are often treated as a smokescreen, as resistance disguising a deeper, different truth.

Historically, psychoanalysts here are products not only of a particular theory (however useful or true), but more largely of their historical conditioning by a century in love with the latent. For the purpose of understanding Greek madness, I'd like to put in a plea for them to respect the way their own views have been constructed.[38] A specific cultural process of about a hundred and fifty years (now analyzable, itself, by cultural historians and historians of science) made it possible for a culture to formulate the idea that madness builds within a personality and breaks out. It is inappropriate to turn this idea, produced by only one of many cultures of this world, onto perceptions of madness outside the West or onto those of the West before the eighteenth century.[39] The notion is anachronistic for fifth-century Greece even though its popular tokens, which can be used, à la Carter Dickson, to conjure up an un-Greek picture of madness, are themselves Greek.[40]

Tragic madness language suggests that madness involves temporary damage to innards. Like Dionysus, madness is evident in the verb. When innards are still again, their owner is sane. After his frenzy, Ajax is *emphrōn*, "in his mind," that is, his right mind. He "seems to *phronein* [think, be sane]" again.[41] It is the activity, the verbs, that matter. The judgment "X is

---

[38] See Chapter 21, nn. 19, 34. Showalter 1987:165–215 concentrates on the "feminization" of the mad, but is still a model historical overview of the making of (British) psychiatry from 1890 to the 1960s.

[39] See, e.g., Clarke 1975:1–24; MacDonald 1981: ch. 4; Porter 1987:268–76 and passim; and more fully below, Chapter 21.

[40] Cf. English use of Greek passion and disease imagery for non-Greek physiology: Padel 1992:76, 85.

[41] *Aj.* 306, 344. *Phronein*: Padel 1992:20, 44. Mobility of "ills": Padel 1992:65–68; cf. below, Chapters 11, 13.

mainomenos," "X *mainetai,*" "is raving," comes only at the moment when X is doing something abnormal. You "are mad" when and only when you do a mad act. The play we call *The Madness of Heracles* is in Greek *Heracles Mainomenos*, "Heracles Raving." Heracles, Ajax, Agave, Athamas, Lycurgus: all do something terrible in a single mad fit and then recover sanity.[42] Mad *adjectives* proliferated in the seventeenth century, a growth which implies that madness "was conceived more in terms of deeds and demeanour than of disease, or any permanent internal disposition."[43] As if seventeenth-century English put into adjectives what fifth-century Greek put into participles and verbs: an intensely diverse account of madness as a temporary condition.

[42] Athamas, Lycurgus: see Chapter 4, n. 36; *HF* 1138–41; *Aj.* 306–25; *Ba.* 1122–28, 1280–90.
[43] Porter 1987:22–23.

TEMPORARY VERSUS LONG-TERM MADNESS

CHRONIC SUSCEPTIBILITY

GREEK CULTURE outside tragedy suggests, on the whole, the same assumption implied by tragedy's language. Madness is temporary. Aristotle illustrates "the condition of men under the influence of passion," who "have knowledge in a sense and yet do not have it," by someone asleep, drunk, or *mainomenos*. "Mad" is part of his model of temporary aberration, momentary loss of normal consciousness. Mad, drunk, asleep. "Angers and sexual passions and other such states change the body, and in some men even create *maniai*." A contemporary medical writer implies that you stop being normal when you lose *phronēsis*: clear thinking, sanity. When you get this back, you are normal again. "When we abandon our accustomed habit, our *phronēsis* is destroyed."[1] Madness, therefore, is a temporary state.

But sometimes, in tragedy and outside it, we get a whiff of an idea that madness can be long-term. The house of Oedipus is *theomanēs*: permanently "maddened by gods." An "evil desire" to rob temples, says Plato, is neither *anthrōpinon*, human, nor *theion*, divine. It is an "itch," *oistros*, "bred in" someone "from ancient and unpurified crimes." Its victim should ask curse-lifting deities for help. Then the *nosēma*, "sickness," may lessen.[2] Herodotus, discussing the causes of Cleomenes' madness, weighs the possibility of long-term divine anger against a lifelong habit of drinking unwatered wine. (Antiquity always thought this very dangerous. It could kill instantly rather than gradually. "Asclepiades, son of Anaxippos, an Ephesian, twenty-two years old," drank "in one gulp a large amount of unmixed wine and died, spitting blood".)[3]

One comic character is incurably addicted to jury service:

> I'll tell you my master's illness:
> he's a jury-addict . . . wild to give verdicts; cries
> if he misses the front row. . . .
> He's mad. . . . So now we've locked him up. . . .

---

[1] Arist. *EN* 1147A12–18 (see Chapter 15, n. 39); Hp. *Breaths* 30 (Loeb 2:250).

[2] *Sept.* 653 (cf. *Ion* 1402 and *Or.* 854, where the word denotes temporary madness); Pl. *Legg.* 854B. *Oistros*: see Chapter 2, nn. 9–14.

[3] Hdt. 6.75–84; *Bulletin épigraphique* 20.385 (1978), quoted in Meillier 1980:98.

> His son's taken his illness very hard.
> First he tried curing him with words. . . .
> No good. Then purifying. . . . Useless.
> Then he tried religion. . . . As a last resort
> he sailed to Aegina, put his dad
> to sleep the night there in Asclepius's temple. . . .
> At dawn he turned up by the railings [of the court].[4]

It is likely that male Athenians could take over family property if they could prove their father incapable: that suggests it was possible to think someone was permanently unable to act responsibly.[5]

Finally, the Hippocratic author of "On the Sacred Disease," who thinks the brain, not the guts, is the center of consciousness, also thinks moisture on the brain causes madness. Phlegm produces quiet madness, bile makes for noisy. "If people rave all the time, these are the causes." Changes in the brain cause sudden attacks of raving terror or delirium.[6]

These examples suggest that fifth- and fourth-century imagination did consider long-term madness a possibility in some contexts, often relating to an ancient curse on individuals or families. Erinyes, for instance, are divinities of relationship (especially family ones) gone wrong. They send madness: they are also primally involved with cursing.[7]

This possibility of the long-*term* does not necessarily involve, as it began to do in the nineteenth century and does for us still, the quite separate idea of the long *hidden*. What the fifth- and fourth-century examples imply is chronic susceptibility to obvious, temporary mad fits.

The sharpest model is Plato's *oistros*: the "gadfly" word for "madness." Being susceptibile to mad attacks is (or, is like) being bitten by a fly. Maddening, when it happens. But when it is not happening, you are not mad. *Oistros* is not like tsetse fly (known to the nineteenth-century British in Africa), whose poison stays and works in the blood. (You know your cattle were bitten only when they start to die.) That you could have a virus, or madness, and no one know, is not a concept available in ancient Greece. When *oistros* is absent, you are sane as anyone else. The only difference is that you are likely to be the one it bites again.

Io and Orestes

Extant tragedy has three figures who are chronically susceptible to mad attacks. Cassandra has repeated pangs of prophetic frenzy. Io and Orestes

---

[4] Ar. *V.* 88–124.
[5] Harrison 1968:79–80; Dover 1974:126–28, 148–49.
[6] Hp. *DMS* 18: cf. Chapter 5, nn. 24–25.
[7] Padel 1992:164–77.

undergo long-term wanderings with repeated mad attacks. Wandering is a core Greek image of madness (see Chapters 10, 11, and 12) and their wanderings are an external image of the repeated mad fits with which they are afflicted. When sane,

> lightened of the disease,
> Orestes weeps, *emphrōn*. But
> sometimes he leaps from his bed,
> running like a colt unyoked.

Orestes never knows when madness will strike. The switch from sanity to madness is "swift." Remember the plural name, Maniai, for the Arcadian landscape round the Orestes monument.[8]

Unsurprisingly, a key word in passages of repeated *maniai* is "again." "Again the pain of prophecy spins me round. . . ." "Again the spasm and mind-beating *maniai* burn me."[9] The mad fits of these figures braid images of repeated storm and fire with images of twisting, driving pursuit.[10] Madness is wind, fire, storm. But storms and fires end. Madness "dies down," "like the sharp south wind."[11] Then the same people are sane.

Here is the heart of difference between our assumptions about madness, and those of tragedy. *We* might argue that when the attack is over, the character is still mad, but the madness has gone dormant or underground. All mad tragic characters have been interpreted at some time or other like this (see Chapter 21). I have heard an analysis of Ophelia's speech patterns in *Hamlet* designed to prove her "mad" before her madness. But in the terms that Greek dramatists, at least, set up, characters not said to be mad are sane as any others.[12]

Maniai are limited, finite. In tragedy (if not outside, in real life), chronic susceptibility to *maniai* is finite too. In the *Prometheus* play and trilogy, an end to Io's suffering, to her wanderings, *maniai*, and persecution, is vital to the plot. From the child Zeus gets on her in that moment of cure comes the deliverer of Prometheus, who foresees this end for Io.[13]

An end to Orestes' madness is likewise crucial to his story. Pausanias uses it, for instance, to explain the finger-monument at *Maniai*. In Aeschylus's *Oresteia*, which defined Orestes' aura in Athenian imagination, Orestes begins with a chronic susceptibility to madness, and recovers: partly

---

[8] *Or.* 43–45, 791, 254, 276. Maniai: above, p. 20.

[9] *Ag.* 1215; *PV* 878 cf. 566.

[10] *Ag.* 1215, 1256, cf. 1172; *Cho.* 1024, 1054, 1063 (cf. Erinyes as hunters: Padel 1992:118, 176–77); *PV* 572, 586, 879–86.

[11] *Ag.* 1178 (*ouketi*); *Aj.* 258; see Padel 1992:81–91.

[12] See Chapter 21, n. 18, cf. nn. 44–45, 49, 56, 58, 66.

[13] *PV* 848; cf. Conacher 1980:64–65.

through a change in the nature and status of the Erinyes, who inflict his madness. They stop hunting him and turn into Eumenides, Kindly Ones, who keep harmful passion away from Athenian citizens. Their attack on him was "binding." Athene "saves" him from them. He, like his mind, is made "safe."[14]

We have met *aphrōn*, "without *phrēn*," "mad," and its opposites *emphrōn*, "in your *phrēn*" (Orestes is *emphrōn*, sane, till Erinyes appear), and *sōphrōn*, "with a safe *phrēn*," a vital word in the *Oresteia*. Aegisthus taunts the chorus of the *Agamemnon* with "missing a *sōphrōn gnōmē* [safe-minded opinion]," because they insult their new ruler. At Delphi, Orestes holds his suppliant branch *sōphronōs*: in a "safe-minded" way.[15] At the end, Orestes is "saved" while the creatures who maddened him are changed to "kindly ones." Their target in him, or anyone, is the inside: *phrēn* or *splanchna*. His life is "saved" when his innards are "safe." He was open to fits of being *aphrōn*; now he is *sō-phrōn*. Safe-*phrēned*.[16]

Aeschylus ends Orestes' chronic susceptibility to mad fits by changing the maddening agents, and how they are seen. But Euripides, in two plays, explores the possibility that this change did not "take," sending Orestes on further Erinyes-ridden travels where fits of madness still chase him. Eventually, these lead to a crisis that ends his susceptibility to madness.

At the end of *Orestes*, Apollo promises Orestes "victory" in the trial. No more is heard of his madness (unless you think he is mad to fear he may be hearing an evil daemon, *alastōr*, while seeming to hear Apollo).[17] In *Iphigeneia among the Taurians*, Athene says Orestes came to the Taurian land "escaping the Erinyes' anger." The memorial shrine he builds will be named

> from your sufferings, going round Greece
> with Erinyes' *oistroi*.[18]

Oistroi: repeated attacks of biting madness. The shrine will memorialize these, and put them in the past. No more susceptibility to Erinys fits. Orestes' journey to the foreign land, the journey that is this play, ends his persecution and his attacks. Io and Orestes alike suffer repeated attacks of madness. But their susceptibility to these attacks is finite.

---

[14] See *Eum*. 332, 978–83, 754 (*sōsasa*, addressed to Athene), 306, 781 (*sōizei me*). Orestes at Athens: Padel 1992:170–85.

[15] *Cho*. 1026; *Ag*. 1664; *Eum*. 44. *Aphrōn, sōphrōn*: see Chapter 3, n. 21, and Chapter 12, nn. 59–60.

[16] *Eum*. 799, 330, 859–60. "Saving" his life: *Eum*. 746. *Splanchna*: Padel 1992:13–18. Target of Erinyes: Padel 1992:174, 180, 191.

[17] *Or*. 1652, 1669.

[18] *IT* 1439, 1456.

CASSANDRA

Before she dies, Cassandra too seems to find some ending to the god relationship that gave her those fits of prophetic frenzy. In *Agamemnon*, she still has the painful relation with Apollo that marks her life, but "sends to destruction" her wand and wreaths, insignia of that relationship. The god himself strips her of them, and speaks through her actions and words.[19] She accepts death. "There's no escape." She prays her murderers be punished. She says of human life, "I pity it." She leaves madness, and Apollo, behind.[20]

In Euripides' *Trojan Women*, Cassandra tells the Greek herald he will "bring her from this land, as one of the three Erinyes." She knows she will help shatter the Atreid house, which shattered Troy. Here too she says goodbye to Apollo's insignia, and gives them to winds, which blow them to the god.[21]

In both plays, she swings between spasms of prophetic madness and lucid, explanatory moments. In *Agamemnon* she starts off silent. Clytemnestra and the chorus think her language will be foreign as birdsong. They compare her to a new-caught wild animal. They think she doesn't understand, needs an interpreter, has to use sign language. She "is mad" (*mainetai*), "listens to bad *phrenes*." When she does speak, it is first to Apollo. The chorus think she will "prophesy about her troubles." They see this as *to theion*, "the divine [thing]" that "stays in the *phrēn* even of a slave."[22]

In her fits, Cassandra sees and smells the local murders, past and future. "What sort of house is this?" she asks Apollo. The chorus answers simplistically, "That of Atreus's sons." "No," she says. "A house hated by gods." She responds to them. She is not isolated. Mad joins sane within one framework.[23]

Cassandra has three spasms of frenzied vision. First, she "sees" four separate things: the house's bloody history, Thyestes' feast, Clytemnestra's plot, and her own death. Second, she describes the links between these (symbolized in continuous speech rather than fragmentary utterances). Thyestes' feast *led to* Aegisthus's plot and the approaching murder. She sees Agamemnon unaware of Clytemnestra's treachery. All this is inevitable: it will happen whether she is believed or not. Third, another continuous speech. This is linkage and argument rather than vision. Clytemnestra will kill her. She strips off her priestess clothes. Look, Apollo is destroying me!

---

[19] *Ag.* 1265–67, 1270.

[20] *Ag.* 1280–85, 1290, 1299, 1323–26, 1327–30.

[21] *Tro.* 457, 461, 451–54, 410–11.

[22] *Ag.* 1047–64, 1081, 1083–84. *Phrenes*, listening to innards: Padel 1992:20–23, 73–75. Madness and possession: Padel 1983:13; above, Chapter 3, n. 27.

[23] *Ag.* 1087, 1311; *men oun*, 1087–90.

She'll die. Orestes will avenge her. Why complain? She makes a final rational prophecy of, which is also a prayer for, vengeance.[24] Mixed with all
this are passages of dialogue with the chorus. They quiz her on her relation
with Apollo, her prophecy of Agamemnon's death, and her own courage,
facing foreseen death.[25]

Running through frenzy and rational communication is her self-
awareness. Cassandra is aware. Of people, of communicating. Aware she is
not understood or believed. She mourns her brother's affair with Helen,
and Troy's fall, which leads to her death. She will no longer speak in riddles; she "will be sane." The chorus must listen. She sees Erinyes in the
house, rising from the first crime, Thyestes' seduction of his brother's wife.
She asks the chorus to "witness" to her truth. Even in prophecy she addresses them. "I speak *to you* of fate in a treacherous murderous bath."[26]

Her relation with Apollo is part of her self-awareness. As she strips the
tokens of her relation with him she says,

> Look, Apollo himself is unclothing me
> of his prophetic dress.

During the pangs of prophecy and lament for her city, her fate, she seems
to the chorus to suffer from *daimōn*:

> Some *daimōn*, evil minded, falling upon you,
> heavy from above, makes you chant
> pitiful, death-bringing sufferings.

The madness and its repetition come from her relation with Apollo, who
maddens her. *Daimōn* "makes her sing."[27]

Euripides showed Cassandra in prophetic frenzy at least twice: once in a
lost play, *Alexandros*, once in *Trojan Women*. Both followed the Aeschylean
swings of rationality and frenzy. In *Trojan Women*, Cassandra enters singing of fire, celebrating her sexual enslavement to Agamemnon as a wedding. Her appalled mother and chorus call her *baccheuousa*, "raving," and
mainas, "madwoman":

> even misfortunes have failed
> to make you sane. You're still
> in the same state.[28]

---

[24] *First*: *Ag.* 1090–149; i.e., 1090–21, 1095–97, 1100–29, 1136–49. *Second*: 1214–22,
which has led (*ek tōnde*) to Aegisthus and the coming murder: 1223–26, 1227–38. *Third*:
1256–63, 1264–76, 1277–85, 1315–19, 1323–26.

[25] *Ag.* 1198–213, 1245–55, 1298–1312.

[26] *Ag.* 1156, 1167, 1182–90, 1196, 1129.

[27] *Ag.* 1269–70, 1174–76.

[28] *Tro.* 307–40, 341, 349–50. Cassandra-scenes in *Alexandros*: Coles 1974:23–32,
Scodel 1980:22–23.

As if to refute them, Cassandra abandons her lyrics for their iambics. Like Aeschylus's Cassandra, this one responds to others. Sanely, she explains the way *she* sees. Taking her will be fatal to Agamemnon. Yes, she is *entheos*, "possessed." But ("so far I'll stand outside bacchic raving") devastated Troy is better off than the Greeks, who face terrible *nostoi*, "returns." Odysseus does not know what agonies await him.[29]

The chorus, illustrating Aeschylus's words that Cassandra "persuaded no one," doubts this will happen. The Greek herald says she would be punished for this prophecy "if Apollo had not maddened your *phrenes*." Apollo "sent her out of her mind."[30]

Ending long-term vulnerability to mad fits means changing your relation with divinity. Cassandra's bond to divinity is different from any other in tragedy. The end to her susceptibility to madness is the end of her life. Cassandra promised sex to Apollo. He gave her the prophetic gift in advance. She broke her promise. His interest marks her story like the city's name in Brighton rock: that peppermint stick of candy, which kept its red letters while you sucked the white away. Their relation, her life, her susceptibility to madness, end together.

TEMPORARY AND LONG-TERM: THE DIFFERENCES

Cassandra apart, there are significant differences of cause and result between madness that comes only once and repeated bursts of madness.

Like Io, Heracles is caught in the erotic relationship of Zeus and Hera. But he differs from Io and Orestes: only one of these gods makes demands on him. His madness comes only from Hera, and only once. One go of punitive madness from Athene destroys Ajax, one from Dionysus destroys Lycurgus, Athamas, Agave, Pentheus. Once is enough for an act with permanently terrible results.[31]

Io and Orestes differ from these figures in three ways. First, their madness rises out of conflicting demands, from a divine, conflicted, plural universe. In his *Anatomy of Melancholy*, Burton set melancholy in the context of the universe's moral, physical, and spiritual disorder. Greek tragic madness too can be both the result of, and image for, cosmic disorder. Io and Orestes are caught in a cross-fire of male and female divine authority-figures.[32] Second, their madness wanders on a huge geographical scale,

[29] *Tro.* 367, 431. *Entheos*, "possessed": Padel 1983:13; above, Chapter 3, n. 27; below, Chapter 12, nn. 47–57.
[30] *Tro.* 407–408 (*exebaccheusen*); cf. *Ag.* 1212.
[31] *HF* 1260, 1309 *lektrōn phthonousa Zēni*: cf. *PV* 650, 900; see Chapter 20, n. 41. For Heracles, Hera is the only active side of the "double bind": see Chapter 19, n. 40.
[32] Fox 1976:17, below, Chapter 20, nn. 28–39.

reflecting the cosmic conflict (Hera versus Zeus, Erinyes versus Apollo) that drives it. Other mad "wanderings" are inner, or small scale.[33]

Finally, neither Io nor Orestes is murderous in madness. Orestes' madness comes after his murder, as punishment for it. In *Orestes*, Orestes is murderous, but not when mad (unless, against the play's own terms, you read him as permanently mad with different phases of madness). His attacks on Hermione and Helen are acts of revenge conceived by other people. Pylades plans Helen's murder. Electra sees Hermione approaching "into the midst of murder" and thinks her fair game. Orestes and Pylades, terrorists together, take her hostage. None of this is madness. When mad, Orestes tries to shoot Furies no one else can see.[34] He does not try to kill people but to scotch the source of his madness.

Not all tragic madness is murderous. Phaedra in erotic frenzy, Pentheus under Dionysus's spell are not. But the commonest paradigm is (Ajax, Heracles, Athamas, Lycurgus). Even acting these roles made for aggression. Lucian (the second-century A.D. satirist) describes an actor playing Ajax who went mad and hit the actor playing Odysseus on the head with a flute. Afterwards he was sorry, fell "ill from grief, and was given up for mad in very truth."[35] But Io and Orestes in madness are victims not agents of violence.

They are victims also of a clash in the world outside. Against those who go mad only once is a single angry divine figure, displaying a divine aggression that brings about its own double. The god causes murderous violence in the person she or he is angry with. Divine anger and punishment come through the single murderous act. Agave, Athamas, Lycurgus, Heracles: murder is the perfect one-way, irreversible act that an angry god gets a mad person to do.[36]

Orestes and Io are revealing exceptions to the rule that tragedy mostly stresses madness as a single acute attack, only present while apparent in action. As the only extant tragic examples of punitive, persecuting madness repeated over time, they expose the trap created by multiple divine demands on human beings.[37] Their madness is emblematic of something innate, not in the person, but in the human condition: in its vulnerability

[33] See below, pp. 105 (Phaedra's wandering mind; cf. Ajax's "wandering" movements on the beach, *Aj.* 59), 105 (rolling eyes), 132 (jerky, dancelike twisting of mad bodies), Chapter 13.

[34] *Or.* 1105, 1302, 1313, 1316, 1491–96), 1536, 1610–12; cf. 251–77, 268, *IT* 298–99. Cf. Chapter 21, nn. 42, 46–51.

[35] *Hipp.* 214; *Ba.* 850; Lucian *De saltatione* 83–84. Murderous paradigm of madness: Padel 1981:112.

[36] Athamas: A. tr. 1. Lycurgus: above, Chapter 3, nn. 6–9.

[37] Padel 1981:111–12; see Chapter 20, nn. 21–27.

to the world as it tragically is. But this vulnerability is most often evident, in tragedy, in a single attack.

There are two main images of mind in tragedy. Most sketch the mind as female-like, vessel-like, passive, entered by emotion from outside. But a few, more ambiguously, suggest mind as active, with emotion as live growth in it, springing from within.[38] Something similar is true, I think, for madness. Tragic insistence is towards the exterior cause of internal change, which is also sudden and finite. But this interacts with a less common alternative: that some people, held in a permanent painful divine relation, are subject, long-term, to repeated pangs of madness.

MEDICINE

There are two reasons, I think, why tragic madness is mainly temporary. One is medical. An important model of madness, in ancient times as our own, is disease (see Chapter 15). Greek doctors did write about chronic conditions, but they spent far more time on acute ones. Our own medical knowledge and practice give us a different relation to both. Very crudely, the fact that we can keep alive people who would then have died means we are familiar with chronic states in a way they were not. From Homer on, poets sometimes mention a "long-wasting-away," consuming disease, which ends in death.[39] Heraclitus was said to suffer from dropsy, of which he eventually died. There were endemic fevers, especially malarial, chronically present in Greek communities.[40] But the model was Pandora's jar, full of ills that escaped and "wandered the world, harming people," permanently present in the world, not in people. *We* know malaria stays in the body and recurs with further bouts of the same disease. But what Greeks saw was another fever. "The body stormed with summer fever, or chill." When the *kausos*, fever (literally, a "burning"), was not apparent, it was not there.[41]

Of course there was a notion of "being sick for a long time." Such sickness was mostly visible, and usually ended in death.[42] Much later in the Greek tradition, it gets defined. Possibly by the Herophileans, Alexandrian doctors who called it a *pathos* (affection) "hard to resolve and move," caused by the body's moistures; and certainly in Roman times, by a Greek

---

[38] Padel 1992:56–59, 95, 134.

[39] *Il.* 13.667; *Od.* 5.395, 11.201; *Ant.* 819: Grmek 1989:36. Tuberculosis in the ancient world: see Grmek 1989:401 n. 2, 403 n. 23.

[40] D.L. 9.3. See Grmek 1989:41, 37–38.

[41] *Erg.* 100–104; Pi. *P.* 3.53.

[42] See Hp. *Epid. I* 3 (Loeb 1:148). *Kausos*: Grmek 1989:290–92.

doctor who calls *emmonon* ("remaining") disease a "chronic constitution contrary to nature."[43]

In Hippocratic writing, diseases are often identified from signs, with no firm distinction between a word used descriptively, of a sign, and the same word used interpretively or diagnostically, of its disease. The disease is, or is shown in, the sign. The same word stands for both.[44] If the sign is absent, so is the disease. You know about what is within from what is temporarily apparent.

Hippocratics often focus on the *krisis*, the turning point. After it the patient either recovers or dies. If the cause of disease "leaves," you recover. "Breaths" cause apoplexy. If they "go away the disease comes to an end." Disease is finite martial attack. If it leaves, the patient gets better.[45]

There are references to long diseases also in the records of religious healing centers, like Epidaurus. But there is far less concentration on chronic disease than we are used to. "Acute diseases kill most people: . . . pleurisy, pneumonia, *phrenitis*, ardent *kausos*. . . . For whenever there is no general type of plague around, but diseases are sporadic, many more people die from these than from all other diseases put together," says the author of *Regimen in Acute Diseases*. He is riding his pet subject; but the same assumption is found in other treatises. To restore everyone to health is impossible. Patients often die before the doctor can fight the disease. The result of disease is death or health.[46]

The medical model is one good basis, therefore, for taking tragic madness as an acute, temporary, visible event that results in recovery or destruction.

NARRATIVE

The other reason for taking tragic madness as one finite episode is literary, a question of narrative function: the role of madness in each story. Hera maddens Heracles to make him kill his family. Athene maddens Ajax to stop him from killing the Greeks and thereby humiliates him. When this, the madness's purpose, is accomplished, madness is no longer needed. Heracles cannot kill his family twice. Ajax is humiliated: his self-image is changed. He will not try again to kill Greeks. Athene says she will "show this amazing *nosos* to you, that having seen it you may utter it to all the

---

[43] [Galen] *Definitiones medicae* 149.xix (Kühn, p. 391).

[44] See Lloyd 1979:22; Padel 1992:52, 55, 88–98.

[45] *Krisis*: e.g., Hp. *Progn.* 2 (Loeb 2:8–10); cf. Hp. *Breaths* 13 (Loeb 2:248). Martial attack: Padel 1992:55, 56.

[46] Hp. *Reg. Acut. Dis.* 5 (Loeb 2:66), *Progn.* 1 (Loeb 2:6), cf. 2.1, 4; 6.1 (Loeb 2:8, 14). Cf. Parker 1983:240 (with n. 25).

Greeks." She wants to publish Ajax's madness. The absurdity agonizes him: he imagines Odysseus, "the whole army" laughing. Because of this, though he still wants to kill his enemies, he plans his own death, not theirs.[47] Heracles will learn from madness

> how great against him is Hera's anger. . . .
> Gods are nowhere, mortal things are great,
> if he does not pay the penalty.[48]

This learning is accomplished in one attack. In each case the play's interest, and the story's, migrates to another issue. The heroes now have to deal with the change their mad act has effected in their lives.

The idea that madness is temporary matches Greek images of other inward experience, of passion and disease. Damage done to *phrenes* is momentary. The mind mysteriously recovers. *Phrenes* somehow survive being destroyed. The continued vulnerability of the mind to the nonhuman aggression of tragic passion is a core image of tragedy.[49]

Like *atē*,[50] madness may have permanent consequences. But this does not mean it is permanent itself. Quite the opposite. Tragedy depends on the terror and irony of the fact that one act or word erupting from a temporary state of mind can do permanent damage. Madness, not a permanent condition, not a hidden, innate aspect of a person but a single seizure coming at them from outside, is the perfect tragic example of that temporary thing.

---

[47] *Aj.* 51 52, 66–67, 367, 382, 408, 389, 361, 391.
[48] *HF* 840–42.
[49] See Padel 1992:117–38, 152–61. Mind as tragic hero: below, p. 244.
[50] See below, pp. 174, 188, 192.

Darkness and Vision

Chapter 5

INNER SHADOW

Madness Is Black

WHAT MADNESS "is like" is fabricated in a culture's mind by the sane. It is what *they* make, from what they see—mad people—and from what they imagine. Tragedy, whether Shakespearian, Jacobean, or Greek, represents madness from the viewpoint of, and in relation to, its own sanity. Two sane acts are behind Greek tragic images of madness: acts of imagination (how the sane imagine madness to be, inside) and observation. How they perceive it, from outside.

These two acts get mixed up. Here (Part 2), I tackle mainly the inside. What the culture, and the genre, imagined it was like on the inside, to be mad. This blends with how society perceived it from outside (see Part 3). Fantasies about madness were embedded in, and given meaning by, a network of Greek images for inner experience whose key element is inner dark.

Inner darkness is a *mille feuille* image, many layered even in tragedy's time. The layers thickened and twisted on themselves as Western societies reused the image. We inherit, as tragedy did, an ancient discourse of darkness about the mind. But many resonances are different, for us. The fifth century lacked associations of the intervening centuries. We, for our part, lack resonances the image held for them. They have faded away, or been overlain by others. Most important among these was the relation of inner darkness to the site of consciousness. Not the head, but the innards. Dark innards, whose darkness intensified in passion, and in madness.[1]

Mind is dark, and madness, mind's disturbance, especially so. Ajax's eyes are "darkened" in madness. Biological and daemonic causes of madness are black. Daemonic madness-senders are "dark-faced children of Night": Lyssa, Erinys, rising from black Hades. Magico-medical organic causes of madness include black roots cut from black earth in the dark: a root-magic still at work in Shakespeare's day. "Have we eaten of the insane root, that takes the reason prisoner?" asks Banquo when the witches disappear. Internal organic causes include black bile.[2]

---

[1] See Padel 1992:75–77.

[2] Padel 1992:69, 101, 175; *Macbeth* 1.3.84. Hellebore: below, nn. 7–8. Eyes darkened, "darkness, my light": *Aj.* 85, 396 (cf. the night timing of his madness 180, 217). Cf. dark stormy words from the "Stygian *atē*" of Io's madness: *PV* 885.

Hellebore, Black Bile

Borage and Hellebore fill two scenes,
Sovereign plants to purge the veins
Of melancholy, and cheer the heart
Of those black fumes which make it smart. . . .
. . . .
The best medicine that e'er God made
For this malady, if well assay'd.
 —Robert Burton, "Argument to the Frontispiece" to
  The Anatomy of Melancholy

In the late fifth century, under the influence of burgeoning medical theory and treatment, two madness verbs arose that had an impact on medical and ethical ideas for two thousand years.

Melancholaō, "I'm full of black [*melas*] bile [*cholē*]," appears first in Aristophanes, spoken by a "fool" bird salesman. Someone else must be "mad" because he's following a blind man, or his behavior has suddenly changed. A rude informer asks rhetorically "Am I mad?" All these are *melancholaō*.[3] *Mainomai* and *melancholaō* mean the same, but *melancholaō* is ruder: a coarse synonym for *mainomai*. In Plato, a medical tutor who does not tell pupils whom to treat and when "is mad," *mainetai*. But a true musician would *not* say *melancholas*, "Are you crazy?" to a layman claiming to teach harmony: he would just comment that the man did not know his subject.[4]

Melancholaō does not appear in tragedy, perhaps because it sounded slangy. But also because, in tragedy's day, black bile did not have the professional medical involvement in madness that the following centuries gave it. *Melancholaō*—and also *cholaō*, "I fill with bile"—to mean "I'm mad," plus the madness implications of black bile, are common in the fourth-century comic poet Menander and Menander-influenced Roman poets.[5]

Hellebore madness-words also figure in comedy, not tragedy. Greek doctors came to use hellebore widely as an emetic, but from the last quarter of the fifth century popular imagination saw it particularly as a cure for madness. *Helleboriaō* is "I need hellebore": am mad, have a fit of madness. *Helleborizō* is "I drink hellebore," that is, as a remedy for madness. "Drink hellebore!" means "You're crazy!" Like *melancholaō*, these words bubble up in comedy: Aristophanes, the fifth- to fourth-century Callias, and the slightly later Diphylus, who wrote *Helleborizomenoi*. "The Hellebore Drinkers," "The Mad."[6]

---

[3] Ar. *Av.* 14, *Pl.* 12, 364–66, 903.
[4] Pl. *Phdr.* 268C–E.
[5] E.g., Men. *Samia* 218, *Epitrepontes* 217, 560–61; Plautus *Amphitryon* 727, *Captivi* 596.
[6] Call. fr. 28; Ar. *V.* 1489; cf. Hp. *Fract.* 11; Strabo 9.3.3.

Greek doctors called two plants "hellebore." "Black" hellebore was what we now call *Helleborus*. Their "white" hellebore was not true hellebore, but a *Liliaceae*. What the two have in common, chemically, is poison. Both are fatal, but, as a modern doctor puts it, "before killing they have side effects. . . . One might as well shoot a gun blindly to enjoy the noise and smell."[7] These side effects, which Greek and Renaissance doctors were after, are violent diarrhea and vomiting. Hellebore is an instant emetic. Patients vomited the poison up before it killed them.

To be fair, some later ancient writers did say hellebore was poisonous. Even early on it was known that "Convulsion after hellebore is deadly." But Burton, recording these opinions in 1621, writes: "Notwithstanding these cavils and objections most of our late writers do much approve it." Drinking hellebore was appallingly common. Greeks drank wine laced with it. ("Flavored," says the lexicon.) The "ill-bred" man tells you at table the bile he shat when he took hellebore was "black as this soup."[8]

Here is a constellation of blackness and angry violence: black bile, black hellebore, mad raving, emetic spasms. In Greek root-magic, it was the darker part of the plant, the part growing in "black" earth, that cured, and caused, madness. "The root of it only is in use," says Burton.[9] There is a homeopathic tone about this that fits Greek apotropaic magic. Treat dark inner violence with what is dark, inner, violent. Cause and cure resemble each other.[10]

But the black bile–hellebore relation also fits Greek poetry's images of emotion, and Greek medical images of battling disease. Doctors in the Greek tradition thought of cause and treatment in terms of invasion and eviction. Disease got in. Doctors had to get it out. Greek doctors go on about what goes into and comes out of their patients. Diet versus vomit, feces, urine, mucus.[11] Inevitably, then, there is an excremental resonance to black bile. Burton remembers a doctor who cured, "with one purge of black hellebore," a madman "thought to be possessed": "The receipt was there to be seen; his excrements were like ink, he perfectly healed at once."[12] I suppose it left you weak.

Greek poetry generally speaks of passion, especially anger, as dark boiling turbulence: an inner storm, darkening the innards. In Sophocles, the "terrible flowering *menos* [force, or fury] of Lycurgus's *mania* flowed away." *Menos* is "black." The "black *phrenes*" of Homer's Agamemnon

[7] Majno 1975:189.
[8] Hp. *Aph.* 5.1 (Loeb 4:158); Burton *Anatomy of Melancholy* 2.4.2; Pliny *NH* 25.58; Thphr. *Char.* 20; Dioscurides *De materia medica* 5.72 (Wellman).
[9] Padel 1992:69–70, 101; Burton *Anatomy of Melancholy* 2.4.2.
[10] See Faraone 1992:36–53. Cf. Padel 1992:68–75.
[11] Timken-Zinkann 1968:289; Padel 1992:55–56.
[12] Burton *Anatomy of Melancholy* 2.4.2.

"filled round greatly with *menos*" in his rage. Organs swell and blacken in passion.[13] If you put these ideas together—invasion and eviction, plus black flooding passion—the image of madness as a black, angry, inner flood seems inevitable. It must be evicted. Hellebore, forcing out black liquid, did just that. There was black liquid inside: now it comes out. Madness was raging within. Now it has gone.

The two new roots for madness verbs in the late fifth century speak, therefore, of new, medically influenced perceptions, which build on already existing imagery. Cause: black bile. Cure: black hellebore. The colors match those of existing daemons and images. We cannot see black bile today. Some medical historians argue the Hippocratics did not see black bile but only posited it as a "theoretical product," "hypothetical fluid."[14]

However, like others since, Greek doctors did see blackness coming from their patients in various forms. Shit "black as soup" (or as ink, once this is invented). "Black" urine: for Greek *melas* means "darkish" as well as "black," and its opposites are "pale," "light," rather than "white." With *melas* it is not a case of pitch-black, coal-black urine, but darkish. And darkish urine ("mahogany colored," according to recent observers) is an observed symptom of "blackwater fever," a form of malaria then probably endemic in Greece. This might have been one commonly noticed "darkness" that made doctors think they had seen bile they could call *melas*. "Black" urine seems to be associated with black bile in Hippocratic texts. A woman who passes it also has "melancholic fits."[15]

Other "black" liquids could also have made them think they saw black bile. Feces of patients with bleeding gastric ulcers. Vomit of patients with carcinoma of the stomach.[16] The modern consensus is that black bile was something Hippocratic doctors thought they saw.

The role of black bile changes round the end of the fifth century. In the twenty years on either side of 400 B.C., black bile, the paradigm black inner liquid, became the main inner determinant of mental disturbance.[17] This was formalized over the centuries within increasingly complex systems of explanation both of madness and of character. The organic source of madness is black liquid.

The humoral system, within which black bile acquired this status, began essentially with the Hippocratics, but they were deeply influenced by the fifth-century pre-Socratic philosopher-poet, Empedocles. Taking for

---

[13] *Ant.* 960; *Il.* 1.103; Padel 1992:136, 25, 68, 81, 84–88. See also Rütten 1992:66–74.

[14] Ribbert 1899:92; Mani 1959:34; G. Gruber 1952:22 (see also Kudlien 1973, followed by Simon 1978:232–35). This approach is documented by Schoener 1964:56.

[15] Hp. *Epid. III* 17 (Loeb 1:260–63). Blackwater fever: Timken-Zinkann 1968:291; Grmek 1989:295–304.

[16] See Timken-Zinkann 1968:290 for specific hypotheses and their authors.

[17] Flashar 1966; Timken-Zinkann 1968.

granted the principle that human interiors and the outside world are made of the same fabric, Empedocles argued for four elements within this fabric. The same four "roots" are in us as in sun, earth, sky, and sea. In us, the mix (*krasis*) of these elements determines constitution and character. As Theophrastus, Aristotle's pupil, reports him, Empedocles thought that if the mix in us is perfect, we are healthy and intelligent. If the mix is best in one part of us, we are especially intelligent there. If best in the hands, we'll be artists. If best in the tongue, orators.[18]

Alcmaeon of Croton, on the other hand, talked instead of several *dunameis*, qualities or powers: "moist, dry, cold, hot, bitter, sweet, and the rest." Health is the balance of power among these. Sickness is caused by monopoly rule by any one alone.[19] In the fifth century, black bile is not a humor but a pathogenic agent. Treatises from the last third of the fifth century treat black bile as a diseased condition of ordinary bile, not a humor. By about 400 B.C. (when our extant tragedies stop), medical writers were integrating ideas derived from Alcmaeon and Empedocles and applying them to humors, *chumoi* (modern Greek for "juices"): the elements on which they based their vision of the body, identified as both cause and symptom of illness. Humors fitted poetic imagery of passion as something liquid, flowing and dripping within.[20]

In the fourth century, Hippocratic writers synthesized all this into humoral theory as the rest of the world has known it since. As the key treatise in this process, *On the Nature of Man*, puts it: "The body of a human being has in it blood, phlegm, and bile, yellow and black." The humors matched the seasons. Blood's season is spring, warm and moist. Yellow bile is summer, warm and dry. Black bile is autumn, cold and dry. Phlegm, cold and moist, is winter. "If you give the same man the same drug four times in the year, he'll vomit most phlegmatic stuff in winter, most moist in summer, most bilious in summer, and the blackest in autumn." Observation of the local kinds of illness meshed with theory. Humoral theory was "the logical consequence of Ionian [i.e., pre-Socratic] philosophy, and a faithful reflection of the pathological and clinical features of the ills actually suffered by Mediterranean populations."[21] A mixture, therefore, of historical accident and philosophical development.

Later writers connected four seasons, four humors further with the

---

[18] Emp. DK 31A28; Thphr. *De sensibus* 11; see Klibansky, Panofsky, and Saxl 1964:5. Same "stuff" inside and outside humans: Padel 1992:43, 51.

[19] Aetius 5.30.1; see KR 234.

[20] Padel 1992:81–88. See Müri 1953, and Hp. *AWP, DMS, Epid. I, Epid. III* (treatises preceding *Nat. Hom.*) with Flashar 1966:36

[21] Grmek 1989:1. See Hp. *Nat. Hom.* 4, 7–8 (Loeb 4:10, 18–24). Empedocles and Alcmaeon as precursors to humoral theory, *Nat. Hom.* as key amalgamating text: Klibansky, Panofsky, and Saxl, 1964:5–8.

"Four Ages of Man." Childhood, adolescence, maturity, old age—in various versions, this matchup stayed in place for two thousand years: a core theory of European medicine, European images of human beings in relation to the outside world.[22]

In Greek post-fifth-century writings, each humor produces its own lot of diseases. On black bile's list are several, including skin-sores. But it also causes madness. Any mental disturbance connected with the others is referred to black bile. *Phrenitis*, for instance (from which we get "frenzy"), is compared to *melancholia*. Both are caused by bile getting into blood:

> Blood in a human being contributes most . . . to intelligence. When bile is moved and enters veins and blood, it stirs the blood, changing its consistency and movement, heating it. The blood heats the rest of the body. The patient loses his wits and is no longer himself. . . . Patients with *phrenitis* are deranged, like melancholics, who also grow *paranooi* [delirious]—some rave [*mainontai*]—when their blood is corrupted by bile and phlegm.

People with excess black bile are "noisy, restless, and do bad, inappropriate things," when delirious.[23]

Another author, the eccentric who imagined (unlike most Greek writers) that the mind might be in the head, argues that mad raving is caused by moisture in the brain. Sudden changes in the brain cause sudden mad terrors: "The brain changes when it is heated. It is heated by bile which rushes to the brain from the rest of the body, through the blood-veins. . . . Shouts and cries at night happen if the brain is heated suddenly. The bilious suffer from this. . . ." Later Galen explains, "As outer darkness fills everyone with fear . . . so the dark color of black bile generates fear: it darkens the seat of reason."[24]

The force of this idea—black bile causes madness—played off Greek magical and religious associations of darkness. Madness's darkness interacts also, I suspect, with a sense of madness as unreadable: as "obscure," and in that sense dark, to the sane. And it interacts with images of the mind as underworld: a place of death and putrefaction, the bowels of the earth. The place fear came from. Hades had black rivers running through it. The mind, which generated and felt these fears, flowed with dark passions. Hades and the mind are parallel habitats: of madness, Erinyes, black dreams. As late as 1482, Marsilio Ficino sees a connection between the

---

[22] Klibansky, Panofsky, and Saxl 1964:10.

[23] Hp. *On Diseases I* 30 (Loeb 5:178).

[24] Hp. *DMS* 18 (Loeb 2:177); Galen *De locis affectis* 3.10 (Kühn 8:91); Klibansky, Panofsky, and Saxl 1964:14–16. Greek siting of "mind" in innards, not head: Padel 1992:12 n. 3, and above, n. 1.

under-earth and the mind. Black bile "obliges thought to penetrate and explore the center of its objects, because black bile is itself akin to the center of the earth."[25]

BLACK ANGER

So, from the late fifth century, organic explanations of madness homed in on black bile. But early on, blackness and bile also suggested "anger." *Mania* and *mainomai* are philologically related to *menos*, an early anger word. It can mean a black violent liquid anger in the innards.[26] Another anger word is *cholos*, or *cholē*, the word Hippocratics and other writers use for bile and black bile. Normally, in Homer and tragedy, *cholos* means "anger," though it can mean "bile"; whereas *cholē* normally means "bile." But from Aristophanes on, writers also use *cholē* for "anger."[27]

These philological basics suggest that in Greek thought, madness is indissoluble from images of anger. *Mainomai* and *lussa* start in battle rage and never quite lose their violence.[28] As *mania* belongs with *menos*, *melancholia* belongs with *cholos* and *cholē*. Madness is a fury-nexus of black, bitter, bloodlike fluid in the guts. Violent, often murderous. As Cicero says of the Greeks, "*Quem nos furorem, illi melancholiam vocant.*" What the Greeks called *melancholia*, Romans called *furor*: the great Roman word for madness, from which we, of course, get "fury."[29]

The anger element of black bile, of madness, illuminates more recent diagnostics. "Melancholia" is the old name for melancholic depression, or the manic phase of manic-depressive psychosis. Melancholic depression is pathological mourning. Not of a real person, but of a lost, internal object you feel you have destroyed. You are ambivalent about it: both dependent and hostile. You feel you cannot live without it: hence the mourning, and delusional self-accusation. You hide from yourself the hostility you feel. Melancholic depression (the highest suicide risk) is "designed to prevent the emergence of hostility." Its symptoms are "a response to some recognition that a leak has developed in your defences" against this hostility. Deep unacknowledged hostile anger is basic to it all.[30] Which fits the Greek taproot of "anger" in *melancholia*. In madness.

[25] Hades and mind: Padel 1992:78–81 (also 102–106, 156–57); Ficino *De vita triplici* 1.4; Klibansky, Panofsky, and Saxl 1964:259.

[26] See Chaper 2, n. 24; Padel 1992:23–26.

[27] E.g., *cholos* as "bile," *Il.*16.203; *cholē* as "anger," Dem. 25.27. Cf. overlap between *cholaō* and *melancholaō*: above, n. 5.

[28] See Chapter 3, nn. 4, 17. *Lussa*: see Chapter 2.

[29] Cic. *TD* 3.11. *Furor*: cf. Poliakoff 1992:75.

[30] Rycroft 1968b:30–31, 89–90, 160; Rycroft 1968a:45; cf. Kristeva 1989:9–14.

MELANCHOLIA

A great physician, when the Pope was sick
Of a deep melancholy, presented him
With several sorts of madmen, which wild object
Being so full of change and sport, forc'd him to laugh,
And so th'imposthume broke.
　　—Webster, *Duchess of Malfi* 4.2

If Aristophanes is anything to go by, *melancholaō* was vernacular in the late fifth century, the time the doctors got hold of it, for "I'm crazy." From the fourth century on, medical and philosophical speculation split and spread the resonances of the noun, *melancholia*, and the adjective *melancholikos* (which is commoner in the Hippocratics than the noun).[31] Noun, verb, and adjective are now important in two contexts, which keep going into the Renaissance. First, pathologically, Hippocratics use *melancholia* (often in the plural) to mean a fit of madness. Second, the terms appear in humoral theory: in accounts of people's characters based on the doctrine of humors. Those people who permanently have in them more black bile than other people, are prone to outbreaks of black bile–related diseases: piles and skin-sores as well as raving fits. They also have various behavioral traits.

In the fourth century, before medical humoral theory set hard and fast, ethical writing (Aristotle especially) gives the *melancholikos* a violent, impulsive nature.[32] Later ethical as well as medical writing develops the image of the melancholic type within a medical framework of humoral types and their diseases.[33]

Through centuries, black bile fuelled Western speculation about the best as well as the blackest things the human mind can do. We use the word "melancholy" now in roughly three ways. Temporary state of mind: melancholy. Character type: "melancholic." And long-term illness: the "melancholia" of early psychiatry. The Renaissance used the word mainly in two ways: the name of an illness and of a temperament. But the different meanings belong together. "Although new meanings emerged, old meanings did not give way to them." The basis of all these different meanings was physical black bile.[34]

---

[31] Flashar 1962:712 collects Hippocratic references to *melancholia*; see also his discussion, Flashar 1966:21–49.

[32] Arist. *EN* 1152A19; cf. Pl. *Rep.* 573C. Flashar 1962:712–13 collects and evaluates Aristotle's references outside *Problemata* to the *melancholikos*.

[33] Starobinski 1960:9; Flashar 1966:16–17, 32–36, 43, 46–49.

[34] Klibansky, Panofsky, and Saxl 1964:2–3; Screech 1991:25.

Chapter 6

THE AFTERLIFE OF INNER BLACKNESS

The self-recognition of modern genius could only take
place under the sign of Saturn and melancholy.
—R. Klibansky, E. Panofsky, and F. Saxl, *Saturn and
Melancholy*

"PROBLEM 30"

BLACK BILE made its long impact on Western thought through interaction
with three other powerful Greek images of madness. One comes from the
fourth century: Plato's images of ecstatic frenzy and inspiration in the *Phaedrus*, which I shall discuss in detail later (Chapter 8). It belongs with ideas
of true seeing: seeing in the light not the dark.[1] Another dates from Hellenistic times: the fictive confrontation of Hippocrates and Democritus,
which I shall also discuss later (Chapter 9). And one comes from the fifth
century, interacting with Homer: tragedy's mad heroes.[2]

But these images met and merged in Renaissance obsession with a supposedly Aristotelian text, *Problem* 30. This little text put mad heroes (especially Heracles, killing his children) center stage with Plato and Empedocles, as paradigm melancholics.[3]

Problems, attributed to Aristotle from antiquity on, has thirty-eight
books, some written as early as 300 B.C. But not, as the Renaissance supposed, by Aristotle himself. The work has more Hippocratic ideas and
language than Aristotle's own writings, and gives a very different picture
of *melancholia*, for Aristotle himself takes *melancholia* negatively. For him,
it is mainly a disease.[4] In the Renaissance, *Problems* was one the most
widely read "Aristotelian" works. Especially two or three pages—*Problem*
30, paragraph 1—which "influenced the interpretation of human genius
as much as anything ever written."[5]

---

[1] Pl. *Phdr.* 244A–45A, 249D–E, 265A–D: see Ferrari 1987:113–19, 180–81, 197,
274–75 n. 89; below, pp. 95–96.

[2] Rütten 1992:55–65 discusses Ajax, Bellerophon, and Agamemnon as *Homeric* heroes
later held to be melancholic types. But *tragedy* crystallized the image of mad heroes: Rütten
1992:62; below, Chapter 22.

[3] Klibansky, Panofsky, and Saxl 1954:15.

[4] Flashar 1962:713.

[5] Screech 1991:27.

Problem 30 tackles "Problems about thought, intelligence, and wisdom." It connects genius and inspiration with madness: all due to *melancholia*.

> Why are all those who become eminent in philosophy, politics, or poetry, melancholics? Some so much that they are affected by diseases caused by black bile? A heroic example is Heracles, who apparently had this nature, and so epileptic seizures were called "the sacred disease," after him. His mad fit, in the episode with his children, points to this. So do the sores that erupted just before his disappearance on Mount Oeta. With many people this is a symptom of black bile. Lysander the Spartan also suffered these sores before his death.
>
> Ajax and Bellerophon too. One went out of his mind completely, the other sought out desert places to live in. . . . Among the heroes, many evidently suffered in the same way. Among men of recent times, Empedocles, Plato, Socrates, and many other well-known men. Also most poets.
>
> Many people have bodily disease as a result of this kind of temperament (*krasis*). Some have only a natural tendency to such suffering. But all are melancholics by constitution.

The effects of a melancholic nature on different people are like wine's effects on different people. Having surplus black bile disposes people to certain characteristics and diseases. Because black bile varies, these show up differently in different people. Cold black bile makes for apoplexy, numbness, *athumia* (despair), anxiety. Hot black bile causes cheerfulness, bursts of song, ecstasies, skin-sores, and euphoric, erotic, impulsive behavior. If hot black bile is too near the seat of intellect you are manic, enthusiastic: godstruck, like Sibyls or bacchants. But if you have the right amount of extra black bile you are unusually intelligent, gifted in education, politics, the arts. All melancholics are exceptional *and* predisposed to a particular set of diseases.[6]

This was the beginning of the glamorization of melancholia. But, once written, it was almost immediately forgotten. For centuries it was submerged by the picture of *melancholia* as illness. Bad.[7] It was rehabilitated twelve hundred years later, in the Renaissance.

It was probably Marsilio Ficino, translator of Plato and Plotinus, who connected *Problem* 30's melancholy of outstanding men to Plato's image of divine frenzy in the *Phaedrus*. The combination had a deep impact on Renaissance thought. For Montaigne, writing 1580 to 1600 (the time of the young Shakespeare), madness underlay much contemporary thought, worship, and morality.[8]

---

[6] Translation and discussion in Klibansky, Panofsky, and Saxl 1964:18–41.

[7] Klibansky, Panofsky, and Saxl 1954:41–54, 67.

[8] See Klibansky, Panofsky, and Saxl 1964:259; Campbell 1961:81–13; Screech 1991:xvii. Divine frenzy: see below, Chapter 8.

The idea that madness could be close to genius was available from Plato. But it gained physiological authority through the Aristotelian *Problem* 30. *Melancholia*, the black of and in human nature, was the foundation of genius. In organic terms, there was no distinction between the madness that made Heracles kill his children, and the genius that produced the works of Plato. Melancholy was at the back of both. Melancholics were the best and worst people. Melancholy might lead to genius: put you "outside yourself," as in Plato's images of ecstatic inspiration, or into the madhouse.[9] As happened to the poet Torquato Tasso, the most powerful historical image, for the Renaissance and afterwards, of genius gone mad, genius caged. Delacroix's painting of Tasso in the madhouse fascinated, for instance, Van Gogh. He asked his brother to send a lithograph of it to Arles.[10]

Problem 30 put madness at the center of ideas about genius for the modern world.[11] "For the first time," say the classic historians of melancholy (writing, rather surprisingly, as if the idea were objectively true, rather than culturally constructed), "the dark source of genius was uncovered."[12]

BLACK STAR, BLACK SUN

Je suis le Tenebreux,—le Veuf—L'Inconsolé,
Le prince d'Aquitaine à la Tour abolie:
Ma seule Etoile est morte—et mon luth constellé
Porte le Soleil noir de la Melancolie.
—Gérard de Nerval

But an essential pulse in Hippocratic tradition is external cause: of what is, and what happens, in people.[13] So, what about external causes of melancholia?

We might work back from the modern world. In the nineteenth century, a desolate external image of madness acting on self was found by a writer who later killed himself "in that accursed backstreet down by the Seine, the *rue de la vieille Lanterne*."[14] Melancholia's "black sun" appears in Gérard de Nerval's poem "El Deschidado," "The Disinherited," published in 1853 (and again a year later, slightly revised).

[9] Screech 1991:23–29. The linkage of melancholy with Platonic *mania* (see Chapter 8), which puts you "outside" yourself, is crucial: Screech 1991:31–33, 37–41. The most dangerous melancholy was "burnt melancholy," "melancholy adust." It was precipitated by any humor "burning": Campbell 1961:75–78; Screech 1991:25.
[10] Tasso, Delacroix, Van Gogh: Gilman 1982:131 (plate 168), 221.
[11] Cf. Burton's interest in *Problem* 30: Babb 1951:63. As Schiesari 1992:191 notes, there were no women on its list of famous mad people.
[12] Klibansky, Panofsky, and Saxl 1964:41. The word "genius" is from Latin. The concept was not available to Greek writers.
[13] Padel 1992:54.
[14] Holmes 1986:210, quoting the photographer Nadar's memoir of de Nerval.

As an individual creation, the image owed much to Tarot and alchemical symbolism, the "magical geography of his childhood," de Nerval's self-mythicizing, and the madness that first attacked him in 1841 and continued in bursts until his suicide.[15] But Osip Mandelshtam, deeply read in French poetry, reacting to a performance of Racine's *Phèdre*, saw the breakup of St. Petersburg in 1916 in similar terms: the quenching of a sun goddess and her culture. "With my black love I have sullied the sun," says Mandelshtam's Phaedra. His poem looses de Nerval's image onto Phaedra and all she symbolized to Mandelshtam:

> a black sun shall rise
> for an amorous mother.

He used the image in another poem fusing political with personal pain for his mother, who died in 1916:

> At Jerusalem's gates
> A black sun has risen.
>
> . . . .
>
> I woke in a radiant cradle
> Lit by a black sun.[16]

The image turns up also in a less literary imagination. A twentieth-century schizophrenic told Laing she "was born under a black sun": "The ancient and sinister image of the black sun arose quite independently of any reading. Julie had left school at fourteen, had read very little. . . . Her language [was] an expression of the way she experienced being-in-her-world. . . . Under the black sun she existed as a dead thing."[17]

In the individual lives that produced this image—the French writer who doused his own light in the "street of the ancient lamp," the Russian poet seeing his culture and city burn, and Laing's doomed schizophrenic—the image fits very precisely the mourning element, the lost object, in psychoanalytic perception of melancholic depression.[18] As an image at large in European imagination, the black sun is heir to something more. Laing's understanding of Julie resonates with his own response to the black sun of alchemy and the image from which the alchemical black sun derives. The black "star" or "planet," Saturn.[19]

[15] Holmes 1986:215, 226, 249, 262; Kristeva 1989: 147. De Nerval's madness: Holmes 1986:235–40, 251 (see his "alternating pattern of illness and creativity," 255).

[16] Mandelshtam 1991:25–26 (with Rayfield 1991:xxviii–xxix). Thanks to James Greene for directing me to these poems.

[17] Laing 1965:193, 200, 202, 204.

[18] Kristeva 1989:145; above, Chapter 5, n. 30 (cf. Schiesari's critique of her, 1992:93–99). Julie is diagnosed schizophrenic, not melancholic, but there are many mourning elements in her communications: Laing 1965:179, 194, 202. Cf. Ficino's "celebration of loss": Schiesari 1992:112–41.

[19] Jung 1967:76 (with n. 40), 266.

Saturn's influence on melancholia goes back to ninth-century Arab astrologers. It was they who matched the colors of humors to those of the stars.[20] The European Middle Ages were profoundly influenced by translations of their work, especially of Alcabitius: "Saturn's nature is cold, dry, bitter, black, violent, and harsh."[21] From then on, Saturn, "black and bitter" as black bile, with the mythographic weight of pagan gods behind it, was responsible for the melancholic's constition and destiny.[22] From the twelfth century, inner blackness is overdetermined, with an external as well as internal cause. Ancient Greek emphasis on external conditions as cause of disease translated into the new art, astrology.

Mandelshtam, not mad but politically, cosmically agonized ("political" seems a weak word for what was going on round him), highlights the image's aptness for the twentieth century. Its poets and schizophrenics summon a mediaeval image to express their recognition that external forces, beyond individual control, act on our lives like a malign dark sun. In Mandelshtam's lines, a ten-century-old image for the source of madness expresses a new sense of world loss. It acts, perhaps, as the self-recognition of a world it might be mad not to go mad in.

Until the mid–fifteenth century, the black star's influence, like the melancholic temperament, was mainly bad and sad. "The hour of Saturn is the hour of evil. In that hour the son of God was betrayed and delivered to death." Judas was a melancholic. Through centuries of blaming humors on planetary influence, melancholics, children of Saturn ("planet of tears, solitary life, soothsayers") got a bad press. Ill-favored, ill-natured, ill-destinied.[23]

And then the whole thing turned round. The Florentine Neoplatonists rehabilitated Saturn, "highest of the planets," as the source of human greatness.[24] And *Problem* 30 was hauled into the limelight by Marsilio Ficino.

Like other writers on melancholia (Montaigne, Robert Burton), Ficino suffered it himself. But he was luckier than de Nerval. *Problem* 30 was a godsend. That opening question, by Aristotle, no less, must have changed his life. "Why are all great men melancholics?" It offered a wonderful reinterpretation of blackness. Saturn, the ultimate source, was outside him. But even black Saturn was no longer only bad: it was the source of genius. "Saturn seldom denotes ordinary characters and destinies, but rather people set apart from the rest, divine or bestial, or bowed down by the deepest sorrow." Melancholia is Saturn's "unique and divine gift." "I will agree," says Ficino (it is hard not to hear a note of triumphal homecom-

[20] Klibansky, Panofsky, and Saxl 1964.127–32; Kinsman 1974c:309.
[21] Quoted in Klibansky, Panofsky, and Saxl 1964:128.
[22] See Wittkower 1963.
[23] Babb 1951; Klibansky, Panofsky, and Saxl 1964:127, 195, 121, 159.
[24] According to Klibansky, Panofsky, and Saxl 1964:241–47.

ing) "with Aristotle."[25] Ficino, more than anyone, crystallized madness-risk as a positive thing. "Genial" melancholy. Melancholic genius.

Here begins the modern world's valuing of the dark. Of internal dark, "black bile," the dark we have in us: our potential for madness and badness. An external black influence governs this. You may feel this to be wholly malign, as it was before Ficino turned things round. But Melancholia's black star is de Nerval's, Mandelshtam's, and Julie's black sun. Our century is drawn magnetically to its darkness.

"WHERE THERE IS LYTEL LIGHT"

> Good Sir Topas, do not think I am mad: they have laid
> me here in hideous darkness.
> —Shakespeare, *Twelfth Night* 4.2

Even in the fifteenth century, not everyone bought Ficino's valuation of the dark. Melancholia was credited with the gift of divination, which related it, very problematically, to politics and to theology, and sharply divided Renaissance thinkers.[26] "Genial" melancholy was vehemently attacked, especially by doctors and churchmen.[27] Luther loathed it. "All sadness," he said, "is from Satan." He cited examples of melancholics who needed, and found, cure for their disease. The devil's access to imagination is through the black humor: ideas of melancholia interact with responses to witchcraft. Despite humanist enthusiasm for genial melancholy, melancholia was still seen in the Renaissance also as a curse.[28] As disease, darkness of soul. It needed cure or exorcism.

Darkness must be treated by the dark. Pharmaceutically, melancholia can be tackled with, for instance, hellebore. But enclosure in the dark will also do. In classical times, we do not hear much of this option. Any such enclosure was not therapeutic but protective. Socrates was accused of saying that a son could get a verdict of *paranoia* for his father, and then imprison him. Xenophon's reply is that Socrates did think it expedient for *hoi mainomenoi*, the raving mad, to be imprisoned, for their own sake and that of their *philoi*, their family.[29]

---

[25] Ficino, *De vita triplici* 3.2: Klibansky, Panofsky, and Saxl 1964:158–59, 259. See also Babb 1951. Ficino's gloom: Klibansky, Panofsky, and Saxl 1964c:256; Kinsman 1974c:310. His triumph: Schleiner 1991:25. Schiesari 1992:160–66 thinks Ficino is "celebrating death as life."

[26] According to Schleiner 1991:27–29, 109–122, 233–62.

[27] Schleiner 1991:11–12, 31–32, 38–54, 66–72 documents and evaluates increasing Renaissance opposition to genial melancholy, which began among the clerics.

[28] Schleiner 1991:67, 14, 171–89; Schiesari 1992:141–58, 159.

[29] Xen. *Mem.* 1.2.49–50; cf. Bdelycleon's law-mad father, and the solution: shutting him up at home (Ar. *V.* 69–132).

Imprisoning the mad, for protection but increasingly also with some (often pretty mad) ideas of cure, is a feature of early modern Europe.[30] The late Renaissance evolved moral and therapeutic reasons for enclosing the mad in the dark. The homeopathic principles behind this are drawn from Greek magic and medicine, but the systems are homegrown: "Every man, the which is mad or lunatycke, or frantycke, or demonyacke, to be kept . . . in some close house or chamber where there is lytel light. . . ." So Andrew Boorde, in the mid–sixteenth century.[31] Lack of light is therapeutic, as it is pretended to be for Malvolio in *Twelfth Night*: a scene that parodies contemporary exorcism.[32]

Even by 1400, Bedlam is an asylum but also, it has recently been argued, a place of attempted cure.[33] A shift in treatment of the mad, from exile to inward confinement, grows though the sixteenth century, and is axiomatic by about 1650. The curative aspect of enclosing the mad seems to figure in some seventeenth-century perceptions.[34] But Bedlam scenes in plays from 1600 to 1650 (Dekker's *The Honest Whore*, Middleton's *The Changeling*), do not show cure, only control. The Keeper whips inmates to keep order.[35]

From the Greeks onward, Western culture has had a sense of women, too, as innerly dark. In Athens, women were typically relegated to a darkness which contained them: the most inward, darkest, chambers of the house.[36] Modern Europe extended this to the mad, who were also traditionally perceived to have darkness in them, and a special relation with the dark. "Her body was created blacker than coal," says an anonymous mid-thirteenth-century romancer, of a mad wild woman. The association of madness and blackness is a commonplace in, for example, the German mediaeval tradition.[37] A dark body is a sign of madness. Inner darkness is expressed but maybe also cured by external darkness, in which the sane confine the mad.

[30] Stressed in Foucault 1971, especially 38–64.

[31] Boorde 1567.

[32] See Schleiner 1991:263–74.

[33] Allderidge 1985 unpacks the mythology of Bethlem as an exclusively imprisoning place. In her view (29), the first written reference to it as a place of *cure* is c. 1450.

[34] See Kinsman 1974c:285–89 (following Foucault 1971).

[35] See Salkeld 1993. Seventeenth-century "Abraham men," ex-Bedlamites discharged after a year, begged to pay their Bedlam arrears for maintenance. They put on a show, at least, of continued derangement: no one seems to expect a year in Bedlam to cure them. Their autobiographical mad ballads were an important part of their show: Beier 1985:116–17; Porter 1987:22.

[36] Padel 1981:5–12. Cf. women as nineteenth-century paradigms of madness: Showalter 1987.

[37] Quoted in Gilman 1982:2.

BLACK TRAGEDY

Alack, the night comes on. . . .
—Shakespeare, *King Lear* 2.4

As Lear takes his first steps to madness, Gloucester says "the night comes on." "Night" marks the outer and inner gathering of dark. Storm and night mirror Lear's madness.[38] The imagination that makes them do so was formed by a Greek tradition: madness as tempest, madness as blackness, in the mind.[39]

Madness is peculiarly appropriate to tragedy partly because of its blackness. "Give me the sun," says Oswald at the end of Ibsen's *Ghosts*. Before he goes mad, he explains: "The disease I have as my birthright [*he points to his forehead and adds very softly*] is seated here." The play ends with him in a mad unreachable state, "his face expressionless, his eyes with a glassy stare," demanding, over and again, "The sun. The sun."[40]

Madness, summed up in the absence or loss of light, is appropriate for tragedy because tragedy itself runs on blackness. Grief, death, failure, loss. Iras does not know Cleopatra has been ordering the asps, but after Caesar's unbearable magnaminity, she tells Cleopatra, "Finish, good lady, the bright day is done. / And we are for the dark."[41] From Greece on, tragedy is the concentrated imagining of forces that make people do things unthinkable to those housed in sanity. It has always imagined these forces, and the states they produce, as black. Its heroes are "for the dark." Absolute tragedy is absolute black. "Black on black." Few tragedies manage this entirely, but even those that do not are shot through with darkness.[42] Tragedy itself is a place "where there is lytel light."

Astrological, theological, and medical accounts of madness in the seventeenth and eighteenth centuries had darkness in common: madness is spiritual night caused by "noisome fumes, black and gross, vapouring up to the brain like the foot of a chimney."[43] This darkness is a drum of ancient images heard repeatedly in psychiatric writing. Dark is felt to be a "natural" metaphor for mad.

For the Italian humanists, "the most profound analogy between Saturn and melancholy" lay in a power to generate in the self the greatest good *and* greatest harm. They valued this polarity. It gave what the historians of

[38] *King Lear* 2.4.278–85, 299.
[39] Padel 1992:85–88.
[40] A causal connection between syphilis and insanity was proved only in the late nineteenth century (see Chapter 3, n. 35), though random associations were made earlier (see Chapter 14, n. 37). See Ibsen 1957:282–85.
[41] *Antony and Cleopatra* 5.2.192–93.
[42] G. Steiner 1990:147, 150; Padel 1994.
[43] Deacon and Walker 1601:325; cf. Foucault 1971:104–7.

melancholy call "a tragic color" to the humanist view (the foundation of most modern views) of human greatness.[44] This tragic color stands out because tragedy, I believe (not all agree), has joy as well as desolation. Light and hope pierce and illumine its black staging of the human condition.[45]

The idea that greatness comes from the same source as madness is a Renaissance input, not a fifth-century idea. For fifth-century tragedy, madness is a curse, an imposition from outside.[46] All the same, fifth-century tragedy and the myths it handles gave the theory its prize evidence. "Heracles, when about to kill his children." Many of the elements that came together in this theory are fifth-century, epecially tragic, perceptions.

Whether we like it or not, the madness of Greek tragedy, the blackness of Greek madness, and the blackness of tragedy are part of our own imagination. Human potential for greatness is tragedy's business, we feel, because we owe our potential for greatness to our potential for blackness. For madness. But it is the Renaissance, not the Greeks, that made this insight a tragic one. For the Renaissance, and for us, the outstanding person has special blackness within. But this very blackness, from which the power comes, may suddenly plunge that person into bestial madness.

Many modern tragic works would be impossible without all this. Conrad's *Heart of Darkness*, for example: that journey into the "heart," the maddest, most murderous part, of humanity. Into, in Hippocratic terms, the place where blood (the "part" most responsible for intelligence) is "corrupted" by blackness. Conrad's novel operates through Greek and mediaeval images. An outer, corrupting dark, of place, of society, works on an individual's inwardness and calls up his own, inner, corrupting darkness, which Hippocratics would sum up, materially, as black bile. The "heart" is the man's, but also that of the world in which he becomes bad. Corrupting darkness, outside and inside: madness, and badness, is seen as your own blackness swamping you,[47] under the influence of blackness from outside. It is a perfect Renaissance image: external blackness, working on the man with "black" in him. Also a perfect tragic image.

The Renaissance view is closer to our own than fifth-century Greek ideas are. It used Greek ideas, both tragic and medical: of madness as a black angry inner flood, of a balance between external and internal cause.[48] But Greek tragic madness is caused by gods. The Renaissance rerouted tragic blackness far from its Greek beginnings and expression in Greek tragedy.

---

[44] Klibansky, Panofsky, and Saxl 1964:158–59, 247.

[45] See Padel 1994, arguing against G. Steiner 1990.

[46] Kinsman 1974c:310. On fifth-century tragedy, see above, Chapter 2, n. 17, and below, Chapters 15, 18, 19, 22.

[47] Cf. Poliakoff 1992:80.

[48] Padel 1992:56–59.

Yet the image elements lived on. You might say Renaissance tragedy reshadowed a blackness begun two thousand years earlier, but more self-consciously. Madness was implicated in new ways now, in the new self-images available.[49] Tragedy had to deal with blackness, inside and out, the black of badness and madness, and did so brilliantly. It is the color of *Hamlet* and *Macbeth*. But black was tragic differently now: it marked a potential for greatness. The black of broken potential, lost personal greatness, belongs with our chaotic ideas of the tragic today. But it was Elizabethan tragedy, not Greek, that brought this about, exploring the blackness of human potential lost:

> Cut is the branch that might have grown full straight,
> And burned is Apollo's laurel bough,
> That sometime grew within this learned man.[50]

Greek culture was the basis of the modern valuing of madness. Yet the sum of Greek elements, as they operate in us today, is alien to Greek tragedy: a whole, foreign to the origin of its parts. As if you took feathers from British songbirds to make a model of an American bluejay. The result bears no relation, or at best a very skewed relation, to the original habitat.

So black bile, a professional medical expression of a general Greek sense that when things go wrong inside they are black, influenced theories of madness and character for two millennia; while tragedies themselves went on shooting a general mad blackness, daemonic and organic, into the Western bloodstream. It is, you might say, black bile's fault that we think of madness as black.

[49] See Kinsman 1974c:312.
[50] Marlowe, *Doctor Faustus*, Epilogue.

Chapter 7

DARK, TWISTED SEEING

DARKNESS: CONSCIOUSNESS, OR ITS LOSS?

IF MADNESS is inner blackness, how do the mad see? To live is normally to "look on light." What do the mad look on? What does Greek tragedy think is it like, to look on the world, mad?

We should place beside this question a paradox that profoundly affected Western reception of Greek ideas of madness. A paradox about darkness, implicit in Greek images of innards. Innards, the equipment of consciousness, and the fluids they contain, the stuff of feeling, are dark.[1] But *loss* of consciousness is also dark. Sleep and fainting are a pouring night, like death. The darkness of the living, passionate mind mirrors that of the underworld, world of the dead. Black is the color of consciousness and passion and of their opposite: nonconsciousness, death.[2]

In the Greek context, this paradox is made sense of by standard images of the blind prophet. Prophets "see" from nonlight: they are blind, they inhabit caves. Darkness in the Greek world had many resonances of danger and death, as for us. But it was also where you might encounter gods, "see" truths unavailable in the light. The image of the darkened seer, familiar all over Greek myth, is reflected in oracular cave shrines and "incubation": institutionalized sleep in a temple through which you find healing. Greek myth, literature, and cult are full of truths seen or heard in the dark: in caves, the night, the underworld. The earliest Greek oracles are shrines to Night.[3]

This notion is iconically available, with multiple facile or stale Romantic resonances, also to us. It crops up easily in popular fiction: in fantasy blends of sci-fi and Camelot, for instance. But for us it has no real-life underpinning such as cult experience, and contemporary images of innards, gave the Greeks. For them, the equipment of consciousness was black. Black innards: which darkened further in passion. Their blackness was inseparable from what they might know, feel, or prophesy.

Unseen, from a cavelike darkness, innards know and speak: the image crystallizes Greek responses to the mysteries of insight, of where knowing

---

[1] Padel 1992:68, 75; above, Chapter 5, nn. 1–2.
[2] Padel 1992:78–79.
[3] Padel 1992:71–75. Incubation: see Ar. *V.* 122.

comes from. It informs the work of Greek philosophers as well as poets.[4] In this context, darkness is an apt image for two opposing things. For death and other cancellations of consciousness, and also for the vessels and site of consciousness: the place where you "see" in the dark.

If both the stuff of consciousness and its negation are black, where does this leave madness, which is so particularly black? Which black is madness? A loss of consciousness, like sleep, fainting, death? Or, like passion, an intensification of consciousness and its darkness: a black from which innards prophesy? Does it see dark, and wrong? Or, like a blind prophet, light and right?

Tragedy's answer, I think, is both. As the opposite of consciousness, madness sees wrongly. Darkly, as Ajax sees. But as the intensification of consciousness, madness sometimes sees more clearly than the sane. Both thoughts turn up in tragedy. Both left their mark on us; for this paradox, and the prophecy resonances that resolved it, have empowered, differently, at different times, modern understandings and revaluings of madness. Madness is the blackest, wrongest possibility of consciousness, a blackness without light. *And* it is a way of seeing in and through the dark, seeing truths unavailable to normal minds: a dark through which someone (not always the mad person) may see more clearly. Two possibilities. Greek tragedy set going the long echoes of both.

AJAX: MADNESS AND SIGHT

First, some dark, wrong seeing.

After Achilles' death, the Greek leaders must award Achilles' armor to another champion. They choose Odysseus. In fury, Ajax plans to kill Odysseus, and them. Athene maddens him, so he kills cattle (and a herdsman) instead. For other people, his madness is a saving thing. It makes Ajax see cattle as men. For Ajax, the madness, and the absurd violence that results, is the worst humiliation. It is Athene's punishment for rejecting her help; for wanting to get glory on his own.

This play pivots on madness, a disturbance of the inner world. But its hero is invested entirely in the outer. Like Heracles, Ajax is all body. He is the pattern of physical strength, of the male body's supreme possibilities[5] —but also of body's limits. "Bodies" fail when thinking fails: when someone "does not *phronei* [think] as a human being."[6]

---

[4] Padel 1992:68–69, 74, 80, 112–13.

[5] From first (as Athene describes him, head dripping sweat, with "murderous hands") to last (when his son must touch the corpse whose "hot pipes still blow their black force"): *Aj.* 10, 1410–14.

[6] *Aj.* 758–61.

"Thinking as a human being" is represented by Odysseus, Ajax's foil and opposite, the supreme intellectual hero. The two men are opposed in Homer. Odysseus sees Ajax among the the dead:

> Alone and apart stood Ajax's soul,
> still angry because I won,
> competing against him for Achilles' arms. . . .
>
> . . . .
>
> I wish I'd never won the prize,
> since afterwards earth covered
> such a noble head: Ajax,
> most beautiful of all Greeks
> after Achilles, and best at war-work.[7]

Ajax, visible but mute, has "beauty and deeds." Odysseus, through whom the *Odyssey*'s listeners see the dead, has compassion and understanding. He speaks. He is sorry. But dead Ajax goes off silently, "on his way to Erebos," everlastingly angry.

In this scenario of redneck versus intellectual, the narrative gives weight to both. It does value the physical: the fierce glory rooted in physical strength. But this valuing comes over through a voice that the narrative implies is somehow superior. Odysseus survives by more than physicality: by "safe-thinking."

Ajax's madness was an early part of his epic persona. Investing only in body leads to madness where body is worse than useless. It turns against you. Heracles' bow by which he *saved* his friends becomes the tool by which he kills them. Ajax's murderous hands, tools of his greatness, bring him shame that leads to suicide.[8]

This story of physicality that turns to madness and self-destruction needs intellect, represented by Odysseus, to "see" it. Sophocles' Odysseus begins in a state of not-seeing, not knowing. Athene can see Odysseus. He cannot see her.[9] He guesses but does not know the criminal is Ajax. An "observer" spots Ajax leaping over the plain. Odysseus follows a trail and sometimes loses it. "We know nothing clearly: we're wandering."[10] In fact it is Ajax who does not see clearly. Who is "wandering," in the sense of "mad."[11]

Athene displays him, mad, to Odysseus and the audience. She calls Ajax

---

[7] *Od.* 11.543–51.

[8] *HF* 571–74, 942, 970, 1062, 1098–100, 1135, 1377–81; *Aj.* 10, 43, 618, 772, 908–909; cf. his sword, 816–22.

[9] *Aj.* 15. Commentators have asked "Why can't Odysseus see her? Is it still night? Is she invisible?" More important is this scene's role in the play's pattern of seeing and not-seeing.

[10] *Aj.* 5, 23, 29–32.

[11] "Wandering," twisted eyes: *Aj.* 447; cf. Chapter 12.

out from his tent, where he believes he is torturing Odysseus. Odysseus himself asks her not to. Athene says she'll protect him by averting "the rays" of Ajax's eyes. Odysseus still worries. "Do you shrink from seeing a raving man clearly?" asks Athene. Yes, he does. Don't worry, says Athene:

> ATHENE: He won't see you now, when you're near.
> ODYSSEUS: How come, if he sees with the same eyes?
> ATHENE: I'll darken his eyelids as he sees.[12]

Sophocles underlines differing ways of seeing. When the audience themselves first "see" Ajax, his eyes have been "darkened." The sane man sees the mad. The mad man does not see the sane. Madness changes sight, can darken it.[13]

The night setting, the surrounding dark, is vital to the play and colors Ajax's whole persona. "Night-Ajax" was "captured by *mania*." His madness, a "dark-turbid storm," is treated—rather like Lear's—as if it were part of the night in which it came. He killed herds and herdsmen "with dark sword blades":

> at night's climax, when evening torches
> were no longer burning.[14]

Even divinity seems shadow here. For Tecmessa, Ajax's talk with Athene was part of his madness. That dialogue which the audience saw and heard, with a goddess they could see but Odysseus could not, was to her mad "words with some shadow."[15]

The darkness before dawn is the setting that this "shadow"—this goddess of reason and wisdom—chooses for displaying madness to Odysseus and to the audience. Athene quizzes mad Ajax on what he's done. Has he killed Agamemnon and Menelaus, tied Odysseus to a pillar? "Don't torture him so savagely." But Ajax insists. Well, go on then, if that's what you want, she says. She is playing with him, cat-and-mouse, while he thinks he's playing with Odysseus.

She turns to the real Odysseus.

> See the gods' strength, Odysseus—how great it is?
> Was any man more careful than him, better
> at doing right things at the right time?[16]

---

[12] *Aj.* 69–70, 81–85.

[13] See Goldhill 1986:182–84.

[14] *Aj.* 285–86, 217 (cf. *nuktōr* . . . , 47), 35–51, 141, 208 (*tholeros*, contrasted with *lampros* at E. *Supp.* 222, suggests darkness; cf. Padel 1992:87).

[15] *Aj.* 301.

[16] *Aj.* 110–20.

Her lesson is divine strength. Odysseus sees the other side of it: human weakness, exemplified by madness. "I know no one," says Odysseus, answering Athene's question. With a slight difference in one accent, his words could also have sounded like "I know nothing."[17] Ajax mad makes Odysseus see how nearly nothing, how shadowlike, *all* human beings are:

> Although he hates me, I pity him
> in his ill-luck, yoked up
> to this terrible *atē* [disaster/madness]:
> thinking of myself as much as him.
> For I see we are, all of us, nothing
> but images and an empty shadow.[18]

Whose darkness is it? Ajax's, or ours? This vision of the human condition is one high point in the play's dance of seeing and not-seeing. From a god he cannot see, Odysseus learns "clearly" about darkness: Ajax's dark behavior, darkened seeing, darkened life. What he does with this insight pre-echoes, a hundred years beforehand, Aristotle's famous summary of what tragedy makes its audience feel. Pity: for you see other as other, other in a mess. Fear: because you also see other as self, image of a vulnerability in which self shares. "I think of myself as much as him." Odysseus's words in Sophocles are the first example I know of a motif developed in Renaissance drama: madness as tragic mirror. Ajax's madness illustrates—makes clear—the tragic human condition, as dark. As shadowy.[19]

"We're all an empty shadow." The first person plural is characteristic of Odysseus in this play. He voices "us." At the end of the play, he argues for community values, common humanity. Agamemnon opposes Ajax's burial, but even he will "come to this": he will need burying one day. Odysseus stresses human beings' need to "share," be with each other. His word is "with."[20]

Ajax's lonely dark fall resonates against this communal background. All of us in the light go into the dark: all of us "come to this." That is Odysseus's perception. Anyone not agreeing is *mōros*, foolish. Agamemnon, who insults dead Ajax, is *epibrontētos*, "thunder-struck," "crazed," and will pay for his uncaring stance.[21] As the audience knows he will, back home.

[17] Aj. 121, *egō men ouden' oid'*; cf. *ouden oid'*. The difference in sound, unknowable to us, is between an acute and grave accent on -*den*.

[18] *Aj.* 121–26. *Atē* as madness, as disaster: see Chapter 18, nn. 2, 13; Chapter 19, n. 39; Appendix.

[19] See Chapter 22, n. 48. Pity and fear: Arist. *Poet.* 1453B12.

[20] *Aj.* 21–25, 125, 1322–69, 1328, 1334, 1340, 1357, 1343, 1365; 1378–80: a speech whose center is *ton thanonta tonde sunthaptein*, backed by another *sun*-compound, *sumponein*.

[21] *Aj.* 121–26, 1375, 1387. Odysseus accuses Agamemnon hyperbolically of madness: see Chapter 18, nn. 40–47.

Athene's moral to Odysseus is, If you are stronger or richer than others, don't be proud, "Don't boast against the gods":

> Day bends down and lifts up
> all human things. Gods love those
> who are *sōphrōn*. And hate the bad.

For some of the audience, this would resonate against a familiar line from the *Odyssey*:

> such is the *noos* [mind] of earth-born human beings
> as is day which the father of gods and men brings on.

"Mind" and day, mind like day, depend on gods. Some might remember Archilochus's reworking of that image, in which human *thumos*, spirit, is changeable as day. Some might know Parmenides' oblique use of both, in which "we" are a mix of night and light. "According to their balance within us, so is our *noos*."[22] Whether listeners knew or remembered all this or not, the thought would bite true in them from their sense of the tradition. Human minds are as much at gods' mercy as human bodies.

AJAX THE SHADOW

Ajax seeing wrong in madness, eyes "darkened" by a goddess who seems shadow to Tecmessa—image of humanity as "shadow," of human "day" bounded by the dark—underlines the permanent presence of shadow. He is darkness visible, a shadow in the light. The brief madness on which his story pivots turns him permanently inside out. In the *Odyssey*, he is shade seen by the light of understanding and compassion. He belongs in Erebos. In Sophocles, who shares with his audience the "fact" that madness is dark, the shadow that marks his mind also marks his life.

Other madnesses make people do decisively terrible things. Kill their children, for instance. Heracles did not want to murder, and does. But Ajax wanted to murder, and fails. His madness makes him do something ridiculous: Ajax, "best-looking, best at deeds, of all Greeks after Achilles." No one laughed at Achilles. Heracles is polluted by his murder; Ajax is darkened forever by the madness that prevents his, and continues dark when sane. "O darkness, my light! O Erebos, most shining to me!" "Day," life, will not bring pleasure. Everything is back to front. Time inverts "unclear" and "clear": unclear things grow, clear ones get hidden.[23]

He exemplifies this in his "deception-speech" (the critics' name for it).

---

[22] *Aj.* 127–33; *Od.* 18.136–37; Archil. 131 (West); Parmenides fr. 16; Padel 1992:33, 43, 71.

[23] *Aj.* 395–96, 475 (cf. 361), 647–49.

He says he will kill himself, while seeming to say he'll give the idea up. (Or, he says he'll give up, while seeming to us to say he'll kill himself.) He who called on darkness as light now speaks truths that sound like lies:

> I'll hide this sword of mine . . .
> digging into earth where no one will see.
> Let night and Hades preserve it below.[24]

The chorus think he'll bury his sword in the earth. The audience knows he'll put it there to bury it in himself. Aeschylus's Ajax-play highlit earlier the physical difficulties of this operation. Pindar says Ajax "stabbed his *phrēn*" with the sword.[25] In Sophocles, Ajax's first mention of the stabbing stresses the darkness in and surrounding him. Unwittingly, he continues Athene's theme, the instability of human "day." The play says he is under her anger for one day.[26] He does her will this day in everything, even his rhetoric. In the madness she sent, he saw wrongly, saw animals as men. In sanity, despairingly, he saw dark as light. Now he speaks of *night*'s fleetingness, not day's. His language refutes him, telling of everlasting night, not light:

> The everlasting circle of night
> gives place to white-horsed day:
> that it may burn its light.

To say night does not last he calls it "everlasting": *aianēs*. The word chimes with his name, Aias, and the tragic cry *aiai*, "alas!"[27] He is everlastingly dark. He will not lighten, even in Hades.

"Everlasting" brings Erinys echoes from Aeschylus's *Eumenides*, written ten or fifteen years earlier, in which the Erinyes, introduced to Athens as "*everlasting* children of Night," say *nosos* (disease) may spill from their anger as an "everlasting," Chernobyl-like pollution in human earth. Other, more hopeful things—the Athenian court, the love of Orestes' heirs for Athens—also last "for ever." But "everlasting" is the Erinyes' word first. Darkness is forever. You make terms with it, or go under. Sophocles' Ajax uses for "night" an Aeschylean word for Erinyes, Night's children, and for their damage they do to "ground": to the human relationships and minds that they, the madness-bringers, rule.[28]

When Sophocles wrote *Ajax* he was still much influenced by Aeschylus. His Ajax expects Erinyes, who "always see sufferings among mortals," to

---

[24] *Aj.* 658–60; see Goldhill 1986:181 n. 28, 189–92.
[25] Pi. *N.* 7.26. On Aeschylus's *Ajax* trilogy, see *Aj.* Jebb ed., Intro. §§5–7 (xix–xxiii); and see below, n. 35.
[26] *Aj.* 753–561, 778.
[27] *Aj.* 672–73; cf. 430–32.
[28] *Eum.* 416, 479, 942, 572, 672; Padel 1992:189–92.

punish his enemies. His half brother Teucer expects Zeus, "remembering Erinys, and end-bringing Justice," to punish Agamemnon and Menelaus.[29] When Ajax says night makes room for day, he reminds his audience of an everlasting Aeschylean presence. Night and Erinyes, plus the madness, death, and pollution they incarnate, are permanent residents in human lives and minds.

Ajax's madness is part of the play's fabric of night, darkness, not-seeing. His "dark" seeing is mirrored by the play's closing issue, burial. How to put his body in darkness (where no man really will see it), now he is "no longer a man but a shadow."[30]

Becoming a shadow: the audience see it happen. Uniquely for Greek tragedy, this Ajax kills himself on stage. He was the pattern of physical strength. Through Odysseus's eyes, the audience saw his madness as image of universal human frailty. In his suicide, they see this image cashed. The destruction of his body was foreshadowed in that momentary destruction of mind.

"Destroy Us in the Light"

Sophocles could find Homeric links between Ajax and darkness elsewhere in epic, outside the *Odyssey*. An ancient commentator on *Ajax* relates the hero's darkness to a passage in *Iliad* 17, where Ajax keeps Trojans off the corpse of Achilles' friend, Patroclus. He kills many, he rallies the Greeks, he is amazing: but the battlefield mists up where they fight, while Trojans fight in clear air.[31] He and Menelaus cannot see the other Greeks. "They are wrapped in mist, along with their horses." Ajax realizes Zeus is helping the Trojans. He prays:

> Zeus, father, draw the Greeks
> from under the mist! Clear the sky!
> Let us see with our eyes! Destroy us,
> since this is what pleases you!
> But do it, at least, in the light!

Zeus pities him

> and at once scattered the mist,
> pushed away the cloud. The sun shone.
> All the battle was made clear.[32]

---

[29] *Aj.* 836–844, 1390–91; cf. *Il.* 19.86–87. Aeschylus's influence: *Aj.* Jebb ed., Intro. §21 (lii).

[30] *Aj.* 1257.

[31] *Il.* 17.236, 279–80, 356–60, 368.

[32] *Il.* 17.626, 644–50.

"If you are going to destroy us, do it in the light." As the ancient commentator saw, this plea unites Sophocles' play with the Ajax of the *Iliad*. In the *Iliupersis*, "Sack of Troy," of which fragments exist, the Greek doctor

> was the first to spot the lightning-flashing eyes
> and heavy thought of Ajax in his anger.

Lightning-flashing eyes; "heavy," angry mind. Sophocles' *Ajax* picks this up too.[33]

Yet another epic, the lost *Aithiopis*, was the source for Ajax's madness and suicide. In it, Ajax killed himself "about dawn": at the boundary of light and dark. Pindar kept this timing.[34] In Aeschylus's *Thracian Women*, the second play of his Ajax trilogy, an eyewitness described Ajax's suicide. Ajax could not manage it alone. His sword bent, like a bow, "till one of the *daimones*, being present, showed . . ." Here the fragment ends. Showed what? Showed the sword the way in? "One of the *daimones*?" It must have been a female one, for the participle is feminine. This, presumably, was Athene, "showing" a sword a way into "flesh that gave no place to death."[35]

Darkness, madness, suicide; *daimōn* darkening the field where Ajax fights, *daimōn* showing death a way into the body, *daimōn* that is "shadow" to other people; lightning-flashing eyes, a heavy mind: tradition drew this net of associations tight round Ajax's name. Sophocles gathers it in and pins it to dark seeing. Athene darkens Ajax's eyes before the audience sees him. He stays darkened through the play until, the only tragic character killed on stage, he gets destroyed in the light. Precisely as he asked to be, in Homer.

"Twisted" Seeing

PANDULPH:	Lady, you utter madness, and not sorrow.
CONSTANCE:	I am not mad: this hair I tear, is mine;
	My name is Constance; I was Geffrey's wife;
	Young Arthur is my son, and he is lost.
	I am not mad;—I would to heaven I were!
	For then, 'tis like I should forget myself.
	O, if I could, what grief should I forget!
	Preach some philosophy to make me mad.

. . . .

---

[33] *Iliupersis* 5.8; *barumēnon noēma*, Homer OCT 5:139; cf. Schol. *Il.* 11.515; *Aj.* 41, 257.

[34] Pi. *I.* 3.35 says he killed himself *opsiāi en nukti*, "at the end of night." A scholiast *ad hoc.* says, "Writing the *Aithiopis* he says Ajax killed himself *peri ton orthron.*"

[35] A. fr. 83.

For, being not mad, but sensible of grief,
My reasonable part produces reason
How I may be deliver'd of these woes,
And teaches me to kill or hang myself.
If I were mad, I should forget my son;
Or madly think, a babe of clouts were he:
I am not mad. Too well, too well I feel
The different plague of each calamity.
    —Shakespeare, *King John* 3.4

Ajax sees animals as men, sees dark as light. He is hung round with images of animality as well as darkness. Other mad people do the opposite: they take human beings for animals. Agave sees her own son as a lion. Other mad figures in lost tragedies killed their children seeing them as some other living thing. A deer, a vine.[36]

Inverted vision, therefore, is central to tragic images of madness. What it inverts—animals and people, dark and light—points to Greek perceptions of madness as dark, and also as nonhuman (see Chapter 13). The mad are perceived as isolated (see Chapter 10) by how and what they see. They are alone in the dark, like seers. We should also notice the fact of inversion itself. The twist of it, *away* (see Chapter 12) from the norm.

The mad do not look normal to other people. They are not supposed to see normally either. Madness skews the two-way flow between what self sees and how others see self.[37] Mad eyes roll, twist. The word is *dia-strophos*, "cross-turned." Translation through Latin would give "per-verted." Io's shape, mind and eyes are *diastrophoi*. In tragedy and medical writers, *diastrophoi* eyes are a sign of madness.[38] Mad eyes are also blood-shot: as if blood is one of the things the mad see when other people do not.[39] Perversion, in the normal route of communication between self and other, is blood-filled.

The mad perceive wrongly, like the drunk.[40] They take pleasure in situations that are desolating. Their mad joy intensifies grief others feel for them. Euripides shows us this with his own twist. Mad Cassandra sees truly, though others do not know it. In *Trojan Women*, she must be

---

[36] *Aj.* Stanford ed., Intro. v; A. frr. 1, 57–62(N) (Loeb 2:398–401); below, nn. 48–49; Chapter 19, n. 56.

[37] See Padel 1992:59–63.

[38] *PV* 882; *HF* 868; *Ba.* 1123; *Or.* 283; Hp. *Progn.* 7 (Loeb 2:16); Padel 1992:60.

[39] *HF* 933–34; Fraenkel *ad Ag.* 1428. With Orestes, the image reminds listeners that his madness entails seeing Erinyes who drip blood from their own eyes: Padel 1992:60, 176.

[40] Drunk companions feel they are "swimming to a false shore": Pi. fr. 124 (127 Turyn); see van Groningen 1960:93–95. Drunkenness and madness: cf. Dionysus, above, Chapter 3, nn. 17–19.

Agamemnon's sex-slave. Introduced as *mainas*, a "raving woman," *bac-cheuousa*, "bacchic-mad," she sings of union with Agamemnon as if it were a wedding:

> Blessed the bridegroom! blessed am I
> in a royal wedding-bed. . . . Dance, mother!
> Sing the wedding-song—oh! with happy songs. . . .
>
> . . . .
>
> Come, daughters of Troy in your lovely dresses,
> sing of my marriage, hymn my husband, fated for my bed.[41]

Hecuba says her suffering has not made her *sōphrōn*. "You stay in the same [state]." "Give her tears for these wedding songs of hers," she tells the chorus.[42] She thinks Cassandra, embracing humiliation and captivity as cause for joy, is seeing them wrongly.

But Cassandra switches from mad lyric song to sane iambic rhythm, marking her understanding of conventional perceptions. Her joy is not deluded but prophetic. Sex with her will be fatal to Agamemnon. (The audience knows this. In Aeschylus, Cassandra is Clyemnestra's extra excuse for killing Agamemnon.) "I'll kill him," says Cassandra. She will avenge her father and brothers.[43]

Cassandra is a prophet. She does not see wrongly, when mad. But Ajax does. He sees bad (the dead cattle) as good. The chorus is glad to hear he is sane again, but Tecmessa asks, Is it better to be unfortunate and enjoy yourself, while your friends grieve for you? Or to share awareness of your misfortune with your friends? The fewer people unhappy, the better, says the chorus. Then we should wish Ajax to stay mad. When mad,

> he took pleasure in the evils he had
> though we, who were sane, were saddened
> to be with him. But now he's stopped,
> relieved of sickness, he grieves . . .
> and, no less than before, we're sad too.[44]

BAD AS GOOD, BELOVED AS ENEMY

Mad people see tragically wrongly. Bad seems good. Their nearest and dearest seem enemies. Orestes suddenly sees his caring sister as "one of the bad ones," initiating one of his Erinys-fits. She restrains him. "Let go!" he cries:

[41] *Tro.* 307–40; cf. 306, 341.
[42] *Tro.* 350–51. *Sōphrōn*: above, Chapter 3, n. 21; below, Chapter 12, nn. 58–61 (cf. Chapter 2, nn. 6, 33).
[43] *Tro.* 347–60.
[44] *Aj.* 265–76.

> One of my Erinyes, you clutch my waist
> to throw me into Tartarus!

Heracles sees his own father as his enemy's father, his own children as his enemy's children.[45]

The mad take with joy the things that damage them. They see those they love as enemies. As the chorus of *Antigone* sings,

> bad seems at some times good
> to the man whose *phrenes*
> god drives to *atē*.[46]

The most searing example of inverting friend and foe is Agave at the end of *Bacchae*, seeing her son's head as a lion's.

When she holds it up, the moral spotlight turns, a moment, on the chorus, observers of her mad seeing. They are maenads too. But they followed Bacchus willingly, while he made Agave a maenad to punish her. Pentheus has persecuted them, they were glad of his death.[47] But now they see mad Agave glorying in Pentheus's head, and they are shaken. "Share my banquet," she demands. "What shall I share, unhappy that I am?" returns the chorus leader. *Tlamōn*, "unhappy, wretched": not a word they used before of themselves in relation to what Bacchus did. They are "wretched" seeing this. In their last speech they call Agave, too, *talaina*, wretched.[48] Their last stance to her is a pity in which, you could say, they also share. For their voice of celebration for wild innocence is impossible to sustain, now they see what their Dionysus made Agave do.

Both parties here are "maenads": that word which means both Bacchic worshippers and "madwomen." Yet they are sane, she mad. Then Cadmus, her father, takes over. There is a wider gulf here between his seeing, his relation with Dionysus, and Agave's. Though he worshipped Bacchus, he never ran mad on hills. Now he cries for her sorrows, and for his own. Agave does not know why. She explains it by Cadmus's age: "How bitter is old age, how sullen in its eyes." "Eyes" sum up the difference between them.[49]

Like Tecmessa, Cadmus feels the mad person would be happier if the madness did not pass. "When you think sanely about what you have done," he says, "you'll grieve with terrible anguish":

---

[45] *Or.* 251, 264–65; *HF* 968, 970–1000.

[46] *Ant.* 621–23; see Chapter 1, n. 3, and Appendix, nn. 43–47. *Phrenes*: Padel 1992:20–22. *Atē* as "harm," damage-chain: below, Chapters 16, 17. As "disaster": Chapter 18, Appendix.

[47] *Ba.* 1020, 1035.

[48] *Ba.* 1186, 1200.

[49] *Ba.* 1248–52, cf. 251.

> If you stayed as you now are for ever,
> you would not seem to be miserable:
> though you wouldn't be fortunate.[50]

All the same, he brings Agave back to sanity, to a life of everlasting anguish, by making her see that head correctly.

The mad see twisted. The twist may go either way. A good thing, a beloved person, a child, seen as an enemy, a bad thing. Or a bad thing—a dead child, slaughtered sheep, sexual slavery—seen with glee: as a slain lion, slain enemies, a wedding. Animals seen as people, people seen as animals. Madness is inner dark. The "per-version" of its ways of seeing is dark in the sense of dangerous, wrong, bad.

---

[50] *Ba.* 1259–62.

Chapter 8

TRUE SEEING

WHAT OTHERS CANNOT SEE: CASSANDRA, ORESTES, IO

> I'll tell thee a miracle—
> I am not mad yet, to my cause of sorrow.
> Th' heaven o'er my head seems made of molten brass,
> The earth of flaming sulphur, yet I am not mad.
> —Webster, *The Duchess of Malfi* 4.2.

MADNESS inverts seeing. Darkened forever by his moment of madness, Ajax sees dark as light. But the inversion may not always be wrong, either empirically or morally. We, from where we are, can imagine ways in which taking dark for light can mean seeing not falsely, but more truly. Seeing where others see nothing. Seeing in the dark. This possibility operates in fifth-century imagination too, but with specific resonances, very different from ours.

There are important differences between seeing false and seeing true in tragic madness, which seem to depend on whether there is something there for mad and sane to see. When the mad see wrongly, they are usually looking at something the sane can see too: only they see it different. Their own child as a lion. Cattle as human enemies. But they see more truly ("truly" according to religious perceptions of their day, a "truly" validated by the text) when they see something where the sane see nothing. Madness can see things that really are there, but that it is normal not to see. Erinyes are known to exist, but most people do not see them. Orestes' madness is to see them as they really are.[1]

All this is close to prophecy: and the innards, equipment of knowing and feeling, are sometimes prophetic. They "speak" and "prophesy" in passion, when they "darken" and "move." Darkness and blindness belong with the mind and passion, and with prophets and earth shrines. The common denominator is seeing what normal people cannot see.[2] Inner blackness sees like a prophet. Eteocles interprets the arrogant stars on Tydeus's shield as foretelling Tydeus's destruction: "Madness [*anoia*] may become a prophet for a man."[3] Dionysus, "mad" god, is also *mantis* (prophet):

---

[1] Padel 1992:178–89.
[2] Padel 1992:16–17, 68–77; above, pp. 65–66.
[3] *Sept.* 402; cf. *margon*, 380.

bacchic raving and madness have great prophetic power.
When the god comes to the body in strength,
he makes those who are raving speak the future.[4]

The mad tragic figures who see something where others see nothing,
and see it truly, are Aeschylus's Orestes, Cassandra, and Io. I have linked
them already, in another context. They are the ones open to repeated,
rather than single, fits of madness (see Chapter 4). Whether you see truly
in madness depends on the gods' intention in sending the madness. For
Heracles, Ajax, and ultimately Agave, madness is sent in divine punishment or anger, precisely to make them see falsely for a moment, and act
disastrously while at that moment. For Io and Orestes, the long-term
bursts of madness *are* the punishment. In them they see or hear truly the
daemonic causes of their suffering.

Prophecy is one example of true seeing in madness, and one of these
figures, Cassandra, is a prophet. Coming to the house of Atreus, she sees at
once what is in it:

> A chorus singing in unison. Not tunefully.
> They never leave this roof. Family Erinyes,
> a mad band, hard to drive out,
> who've drunk human blood to be bolder,
> stay fixed in this house.

She sees and describes past murders here. The locals marvel:

> I am amazed that you,
> though raised across the sea,
> speak truth of a foreign city,
> as if you'd been here.

She is right to see murders, to see Erinyes here like a gang of muggers.
This is true vision. She has it because she has bursts of mad prophecy in
which she sees truth others cannot see.[5]

At the end of the next play, Orestes too, beginning his madness, sees
Erinyes. Again the chorus cannot see them. This chorus explains them
away as *doxai*, "seemings, imaginings":

ORESTES: Ah! Ah! women! maidservants—like Gorgons!
          Black-robed women, mixed with dense snakes!—
          I can't stay longer!

[4] *Ba.* 298–301. See below, p. 87.
[5] *Ag.* 1183, 1186–90, 1199–1201. Orestes, Cassandra, Io: see Chapters 2, 4.

CHORUS: What *doxai* whirl you round,
            you dearest of sons to your father?
            Stop! Don't be done over by fear!
ORESTES: For me, they're not the imaginings of pain.
            These are clearly my mother's avenging hounds!
CHORUS: Because blood is still fresh on your hands.
            Confusion falls on your *phrenes*
            because of this.
ORESTES: Lord Apollo! They are coming in gangs now,
            and foul blood drips from their eyes!
CHORUS: There is a way of cleansing it.
            Apollo's touch will free you from these pains.
ORESTES: You don't see them. I see them.
            I'm driven. I can't stay.[6]

With one of the loneliest lines in tragedy, "You do not see them: I do," Aeschylus pinpoints the gulf between mad and sane. It is defined by how and what each sees.

In the next play, he confirms that what mad Orestes, and mad Cassandra, saw was real. The audience themselves now see it too: Erinyes, squatting at the world's center, Delphi's shrine. In the two first plays, the chorus members had to say they could not see Erinyes. Now they are themselves Erinyes. The trilogy shows the audience that what madness saw was true. Everyone sees it.

Io's madness is accompanied, and incarnated, by the sting of *oistros* and the *eidōlon* ("image") of hundred-eyed Argus. Argus spied on her till Hermes killed him. His ghost still hounds her, accompanied by a mysterious piping sound.[7] In her madness, she hears this piping sound, and dances to it. It may have been represented by flute playing on stage. No one else comments on the sound, but there is no suggestion that what Io hears and sees is not as "real" as her madness. Mad, she hears and sees things other people cannot. Things really there, really sent by gods.

One other figure, arguably, sees more truly in his madness than when he was sane. This is Pentheus. His case is a little different. When he appears dressed as a woman, under Dionysus's orders, his vision and mind change along with his figure: so madness transforms Io's shape and mind, and twists her eyes. Pentheus sees things others might see, the city, the sun, the Stranger. But he sees them double, or transformed:

DIONYSUS: Your figure looks like one of Cadmus' daughters.
PENTHEUS: I seem to see two suns. Two of Thebes,

---

[6] *Cho.* 1048–62.

[7] *PV* 569–76. *Hupnodotan*: Some have suggested Io heard Hermes' pipe charming Argus asleep. In Sophocles' *Inachus*, Argus himself sang lyrics (see Griffith *ad PV* 567).

the seven-mouthed city. And you—I think
you go before me as a bull. Horns have come up
on your forehead. Were you perhaps
an animal all the time? You're certainly bull now.

DIONYSUS: The god's with us. Before, he was not kind.
He's with us. *Now you see as you should.*[8]

In this scene of saw-toothed ironies and double entendres, Pentheus has a
true epiphany. Dionysus was known to appear as a bull. Other people in
the play have seen the Stranger in human disguise. Pentheus tried to dis-
mantle that disguise, stripping off the long hair and thyrsus. Now he sees
Dionysus in a sense correctly: god as bull. Pentheus is under Dionysus's
spell now. Mad. Dionysus talks to him as Athene talks to mad Ajax, when
she calls him out to be mocked: god talking man into displaying himself in
the trap.[9]

Pentheus sees double, like someone drunk. The "god of" drink has maddened him.[10] Seeing double, seeing a human shape as animal, seems
wrong to the sane and the sober. But Dionysus's human shape was a disguise. There *are*, in a sense, two of Thebes: the civilized safe city run by
human beings, and the place where divine violence erupts, a broken world.
There *are* two "suns" here: the rules that people see and live by, and the
anarchic radiance of gods. The audience knows the disguised god's plot.
They see here madness seeing wrongly seeing true.

"FINE FRENZY" AND PLATO'S *PHAEDRUS*

Lovers and madmen have such seething brains,
Such shaping fantasies, that apprehend
More than cool reason ever comprehends.
The lunatic, the lover, and the poet
Are of imagination all compact.
One sees more devils than vast hell can hold.

. . . .

The poet's eye, in a fine frenzy rolling,
Doth glance from heaven to earth, from earth to
    heaven. . . .
    —Shakespeare, *A Midsummer Night's Dream* 5.1

For us, now, in some contexts, it is a familiar idea that mad perceptions
may be more, not less, true than sane ones. The idea may feel like ours.

---

[8] *Ba.* 917-24; cf. *PV* 673, 882.
[9] See Dodds *ad Ba.* 912–76; *Aj.* 89–95. God as bull: Padel 1992:144 n. 10. Pentheus
stripping Dionysus: *Ba.* 493–96.
[10] Dodds *ad Ba.* 918. "God of": see Chapter 3, nn. 19, 22.

Something like it contributed, for instance, to the revaluing of madness and psychiatry in the 1960s.[11] Yet in the form in which we entertain it, this idea simmers with ingredients from many different centuries and societies.

In this and the next chapter, I shall isolate three ingredients which, from mediaeval times through the Renaissance down to us, helped to privilege mad seeing as true.

The first, closest to tragedy itself, is Plato's *Phaedrus*. It stamped on European imagination the image of divine "fine frenzy" important to Montaigne and the Italian humanists, in which lovers, the mad, the poets, see truths the sane cannot.[12]

In setting this idea loose in subsequent imagination, the dialogue established a gulf between ways of seeing madness in tragedy, and ways of seeing madness after it. No one in tragedy *wants* to see daemons like Erinyes, or see Dionysus as a bull. No one wants Cassandra's prophetic thrills, Cassandra least of all. The maenad chorus of *Bacchae* may sing how wonderful it is, running through forests mad with your hair loose, but at the end, faced with what Dionysus's madness did, they call themselves "wretched." They do not value the madness in itself.

The idea that madness brought anything as positive as "blessings"[13] comes primarily from Plato, from the *Phaedrus*. It is Greek, in that it is written by a Greek. But it did not represent its culture's beliefs even then. It is not fifth-century. Tragedy's spectators and poets would not have felt it.

The *Phaedrus* is one of the most ironic, rhetorical, subtle of texts. Nothing in it is simple evidence for anyone's views of madness: not those of Plato, nor those of Greece generally. Its images of *mania* are multiple and self-contradictory, and must have been startling at the time. The dialogue introduces them for purposes of its own. Embedded in this filigree of original ideas is the statement which had such influence on the Renaissance and on us: that god-given *mania* can bring "goods."

MANIA CLASSIFIED BY HUMAN ACTIVITY

The *Phaedrus* has two accounts of god-given madness. The first rises from a rebuttal of the sophistic claim that you should prefer lovers who do not

[11] See, e.g., Bateson 1973:197, 172, on a schizophrenic shaped in childhood by "false interpretation of his messages" when he faced something he knew was false, whose falseness was never admitted. Laing 1965:11–12 began, "In the context of our present pervasive madness that we call normality, sanity . . . , all our frames of reference are ambiguous and equivocal. . . . Our normal 'adjusted' state is too often the abdication of ecstasy." See below, Chapter 9, n. 21.

[12] See Chapter 6, nn. 1, 8–9.

[13] See Chapter 9, n. 17.

truly love you to those who love you madly. Socrates argued playfully *for* the notion that true lovers are mad and should be avoided. Now he turns against it:

> It would be true, if it were a simple fact that *mania* is bad. But in fact the greatest goods come to us through *mania*, as long as it is given by divine gift. When mad, the priestess at Delphi and those at Dodona did many fine things for states and individuals. When sane, they did little, or nothing. By prophesying in divine possession, the Sibyl and others have foretold the future to many people, and guided people right.[14]

Prophecy in madness: not quite a new idea. Heraclitus had said the Sibyl prophesied "with raving mouth." But we do not know how straight this was received in *his* time. Socrates is flirting with wordplay already invoked by another paradoxical writer (who likewise is no good evidence for what the culture generally believed). Modern language "puts in an extra letter" and calls prophecy "mantic." First, truly, it was "manic." *Mania* from god is better than human sanity (*sōphrosunē*), the mental state in which people interpret signs. Mad, true prophecy is better than augury, when sane people, *emphrones*, tell the future by bird-watching.[15]

The first model of good-giving, god-given *mania*, then, is prophetic. The next is more problematic, at least for readers from our own world. This *mania* has broken out in, and also healed, unspecified families of "diseases and most terrible sufferings" inflicted by ancient *mēnimata*.[16] A rare word, which means, essentially, "causes of anger."

Mēnimata appear in relations between the dying and the living. Dying Hector warns Achilles, dead Elpenor warns Odysseus, to bury him, "Lest I become to you some *mēnima* of gods." One tragedy speaks of Ares' ancient "angers" against the race of Cadmus, Thebes' founder, because Cadmus killed his *drakōn* (snake, "dragon"). Ares' *mēnimata* demand that Creon, Thebes' present ruler, must have his own son killed in the cave where Ares' *drakōn* lay. *Mēnimata* in the *Phaedrus*, here, must show Plato thinking with tragic, perhaps especially Theban, families. He may be quoting from the play, something Plato is known to do.[17]

After mentioning these "angers" in families, Socrates says *mania* has helped with them, in a mad, much argued-over sentence whose grammatical subject is *mania*:

---

[14] Pl. *Phdr.* 244A.

[15] Heraclitus fr. 92DK; Pl. *Phdr.* 244C–D. Cf. Padel 1992:167 n. 14.

[16] Pl. *Phdr.* 244D–E.

[17] *Phoen.* 931–35; Linforth 1946b:165. *Mēnimata*: *Il.* 22.258, *Od.* 11.73; cf. Lobeck's conjecture *ad Cho.* 278; below, Chapter 20, n. 29.

Madness has entered in and prophesied and found release for those who
needed it, fleeing to prayers and the service of gods, from which it has found
purifications and rites [*teletai*] and made healthy for the present and future
the one who has it [who has the *mania*?], finding solution for present ills for
the one who is mad in the right way, and possessed.[18]

The sentence is difficult: no Plato expert I have consulted, in commentaries
or in person, is entirely sure of its interpretation, or even punctuation.
Greek often uses *mania* as *nosos*, "sickness." The dialogue has already suggested mad love is sick ("the lover is sicker than the nonlover") but this is
later corrected.[19] The idea of sickness here is problematic. Is madness one
of the sicknesses, or their means of cure?

The sentence starts as if *mania* is one of these "greatest sufferings" inflicted on families because of angry gods, or angry dead. But it continues
as if madness itself, like a clairvoyant, has "discovered" rituals to avert
these sicknesses.[20] *Mania* turns out to be not sick, but prophetically
healing.

These ancient families sound very like tragic ones—the house of Laius
or Atreus, for instance—where a curse, embodied in Erinyes, makes family
members continue mad destructive acts.[21] But in the sentence as we have
it, it is unclear who experiences this madness. Family members themselves?
Or clairvoyants?[22] Whichever it is, they must be mad *orthōs*, "in the right
way." As in the prophecy model, the benefits of real madness are contrasted with the flat sane exercise of human craft.

The third example is poetic: madness of Muses. As in the second, *mania*
is the grammatical agent. Madness "takes a soft, untrodden soul, and
wakes it, inspiring it [*ekbaccheuousa*] to songs and poetry." Poets who think
they can do without *mania* get nowhere. The poetry of the mad makes that
of the sane fade to nothing.[23]

Of course others before Plato had connected poetic, like prophetic, inspiration with madness. Notably Democritus, who said the best poems
were made "with divine frenzy and holy breath." An old idea: one that
deeply engages Plato. He says elsewhere that poets do not know what they

---

[18] Pl. *Phdr.* 244E.

[19] Madness as *nosos*: see Chapter 15, nn. 12–37. Mad lover as "sick": Pl. *Phdr.* 236B.

[20] See Thompson ed. (1860) *ad loc.* Though satisfied "on the whole" with Lobeck's reading, he enumerates difficulties to it. Robin's translation (Budé ed.) starts a new subject half-
way through.

[21] E.g., *Sept.* 686–711; see Padel 1992:171–75.

[22] Pl. *Phdr.* 244D5. See Linforth 1946b, followed by Ferrari 1987:113.

[23] Pl. *Phdr.* 245A.

are talking about, or meaning. Poetry is due to "Muse within you,"[24] not to you yourself.

No one asks who gets the "goods" from madness. In the first example, the clients benefit, not the mad priestesses. In the second, it is hard to know who is going mad. Madness benefits families. Do they or their clairvoyants go mad? It would fit the first example if the professionals go mad, the sick families benefit. The third example is moot. Who are the beneficiaries of great poetry? Audiences? Poets? Plato does not ask.

The passage ends with the claim that god-given *mania* produces "noble works."[25] This wheels in one of antiquity's most enduring images: the wings, chariot, and horses of the soul. It comes in a speech on the "fourth *mania*," erotic madness, "best of all frenzies." Socrates describes what happens to souls who truly love. Their wings sprout: this is salvation via mad loving. The mad lover also brings blessings *to* the beloved. A sane lover's attentions "beget in the loved soul a nonfreedom [i.e., meanness, pettymindedness] which the masses praise as virtue, and will make the soul roll around the earth for nine thousand years and be *anous* [mindless] under the earth."[26] A paradox. Sanity makes the beloved do what is traditionally mad: wander (see Chapter 11). It makes the beloved *anous*, mindless, mad. Mad lovers are better after all.

The silence of the first three examples, over who receives *mania*'s goods, is carried on here. Who gets the "goods" of mad love, the beloved or the lover? Socrates is really gunning for the mad, actively *loving* soul. But the loved soul benefits too.

The whole piece is mad, in a way: a kind of "mythic hymn" delivered inspirationally, like the work of mad poets. Later on, Socrates looks back on it as "play."[27]

One point important for later readers is that the sprouting wings, the soul's development through mad love, go with "seeing truth."[28] If the greatest goods come to us through madness, their climax is true vision. It is love that makes wings sprout. Love is only the fourth madness, and not all madness is love. But this hymn on sprouting wings is embedded in a discussion of madness.

This image of spiritual development was magnetically compelling. In the long reception of the *Phaedrus*, another, separate idea can be read, by

[24] See Democritus frr. 17–19DK; Pl. *Crat.* 428C. See Delatte 1934:28–30; Dodds 1951:82, 101 nn. 125–26; Harriott 1969; Murray 1981.

[25] Pl. *Phdr.* 244B.

[26] Pl. *Phdr.* 249D–E, 256E.

[27] Ferrari 1987:111, Pl. *Phdr.* 262D.

[28] Pl. *Phdr.* 247A, 247D5, 248C–D, 249E.

association, in or from the text: *madness* makes your soul's wings grow; madness lifts the soul to higher planes, to see truths inaccessible to the sane.

MANIA CLASSIFIED BY GODS

The second account of madness is a misleading description of the first. Commentators have tried to reconcile them but the differences are obviously part of the design. Plato is an exact, and exacting, writer.[29]

This new account starts off by saying that "we" (Socrates and Phaedrus) said "there were two kinds of *mania*, one from human ills [*nosēmata*], the other from a divine release from accustomed habits."[30] "We" never did. On the contrary, *mania* was said to heal ills. It had been suggested, earlier, that true lovers were "sick,"[31] but this was set up to be knocked down. The first account did not say madness itself was sick. It began by saying the greatest goods come from madness, "as long, however, as it is god-given" and then explored god-given madness. The new account uses some of the same language, but in different places, to say different things. In the first, *mania* brought "release" from ills. Now, there are two classes of *mania*, one due to ills, another that brings "release" from habit. "Release" is still a good, but in a different context.[32] So this opening warns readers that the new account may not tell it as it was about the first.

The main difference is in the way of classifying *mania*. The new way is what everyone remembers (reading it back, as the dialogue misleadingly invites us to do, into the first) from the *Phaedrus*. Dodds, for instance, amalgamates them in his "Blessings of Madness" chapter in *The Greeks and the Irrational*.[33]

This second account classifies madness by the gods that inspire each one: "We divided divine madness into four parts: mantic, inspired by Apollo; mystic [or "pertaining to rites," *telestikē*], inspired by Dionysus; poetic, inspired by the Muses; and fourth erotic, inspired by Aphrodite and Eros, which we said was the best."[34] This was *not* how the first account classified things. It was much messier; and done from the human perspective. Except for Muses, no gods appeared in it. The prophetic examples included Sibyls, and priestesses at Dodona as well as Delphi. Now everything except

---

[29] Hackforth's commentary "admits" the second account is "inexact": see his notes on 265B, 266A. Staggeringly, he rewrites the Greek to what "a writer with more concern for exact statement than Plato had would have made Socrates say." For a corrective, see Ferrari 1987:60–61.

[30] Pl. *Phdr.* 265A.

[31] See above, n. 19.

[32] *Exallagē* 265E; cf. *apallagē*, 244E.

[33] Dodds 1951: ch. 3.

[34] Pl. *Phdr.* 265B.

for Delphi, and Apollo, is missing. No Sibyls, Dodona, or Zeus (whose prophetic shrine was Dodona). Prophetic *mania* belongs only to Apollo. The second example was ambiguous, but certainly mixed prophetic powers with healing. Prophecy is kept out here and, again, one specific god is assigned to this *mania*: Dionysus.

One thing happening here is a distorting simplification. The taxonomy is now *via* gods, but given spurious authority by the false claim that "we" said it before. Side issues are left out. No Zeus under "prophecy." No prophecy in Dionysus's *mania*.

Though it was not his central feature, Dionysus's madness was in fact known to have prophetic power. "Bacchic frenzy and madness have much prophecy."[35] As for *telestikē*, which means "associated with *teletai* [rites]": Dionysus was not the only god with rites, nor even the only one with initiatory, mystic rites (the main fourth-century use of the word). So why Dionysus, here?

Telestikē picks up *teletai* from the first account, where this *mania* "discovered" healing "rites." Through the fifth century, *teletai* is used for "rites" generally, in many cults: of Athene, of divine Heracles, at Eleusis. At the end of the century, Aristophanes uses it of Orphic rites.[36] By this time it is mainly, but not only, used for rites in mystery cults, like those of Eleusis. But at this time, in *Bacchae*, Euripides' Dionysus uses it of his own cult and his chorus sings,

> Happy is he who knows the rites of gods,
>
> . . . .
>
> *baccheuōn* [raving in bacchic frenzy]
> on mountains in holy purifications.[37]

This reflects how the word increasingly, in the late fifth century, means secret, initiatory rites, often connected with "purifications." Plato himself, elsewhere, speaks of releases and purifications from crimes, through sacrifices that people call *teletai*. He also connects purifications (*katharmoi*) and certain *teletai* with Dionysiac dances.[38] For Plato, *teletai* often seems to mean initiatory rites. In Alexandrian times, the word is increasingly attracted to secretness, and often means a "rite" with some hidden philosophic meaning. By Philo's day it can even *mean* "inner meaning."[39]

But for fourth-century readers of the *Phaedrus*, *teletai* might mean

[35] *Ba*. 299; above, n. 4.
[36] Pi. *O*. 3.42, *P*. 9.71; *N*. 10.34; Hdt. 2.171; Andocides 1.11; Ar. *Ran*. 1032, *Pax* 418. At *IT* 939, Orestes' arrival is commemorated in the "rite" of the Anthesteria: see Padel 1992:182–85.
[37] *Ba*. 22, 73–77. See Linforth 1946b.
[38] Pl. *Rep*. 356A, *Legg*. 815C.
[39] See Zijderveld 1934; Dodds *ad Ba*. 72–75.

"rites" of any kind; *or* especially (but not only) "secret rites"; *or* purely initiatory, purificatory rites. At this distance, we cannot know. Whatever they thought the word meant, I suspect it reminded them also of *Bacchae*. Release, purification, crime and cleansing, *teletai*, and tragic resonances figured in the second example, in the first account of *mania*. There, they were not specifically associated with Dionysus. But they *are* important to *Bacchae*, the play that featured Dionysus himself. Its chorus connects *teletai* and purifications. Teiresias speaks of "goods that come through" Dionysus, a line suggestively similar to Socrates' claim that goods come to us through madness.[40]

The play says that Dionysus, by ending grief and bringing the blessed forgetting of sleep, brings *pharmakon ponōn*, "cure for sufferings. The dialogue's first account of madness says one particular type of madness does the same thing: cure sufferings. And this type is, of course, the one that the second account assigns to Dionysus. The play says Dionysus is prophetic. So is this *mania*, in the dialogue's first account.[41]

In the play's polarization between Pentheus and Dionysus, opposed young males, Pentheus stands for insanely sane human containment, for imprisonment. Dionysus stands for the sanely mad, for not being bindable, for divine release: physical, psychic, moral, social.[42] Divine "release" is a good in the *Phaedrus*, whose uniquely wild setting frees its protagonists from the colonnades, from normal civilization.[43]

In the play these cousins, one mortal, one divine, offer two ways of male being, which seem central to the *Phaedrus*'s exposition of different ways of loving. (We might remember that *Bacchae* starts from the desire of a god to be honored and in some sense loved: to this end he has taken on "mortal *eidos*," mortal form.) Their opposition is alive in Socrates' turnaround. From arguing that the nonlover is preferable, because not mad, he ends up saying the nonlover makes the beloved *anous*, which in tragedy means "mad."[44] While mad, lovers see truth.

The play, then, offers a context in which it is sane to be mad. So does Plato's dialogue.

There were hints in the first account that could have prepared readers for attributing the second *mania* to Dionysus. They pointed to Dionysus via

---

[40] *Ba.* 285; Pl. *Phdr.* 244A.

[41] *Ba.* 280–82, 298; Pl. *Phdr.* 244D–E (see *ponōn*, 244D; *prophēteusasa, apallagē*, and *lusin . . . kakōn*, 244E); and see above, n. 18.

[42] *Ba.* 232, 239, 615–22, 636.

[43] From *Exō teichous*, Pl. *Phdr.* 227A. On words: Ferrari 1987:3–4, 22; above, nn. 32, 41. At *Phdr.* 256E, the nonlover's friendship is flavored "with mortal *sōphrosunē*," offering "sparse, mortal goods," and engenders in the other soul *aneleuthereia*, nonfreedom "which the world praises as virtue."

[44] Pl. *Phdr.* 257A; see Chapter 2, n. 33. *Ba.* 53.

tragedy; specifically, two late fifth-century plays, *Bacchae* and *Phoenician Women*. Theban plays. And it is often Thebes that offers the sharpest examples of what the first account alludes to: ancient families, mad cursed suffering, rites, release. All tragedies are under the auspices of Dionysus, but Thebes is his own home town. Furthermore, Plato elsewhere connects release, purification, and some form of prophecy with Dionysian "rites" and dance. Tragedy itself is one of Dionysus's rites and dance: rites whose effect Plato's pupil Aristotle would later describe as *katharsis*, "purification."[45]

I am not suggesting that by "rites" Plato means tragic performances. Simply that in both accounts of this madness, Plato is thinking with Dionysus's own violent genre; and possibly also with the most violent play of all, whose protagonist is torn to bloody pieces. Plato is responding, I think, to tragedy's interest in madness, as well as to the madness of its god.[46]

In the first account, Socrates classified madness through human beings who felt it—priestesses, sick families or their healers, poets, lovers—and what it made them do. In the second, madnesses are classified by their gods. The dialogue moves from human phenomena and feelings to their divine source and meaning. Madness is one vehicle of that movement. Plato plays with tradition, for his own idiosyncratic ends.

He also, I think, makes his own use of madness as tragedy represents it: that it may be both human, and divine. There are always two ways of seeing it.[47]

As far as later ways of seeing madness are concerned, Plato turned a new corner. The *Phaedrus* implies that most people in the fourth century think madness is shameful.[48] But in suggesting that for those in the know there are better ways of thinking about it, the dialogue freed European imagination to value madness. Henceforth in prophecy, poetry, ritual, and love, madness may see "more than cool reason ever comprehends," as Theseus, that paradigm of cool and kingly Athenian reason, says in Shakespeare.

[45] Thebes: Zeitlin 1990. *Katharsis*, purifications: Arist. *Poet.* 1449B27; above, n. 38.
[46] Violence: Padel 1990b:336, 365. Tragedy's interest in madness: 1981:118–25; above, pp. 8–10, and below, pp. 189–94, 239–48.
[47] See Chapter 18, n. 39.
[48] Pl. *Phdr.* 244B; see Dodds 1951:82–83 n. 2.

Chapter 9

A LEGACY OF TRUE MAD SEEING

SEEING "A COUNTRY OF TRUTH": DEMOCRITUS AT ABDERA

Nothing but noise and folly
Can keep me in my right wits, whereas reason
And silence make me stark mad.
—Webster, *The Duchess of Malfi* 4.2

THE *Phaedrus* slid into Greek imagination a hieroglyph of seductive new thoughts about madness. These could work two ways. First, the way things are put overtly in the *Phaedrus*: that true madness may engender privileged, truer seeing. Second, a more elitist idea, implied in the dialogue's playful somersault over loving and nonloving, madness and sanity: that privileged seeing may *look*, to noninitiates, *like* madness. There may be superior ways of seeing that other people wrongly call madness.

For the first time, then (except, perhaps, for the paradoxes of Heraclitus), the idea arises in Greek thought that not everyone may agree what madness is. What the stupid or uneducated call madness may in fact be truer vision.[1] For Plato, this truer vision would mean philosophy. In the *Phaedrus*, remarks in the second account of *mania* about "release from accustomed habits" remind us this is a philosopher speaking. Philosophers are now perceived as living differently from normal people. But later readers could focus only on the idea that in other areas as well as philosophy, especially the arts, madness may see more truly.

A century or so later, this idea is distilled in a portrait of a meeting between another philosopher and a doctor, given novelistic treatment in a sequence of fictitious letters composed between the third and first centuries B.C.[2] The Abderites, Democritus's fellow citizens, ask Hippocrates to come to Abdera and cure Democritus, who is mad "through too much wisdom." He has three kinds of symptom: odd ideas, insomnia and solitary behavior, and laughter. (In the Renaissance, this laughing is Democritus's talismanic image: he is "the laughing philosopher.") The Ab-

---

[1] Homeric characters get accused of being mad when they are sane, e.g., Eurycleia, above, p. 22. This does not mean disagreement over what madness is. Penelope just thinks Eurycleia wrong: it's mad to say Odysseus has come back. False opinions when mad: above, p. 74.

[2] The letters in Greek philosophical context: Temkin 1985; more recently, Smith 1990:21–32.

derites complain, "He laughs at everything, big and small, and counts all life for nothing." He writes about the lower world, says the air is full of images, listens to birdsong, sings songs to himself, softly, at night. His complexion has gone off along with his mind.

From their letter, Hippocrates doubts the madness. He thinks of melancholics. He'd like to remind Democritus there is joy as well as grief in the world, but thinks he shows strength of soul in ignoring mundane things like family and property. Some unusual mental conditions, like people pursuing wisdom, people who look down on human affairs (all this corresponds, though he does not say so, to current philosophical positions), do need solitude. They are not morbid, but need *ataraxiē*, freedom from disturbance. A freed mind surges upward and sees "a country of truth" untouched by relatives, nuisances, daemons, or human maxims and projects, where "the large vault of heaven is decorated with the restless stars." If wisdom transports Democritus there, of course the uneducated Abderites cannot understand him. (Hippocrates is not writing to the Abderites.) The Abderites may be misreading desire for solitude, as madness. Maybe *they* need treatment.

In Abdera, Hippocrates' suspicions are confirmed. Democritus is not mad. Quite the contrary. Scorning human affairs, he is writing "on madness": what it is, how it begins, how to relieve it. He dissects animals to learn about bile, the cause of madness. Impressed, Hippocrates wishes he had time for such research. What's stopping you? asks Democritus contemptuously. Property? Children? Money, disease, death? Weddings? Mocking Hippocrates, Democritus derides people who squander their lives on senseless things and cause their own misfortunes—at which he laughs.

Hippocrates disagrees. The fault is not in human beings but in the necessities of life, and in nature, who put us here. Democritus converts him with a Cynic diatribe on the uselessness of "man." No match for the philosopher, Hippocrates thanks the obtuse Abderites for the opportunity to meet this wisest of men. Yes, people waste their lives uselessly. The Cynic moral wins.

In its time, this story was related to and comes from the complex interaction of competing, overlapping Hellenistic philosophies,[3] plus the legacy of Plato. Democritus's symptoms express popular Greek images of madness. But that he sees truths about human life which ordinary people cannot see: this is ultimately from the *Phaedrus*.[4]

The Northern Renaissance loved this story. Hundreds of translations, exegeses, interpretations, reworkings and discussions give it new values

---

[3] Stoic, Cynic input: Rütten 1992:14–27.
[4] See Chapter 8, nn. 12, 15, 41–44.

and resonances. Paintings and engravings show what an imaginative pull this confrontation had.[5] It became related, of course, to *Problem* 30 and "fine frenzy."[6] The idea that madness sees truth, that what looks like madness to others is really truer seeing, gets a triple guarantee: Plato, "Aristotle," "Hippocrates." Democritus, sitting in melancholic pose in a garden, classic *"locus melancholicus"* (as one scholar calls the removed place of melancholic insight and meditation),[7] is supremely associated with seeing more truly. For Thomas Walkington, in *The Opticke Glasse of Humours* (1607), Democritus is the ancient melancholic seer "who put out both his eyes voluntarily in order to be given more to contemplation." The type of the sanguine melancholic, he does mad-seeming things to see more clearly.[8] Possessing the special sight (insight, foresight) of melancholia, Democritus is the chosen alias of Robert Burton.[9]

MELANCHOLIC DIVINATION AND CHRISTIAN FOLLY

The idea that melancholy has a special way of seeing seems to matter increasingly through the Renaissance. Humanists and physicians from 1500 to 1550 marvel at the melancholic's powers of divination. Sometimes this means predicting the future. Sometimes it means showing sudden knowledge of languages or natural philosophy. Prosper Calanio, whom Burton read and annotated, said that in melancholia the soul overcame its bodily prison and reached through to pristine knowledge. Even women, and uneducated people, have shown knowledge of celestial and philosophical matters when they were melancholy, "for *atra bilis* itself lends *ingenium*."[10]

In these early Renaissance texts, unlike the *Phaedrus*, divination is not one gift of melancholia beside others. Rather, divination is common in various degrees to all gifts of melancholy. But by the early seventeenth century things have changed. The melancholic's powers of divination are a "disputed subject." It may have been its powers of divination that led some to react against the potent glamorization of melancholia, and to represent it as sick, as "harmed" imagination.[11] But even this reaction shows how potent the image was. For good or ill, melancholy engenders a special way of seeing.

---

[5] Rütten 1992, with illustrations; Schleiner 1991:52, 201, 205, 250–54.

[6] Pigeaud 1981:454; Rütten 1992:124–30. *Problem* 30: above, pp. 55–57. Fine frenzy: above, pp. 81–86.

[7] Watanabe-O'Kelly 1978.

[8] Walkington quoted in Schleiner 1991:119, Rütten 1992.

[9] Schleiner 1991:204–207, who discusses melancholic divination in detail.

[10] Quoted in Schleiner 1991:28–29.

[11] According to Schleiner 1991:29, 74, 84–108.

The Renaissance did not love real-life madness. Alongside learned glamorizing of madness and mad seeing, and the exploitation of this for philosophical or dramatic ends, run fears of madness, and its connections with poverty, vagabonds, violence. And a devaluation of madness, as unreason at random from the truth.

Yet at many levels, as literature and philosophy do testify, they were fascinated by this unreason. Their fascination was expressed in another mediaeval and Renaissance image of mad true seeing: "Christian folly."

Christian folly gathers impetus around the same time as melancholic divination, whose opposite in a sense it was. In melancholic divination men of genius—sometimes even the uneducated, even women—see truths inaccessible except through black melancholy. But Christian folly is the simple soul seeing religious truth through clear-eyed simplicity, seeing truths from purity, not darkness.

Christian folly was embedded in European religious and philosophical discourse by at least 1450, when Cusanus argues in *Idiota de sapientia* that the idiot sees more clearly than the philosopher. Several works of around 1500 praise folly at the expense of conventional wisdom. The "holy fool" such as Percival wins religious perceptions and experiences unattainable to others.[12] A spiderweb of learned images spread the idea of the "madness" of Christianity, with its "transvaluation" of ordinary values, its possibilities of "the fool in Christ." It had impact on popular thought as well as on scholars.[13] The many real-life court fools, in the Middle Ages and Renaissance, influenced the fool's role in popular imagination and drama.[14]

All this is part of Erasmus's context. His *Laus stultitiae* comes out in 1511. Christ emerges as a special madman, and Christianity as the highest form of the inspired madness praised in the *Phaedrus*.[15] These ideas were profoundly magnetic. Ben Jonson quoted him, and Shakespeare changed his use of fools under the influence of Robert Arnim, a learned fool who borrowed Erasmus's term "foolosopher." When Arnim joined his company, Shakespeare assimilated his joking style to Arnim's, working into his plays Erasmus's vision, and More's, of this world as a world of fools. The Fool sees Lear's relationships and life more truly, in the play's terms, than does the king.[16]

In the mystic tradition and in Erasmus, ecstasy, like the Platonic "fine

[12] E.g., Jung and von Franz 1971:2, 295, chs. 2, 12.

[13] Kinsman 1974c:276–83. Kaiser 1963:19–17, 51–83, 84–90. Christianity's "madness" in relation to *mania* in the *Phaedrus*: Screech 1985. Popular thought: Kaiser 1963:277, 296.

[14] Real-life "fools": Welsford 1935; MacDonald 1981:121. Influence on drama: Welsford 1935:113–96, 197–240, 245–72.

[15] Screech 1980:67–72, 78–83, 140–41, 180–82, and passim.

[16] See Kaiser 1963:296; Bradbrook 1979:51–73, 69–70.

frenzy" of lunatic, lover, poet, and inspired devotee, is supremely important: a madness that sees truths beyond normal seeing. Though it might
seem its polar opposite, Christian folly worked *with* the image of melancholic divination, in providing the early modern imagination—and ultimately our own—with an vast jungle floor supporting the idea of mad
seeing. Pure madness or dark, simple or complex, genius or "fool": visions
of the laughing philosopher mesh with fascination over the vision and
speech of fools, of madness.

Plato's *Phaedrus* and fine frenzy. "Aristotle"'s *Problem* 30. Melancholic
divination. Christian folly. Mystic vision. How could we escape this com-
post of ideas? How not inherit some feeling that madness can see truth?
These are seams of thought, deeply embedded layers in the quarry of ideas
that underlie our attitudes to madness: its goods, values, its ways of seeing.
They are alive and at work in us. They may seem to us like archetypes,
universally true. This is because they have worked into the skin of our
minds. They were shocking and passionately argued-over ideas in their
day, when they were new. Then they lived on as cultural constructs, form-
ing attitudes in subsequent societies. Now they are wraiths in our less
learned imaginations, still potent shadows of long-past controversies. We
may even react to them as if they were our own ideas. They are not, of
course. We use them as coin of the realm, but they were there before us.
They own and ride us, rather than us owning them.

WHO GETS ANY "GOODS" FROM WHAT MADNESS SEES?

This fallout from the Renaissance is an element in our own attitudes to
mad seeing that separates us from attitudes in fifth-century tragedies, pre-
Plato. Divination and poetic inspiration were around in the fifth century.
But no one then wanted to be mad, to see madly. "The Blessings of Madness" is the title of a famous chapter in Dodds's book *The Greeks and the
Irrational*, where he considers prophecy, inspiration, and maenadism in the
classical age.[17] The investigation itself is wonderful, and directed subsequent research. But to line all the material up under Plato and call it all
"Blessings" does not match the fifth century, whose responses to madness
are expressed rather by tragedy. The *Phaedrus* is talking of special sorts of
madness. Plato does not think there are blessings or truths available to mad
Ajax, for example. The poets who make Cassandra are clear that what she
has is not a blessing. No one gets goods from it, least of all her.

Our own age is peculiarly placed to value, even idealize, truths available
to madness. Hence the title of Dodds's chapter. His organizing image reflected a groundswell, a reevaluation of madness, emerging in anthropol-

---

[17] Dodds 1951: ch. 3.

ogy and psychoanalysis in the mid–twentieth century. Literature on schizophrenia brought out ways in which schizophrenics disregard the fictional communications and conventional assumptions on which ordinary life runs, and express emotional truths that sanity deliberately, conveniently, obscures.[18]

In popular responses to this work, such insights were sometimes distorted (while the real pain of schizophrenia could be ignored) into the idea that schizophrenics see the world more truly than the sane. One could track in many different social, scientific, literary, and filmic contexts, Western culture's multiple responses to madness as a means of seeing truly. "In madness, Lear finds the wisdom he never knew as king."[19]

Our minds are conditioned to react to the idea very differently from the Athenians of the fifth century, who faced madness before Plato, before Christian folly: before the Renaissance and Romantics, in their different ways, for different reasons, found value in unreason.

The line of thought culminating in, say, a fine 1935 study of the Fool, which valued the "unambiguous wisdom of the madman who sees the truth," rested on a humanist faith that took for granted everyday truth about the world, and also the desirability and even possibility of grasping it correctly. The last thirty years of philosophy, linguistics, and deconstruction have invited us to think differently.[20] It is now possible (partly because of Laing's work), but it was not for all Laing's first readers, newly hit by his care for the truth of what the schizophrenic saw and said, to evaluate true seeing in madness differently. On the one hand to see madness in Shakespeare, for instance, as a product of particular historically specific festivals. And to see, on the other hand, that "there is no *a priori* relationship between madness and truth in the plays. Both the Fool and the mad man mobilise language to an extent where sense and non-sense—truth and untruth—are indistinguishable and no longer seem to matter. Some of what the Fool says is actually pointless."[21]

As a result of the revisions of psychoanalysis, it is also possible (not that it helps) to believe that true seeing in madness is not necessarily good for the person doing it: "the insane person is not 'cut off from reality.' On the contrary, the insane person is inundated with reality, overstimulated, overreceptive, completely porous to the outside world. He is a crustacean without a shell, a bird without feathers, a warrior without armor."[22]

This insight does bear, I think, on such true mad seeing as there is in

---

[18] E.g., Bateson 1973:193–97; Laing 1971:50–51. See Chapter 8, nn. 11, 13.
[19] Sheridan 1980:16–17.
[20] Salkeld 1993:17; see Welsford 1935:269.
[21] Salkeld 1993:19.
[22] Clément 1983:91–92.

Greek tragedy. The maddened person may temporarily perceive *more clearly than usual* the god-haunted world within which human beings really do, according to the tragedies' own terms, exist. Orestes and Cassandra see Erinyes in their madness because the Erinyes are really there. Madness's capacity to see truth is in Greek tragedy ultimately connected, like its every other aspect, to the mad person's relations with divinity.[23]

If there are "goods" in tragedy's use of madness, it is other people, not the maddened person, who gets them. Ultimately, the audience gains. They, it may be, see a truth about human lives, about divinity in human life: light from the dark, a truth it is sad to have to see.[24] But the mad person, no. Cassandra's last vision, before she goes off to her death, is of human life as a writing, or sketch, blotted out by one dab of a wet sponge.[25]

[23] Cf. Cassandra: see Chapters 4, 8.
[24] See Chapter 22, nn. 38–41.
[25] *Ag.* 1329.

PART 3

Isolation: Wandering, Disharmony, Pollution

Chapter 10

STONE: MADNESS IS OUTSIDE

DISTANCE

It is mad to walk out, there is an abyss there, there are
wild beasts.
—R. D. Laing, *The Divided Self*

ONE OF THE paradoxes of madness is that people who suffer it feel deeply
alone, while other people see it as something that affects, perhaps menaces,
themselves. Madness shows itself (to the sane) particularly in relationships
with other people. Killing them. Or avoiding them. The solitude of the
mad expresses a way of seeing that cannot be shared. "You don't see them,"
Orestes tells the chorus (meaning the Furies). "I see them. I can't stay." He
rushes off. Madness is alone. Yet other people see it as very much their
business.[1]

For Ajax's followers, Ajax is "hard to serve."[2] He came to Troy a leader.
Now, "a lonely pasturer of *phrēn*," he inhabits

> the same sheepfold
> as madness sent by god:

a "great grief to his friends." His moment of madness turned him to pain:
for others and for himself. He cannot share his pain *with* them (it is Odysseus who stresses community and "with"), for his mind grazes like one of
the animals he killed, on *his* grief, alone.[3] Madness makes difficulty and
danger for others, while isolating you from them.

I suggested above that tragic images of madness are made from a mix of
imagination and observation. How the sane imagine madness to be, inside, interacts with how they read it from outside. In Part 2, I focussed on
what the culture imagined it was like, from the inside, to be mad. To see
madly. Part 3 explores more external bodily images: symptoms of mad-

---

[1] According to MacDonald 1981:1, this paradox is central to problems confronting historians of madness. Orestes: *Cho.* 1062; above, p. 80.

[2] *Aj.* 609–10. *Dustherapeutos*: "hard to cure"? or "to serve"? In this Homer-bound play,
I'd choose "serve": cf. *Od.* 13.265. *Therapōn* in Homer is "attendant, squire"; what the
chorus members are to Ajax. Maybe both "therapy" and "service" are active in the word. He
is hard to serve because he is hard to cure.

[3] *Aj.* 614–16; cf. above, p. 69.

ness, seen from outside, plus inner movement that the sane, extrapolating from the outside, attribute to the mad interior.[4]

At the center of relations between mad and sane, I think, is brute physical distance. The sane perceive distance between themselves and the mad. This perception is self-fulfilling. They may attribute the need for distance to the mad, but they attribute to the mad an impulse they themselves feel too. Odysseus fears Ajax mad; he would not fear him sane. The distance between them at that moment is organized by Athene. But the one who wants it is Odysseus.

In most contexts, it is the sane who see most acutely the difference between mad and sane. Agave thinks Cadmus a killjoy for not joining her celebration. He sees the gulf between her mad illusion and his own painful sanity. The sane perceive difference, and make sure of the distance, between themselves and the mad. Yet they often (rightly or wrongly) attribute the distance to the mad: "Those [epileptics] who are used to their disease feel an attack coming in advance, and run away from people. Home, if that's near. If not, to the most deserted place, where fewest people will see them fall down."[5] The sane represent the mad moving *away*. Away from sane society. Sometimes, like Orestes, they move away from home. Away from a right place.

This move away is an outer movement made by (or attributed to) the mad. It is also a basis for inner movement, which the sane attribute to the mad mind (see Chapter 12). Images of the mad are full of dis-placement both seen and unseen: displacement of body and of mind. Madness is outside society, outside the norm. The mad mind veers outside its proper track. The mad body "de-viates" ("leaves the road") from its normal place, normal behavior.

STONE

One example of the way the sane contribute to distance between themselves and the mad, while insisting on seeing the mad as *self*-isolated, is a motif that crops up in myth and tragedy. Stoning the mad: the most concrete way of forging distance.

The Taurian herdsmen stone Orestes and Pylades when they see Orestes' mad fit. More complicatedly, in another play, the Argives sentence Orestes to be stoned. This is punishment for matricide, not for his madness. He endangers their city, because he is polluted by his murder. But Ajax is also threatened with stoning. As soon as his followers hear that he was mad and tried to kill the kings, they fear "to suffer stone-thrown war, battered along

---

[4] Above, p. 47. Working from outside to inside: Padel 1990b:336, 1992:66.
[5] Hp. *DMS* 15 (Loeb 2.170).

with him." Again, this response is not purely to his madness but to crime: the crime madness made him commit, the far worse one it prevented. Death by stoning: punishment for crime.[6] But both Orestes and Ajax are men who have been mad.

It has been suggested that stoning the mad was meant to cure them.[7] Unless death counts as cure, this seems unlikely. And, as I argued, there is little sign in the culture of a concept of long-term madness that needs cure. Madness is mostly temporary invasion. It seems to me more important that those marked by even a moment of madness should be driven out of civilization with the physical element of which civilization is built. In Greece, anyway. *Domos*, "house," can also mean a course of stonework in a wall.[8]

It is as if society must wall in or wall out victims of divine hatred marked by an episode of madness.[9] Walling them in was the European decision (see Chapter 6). In myth at least, the Greek way was walling them out, by either exile outside stone walls, or death in the material those walls were made of. "Death from citizens" threatens Orestes.[10] Stone, which separates citizen and stranger, self and other, also separates mad and sane. The sane protect themselves in one of the world's hardest elements, the stuff of which civilization is made. Stone keeps out, kills, controls. Athene stops Heracles' madness by throwing a stone at his chest where Lyssa entered, which "stopped him from mad killing and plunged him into sleep."[11]

Stone is also a material of punishment. Stoning brings out the Greek sense (see Part 4) that madness has something bad in it, which needs punishing. For the victim, it is a sharp, bruising ejection from the safe, normal world. In myth, and in historical times, others as well as the mad were stoned in punishment; mainly they were people who endangered the community. Orestes' pollution endangers Argos. Paris shames Troy if he cannot fight the man whose wife he stole. Hector says the Trojans should have stoned him for endangering Troy. Menelaus sends Helen back to Argos at night, in case parents of men who died at Troy should stone her. You stone someone for a particularly sacrilegious murder. Creusa tried to poison Apollo's temple foundling: the Delphians decide she should die by stoning.[12]

Death by stoning, therefore, suits anyone who endangers the commu-

---

[6] *IT* 310–29; *Aj.* 252; *Or.* 442, 946–49. Death by stoning: Parker 1983:194 (with n. 20), 219.

[7] Simon 1978:152, 306 n. 53.

[8] Hdt. 2.127, 179. Madness as temporary: see Chapter 4.

[9] Madness as sign of divine hatred: see Chapter 14.

[10] *Or.* 442.

[11] *HF* 863, 1004–1006, see above, p. 19.

[12] *Il.* 3.42–52, 56–57; cf. Ar. *Ach.* 282–85, 295, *Or.* 56–59. *Ion* 1112.

nity, anyone polluted by treachery or murder. Historical generals were stoned for failing their troops. This motif of stoning the mad shows how the culture aligned madness with the worst kinds of damage: murder and pollution.[13]

ON THE ALEIAN PLAIN

("The name is Orestes")

> I didn't know where to look. I,
> without a country, toiling here—
> how many laps? I feel my legs give way
> above the axle and wheels, the wild track.
> Knees give way easily when gods want it.
> No one can escape, there's no use being strong. . . .
> —Seferis, *Mythistorema*

The mad side of this distance between mad and sane is expressed through mad wanderings in mountains, forests, deserts. The earliest mad wanderer is Bellerophon, hated by gods, who

> wandered alone over the Aleian plain
> eating his own *thumos*, avoiding the paths of men.

The "Aleian Plain" is literally the "Wandering Plain." This Homeric hero who figures, much later, in *Problem* 30's list of mad heroes, went to the Plain of Wandering, to be alone.[14]

Other mad wanderers include the daughters of Proetus, who wandered through forests and mountains of the Argolid, maddened in punishment by Hera or (in another version) Artemis.[15] Maenads also supposedly wandered wild untamed places. Forests, mountains:[16] places where the wanderer is hard to follow, as mad minds are hard to follow for the sane. Virgil compares maenads and the Proetides to Io, one of the two great tragic exemplars of mad wandering. Like the Proetides, "far-wandering" Io is "driven" from home by angry divinity.[17]

The other mad wanderer in tragedy is Orestes. Like Io, he cannot stay in his right place, is hunted by daemonic anger that is the cause and image of

---

[13] See Parker 1983:194–96 (with n. 20). Damage: see Chapters 16, 17, 20. Pollution: see Chapter 14.

[14] *Il.* 6.201–202. Homer does not say explicitly that Lycurgus and Bellerophon were mad (see Simon 1978:68–70). But both were, in later tradition. *Problem* 30: see Chapter 6.

[15] Hes. fr. 37 (Merkelbach/West), Löffler 1963; Burkert 1983:168–74; Dowden 1989:71–95.

[16] Henrichs 1978:144 (with nn. 72–75).

[17] V. *Ec.* 6.47–52; *PV* 707–35, 790–812, 577, 586 (*tēleplanktoi planai, poluplanoi planai*).

his madness, and of his wandering. He "wanders in madnesses" through Greece (wanderings commemorated at several sites in historical times), and in foreign lands.[18]

Aeschylus presents Io and Orestes in similar terms. Fits of madness accompany their physical wandering and are identified with its cause. Both are "carried off" stage, out of their plays, by a burst of madness which sweeps their minds "off course," their bodies away from society. Io's off-course imagery is stormy waves. Orestes' is a chariot, charging out of control, off the track. For both, the main movement of body and mind is *exō dromou*, "out of the road."[19]

"ALL THROUGH IRELAND"

> Now, when Suibhne heard those great cries . . . in the vault of the firmament, he looked up, whereupon turbulence, and darkness, and fury, and giddiness, and frenzy, and flight, unsteadiness, restlessness, and unquiet filled him, likewise disgust with every place in which he used to be and desire for every place he had not reached. . . .
> —*Buile Suibhne* ("Frenzy of Sweeney")

Mad wandering is not only Greek. In Irish legend the outcast king Sweeney wanders "all through Ireland" and "lives among trees."[20] He fits a common Celtic pattern: the madman who lives wild in the woods, whom we meet in stories of prophets like Lailoken and above all Merlin. Each of these is the antitype of another Celtic figure, the saint who lives wild for love of God. *Wodwose*, "wild man of the woods," comes from *wūdū*, "forest": not from "mad," which is *wod*, related to *woden*, Odin, and *vates*, Latin for "seer." But given the general Celtic connections of madmen with wild woods, the two meanings inevitably tangled in the one word. "'They call me the Man of the Wood', said the madman."[21] Wild man. Madman. Forests.

Celtic heroes go mad in battle, too. Especially when they "look upwards," an Irish motif borrowed into early Norse literature: "I advise you

---

[18] *Or.* 532; Paus. 8.34.2; Strabo 12.2.3; *IT* 84. Cf. Chapter 2, n. 26.

[19] *PV* 882–84; *Cho.* 1062, 1022–24. Mad inner movement: see Chapter 12.

[20] O'Keefe 1952; Heaney 1984:5, 9, 12, 14.

[21] Heaney 1984:56. See Jarman 1960:13, who cites Geoffrey of Monmouth's *Vita Merlini* chapters 72–73. Tolstoy 1985:26–29 thinks them all "originally" "the same figure." (Pitfalls in the "originally" approach: see, e.g., Padel 1992:37–38, 161, 169; above, p. 20, below, p. 168.) Most Celticists, I'm told, would agree there was some exchange between these stories, but would see here a pervasive *topos*, not evidence of a single original.

Loddfáfnir . . . look not up in battle—for the sons of men become mad with terror—lest spells be cast upon you."[22]

These Celtic and Norse images underlie even the mad scenes of *Lear*. Madness begins when Lear enters the wild, the "heath." It reaches a climax in "the country," near Dover.[23] In the much later society of eighteenth-century Europe, we find melancholics who are seen to "wander without knowing where they are going."[24]

There is an erotic angle too. In Celtic contexts the hero sent mad in battle, the outcast king, and the wild mad prophet parallel the hero who runs mad for love. Lancelot takes to the woods when he goes mad.[25] From another culture, compare the Persian story of Majnun, in the twelfth-century poem-cycle *Khamsa*, by Nizami. Separated from his beloved, Layla, Majnun too went mad and fled into the wilderness. In whatever culture they met it—Celtic, Norse, Eastern, European—this motif of a madness (military, erotic, royal, vatic), which causes and is expressed by isolation in the wild, appealed to the Romantics. They had a Greek and a Northern heritage of wandering and madness, geographic and mental, to think with. Hölderlin held that madness was the only logical end for the poet.[26] It was the Romantics who put the topspin on twentieth-century evaluation of mad wandering. Anachronistically, we bring all this to our reading of mad wildness and wandering in Greek tragedy.

MADNESS AS "WANDERING"

> But what are our souls searching for,
> travelling from harbor to harbor
> on rotten, sea-soaked planks?
> —Seferis, *Mythistorema*

In many cultures and languages, madness is called "wandering" and "wandering" means "mad." In Greek, this identification is very deep and very strong. Oedipus, when he hears where Laius was murdered, and begins to realize he may be the murderer, is overcome by sudden "wandering of soul and agitation of *phrenes*." Phaedra's sick delirium is "wandering of *phrenes*." In Greek (says a great commentator on *Hippolytus*), "to be mad is to stray from the path of right reason."[27] You "wander in your soul," "wander

---

[22] *The Hávamál* stanza 129: Martin Clarke 1923:77, 114. The Norse uses *gjalti*, borrowed from Irish *geilt*, "mad." Once, in early Irish literature, this is glossed by Latin *volatilis*, "able to levitate," a feature important in the Irish story.

[23] *King Lear* 3.4, 4.6.

[24] Foucault 1971:125.

[25] Malory, *Morte d'Arthur* 11.8.

[26] Gascoyne 1938:3.

[27] Barrett *ad Hipp.* 141–44; *OT* 727; *Hipp.* 283; cf. *paraplanaomai*, Schol. *ad Eum.* 104.

away," as Phaedra does, from sanity.[28] You are not responsible for what you say when "wandering":

> you should not blame someone wandering
> in stormy grief, who talks against his *nous*.[29]

As we have seen, participles for "mad" are mostly passive. Tragic grammar plays between two suggestions: that madness is due to the self, or is caused by an outside force. But the grammar comes down more heavily in favor of madness caused from outside.[30] The violence of the images reflects this. You are hit and "struck" *by* madness.[31] The violence-from-outside often skews *you* "aside"; it makes you "wander."[32]

"Wandering" images of madness, therefore, often mention daemonic weaponry: whips, goads, and daemonic pursuit emphasize an outside source. Madness is daemonic persecution. Erinyes use goads on Orestes. "A maddened understanding" is "an inescapable goad." Io is "maddened with goad-torturing pains." Lyssa will "drive and goad" Heracles to madden him.[33] Madness is something done to you, painfully, by outside forces, not something you do to yourself.[34] Wandering turns you aside, as when *daimōn* "makes" Odysseus "wander," "turning" him from his goal.[35] Or a spear, thought, or purpose is "turned aside."[36]

Inner and outer, mental and physical belong together. The body's external wanderings, large scale and geographic, like Io's, or smaller-scale rolling eyes and restlessness, are mirrored in the mad mind.[37] It twists aside like the body and eyes. Io's *phrenes* and eyes are *diastrophoi*. Inner movement too is "out of," "aside."[38]

---

[28] *Poi pareplanchthēn gnōmas agathas? Hipp.* 240. *Paraplazō* is common in these contexts, in active (*noēma* as object, *Od.* 20.346; *phrenōn tarachai* as subject, Pi. *O.* 7.31) and passive. You "wander in soul" from lost prosperity, *Tro.* 640. *Planē* is often coupled with *anoia*: e.g., Pl. *Phd.* 81A (cf. *Rep.* 505C).

[29] *Phil.* 1193–95.

[30] See *mainomai*, Chapter 3, nn. 1–6. Fifth-century stress on outside source: Padel 1992:117–31, 157–61.

[31] Padel 1992:117–19; above, Chapter 3, n. 30.

[32] See Dodds 1951:67; Padel 1992:30, 43, 121, 176; above, Chapter 2, n. 34, and Chapter 3, n. 30.

[33] A. *Supp.* 109, 563; cf. *PV* 597, 692; *HF* 837; Padel 1992:118, 163, 177.

[34] See above, n. 30; Padel 1981:110–14; Padel 1992:125–26, 129–32, 158–61.

[35] *Plazō*, "I turn" (transitive), *paraplazō*, "I turn aside": *Od.* 24.307; cf. Chapter 12, nn. 9, 12.

[36] *Il.* 11.351 (a spear turned by armor). *Plazō* or *paraplazō* of thought: *Od.* 20.346; cf. *Hipp.* 240, Pi. *O.* 7.32 (and, absolutely, Pi. *N.* 10.7). Cf. *paragō, paraspaō*: *OC* 1185; Arist. *EE* 1227A21; see Chapter 12, nn. 6–19.

[37] See, e.g., *phoitaō, phoituleō*, often used of a mad body, *and* of daemonic goad into wandering: *Aj.* 59; *Trach.* 980; *PV* 597; *Or.* 327. See Chapter 13; Foucault 1971:65.

[38] *Diastrophē, diastrophos* for mad eyes and *phrenes*: *PV* 673; *Aj.* 447; *Trach.* 794; *Ba.* 1122, 1166; see Chapter 7, nn. 37–38. Mind "twisted," moral *diastrophē*: D.L. 2.87; see Chapter 12.

Sometimes a poet uses "wandering" of intellectual perplexity rather than madness. Oedipus, pondering the plague, has "come many roads in wanderings of thought." Odysseus, looking for the criminal, suspects Ajax but without proof: "We know nothing clear: we're wandering." He means, "We're uncertain."[39] Dreams are also supposed to "wander." So does the soul, in sleep.[40]

But usually in Greece "wandering" means something far more violent, with shaming, negative overtones: chaotic dis-placement.

[39] *OT* 67, cf. 727; *Aj.* 23, see Jebb, Stanford *ad loc.*
[40] Bremmer 1983:132–33; Padel 1992:80.

Chapter 11

"ALIENUS": RESONANCES OF MAD WANDERING

RESONANCES OF WANDERING

Since the soul has come here from elsewhere, [Empedo-
cles] calls birth "a tour abroad." This is euphemism, a
comforting name. In fact, the soul is always a fugitive and
wanderer, driven by decrees and laws of gods.

—Plutarch, *De exilio*

IN ANY CULTURE, to call madness "wandering" gives it specific resonances
tied to local imagination. What wandering says about madness as an image
depends on how you think of wandering itself. The image's value, like the
meaning of a word, depends "on the place it occupies, at the period in
question, in relation to the general system":[1] of the language, commerce,
diplomacy, travel, and a whole pack of cultural associations. Wandering,
like madness, carries specific religious, ethical, and even medical weight in
different cultural contexts.

In mediaeval theology, for example, every human being is a wanderer
between two worlds. *Peregrinus*, a "traveller," "stranger": *viator*, a "traveller" through life. The image held resonances of earthly pilgrimage plus
inner spiritual journeying. From the first or second century A.D. at least,
Odysseus the wanderer was a familiar emblem of spiritual struggle, embodying life as wandering exile, or a permanent spiritual yearning and
aspiration, surviving dangers and desolation.[2] In the early Church Fathers,
Odysseus tied to the mast, the Cross, becomes the prototype of the traveller withstanding this-worldly temptation on his voyage through life.[3]

But even in mediaeval theology, wandering also had a negative charge of
alienation from God. Failing to love Him in the way He ordained, you
"fall" from, are estranged from, His *ordo*, like the fallen angels. Satan is
allotrios, *alienus*, the "other." (A "mad" as well as bad angel.) "Wandering"
resonated with spiritual and moral, as well as geographical, displacement.

[1] Vernant 1980:92.

[2] Stanford 1954:121 thinks later Stoic admiration of Odysseus as ideal *homo viator* came
from Zeno, filtered through Epictetus (a Stoic philosopher of Rome's imperial period). See
Epictetus *Discourses* 1.12.3, 3.24.13; Stanford 1954:175–77; Becker 1937:77–85.

[3] Klauser 1963; Ladner 1967:235–40. The *Odyssey* as spiritual journey: Buffière
1973:413–18.

Hamartia ("sin") is *allotriōsis* from God. *Allotriōsis* means "making other." In pagan Hellenistic writers, it is used of "aversion" (to things you do not like). But in Christian Greek, it means spiritual "alienation."[4]

What about wandering for early Greeks themselves?

In Homer, wandering is disgrace. A shameful, misery-dark state. Achilles' degrading treatment by Agamemnon makes him feel "like a wanderer without honor." Odysseus's disguise as a beggar in his own home expresses the shameful wandering he has endured so far. The disguise quite precisely "brings home" the shame of his wandering. "Nothing is worse than wandering," says Odysseus. A wanderer is "ill-starred, unfortunate."[5] You cannot have honor, which sustains the identity of Homeric heroes, unless you are in place, and are seen to be in place. Odysseus's different false identities express the atopic pain of his untethered wandering.

Homeric beggars are shameful, but may have sunk past feeling their shame. Other people's attitude to wanderers, strangers, or beggars swing between disgust, contempt, suspicion, and fear. Pirates are wanderers: they "bring evil to men of other lands."[6] The suitors at Ithaca and their hangers-on despise wanderers,[7] an attitude condemned by decent folk on grounds of compassion. And of fear, "for all strangers and beggars are from Zeus": "Gods visit cities, looking like strangers from other places."[8]

Homelessness and wandering hint at uncomfortable relations with divinity. A wanderer may be god in human guise, or may carry in his body and story a contagious divine hatred. Aeolus gave Odysseus the closed bag of winds. He refuses to help when those winds escape and blow Odysseus back again. He sent them to Odysseus to "reach his home." If Odysseus failed to get there, that shows he is "vilest of living creatures." It is not "right" to help someone gods hate so much[9] (in spite, apparently, of the feeling that "strangers are from Zeus"). He turns Odysseus away.

The other—foreigner, beggar, refugee—is dangerous at many levels, economic as well as religious:

> Who'd summon a stranger from abroad
> except for public workers: a prophet,
> healer, builder, minstrel? These are invited

[4] Gregory of Nyssa *Contra eunomium* 2.366.8 (Jaeger); see Gokey 1961:171 (with n. 97), Ladner 1967:233–35, 247–48 (with nn. 72, 76); cf. below, Chapter 19, n. 15. Alienation: below, n. 32.

[5] *Il.* 9.648; *Od.* 17.337, 15.343–45, 6.206, 17.483.

[6] *Od.* 3.73, 9.255.

[7] *Od.* 17.217–20, 376–79.

[8] *Od.* 6.208, 17.483–86, 501–504.

[9] *Od.* 10.66, 72–75; see Chapter 14, n. 32.

all over the earth. No one would invite a beggar,
who'd wear his resources out.[10]

It seems uncertain, in this Homeric world, how much divine protection,
and what rights, a displaced person has: but surely not the normal ones.
Odysseus prays for revenge on the suitor who insulted him, "*if* there are
gods and Erinyes for beggars."[11]

Homeric responses to homelessness express fears of contact with moral
disgrace, ill-luck, divine hatred. Something might rub off on you. What
lies behind the stranger's lack of place? Zeus's anger? If Zeus gives someone
only evil fate,

> he makes him reviled. Terrible famine
> drives him over the holy earth. He wanders,
> honored by neither gods nor mortals.

Some ancient commentators, familiar with connections between wandering, dishonor, and madness, interpreted the word "famine" here
(*boubrōstis*) as "madness": a wanderer "driven" by emotional rather than
physical pain.[12] In the Homeric world and for those influenced by it afterwards, madness, wandering, foulness, and mental and physical pain are
very close.

In the archaic world, if you undertake wandering deliberately you do it
for profit. Like Hesiod's father. Hesiod tells his brother to take ship and
build up cargo, "to bring profit homewards, like your and my dad." The
Argonauts went east for the Golden Fleece: myth interacted with history,
with the trade and colonization of the seventh and sixth centuries B.C.
Greek imagination expected the right sort of wandering, a temporary, purposeful displacement, to enrich you.[13]

The story of your wandering might do this for you. In mediaeval times,
travel is "the mother of tidings."[14] In the *Odyssey*, Odysseus makes literal
capital out of his wanderings. In gifts that function almost as payment for
his long, wonderful tale of wandering, he recoups the plunder he earlier
stole from other worlds by force, and lost.[15] As a story, his wanderings
"bring gain homewards," bitter as they were at the time.

It is the same in the fifth century. You did not travel for pleasure but for
profit, war, to consult oracles; or unwillingly, in exile. The *Odyssey* uses
alētēs, "wanderer," of beggars. Tragedy uses it of exiles too. Beggars and

[10] *Od.* 17.382–87.
[11] *Od.* 17.475.
[12] *Il.* 24.531–33; see scholiasts cited by Leaf and Bayfield *ad loc.*
[13] *Erg.* 631–38; Hawkes 1977:1–17.
[14] Tuchman 1978:55.
[15] *Od.* 9.41, 225, 465; 13.10 (the first thing he does in Ithaca is check that all his gifts are
there).

exiles are shameful. Wandering is aligned with all this. It is the worst Greek nightmare: houselessness.[16] When you "wander from" something ("from" happiness or prosperity, for instance), that means you miss it, "lack" it. Wandering is a shaming lack: of position, possessions. Even Clytemnestra's ghost complains, "I wander shamefully." Like outcast Oedipus.[17]

The two poles, therefore, to classical Greek resonances of wandering in ordinary life were shameful loss of place versus profit. But the "god in the stranger" idea continued. In Plato's *Sophist* a "Stranger from Elea" takes over Socrates' usual role in leading the discussion. Theodorus introduces this Stranger, saying he is devoted to philosophy. "Perhaps," says Socrates, "it is no ordinary guest but some god you have brought us unawares. Homer tells us gods attend on the goings of men of mercy and justice. Not least among them, the God of Strangers comes, to mark orderly or lawless human doings. Your companion may be one of those higher powers, who means to observe and expose our weakness in philosophic discourse." Philosophers are heirs to Homeric bards. They "go from city to city surveying from a height the life beneath them. They appear, to the world's blindness, to wear all sorts of shapes. To some they seem useless; to others, above all worth. Now they appear statesmen, now sophists. Sometimes they give the impression of simply being mad."[18] Plato's romanticizing of the wandering philosopher may be the beginnings of Western romanticization also of wandering.

These resonances rang differently in, and were added to by, various subsequent Western cultures. Mediaeval theology, for instance, affected them, and European empire building; so did the nineteenth-century Western appetite for imperially confident travel. So, above all, did the Romantics. Post-Renaissance, post-Romantic readers as we are, we read with these newer resonances in our minds:

> I went hunting wild
> After the wildest beauty in the world.

The Romantics glamorized mad seeing. They also glamorized wandering. Bored with Ithaca's "still hearth," the late-nineteenth-century Ulysses "cannot rest from travel." He burned his restlessness into our imagination, as the pattern of our own:

> Yet all experience is an arch wherethro'
> Gleams that untravell'd world, whose margin fades
> For ever and for ever when I move.[19]

---

[16] *Od.* 17.578; *Ag.* 1282; *Cho.* 1042; *OC* 50, 746; *Heraclid.* 224; E. *Supp.* 280.

[17] Pi. *O.* 1.58; *Eum.* 98; *OC* 444.

[18] Pl. *Sophist* 216A–D; cf. *Od.* 9.270, 17.483.

[19] Wilfred Owen, "Strange Meeting"; Tennyson, "Ulysses." Glamorizing mad seeing: see Chapter 9.

For us, wandering has a depth charge of glamor that goes hand in hand with contemporary glamorizing of madness. Benjamin Britten's *Curlew River* (1964) came out of an encounter with a mediaeval Noh play, cross-fertilized by English religious drama. But the madwoman in it, wandering, looking for her child, however much she owes to the Japanese stage or recalls Celtic and other mediaeval figures who went mad, wandered, and took to the wild, also speaks to twentieth-century audiences through an English Romantic filter. The Madwoman is seeking her child. "She wanders raving, raving and all alone." "How very far," sing the Pilgrims, "comes this wandering soul." But the Ferryman is not touched:

> Any fool can see
> your feet are wa-a-ndering,
> your thoughts are wa-a-a-a-a-ndering,
> wa-a-a-a-a-a-a-ndering too.[20]

The passage echoes Romantic elision of madness and wandering embedded in so much formative English poetry, from Byron and Shelley to Tennyson. Ernest Dowson's famous appalling poem, "To One in Bedlam," values a caged madman's dreams above those of the sane world. The language may strike us irritatingly now, but it expresses an important pulse in late Romantic imagination:

> With delicate, mad hands, behind his sordid bars,
> Surely he hath his posies, which they tear and twine;
> Those scentless wisps of straw, that miserably line
> His strait, caged universe, whereat the dull world stares,
>
> Pedant and pitiful. O, how his rapt gaze wars
> With their stupidity!

The comfortably restless "decadent," roaming his free life in the cafés and drawing rooms of London, France, and Ireland, throws facile glamor over the loneliness of his imaginary caged lunatic:

> Better than mortal flowers
> Thy moon-kissed roses seem: better than love or sleep,
> The star-crowned solitude of thine oblivious hours!

Wandering, solitude, and madness did *not* appeal like this to ancient Greece. We cannot read this indulgence back. Fifth-century Greeks hated travel, even for specific purposes. Except for some philosophers, they hated solitude too. Wandering, in itself and as an image, has no creative overtones in the fifth century, but rather a firm negative charge. In the *Timaeus*, Plato's anatomy of the human interior and the cosmos (until the nineteenth century, the most esteemed and studied of his works), wander-

---

[20] Cf. Chapter 9, n. 22.

ing in the body is the cause of bad. It causes emotional and intellectual "disease": "All humors that are bitter and bilious wander through the body . . . mingle with the movement of the soul, and implant all sorts of diseases of the soul."[21]

CENTRIFUGAL, CENTRIPETAL: TWO PATTERNS OF PUNISHMENT

> I am one too, now. A fugitive from god.
> A wanderer, who trusted in mad strife.
> —Empedocles, fr. 115DK

The gods make Bellerophon wander because they are punishing him. Wandering, like madness of which it is the deepest image, is one of their cruellest punishments.

This punishment can take two forms. Gods inflict a centrifugal wandering, away from home, as on Io, Bellerophon, and Orestes. Or they frustrate and prolong centripetal wanderings, hindering someone trying desperately to get back home—supremely, Odysseus.

The centrifugal punishment is the one often accompanied (Bellerophon, Orestes, Io) by madness itself. Gods drive Tydeus from his father's home; Io is driven from her father's home; daemons drive Orestes over the earth.[22] (By contrast, geographical doubts and disorientation threaten, but never overwhelm, Odysseus.) The wandering may be the image of the madness, but the madness also shows the pain of the wandering. The two belong with each other, illumine each other as two sides of the same torture.

In later Western literature, connections between "driven from home" and "driven mad" resurface in figures like lover, warrior, mad poet: "driven" from society, wandering in the wild. But in Greek tragedy, in the figures of Io and Orestes, it is a product of a particular, punitive, relationship with a god.[23] In centrifugal wandering, the madness is part of the wandering: each is an image of the other. The mad mind is "turned aside," as wanderers (and the mad) are alienated from their society. In centripetal wandering, there is disorientation, but not madness. The man is trying to get back to his home.

This *can* be read as an image of mental activity: someone trying, for example, to get back to his right mind. Or, in the later Stoics, as a spiritual

---

[21] Pl. *Ti.* 86E, cf. "the wandering cause," 48A. This is the context in which the wandering womb, which causes diseases in women (see Chapter 12), is introduced: 91C. Wandering is the cause of bad throughout *Ti.*

[22] *Il.* 14.120 (a guess, by his son); *PV* 665; *Eum.* 76.

[23] See Chapter 10, nn. 17–19. Madness as punishment: see Chapter 18, nn. 30–35, and Chapter 20, nn. 29–38. Cf. stoning as punishment: see Chapter 10, nn. 12–13.

journey and aspiration. Readers of the *Odyssey* have used it all ways, and will again. You can read Odysseus's wanderings as mental disorientation, if you want. But in the poem's own terms, Poseidon's persecution is designed to stop Odysseus getting back to a specific physical island. Poseidon does not inflict madness on him (though the companions, through some unstated daemonic agency, have destructive mad recklessness thrust upon them). Odysseus's wanderings are a frustrated *nostos*, "return."

All the Greek veterans have difficulty getting home from Troy. Some never make it. The lost epic *Nostoi*, "Returns," contained their stories. Gods prevent them, storms blow them off course, daemons turn them aside. Waves, currents, the North Wind, stormwinds; Poseidon, storm and lightning from Zeus, Athene: all these attack the Greek ships going home. These wounded *nostoi*, after so long away, are a magnetic theme in epic and tragedy.[24]

In the *Odyssey*, Odysseus and his companions meet dangers that threaten to "lose" them their *nostos*, even make them forget entirely the home they want a *nostos* to. Threaten even their memory of their right place. Helios "took away their *nostimon ēmar*," "day of return." The lotus, Circe's drugs, and the Sirens take away thought of, desire for, home. The companions are geographically disoriented. This is also an image of the threat wandering poses to their sense of self:

> Friends, we do not know
> where darkness is. Or dawn.
> Where sun, who brings light
> to mortals, goes under earth.
> Nor where he rises.[25]

Divine persecution is expressed in making them forget themselves and their place, in stopping them getting back to their lives, to their proper minds of which "home" is also (but not only) an image. Odysseus, unlike his fatally appetitive companions, never forgets. Self-controlled survivor, he keeps his right mind and identity throughout, and gets his *nostos* in the end.[26]

To later centuries, the *Odyssey* of course suggested all kinds of relationships between emotional and geographical wandering, displacement, loss of identity, and the continuance or development of identity through the experience of a journey-in-the-wild. The *Odyssey* offers the revelation of a directed achieved journey, in and through its opposite: an apparently unpatterned, displacing wandering. The two are often contrasted. When the

---

[24] *Od.* 9.80, 10.48, 54, 1.75; *Tro.* 78–83; *Ag.* 627, 635, 650–57; *Hel.* 407–10.
[25] *Od.* 10.190–92; cf. 1.9, 9.94–97, 20.236, 12.41–43.
[26] See Padel 1985:90–93.

journey became a pre-Socratic image for the process of knowledge (of the world, of truth), Parmenides journeys toward knowledge, while other mortals wander, in ignorance.[27] Odysseus's journey is used as prototype of the life spent in spiritual yearning. His return is image of the soul's return "to its own country." Plotinus links a phrase in the *Iliad*, "let us flee to our own country," to Odysseus leaving Circe and Calypso. He found in that Homeric phrase, "own country," a hidden religious meaning: return to a proper, home relationship with God.[28]

With creative reinterpreters like these at work, who needs enemies? The later Greek tradition expressed the *Odyssey*'s emblematic possibilities through a fantasy etymology, relating *nostos*, "return," to *nous*, "mind."[29] Returning home is returning to your right mind. Or it is arriving there for the first time in this life, which is also arriving at your original home, the being-with-God you enjoyed before your sojourn on this earth. With the right religious topspin, *nostos* becomes arrival at the rightness, the sanity, of the universal *nous*: the city of God.

Specifically fifth-century associations with the *Odyssey* are hard to prise out of its reception, the over-loam of later centuries. Underneath is basic Greek centripetal wandering: a person, a mind, trying to get back to a lost right place. Some gods help, others frustrate and undermine the journey, in anger.

There are two kinds of punitive wandering. We shall see there are also two basic roles of madness in tragedy (see Chapter 18). Madness makes you "err" ("error" is Latin for "wandering"). And madness punishes "error."

In all this wandering and madness, gods are generally seen as the authors of human movement. Angry divine attention is in itself, like madness, something to be ashamed of. Shame touches the outcast wanderer, and the maddened mind. Ajax is ashamed at his mad acts. The Proetides are maddened *and* made physically repellent. Orestes is physically repulsive. One should not play down the physical reality. Beggars, wanderers, those who had been mad, were probably deeply foul in fifth-century Greece. But Orestes' physical condition also expresses the repulsiveness and frighteningness of his madness in itself. Madness is repellent to normal society. One who has suffered it is expected (to a fluctuating degree, no doubt, in different Greek societies) to feel shamed.[30]

[27] Parmenides fr. 6. See Padel 1992:112; KRS 288, p. 242; Becker 1937; Mourelatos 1970:16–17, 21–25.

[28] Plot. 1.6, 8, 16; *Il.* 2.140. This meaning seems self-evident to Augustine (*Civitas Dei* 9.17), who treats the phrase as if Plot. wrote it.

[29] See Carcopino 1956:175–211; Dodds 1965:100–101; Frame 1978:28 and passim (a potent modern exploration of this etymology); above, n. 3.

[30] *Aj.* 367, 426 (*atimos*); cf. *Hipp.* 246. Proetides: see Chapter 3, nn. 4, 10; *Or.* 220–23. Dodds 1951:82 n. 2 suggests *oneidos* attaching to madness had changed by Plato's day. Cf. Dover 1974:127–29, 148–50; see below, Chapter 14.

ALIENATION

> To be human means to live in a world—that is, to live in a
> reality that is ordered and that gives sense to the business
> of living. This "life-world" is social in its origins and in its
> ongoing maintenance: the meaningful order it provides
> for human lives has been established collectively and is
> kept going by collective consent.
> —P. Berger, B. Berger, and H. Kellner, *The Homeless
>   Mind*

The word that comes to a modern mind, in all this, is "alienation," a complex, problematic word with strong psychological and sociological associations. Since Marx, alienation has been seen as an evil inevitable in our own material and political condition. We are alienated from our labor and its product. Capitalism causes an economic and sociological alienation, which affects certain sets of people in society particularly,[31] and which has a vital spiritual dimension.

The term "world-alienation" was first used and described, as far as I am aware, by Hannah Arendt. It refers to estrangement from the human world: a sense of its meaninglessness, and of personal noncommunion with it.[32] Once identified, this could be read back into other societies, where alienation had theological as well as social resonances. The persecutions of the late fourteenth and early fifteenth centuries may have been the first awful flowering, in Europe, of alienation between groups of people: a social alienation continuous with the early mediaeval sense of estrangement from God. It is expressed, for instance, by the fourteenth-century author of *Sir Gawain and the Green Knight*, and also by his hero.[33]

"Alienation" also holds psychological resonances, for us. In the early twentieth century, about the time that Marx's concept of alienation was catching on, and before "world-alienation" was coined, a psychiatrist was an alienist: one who studies conditions and people alien to normality.

Alienation carries, therefore, complex loads of discomfort. But another side to it is desirable, purposeful alienation from the world. This has some roots in the self-images promoted by Greek and Roman philosophical ideals. The philosopher removes himself from the world, like Democritus at Abdera. This self-removal became a coherent Christian ideology in the early Middle Ages, and received a new energy, though also a new set of rules and qualifications, in the twelfth century. It contributed to the *contemptus mundi*: a spiritual attitude that had continuous appeal well into the

---

[31] Sociological alienation: e.g., Nisbet 1966: ch. 7.

[32] Arendt 1958:248–57.

[33] Ladner 1967:255–56; Howard 1974:49–63. In the Church Fathers, *allotriōsis* is alienation from God, not from human community: above, n. 4.

seventeenth century. There are spiritual benefits in estrangement from the world and its worldliness.[34]

When we relate alienation to madness, both in our own and previous ages, this second strand (philosophical self-removal) interacts with other positive evaluations of madness. Alienation from the conventional world suits the romanticizing (as in Ernest Dowson) of mad lonely insight. "I am aware," wrote Laing, "that the man who is said to be deluded may be in his delusion telling me the truth, and this in no equivocal or metaphorical sense but quite literally, and that the cracked mind of the schizophrenic may let in light which does not enter the intact minds of many sane people whose minds are closed. Ezekiel, in Jaspers' opinion, was a schizophrenic." The romanticizing of madness goes hand in hand with the romanticizing of wandering: of alienation in the round. We are also predisposed to it by the pluralization of the mainly Western societies we live in and read from. We value the plural, the multiple possibilities of other worlds. That valuing belongs also with popular valuing of mad seeing.[35]

Greek tragedy offers us ambiguous images of bacchic celebration: source of violence and danger as well as pleasure. The only positive value in madness otherwise is a doubtful one: it stops you realizing how terribly you are destroying yourself, how badly off you are.[36] There is no value in seeing Erinyes, however real. Menelaus asks Orestes about seeing them:

MENELAUS: What *phantasmata* [appearances] make you ill?
ORESTES: I seemed to see three women like night.
MENELAUS: I know the ones you speak of.
                       I don't want to name them.[37]

Menelaus knows them, knows they exist and have a name, but will not involve himself by naming them. He avoids even verbal contact with the source of Orestes' madness.

In popular thought throughout the seventeenth century, deviation from norms of social and family life signified alienation from fundamental religious values. The drama of the inner life was a moral allegory: madness is sin, despair is apostasy, sanity is spiritual grace.[38] Social, spiritual, and psychological alienation were part of each other. What was mentally com-

---

[34] Ladner 1967.

[35] Berger, Berger, and Kellner 1974:65–66; Laing 1965:27 (one side effect of his study was to glamorize schizophrenia: see above, Chapter 9). Romantic madness, wandering, romantic need for madness: Gascoyne 1938.

[36] See Chapter 7, nn. 44, 50. Bacchic seeing: Chapter 7, nn. 47–48. Images of Dionysus: see Chapter 3, n. 14.

[37] *Or*. 407–409.

[38] MacDonald 1981:165–67.

fortable, and right, was to be in a state of normal relations with other people.

Something like this was the essence also of tragic Greek attitudes. Madness was not glad or valuable, but was hung round with shame. Isolation was homelessness not just of the body but the psyche, taking away everything that made you human. Madness displaces: socially, geographically, internally. Self-isolation is a sign of madness. In a fourth-century comedy, a girl seen wandering outside the city must be possessed.[39]

IDIOS: "THE BLACK BIRD GOES ALONE"

If I wanted to remain alone, I longed
for solitude, not for this sort of waiting,
the fragmenting of my soul on the horizon. . . .
—Seferis, *Mythistorema*

Our own associations with alienation, therefore, are mostly foreign to tragic thought, even though many have Greek roots. Working in us, now, they are later and often literary admixtures—from cultures (and segments of society) that can afford to value isolation—onto an earlier thought core. In that earlier thought, and for most people actually suffering it in all eras (in Western history, at least), madness is hurtfully, often angrily, alone. In Cormac's tenth-century *Glossary*, the word *mer*, an early Irish word for "deranged," is associated with the blackbird, Latin *merulus*, because "the blackbird goes alone."[40] Madness's aloneness, before the Romantics glamorized it, was not a welcomed solitude, but painful, shameful, deviant.

Yet, by an accident of linguistic history, it was the Greek for "belonging to oneself, personal," *idios* or *idiōtēs*, that gave English its hardest, most excluding word for "mad": "idiot."

Idiōtēs meant a person in a private capacity, as opposed to public office; then a layman, one not professionally learned; then someone "unskilled" in something. By the fourth century it can mean someone unlearned, an ignoramus; often it is a term of abuse.[41] By the Roman era, related Greek words acquire social coloring. *Idiōtismos* is "vulgar fashion," "vulgar speech."[42]

Idios is "personal to, peculiar to." Also "separate, distinct." And "private." You do something in a *private*, as opposed to public, capacity, for your *private* interest.[43] Plato coined a word *idiōsis*, "privatization," "mak-

---

[39] See Handley 1969.
[40] See Clarke 1975:32.
[41] E.g., Dem. 4.35 ("ignoramus"); Men. *Samia* 71 ("idiot!").
[42] Epictetus *Enchiridion* 33.6; Longinus 31.1; D.L. 7.50.
[43] *Od.* 3.82, 4.314; Hdt. 6.100; *PV* 404, 543; Th. 1.82, 2.61.

ing private." It is a bad thing in his book. The "community of pleasure and pain" binds citizens together; the *idiōsis* of these feelings breaks down community bonds.[44] In later Greek, "to do one's *idia*" is to "mind *one's own* business." *Idios* also means "strange, unusual, surprising," and thus gradually—in Plutarch, for instance—"eccentric."[45] In tragedy, it is sometimes hard to evaluate its force. Euripides' Orestes tells Clytemnestra's father that his daughter, Orestes' mother, sought out "*private* marriage-beds, not prudent ones." She slept with Aegisthus. Does the word here mean "unwisely?" "Secretly?" Or "on her own?" In this context we really cannot tell.[46] But there is none of our inwardness in it. Like *idiōtēs*, *idios* is "private" as contrasted with public.

There is a twist of attitudes in the word's history in English. In the fourteenth and fifteenth centuries, "idiot" means an "uneducated person," or a "layman." But at the same time the word begins its long habit of referring to someone deemed legally to be deficient in reasoning. A "fool."

So, from a society that found personal solitude dangerous, uncomfortable, shameful, and connected it with madness, comes a word that later societies will translate by "private," but that carries in Greek none of the connotations of personal inwardness (a notion for which the fifth century generally had no need or word). Ultimately, this word gave some European languages a word for "mad." Where in tragedy (we might say) private is mad, English abstracts from *idiōtēs* the notion "personal, peculiar to" and derives from it a word for that mental abnormality which fifth-century society associated with isolation.

Is this really accident? Or does the shift in meaning from "personal" to "mad" say something about the journey that elements in Greek ideas of madness have travelled to reach us, and the company they got into on the way? Perhaps this odd linguistic relationship reflects the shifting values and images of madness, some of which I have sketched, in trying to weigh the input of our own response when we look at tragic madness.

As with true mad seeing (see Chapter 9), and mad blackness (see Chapter 6), we inherit Greek images, words, and links between wandering, isolation, and madness: but it is a heritage transformed by the societies that handed it on. Their own transforming values deposited strata in our own attitudes to madness, which color our approach to Greek madness. We interpret in accordance with ideas at work in our own culture: especially modern assumptions about, and fascination with, personal inwardness.

A study of madness in our century belongs with the study of character

[44] Pl. *Rep.* 462C1; see Vlastos 1973:17 n. 48.
[45] Plu. *Moralia* 1068B (*De communibus notitiis*) and 57E (*De adulatore et amico*); *Themistocles* 18.
[46] *Or.* 558.

and personality. But fifth-century madness belongs mainly with ideas about divinity (see Chapter 20), and divinity's hand in shameful (but fascinating) human violence. Not with the intricacies of wandering, so much as with what makes one wander. With what alienates, not alienation in and for itself.

Chapter 12

INNER WANDERING

INNER AND OUTER

MADNESS illustrates a basic principle in Greek thought about mind and body: what is seen happening outside must be going on at the same time inside, unseen.[1] This principle directs many fifth-century and fourth-century comments on human behavior. The medical diagnosis of dreams and diet, for instance. If you dream at night about "struggles" that did not happen in the day, says one doctor, change your diet at once. Your soul is disturbed by secretions caused by surfeit in your body. The same principle drives ideas about what causes madness. It would not be surprising, says Herodotus, if Cambyses' mind was unhealthy, when his body was sick.[2] You expect the inside to be wrong if the outside is; and vice versa.

This principle dominates sane fantasies about what the mad interior is doing, when the mad outer body can be seen wandering. If, externally perceived, the mad go physically away, if their bodies wander, there must be corresponding inner wandering. And so Greek images of madness as displacement and wandering get applied to the internal as well as the external. What the sane imagine happening to the maddened mind is the inner image of what they see (or say they see) happening outside, to the mad body.

PARA AND *EK*: THE MIND ASIDE, OUT OF PLACE

> No one will ever read the wild, sprawling, scrawling
> mad woman's signature. . . .
> —Patrick Kavanagh, "The Great Hunger"

Even in life, one person's inwardness is unseen by other people. You cannot see inside another person's mind: though fifth-century songs and stage figures sometimes wish you could. On stage, such inwardness is not just unseen, it does not exist. A stage character's inwardness is fictional. It builds in the audience's imagination according to local ways of inferring

---

[1] Padel 1992:67.
[2] Hp. *De victu* 4 88.10 (Loeb 4:424). Hdt. 3.33; cf. Dodds 1951:65. Causes of madness: see Chapters 18, 19, 20.

character from words and behavior. The audience project these inferences into the actor's body, which on the Greek stage was likewise unseen, hidden in its showy masked costume.[3] No inner "wandering" can be seen. It happens only in language.

Tragic language presents all emotion as inner movement. Greek thought and myth see madness, the extreme of emotion, as outwardly violent.[4] The mobile violence is inner too. When it has a direction, this is always "out of," "away," expressed through a dense range of further madness-words: images compounded with two prepositions, *para*, "aside," "beside," and *ek*, "out of."[5]

Para combines with striking and hitting verbs to produce an extraordinary number of intricate nouns, participles, and verbs for "madness," "mad," "be maddened." Delirious, impassioned, or mad, you are "hit aside," *parakopos*, in your *phrenas* or *nous*.[6] *Parakoptō*, "I hit aside," with a god as its subject and human *phrenas* as its object, is "I madden."[7] *Parapaiō*[8] and *paraplēssō* both mean "I hit aside," that is, "make mad." *Paraplēssō* engenders the passive adjectives *parapeplēgmenos* and *paraplēx*, "struck aside," "mad": a word used for "mad" laughter, "mad" laws made by drunks, people "mad" with desire, a "mad" self-destructive politician.[9] *Parakrousis*, "striking aside," is used for delirium or insanity. *Parakrouō* can mean "distort" one's judgment, but in a medical context can indicate delirium.[10]

In "hitting aside" verbs, the agent is often a god, the object often *phrenes*. Gods hit the mind with madness. But with words of "carrying aside," the agent is often madness carting you away. Io is carried off by a blast of *lussa*. *Paraphoros* is "carried aside," "mad"; *paraphora*, "carrying aside," is "madness."[11]

Sometimes the mind is "driven" aside rather than "struck." Verbs meaning "I drive aside"—*paragō, paraspaō*—are often used with the mind as

---

[3] Cf. Padel 1990b:358–59. Opening someone's mind to see what's inside: Padel 1992:14.

[4] See Chapter 3, nn. 4, 10, 17, 19, 30; see also Chapter 13. Emotion as inner movement: see Chapter 12; Padel 1992:66–68.

[5] See Chapter 2, nn. 5, 34; see also Chapter 3, n. 30. Becker 1937:160–64, discussing madness and wandering, also collects *ek*- and *para*- compounds.

[6] *PV* 582; *Ba.* 33 (with *phrenōn*), 1000. Cf. *parakopē*, frenzy, delirium: *Ag.* 223; Hp. *Aph.* 6.26 (Loeb 4:184); *Eum.* 329.

[7] See Fraenkel *ad Ag.* 1252; see Chapter 2, nn. 7–8, 30; *Hipp.* 238; Schol. *ad PV* 581 ("in *oistros*-driven fear"): *parakekommenos ton noun*. Photius, s.v. *parakekommenos*, explains "*paraphrōn, phrenas beblammenos*."

[8] *PV* 1056; Ar. *Pax* 90, *Pl.* 508; Pl. *Symp.* 173E.

[9] *HF* 935; Ar. *Ecc.* 139, *Lys.* 831, *Pl.* 242; Hdt. 5.92.

[10] Hp. *Prorrh.* 1.19 (Littré). *Parakekrousthai ton phrenōn*: *Comica Adespota* 705, cf. Hp. *Epid. I* 26, Case 1 (Loeb 2:186).

[11] *PV* 883. Cf. Plu. *Art.* 1 (and, with *xunēseōs*, "carried away from understanding, deranged," Pl. *Sophist* 228D); *Eum.* 330.

object. And they appear in the passive: "I'm driven or led astray; maddened."[12] "Driving aside" suggests either a herded animal or a driver in a runaway chariot, like Orestes when madness begins:

> as if I'm twisting reins in a chariot,
> outside the track. My *phrenes* carry me,
> they're hard to govern; they overcome me.[13]

The image touches that of the *parēoros*, the extra horse harnessed outside the traces, over whom you have less control. *Parēoros* came to mean "sprawling, out of control": sometimes wholly physical but often blending physical with mental floundering. A mind all over the place, in an out of control body.[14] Being off track, mentally or physically, or mentally and physically, is mad.[15]

There are many other mad *para* compounds. There are less violent ones like *paraphrōn*, "with *phrēn* aside," or "beside your *phrēn*."[16] *Paralērein*, "talk deliriously," is also "be mad, be a fool."[17] *Paranoein*, "to think aside," is "to be deranged."[18] *Paranoia*, "thinking aside," is "madness, delirium."[19] By various routes, English absorbed technical words ("paranoia") from all this. Maybe it was influenced by Greek's mad persistent *para* towards images like "beside yourself."

The other madness preposition is *ek*, "out of": as in "out of your mind." *Ekphrōn*, *exō phrenōn*, mean "out of your *phrēn* or *phrenes*, mad."[20] Words meaning "outside"—*exō, ektos*—can mean "mad."[21] Like *para*, *ek* combines with "hitting" verbs. "Struck out," like "struck aside," means "mad."[22]

Departure from right place is the root image here. You "stand out

---

[12] *Ant.* 792; *OT* 974.

[13] *Cho.* 1022–24.

[14] See *Il.* 7.156 (physical), 23.603 (coupled with *aesiphrōn*); Archil. 130.5 (West) *parēoros noou*; *PV* 365 (with *demas* as "accusative of respect"—but Typhon's *phrenes* have already been struck, 363); Theoc. 15.8 (Praxinoa's husband, "that idiot"). Leumann 1950:222, 225, 228–30 (cf. 329) argues that its original use is "forgotten" in these meanings; but this is the sort of thing we cannot know.

[15] Cf. Detienne and Vernant 1978:22–23, 26 n. 67.

[16] *Sept.* 806; *OT* 692; S. *El.* 473.

[17] E.g., Hp. *Epid. I* 2.34 (Loeb 1:150); Ar. *Eq.* 531.

[18] *IA* 838; Ar. *Nub.* 1480.

[19] *Sept.* 756; *Or.* 824; Hp. *Progn.* 23 (Loeb 2:48); Pl. *Legg.* 928E; Arist. *PA* 653B5, *paranoias poiei kai thanatous*, etc. See Chapter 2, n. 5. Cf. "turning" the *phrēn*: Padel 1992:93 n. 49; *paralassei phrenas*, *Ant.* 298.

[20] Pi. *O.* 7.47. *Ekphrōn*: Pl. *Ion* 534B ("frenzied," of poets); Dem. 19.267 ("stupid"); Lucian *Bacchus* 1 (of maenads); Hp. *Mul.* 2.117 (Littré). See Chapter 3, n. 21.

[21] See Silk 1974:121–22 n. 17.

[22] See *Il.* 13.394, "out of his mind" in terror, or *ekpepatagmenos phrenas*, *Od.* 18.327.

from," "slip away from," your *phrenes*.[23] The Latin root of the word "delirium" enacts the same movement: *de*, "out," plus *lira*, "furrow." Derailment, out of the furrow. Phaedra feels she left the right path in her frenzy. She abandoned her proper *gnōmē*, her reason, the perspective she ought to stick to:

> What have I done? Where
> have I wandered
> from a good *gnōmē*? I was mad. . . .[24]

EKSTASIS AND SHAMANISM

This movement aside is reflected in a Greek word with a deeply complicated later history: *ekstasis*, "displacement," "being out of place," from which we get English "ecstasy."

Ekstasis is used through centuries of Greek writing, both pagan and Christian, for a gradually shifting range of violent inner experience. In the classical period, it refers to madness, dislocation, delirium, *melancholiai*. *Ekstasis* means "stepping out": out of normal behavior and sense.[25] In Hippocratic writing, *ekstasis* is physical "dislocation"—of hip joints, for instance—but also mental "distraction" in fever, or delirium. "It's good if dysentery, dropsy, or *ekstasis* come after *mania*."[26] Feverish *ekstaseis* when the patient is silent are deadly. Melancholic *ekstaseis* are not a good sign in epilepsy either. "Those with most blood are best."[27] *Ekstasis* at this period might mean any epileptic-like "seizure." Aristotle uses *manikē ekstasis* and anger as examples of "affective qualities" in the soul.[28]

Classical writers, therefore, use *ekstasis* (and the related verb *ekstasthai*, "to stand out") for any sudden change of mood, any sudden switch from normal ways of being.[29] It indicates physical dislocation, *and* abrupt change of mind, in awe, stupefaction, seizure, madness.

Later Greek began to use *ekstasis* for mystical experience.[30] The mental

[23] *Or.* 1021; *PV* 472 (*exestēn phrenōn, aposphaleis phrenōn*). At *Hipp.* 935, words are *exedroi phrenōn*: see Barrett *ad loc.*

[24] *Hipp.* 239–41. Cf. Lucretius *De rerum natura* 3.464 (*dementit enim deliraque fatur*); Devoto 1940:102. Foucault 1971:99–100 cites the "furrow" derivation from an eighteenth-century medical dictionary.

[25] E.g., Hp. *Prorrh.* 2.9 (Littré); Arist. *Cat.* 10A1. See Dodds 1951:77, 94 n. 84; Bolton 1962:136; Burkert 1985:110. It is unlikely that *ekstasis* visualizes mind "going out" of a body: see Burkert 1985:391 n. 3; below, nn. 32, 37–40, 46.

[26] Hp. *Aph.* 7.5 (Loeb 4:194); cf. Hp. *Arthr.* 56 (Loeb 3:330).

[27] Hp. *Coac.* 65 (Littré), *Prorrh.* 2.9 (Littré).

[28] Arist. *Cat.* 10A.

[29] Dodds 1951:94–95 n. 84.

[30] Plot. 6.9, 11.23; see Armstrong's note in the Loeb ed., and Dodds 1965:71.

displacement becomes specifically religious in Christian contexts. In St. Paul, *ekstasis* can mean religious "trance." In one *ekstasis*, Paul sees a vision of heaven opening. From having meant "displacement," a change or distraction, *ekstasis* is now a visionary ecstasy. Christian writers attribute it to Hebrew prophets. This is the core of "ecstasy" as used today: a seizure of human being by divinity.[31]

Rohde, the great historian of Greek irrationality, thought *ekstasis* "originally" involved the idea of the soul's departure from the body.[32] Both elements in the idea reflect pulses of his own day. On the one hand, there is a lust to explain the near by the far, function by origin; plus the high hope that we accidental latecomers *can* establish "origins" for ancient words in specific beliefs.[33] And on the other, there is a passionate interest (reflecting, perhaps, the Romantic influence on early anthropology) in souls that leave the body.[34]

At this point, our imaginative inheritance, both Christianity and post-Christian flirtation with the occult, has a distorting effect on our responses to classical Greek. In Christian mystics, ecstasy is the standard term for mystic union with divinity, and those connotations linger on in post-Christian imagination. It is easy to read them back, anachronistically, into classical texts.[35]

There is also the modern glamor of shamanism. Anthropological accounts of Siberian shamans hit the West at the beginning of the twentieth century. In the 1930s, scholarship began to apply shamanism widely—too widely—to other societies.[36] Popular imagination fell in love with it too. Since the '60s, shamans have become big business. They are an idealized part of the West's own mythology, now. Urban shamans, and shaman workshops, appear throughout the United States.[37]

The core idea of shamanism, as found in Siberia and some other cultures, is a body lying still while its soul journeys to be instructed in healing techniques that are applied in the community on return. Does anything like this purpose-filled, spiritual, and healing wandering outside the body appear in ancient Greece?

The question of shamanism in ancient Greece is a scholarly war zone. There are a few Greek stories, not told earlier than the fourth century, of men whose bodies seemed to die. Their souls roamed, witnessing es-

---

[31] Acts 27.17, 10.10; Dodds 1965:61; Lewis 1989:15. See above, Chapter 9, n. 21.

[32] Rohde 1925:258–62, 293.

[33] See Claus 1981:14; Padel 1992:37–38, 160, 169, 180.

[34] Soul leaving body: below, nn. 37, 40–41, 45. Romantic idealization of centrifugal or mad wandering: see Chapter 10, n. 26, and Chapter 11, nn. 18–19, 34.

[35] See Dodds 1965:70–71.

[36] See Clarke 1975:7 (with n. 17); e.g., Tolstoy 1985:141–60 calls Merlin a shaman.

[37] See Drury 1989:11–21, 103–105 (shaman centers).

chatological mysteries.[38] From the 1930s onward, scholars suggested these were shamans; especially since the stories seemed to come from the north, and there might be northern influence at work. This idea was supported by both Dodds and Eliade in 1951.[39]

Belief in Greek shamanism, both scholarly and popular, is still vigorous. Recently in a British TV production of *Oedipus Rex* Oedipus called Teiresias a shaman. However, more recent studies, especially those demanding rigid definitions of shamanism, and anthropologists who actually work with shamanic cultures, reject shamanist interpretations of these stories. These Greek soul wanderers are not healers. You can see shamanism anywhere, if you look for it. "Shamanism" gets applied promiscuously to societies having little in common with shamanic cultures. Something like "ecstasy" or "soul journey" is found in too many places to be called by the hold-all title. Just going into trance is not enough. Anthropologically defined, shamanism is restricted in time, place, appearance, and activities.[40]

It has been suggested, instead, that these few Greek stories offer evidence of some nonshamanic "soul belief" of a body lying tranced while the soul wanders outside. The stories have also been linked to possession, seizure by nymphs, and divinatory arts.[41] There is little other evidence of Greek shamanism, and this lot is not enough. One scholar thinks the idea of shamanism was useful, from the 1930s on, in making Greek scholarship take myth seriously in relation to cult practice; but he denies, as many now do, that you can find shamanism in Greek material.[42]

Outside purely Greek scholarship, it has also been argued that shamanism is essentially opposed to possession. In the one, the soul leaves the body and wanders abroad. Its experience outside is what matters. In the other, an alien force enters the body. What matters is what that force says while in the body, not what the host soul does. Shamanism and possession are "essentially opposed" and not found in the same culture, though the term "ecstatic religion" has been used, misleadingly, of both.[43] If this is right, shamanism is unlikely to have been found in Greece, which (almost certainly) did have possession.[44]

However, some students of shamanism as a general phenomenon, rather

---

[38] See Bolton 1962:126, 148–53.

[39] Kagarov 1934 and Meuli 1935 suggested Aristeas of Proconnesus was a shaman; cf. Rohde 1925:300, 328–29. Dodds 1951:141–56 and Eliade 1964 [1951]:389 followed in the same year, encouraging ideas of Greek shamanism. Cf. Burkert 1972:162–65.

[40] See Bremmer 1983:48 (with n. 95).

[41] Bremmer 1983:25–43. Bolton 1962:36, 85, 125–34 (the standard work on Aristeas) denied he was a shaman. See also Burkert 1985:111.

[42] He argues instead for a specifically Greek "free soul" idea: Bremmer 1983:52 and passim.

[43] Dodds 1951:88 n. 43; de Heusch 1981:152–56; see Vitebsky 1993:21.

[44] See Padel 1983; Burkert 1985:391 n. 1.

than its operation in individual cultures, want "shaman" to mean simply, loosely, "master of spirits." They would deny the "healing" element is central to it. They believe possession and shamanism can crop up in the same culture.[45]

The current state of play here seems, therefore, a standoff. What is clear is that we cannot say Greek culture was shamanic. If Greek culture had been shamanic, shamanism might have seemed like one model or extension of madness, in Greek constructions of it: might have seemed to incarnate the wandering mind. But we cannot say this. In fact, the core of shamanism seems quite opposite to tragic images of madness. Greek madness does not separate mind and body.[46] The mind does not leave the body and wander somewhere else. What happens instead is a restless wandering of mind and body both.

Popular modern ideas of shamanism are inappropriate, therefore, for understanding the Greek *ek* of madness. But they do make a useful contrast with tragic images of madness. A shamanic interpretation of *ekphrōn* would stress the free-wandering mind: a mind on its own, outside an inert body. But in tragic madness, before Plato, before any evidence of soul journeys, the *ekphrōn* person is known by a restless physical mobility of mind and body together. This, on the evidence of tragic poetry, is what Greek fifth-century imagination is interested in. Not in experience the mind might have outside its normal housing.

ENTHEOS, ENTHOUSIASMOS

Beside these compounds of *para* and *ek*, now set their apparent opposite: compounds with *en*, "in."

Entheos means "with god inside," possessed.[47] Maenads are *entheoi* with Dionysus; Phaedra seems to be *entheos* with Pan or Hecate; belligerents are *entheoi* with Ares. Zeus made Apollo's *phrēn entheos* with divining "skill."[48] Related linguistically to *entheos*, *enthousiasmos* is inspiration, frenzy.[49] Democritus supposedly said the best poems get made "with *enthousiasmos* and holy breath." Plato claims something similar in the *Timaeus*. No one achieves "*entheos* divination" while *ennous*, "in one's mind." We achieve it when *phronēsis* (intelligence) is "bound up by sleep" or altered by disease

---

[45] Lewis 1986:81–93, 1989:48–49.

[46] The one exception might be the post-fifth-century ideas outlined above (see Chapter 9, nn. 1–9). If you looked for points of similarity with shamanism anywhere in Greek material, it would be here, I think: in philosophy's images of itself. But it would insult Plato (maybe current shamans too) to say they are one and the same.

[47] See Dodds 1951:87; Padel 1983:13; Burkert 1985:109.

[48] *Ant.* 964; *Hipp.* 141–42, cf. Xen. *Symp.* 1.10, "possessed by *erōs*"; *Sept.* 497; *Eum.* 17.

[49] Burkert 1985:109–111.

"or some *enthousiasmos*."[50] Socrates in the *Phaedrus* says he has forgotten, "because of *to enthousiastikon*" (a moment of possession) if he defined love at the beginning of his speech. That he did so, beautifully, demostrates the "technical" word skill of Pan and the nymphs who inspired this definition.[51]

Aristotle, classifying types of tunes, calls some ethical, some tunes of action, and some *enthousiastika*, which have a passionate effect on the soul. They make it *enthousiastikē*: "for *enthousiasmos* is a feeling of the soul's *ēthos* [character]." Ethical tunes are useful in education. But active and *enthousiastika* tunes bring *katharsis*, and relax tension. Pity, fear, and *enthousiasmos* affect everyone. But some people are specially liable to *enthousiasmos*: "under the influence of sacred tunes we see these people, when they use tunes that violently affect the soul, changed: in a state, as if they'd undergone medical therapy and taken a purge."[52] *Enthousiasmos* marks the best poetry, the truest, most authentic prophecy. It is also violent. Aristotle assumes it has physically violent results—like *ekstasis*. Poetry, prophecy, violent religious spasm in response to music, a bringing out of things, in yourself, which is out of your own, human control: this is the word's semantic beat. We might remember hellebore, another violent, spasmodic "purge" and cure for madness.[53]

The related verbs *enthousiaō*, *enthousiazō*, are used mainly by Plato and tragedy. The Greek herald says Hecuba is "enthused" (i.e., "possessed") by her troubles. She is distraught and wants to die in the pyre of her city. In Aeschylus's *Edoni*, Lycurgus's house "*is frenzied*, its roofs rave like a bacchant." Dionysus has possessed the house as he will possess, and madden, its master.[54]

In a context of poetic possession, Sophocles uses a rare adjective *enthriaktos*, which may suggest something divine and alien "in" the human mind: the Thriai, "teachers of divination" given to Hermes by Apollo (who get inspired, themselves, by eating honey). Hesychius, the ancient lexicographer, attributes the line to a lost play, *Sinon*, and links the word to *enthousiaō*. It is as if the Thriai, like Bacchus in *bacchaō*, get into the mind.[55]

Plato uses *enthousiaō* mainly for poetic possession.[56] It has the same

---

[50] Democrit. fr. 18DK; Delatte 1934:28; Dodds 1951:82, 101 (with nn. 125–26); Pl. *Ti.* 71E.

[51] *Phdr.* 263D; cf. 258C and the unusual *enthousiasis*, 249E. See Borgeaud 1988:104–107.

[52] Arist. *Pol.* 1340A11, 1341B34, 1342A7.

[53] See Chapter 5, nn. 6–8.

[54] *Tro.* 1284; A. fr. 58. Lycurgus and *Edoni*: see Chapter 3, nn. 6–9, and Chapter 19, nn. 30, 56.

[55] S. fr. 544 (Jebb/Pearson). Hesychius explains *enthriazein* as *parakinein, apo tōn muntikōn thriōn*. Thriai: *h. Merc.* 551–64. *Bacchaō*: see Chapter 3, nn. 23–26.

[56] Pl. *Ion* 535C, 536B, *Apol.* 22C, *Phdr.* 253A, 241A. See Pl. *Theaetetus* 180C, *Phlb.* 15E (*enthousian huph' hēdonēs*); cf. *Tro.* 1284 (Hecuba, "frenzied by *kakais*").

range as *enthousiasmos*: poetic inspiration, prophetic possession, bacchic frenzy, "distraction" through intense grief or pleasure. Aristotle says an orator may use flowery words once he has "inspired" (i.e., excited) his audience.[57]

THE MIND DAMAGED, LOST

> . . . mind has mountains; cliffs of fall,
> Frightful, sheer, no-man-fathomed. Hold them cheap
> May who ne'er hung there.
> —Gerard Manley Hopkins, "No worst, there is
> none"

Madness as violent inner movement: its opposite is a quiet, still mind. "Sane" or "prudent," *sōphrōn*, means "with a safe *phrēn*," with your mind in the right place, inside, unmoved, undamaged. And you yourself "inside," "in possession of *phrenes*,"[58] living up to the Athenian male upper-class ideal of "self"-control whose inner correlative is an unruffled *phrēn*. The ideal was control over your self, desires, body, mind.[59] Women did not have this (or not in surviving male images of them). Men must control everything (women, their own feelings) they see as turbulent, inner, unsafe.[60]

The opposite of *sōphrōn* is *ekphrōn* or *aphrōn*, a *phrēn* that is damaged, cancelled, lost.[61] Tragedy specializes in this state: people who are *aphrōn*, "*phrēn*-less," "empty of *phrenes*," or "stupid," "insane."[62] Heroes are asked "where are you in your mind?"[63] as if they are lost in it, as in a landscape. Or they may be *ekphrōn*, "out" of *phrēn*, with their *phrēn* out.

When your *phrēn* is safe, you are in your mind, and your mind is in you. You are *emphrōn*, sane. Augury, says Socrates in the *Phaedrus*, is less authentic than any divination done in a state of *mania*. Augury is done by *emphrones*, people "in" their *phrēn*. But prophetesses benefitted Greece most "when they were mad."[64]

---

[57] Arist. *Rh.* 1408B14.

[58] *Ant.* 492, cf. *PV* 444 (*phrenōn epēbolos*, opposite of "raving"). Orestes tells Electra "Be *endon*" (with no location), and *mē 'klageis phrenas*, *Cho.* 233. Does he mean "get in the house"? or "contain yourself"? Cf. *eisō phrenōn, Med.* 316; *phrenōn ouk endon ōn, Heraclid.* 709.

[59] Padel 1992:88 n. 35; Dover 1974:125–29; Williams 1993:40.

[60] Just 1989:153–217; Padel 1983:6–7.

[61] See Snell 1978:70–72; above, Chapter 2, nn. 6, 33, and Chapter 3, n. 21.

[62] *Aphrōn*: *Il.* 5.875; *Eum.* 377 (crazy); cf. *Il.* 3.220, 4.104; S. *El.* 941 (silly, stupid). "Empty of *phrenes*," *Ant.* 754; of *nous*, *OC* 931.

[63] *Ant.* 42; cf. *Phil.* 805. Campbell *ad* S. *El.* 390 asks if *ei* is *eimi sum* ("where are you in your mind?") or *eimi ibo* ("where are you going in your mind?") and gives parallels for both.

[64] Pl. *Phdr.* 244B; see Chapter 8, n. 14–15.

Madness is inner movement that involves inner damage and loss. Your mind "moves out" of you, out of control. In images surrounding wanderers, the safe person or mind is still, at home, in his or her right place; the unsafe one is loose, outside, unhoused.[65] Outside is mad; mad is outside. And dangerous.

OUTSIDE AND INSIDE

Ekstasis, enthousiasmos: their prepositional prefixes suggest opposite movements. "Out," "in." Yet in fourth-century medical and philosophical writing the two have the same effect on body and mind. *Ekstasis* is intense delirium, epileptic seizure, abnormal violence of body, with attendant change and violence of mind. According to Aristotle, *enthousiasmos* is "so powerful for some people it can overpower their soul."[66] Something coming in (the root implication of *entheos* and *enthousiasmos*) has the same effect as forcing the mind "out," making it wander.

Madness, characterized particularly by *ek* words, overlaps possession, characterized particularly by *en* words, but it is not a symmetrical relationship. If you are *entheos* (god "inside"), you are *ekphrōn*. Your mind is "out." But if you are *ekphrōn*, you are not necessarily *entheos*.[67] There is no worked out relation of madness and possession, *ekphrōn* and *entheos*. It may depend on the purpose and identity of the divinity involved. On the whole, Erinyes or Lyssa make you *ekphrōn* but not *entheos*, while Olympian divinities like Apollo and Dionysus make you *entheos*. But possession language gravitates even to Lyssa.[68] The possessed have a wild activity of mind, speech, and body like the mad.[69] Possession is a kind of madness, though not all madness is possession.

THE WANDERING WOMB

I have argued elsewhere that in tragedy's day a "female" image of mind dominates Greek language of feeling and thinking. Tragic language treats mental equipment more like an inward receptacle than an active organ. Mind, as tragedy presents it, is dark, interior, penetrated; filling and flowing with blood, impure and uncontrollable. It has the perceived qualities of the female interior.[70]

[65] See Padel 1994.
[66] Arist. *Pol.* 1342A7; cf. above, n. 51.
[67] Padel 1983:13.
[68] Tambornino 1909:4 takes Lyssa running into Heracles' breast (*HF* 861–62; see Chapter 2, n. 18) as possession. Cf. *lussaō*: see Chapter 3, n. 25.
[69] Bolton 1962:134–36; cf. Padel 1981:107, 1983:14.
[70] Padel 1992: chs. 3–5; cf. Padel 1983:16 n. 27.

So we must compare images of mental movement to contemporary images of the womb's behavior. The womb too is imagined to wander when something goes badly wrong. Like the mind, the womb has a right place in the body. When damaged, it wanders away. Doctors recommend treating it by luring or squeezing the womb back to its right place. The womb is "a kind of animal," hard to control, even for a male doctor from outside. A diseased or unused womb moves round the body, and its wanderings cause disease. This belief is the beginning of hysteria theory.[71]

The "wandering womb" found a place also in Plato's account of the creation of the universe: in the *Timaeus*, wandering is the cause of bad (an image that reflects general Greek assumptions that movement, especially internal, is the cause of change and danger).[72] The wandering womb turns up in Plato's version of the creation of women and sexual desire. The male sexual parts are hard to control, disobedient, self-willed. They try to conquer everything in *oistros*-driven desires. The womb, if it remains "without fruit," gets ill, "and by wandering everywhere through the body, blocking the channels of breath, preventing breathing, it casts the body into extreme distress and causes all sorts of diseases."[73]

These are the background ingredients here: wandering is bad, internal wandering is dangerous. If there is some essential female thing in women that resembles the mind, that too may wander and cause harm. One Greek word for womb is *delphus*. Does this reflect *delphis*, "dolphin," implying that the up-down movement of the womb is sea-lawless, and animal? There is no evidence for this. But ideas of the womb's mobility reflect, I guess, Greek images of the mobility, the too easily moved nature, of the mind.

[71] Hp. *Mul.* 1, 2–7 (Littré), *Nat. Mul.* 2.3.8 (Littré); Leibrand and Wettley 1961:54–59; Simon 1978:238–60; Lefkowitz 1981:12–23.

[72] See Chapter 11, n. 21. Movement as cause of dangerous change: Padel 1992:65–66.

[73] Pl. *Ti.* 91C. Ideas of mobile wombs in the Renaissance and eighteenth century: Kinsman 1974c:314–15; Foucault 1971:150. *Oistros*: see above, Chapter 2.

Chapter 13

DAEMONIC DANCE

"Der Rhythmus der Disharmonie"

When I love thee not,
Chaos is come again.
—Shakespeare, *Othello* 3.3

MADNESS and passion force inner and outer violence on the self. The violent outer body expresses inner violence too, in which heart kicks *phrēn* or spirals beside *phrenes*; *phrēn* shakes on the rack; inner and outer writhe together in hunted, displacing, twisting leaps.[1]

How is this inner movement imagined? What is it like?

A chaotic "pulse" seems the closest we can get. The word *pitulos* means "beat" or "throb." Sometimes it is a rhythmic "beat", like oars, but mostly an irregular jabbing: a "butting" ram, or "thrusting" spear. In passion, madness, or disease, *pitulos* suggests a wild, unpatterned, unrhythmic jerking, both inner and outer. The German scholar Wilamowitz, in his Commentary on *Hercules Furens*, called *pitulos* "der Rhythmus der Disharmonie."[2] Greek doctors take *spasmoi*, spasms, as a sign of disease. When Philoctetes' foot begins to throb, it is a thrust of pain, a savage spasm: like the *pitulos* of terror, drunkenness, physical agony, or Heracles' *mania*.[3]

Other words for the movement of hurt minds and bodies revolve round *taragmos* (or *tarachē*), "disorder, confusion." Passion and disease cause external *taragmos*. Internal *taragmos* disturbs the *phrenes*, or the whole person.[4]

The related verb *tarassō*, "I disturb," takes as its object the thing it confuses: either a person, or a person's *phrēn* or heart.[5] The mind "is dis-

---

[1] *PV* 881; *OT* 153 (see Jebb *ad loc.*); *Ag.* 996–97; *Il.* 22.452; *Cho.* 410; *h. Dem.* 293; A. fr. 387N; *Aj.* 693.

[2] Wilamowitz *ad HF* 816. The *pitulos* of madness is irregular, so not really a "pulse" (as Platnauer calls it *ad IT* 307). Barrett *ad Hipp.* 1464 says the word's core is not noise but repeated movement.

[3] *HF* 816, *Alc.* 798, *HF* 1189; Hp. *Coac.* 350 (Littré), Th. 2.49.4; *Phil.* 744, cf. 792. Cf. eighteenth-century images of madness as intense movement: Foucault 1971:93.

[4] Disturbing *phrenes*: *Cho.* 1056; *HF* 836, 1091 (caused by Lyssa's *taragma tartareion*, 907); Pi. *O.* 7.30. Disturbing whole person: e.g., *Hec.* 857.

[5] *Ag.* 1216; *OT* 483 (*me* as object); *Hipp.* 969 (*phrēn* as object, cf. *Ant.* 1095); *Ba.* 1321 (heart as object).

turbed": so are physical organs: eyes, bowels.[6] Doctors use the related adjective *tarochōdēs* in a passive sense, "disordered," to describe bowels and mind.[7] "Disturbed" air causes *tarachos* and *thorubos*—a noisy rushing—of blood, which shakes other parts of the body. A throbbing hypochondria "means *thorubos* or *paraphrosunē* [senselessness]."[8]

Tragedy and medicine, therefore, expect irregular throbbing in a disturbed mind and body. (For Hellenistic philosophers, sensitive to these traditional associations, the most valued condition is *ataraxia*, freedom from *tarachē*.)[9] In madness, delirium, or violent passion, limbs and eyes twist, innards sing and circle in *tarachē*.[10] Io's limbs and mind are violent, her eyes whirled *heligdēn*, "twisted round" (as in "helix"). She is carried off course, by madness.[11] In such wild movement, "fear is ready beside the heart to sing and dance in anger." The mad writhings of mind and body are disharmony, dis-rhythm, but resemble disordered "dance."[12]

JOINED-UP DANCING

We must bring in here a few local resonances of dance and music. A tragedy was a musical composition. In fifth-century Greece, especially onstage, singing and dancing belonged together. *Mousikē* meant poetry as well as music: poetry was sung. "Music" was an image of civilized right order. As a tragedy is. In dance and song, as in a poem, every component has its proper place. All pieces operate together.[13] Poetry, music, and dance incarnate educated, desirable, controlled, functioning order.

Choros meant "dance." For tragic texts, as they are handed on by Renaissance scholars, the word refers to the singing group, the "chorus," which tends to stand for order—for controlling passion, avoiding extremes. They often sing a belief in moderation, a fear of extreme passion, a care for ordered, rhythmically controlled values that they express in symmetry and meter. Watching Phaedra devastated by sexual passion, the chorus tells Eros: "Don't come to me *arrhuthmos* [unrhythmical]."[14]

---

[6] *Cho.* 289; *Or.* 253 (*omma*); Hp. *Coac.* 205 (Littré) (bowels).

[7] *Ta tēs gnōmēs tarachōdea*; *Epid. III* 150, case 7 (Loeb 1:268). Internal "disturbance": *Breaths* 14.42–48 (Loeb 2:250).

[8] Hp. *Progn.* 7 (Loeb 2:16).

[9] Padel 1992:88 n. 35.

[10] "Rolling" eyes and mind, "twisted" seeing: see Chapter 7, nn. 37–38, and below, nn. 66–67.

[11] *PV* 881–83. Heart "circling": cf. *Ag.* 997. Relation (in fifth-century writing and on the stage) between seen and unseen: Padel 1990b:345, 358, 1992:66.

[12] *Cho.* 1024. Singing innards: Padel 1992:73. Dancing heart: Detienne 1989:57.

[13] See further Padel 1992:126–27; W. D. Anderson 1966:2, 13, 37–40 and passim; Lippman 1964:2–3, 38–44, 62–65; Lonsdale 1993:44–75.

[14] Erotic moderation: *PV* 887–93, 901–903; *Hipp.* 529; *IA* 554. Sometimes (e.g., *Ba.*, *Eum.*, A. *Supp.*) the chorus is not moderate but partisan. In *Phil.* they do *not* base their wish

It is as if "dance" means order: an order that depends on the security of emotional moderation, based on traditional piety, and best praised through controlled meter. The word "meter" comes, in fact, from *metron*, a unit of measuring. From this *metrios*, "moderate," derives.

Another chorus, frightened by scepticism about oracles, by disrespect shown to "seats of daemons," says of ancient laws that "god in them is great and does not age," wishing "bad fate" on anyone who violates holy things (including holy laws). "If such deeds are honored, why should I dance?" Does this mean "serve in a tragic chorus"? Or just "dance"? I do not think it is a sharp self-reference, but I do think it means more than our simple "dance." It means "dance *in a chorus*": that is, take part in the most basic Greek image of harmonious society, based, as choric dance and society both were, on worship. This is a vision of dance very different from disco, where individuals are random atoms. Most middle-aged members of Western society now are too young to know "joined-up dancing" even as simple as the quickstep. It is not theirs, any more. By contrast, in Greek choric dance each person played a known and measured part; the dance cemented ancient rules of joining and cooperation. Rules in which gods lived: for Greek gods inhabited every human activity and relationship, and enforced the rules of these activities.[15]

The dances that accompanied choral songs were the theater's biggest movements. They made public the inner mobility that tragic language attributes to minds in passion. The danced song comments on, but also counterpoints, the tragedy's *dis*ordered passions: mainly those of individual characters. Order versus disorder: plural versus single. Single, mad, or impassioned minds "move out" of their right place, alone and at risk, while plural concerted bodies move in patterns emblematic of right place and security. The musical structure, violent *and* orderly, expressed through the interplay of individual actor and plural chorus, is the basis of tragic tension.

Many theories of tragedy's origins make choral song its starting point. The complex lyric rhythms seem to have been patterned, long before tragedy, by dance steps. Dance patterns and song meters developed and survived together. The meters "controlled the feet of the dancers as well as organizing the words of the song."[16] These braidings of sung and danced thought, of ordered movement in mind and in body, are background for tragic representations of madness as *dis*ordered dance.

for security on a moral stance: within a stanza they sing Philoctetes to sleep, then (833) tell their captain, "Let's go."

[15] *OT* 871, 883–98; see Padel 1992:7–8, 139–41, cf. 165.

[16] Webster 1970:xi, 200. Relation of internal movement described in tragic language of passion, to external moves of choral dance: Padel 1992:66.

"The Song of Erinyes"

Madness-daemons, Lyssa, Erinys, are so pervasive in tragedy that vase-painters often use them as a tragic token: they show that a mythic scene is not any old myth but a scene from tragedy.[17]

Madness-daemons characterize tragedy. But what do they do in the actual plays? How do they affect their victims? They make music. They make their victims dance. Lyssa will pipe music to Heracles, and spark a riot of movement in him.[18] Erinyes inhabit the house of Atreus, and the breasts of its family members. In the *Oresteia*'s first play, they appear to Cassandra as a foul *choros* and *kōmos* ("revel-dance"). In that house, the *thumos*, spirit, "sings, self-taught, the Erinyes' dirge." Erinys-music inhabits the inhabitants' minds. Finally, Erinyes become the last play's *choros*, the singer-dancers, the music's vehicle.

Their "hymn," sung in strange alternating units of trochaic and dactylic stanzas, is their medium of terror. Their "hateful" song is the first musical shock of the play. It says it inflicts madness: and must have sent a frisson through its first audience. Would Athenians, hearing it, themselves go mad? To hear it is to understand what Erinyes do in people's minds. Is this madness?

> Come, let us fasten our dance, make our hated music clear:
> how our company governs humans, discharges its office.
>
> . . . .
>
> Over our appointed victim, this is our tune:
> striking aside, carrying aside (*parakopa, paraphora*),
> damaging minds. A hymn without lyre, the song
> of Erinyes. Withering mortals. Binding their minds.[19]

Other mad-making gods inspire dance. Dionysus forces Theban matrons to be maenads: they run wild over mountains "in dances." Dionysus's Asian maenads are *Bacchae*'s *choros*.[20] As with maenads, so with the daughters of Proetus. Wild dancing is a symptom (maybe also a cure) of their madness too. Their story has various versions. The girls rush mad over mountains like maenads.[21] In one version, men cure them by chasing them "with shouts and a sort of possessed dancing."[22] Some versions compare their activities with Dionysian dance and madness.[23]

---

[17] Padel 1992:163, 170–72.
[18] *HF* 871; see above, Chapter 2, n. 18.
[19] *Ag.* 1186–89, 991; *Eum.* 307–33. Erinyes at Athens: Padel 1992:175–85, 189–92.
[20] *Ba.* 21, 114, 148, 184, 190, 195, 207, 220.
[21] See Hes. frr. 37, 261 (Merkelbach/West).
[22] Apollod. 2.2.2. See Dowden 1989:79.
[23] See Dowden 1989:75, 79, 81.

It is Hera (in most versions) who maddens the daughters of Proetus, and Hera who inflicts Lyssa on Heracles. Afterwards he imagines her dancing, "beating the floor of Olympus with sandalled foot." Only dance could express her glee at destroying him. His madness was a dance: Lyssa played *aulos* for it. Now, in his bitter fantasy, those mad movements are celebrated by Hera's dance.[24]

Outside tragedy, music can be cause or symptom of physical and mental abnormality, and violence. But it can also be used ritually to cure violence.[25] In his blueprint for musical education, Plato suggests dancelike leaping is the basic condition of life. *Choreia*, choral dance, can refer to movements of soul as well as body.[26] In the *Symposium*, he takes Corybantic dancing as an image for inner movements of passion. Listening to Socrates, Alcibades' heart "leaps" more wildly than Corybants.[27]

Corybants? Their dancing was supposed (according to one scholar) to "surpass all others in violence." It is not clear who or what they were. There are not many early references to them, and no very informative ones. Texts compare their rites and music, especially their communal, orgiastic dance, to those of Dionysus.[28] I doubt fifth-century Athenian audiences were deeply familiar with real-life Corybants. Corybants may have been an aspect only of imaginative life, though they may represent something that existed elsewhere. ("Hottentots," rather than mermaids, in Edwardian children's literature.) You could not, I think, prove that Corybants were at work in fifth-century Athens.[29] Still, imaginative life is vital for tragedy, and Corybants clearly play an increasingly intense role in late-fifth-century Athenian imagination. Corybantic madness, linked with cure through wild dance, is bracketed with Dionysian rites.

The Middle Ages and Renaissance also see madness as grotesque dance. A mid-sixteenth-century drawing by Pieter Breughel the Elder, for instance, on the pilgrimage of the mad to Molenbeek, shows mad figures, restrained or half-carried by others, limbs flailing in a caricature of dance. Musicians walk alongside, playing to them. Henricus Hondius did a series of engravings based on this drawing, stressing the power of music over the possessed. So did Daniel Hopfer, who gave the dancing figures leaves and birds' nests in their hair: tokens of fools, wild men, the mad.

[24] Dowden 1989:74–80; *HF* 1303, cf. 871.
[25] See Lloyd 1979:42–43, with references. Dance as disruptive force: Lonsdale 1993:76–110.
[26] Pl. *Legg.* 672E–73A10; Detienne 1989:58.
[27] Pl. *Symp.* 215E.
[28] Starkie *ad* Ar. *V.* 8, cf. *V.* 118–24; Strabo 10.3.21. Corybants: Pl. *Ion* 534A, *Euthyd.* 277D; Linforth 1946a; Burkert 1987:141 n. 32, 162 n. 3, 165 n. 43, 112.
[29] Ar. *V.* 119 is no evidence (cf. Simon 1978:123) for their existence in fifth-century Athens. Trying to cure a mad father? Mix familiar with fantasy cures for a laugh.

There may be a continuous link here: linguistic images, feeding through Latin from Greek texts and culture into the perceptions of madness in the Middle Ages and the Renaissance. Or it may be historical accident: local perceptions in separate societies, arriving at an image of madness as disharmonous dance. Either way, in the Renaissance too madness can be seen and represented as unrhythmical, unmusical dance. In Northern Renaissance iconography, "The idea of the dancing madman, either the fool or the possessed, adds one more level of interpretation to the image of flailing limbs as an icon of madness."[30]

DISORDER THROUGH ORDER

So tragedy articulates a Greek sense, which had important life also in the Renaissance, that madness makes the mad body and mind move violently in ways that seem like dance.

But this movement is also importantly not-dance. Greek dance generally incarnates order: that of the social structure to and in which you safely belong. Its relations and patterns are governed by aesthetic and social rules. But madness is perceived as outside controlled order. In fifth-century Greece, isolation (see Chapter 10) and wandering (see Chapter 11) have nothing to do with dance. The *parēoros* (see Chapter 12) is not *in* harness but *para*, beside. The mad person is out of the right place. Greek choral song and dance put you in the right place, at and in the right time.

There seems, therefore, a vital paradox about the image of madness as dance, which bears on the larger paradox involved in representing the *Disharmonie* of madness through and in the harmonies of tragedy, or any art. Breughel's drawing com-poses, places together, the untogetherness of its subject.

In many epochs and genres, literature has found a useful paradox in exploring madness, seen as essentially dis-ordered, through its own forms, which are an image of order. Ordering the disorder, controlling it while conveying it, makes for resonant and creative tension. Burton's *Anatomy of Melancholy* sets melancholy, "epitome" of human disease, in the context of the disorder of the universe. Ordering itself, it tries "to order the material of chaos." Its structure overcomes that chaos.[31]

But *can* any literature actually write madness? Write about it? Represent it? Can it present something society sees as disordered, in forms of syntax, music, or meter that incarnate human rules and order? Does it falsify it, by presenting it within its own order?

Foucault saw eighteenth-century images of madness as a delirium "of

[30] Gilman 1982:31–36, plates 41–46.

[31] See Fox 1976:9 and passim. Lonsdale's examples of "dance as disruptive force" focusses on "divine prototypes" (Dionysus, Hephaestus), satyrs, maenads: Lonsdale 1993:76–110.

both body and soul, language and image, grammar and physiology."[32] But the end of the eighteenth century makes a division between "the languages of reason and unreason," when madness is reseen as mental illness. Before, in Shakespeare, madness escapes reason and dramatic order. Afterwards, madness is silent. Psychiatry begins its "monologue of reason about madness." You never hear the voice of madness itself again.[33]

There have been many theoretical objections to his position, and to Derrida's attack on him (a debate that resounded through the 1980s and that Derrida is generally agreed to have won).[34] Derrida argued that Foucault may *say* he is writing about madness's silence, but in fact, like psychiatry, he writes about madness from the point of view of reason, thereby bleaching madness's voice out of his own work. By writing *in language*, necessarily syntactical and structured, Foucault aligns himself with the very rationality that he says silenced madness. Language, image of order, is incompatible with madness, image of disorder.[35]

Foucault said he was writing an archaeology of the silencing of madness. Derrida said this was impossible. But both assumed reason and madness were strongly opposed. Recent contributors to the discussion of their debate suggest madness is "only weakly opposed" to reason. Madness is "a degree of confusion within the purview of rationality." It is "somewhere else," at "the place where intelligibility is slipping away."[36]

The question thrown up was whether madness is catchable in the orderings of language. But the original debate did not leave much room for the basic anthropological point that any society's image of madness is constructed by the sane. What surfaces in sane people's literature will be more or less true to sane ways of seeing and hearing madness at that time and place, rather than to a local mad person's own experience. English Renaissance audiences knew the codes and conventions of how a mad person might look and behave in their society. They recognized madness when they saw, not madness itself onstage, but a particular set of shared symbols, with specific medical, social, and sometimes political resonance, which represented madness, then.[37]

[32] Foucault 1971:99–101.

[33] Foucault 1971:x–xi, 31. In the preface to the first edition of *Histoire de la Folie* he included an argument about Descartes that Derrida 1978 demolished. Foucault responded by a defence (Foucault 1979), and by dropping the Descartes preface from, while adding appendices to, his second edition. See Boyne 1990:71, 76–79.

[34] You could say Derrida implies there can be no madness in any literature: all writing shares in "reason," so excludes madness from its discourse. See Felman 1985:35–55; Salkeld 1993:40.

[35] Derrida 1978 For discussion of their debate, see Felman 1985; Boyne 1990:53–90; Salkeld 1993:37–45.

[36] See Felman 1985:50; Salkeld 1993:43–44.

[37] Salkeld 1993:3, 46.

Empirically, Foucault's argument about silence is weakened by written testimonies from people incarcerated and treated as mad both before and after the "monologue of psychiatry" began. This monologue has not been absolute. Even the "silencing" practitioners recorded some of their patients' talk, though they did not, as we would try to do, interpret it.[38]

One could also argue that Foucault's celebration of the insights of the mad was an unexamined expression of the "true mad seeing" tradition not that far from the patronizing glamorization of Ernest Dowson. Foucault, like Dowson, undervalues the fact that most of the mad, however one deciphers that name, are desperately unhappy. Many of the eighteenth-century scraps of discourse from the mad that have come down to us "betray what seems to represent an insupportable degree of pain."[39]

This is something that matters more to therapists than literary critics, but it would not hurt the critics to remember it. I recently heard a Foucault-based talk whose speaker suggested we abandon the word and concept of psychosis, and leave instead "an absence," a black hole: nothingness. Asked how people in pain who wanted a therapist's help would feel, if they thought the person they hoped might rescue them could only put them conceptually in a place without a name, he could not answer. He "didn't know." Despite Foucault's own passion, a kind of patronizing, an arrogance towards "the mad," makes itself felt under the Foucauldian glamor, in its reception anyway.

Sane ways of seeing madness, in Athenian society, must have been an ordered code, available to the sane in construing what they saw, which also provided a departure point for the mad themselves. They were going mad in, and from, this society, not any other. As far as tragedy was concerned, the representing of disorder depended on understanding it in terms of order. Tragic madness was a construct: presented within an ordered dramatic scheme. It must have had direct relation to the ways real-life madness was seen in the society; and maybe also some relation (though more complex) to the experience of madness. In each time and place, sane syntax is something to be mad from.

In Foucault-based madness debates of the 1970s and 1980s, madness is often called "other."[40] But there are many ways of being "other." Greek images present madness not as "opposite" to reason and right order, but astray from it. They do not represent the mad inhabiting a different world: mad people, like beggars and wanderers, are just not in the right place

---

[38] See Porter 1988 passim (especially xxxvi); Ingram 1991:105–54; H. Green 1964. Cf. Felman 1985:66–67, 80–81, on autobiographically "mad" *literature*: Gérard de Nerval's *Aurélia*, Flaubert's *Mémoires d'un fou*.

[39] Ingram 1991:106. True mad seeing: see Chapters 8, 9.

[40] See, e.g., Felman 1985:36, 42; Boyne 1990:33, 44. Cf. above, Chapter 11, n. 10.

within this one. The mad share a world with the sane. In some cases, they see it more clearly than the sane. But they have lost their place in it. They wander in it, unhoused: in the world, in their minds.

STAGE SYNTAX OF MADNESS

Literature's imaginative entry into, and representation of, disorder involves far more than madness. Tragedy is concerned with world disorder, moral disorder. Its madness is part of that. Disorder within a person, a mind, is a potent emblem and illustration of disorder in the world outside.

This is where the music and dance are useful. In the ordered Western investigation of disorder, tragedy puts center stage a specific set of images of music as well as madness, and linked the two together. Music is image of measure, and rule, the basis of right order. Madness is *para*, "beside"; *ek*, "out of," all this.

Dance images of madness express a central paradox, of unseen disorderly inner movement, articulated and ordered within a composed, choreographed performance. Madness is a *non*-dancelike *ek*: expressed through a genre that is itself a very highly wrought, rehearsed dance.

Tragic music and dance combine violence of mind and body with the immobility of mask and elaborate, ceremonial costume. Tragedy's mad violence is a wandering outside prescribed bounds. But tragedy presents it in and through prescribed forms of meter and syntax that incarnate those very bounds.

The audience did not see the physical or mental violence.[41] They saw patterned order, representing imagined disorder. Syntax and meter, organizing mad language, denied their words' insistence on *ek*, *para*, the swerve away from the norm, the violent, wandering *phrēnes*. Madness language speaks of disorder through its own order. Regulated syntax, grammar, and meter contradict the disorder their words express.

When a character swings between madness and sanity, the meter reflects it. Io enters mad, chased by *oistros*, and leaves in the same state, but converses rationally in between. The meters differ for each state. When she talks rationally she shares the sane meter of common dialogue. When mad, she sings in lyrics.[42] But the meters are still recognizable metrical units.

Violent madness, in fact, is lyric. Sometimes, as for Io, the poet uses astrophic lyric. These lines are not balanced by a responding verse, as in choric song. But they are made up of recognizable lyric units. Sometimes mad lyric lines are pierced by cries ("ah!"): quick excited short syllables,

---

[41] See further Padel 1990a:345–46, 364–65.
[42] *PV* 566, 877–78. Sane talk: *PV* 613–779.

giving a feel of confusion. But they are still incorporated into the metrical scheme. Wild cries are usually pinned within lyric order.[43]

The audience heard language expressing inner and outer violence, spoken from masked unmoving faces. The language replaces what it describes. The actual external movements on stage were very different from the anarchic chaos brought forward in the language. When they watched, they *heard about* mad figures with tangled hair, frothing mouth, bloodshot rolling eyes, disordered twisting limbs.[44] But what they saw were masks, topping bodies whose dance gestures, as in a Noh play, conveyed madness in controlled, stylized forms.

"Unmusical Music"

However, there were exceptions to the Greek image of music as order. Some music was licentious, dangerously overexciting. In myth, the Sirens' song is fatal, as well as instructive. There was military music with destructive overtones. War dance.[45] The Spartans, and others, went into battle accompanied by flutes.[46] There were some domestic dances too disgraceful for decent people to dance, like the *kordax*. Music was felt to express and generate good, but also evil.[47] Plato thinks the *aulos*, for instance, is potent for evil and bars it from his ideal city. References to the *aulos* stress its freedom, its excitingness, compared to the adjustable measures and tuning of the lyre.[48]

Yet even flute music was still music. There were worse sounds. They were not-music, yet thought of in music's terms. Battle, for instance. One Thebes-based chorus asks Ares why, possessed by blood and death, he is *"paramousos* [out of tune with] Dionysus-festivities?" Ares' noise and movements are the opposite of music. They are *para*, "beside," music:

> You don't toss curling hair in the circles
> of beautiful dances. You don't sing
> to the flute's breath
> music for dance-making Graces.
> You breathe on the Argive army

[43] E.g., *Cho.* 1047; *Tro.* 307–309; *PV* 561–74, 877–86; *Ag.* 1072–77; *Sept.* 149–62. "Inarticulate cries" generally: Stanford 1983:57–70.

[44] E.g., *Or.* 225–26 (tangled hair); *HF* 834 (frothing mouth); Twisting throbbing movements: see Chapter 3, nn. 20–21; Chapter 7, n. 38; Chapter 12, nn. 9–24.

[45] J. Anderson 1970:77–82, 93. Sirens: Padel 1992:65, 73.

[46] Th. 5.70. Borthwick 1967:22–23 reconstructs a Pyrrhic war dance, supposedly known to Athenians, from *Ag.* 826.

[47] See Ar. *Nub.* 540, 55; Thphr. *Char.* 6.3; Athenaeus 14.631D; W. D. Anderson 1966:2.

[48] Pl. *Rep.* 399D; W. D. Anderson 1966:64–66; Lippman 1964:72, 128.

with its weapon-clatter, inspiring them
with bloodlust against Thebes. You lead
a fluteless dance-troop in the dance.

This is the strophe (a stanza whose metrical pattern is replicated exactly in
the next, the antistrophe). The antistrophe replaces "you lead a fluteless
band in the dance" with words about the Sphinx's "most unmusical odes."
The battle noise, male human beings killing each other, ghastly fluteless
music, becomes a female daemon's destructive riddles. Both are "unmusical music": noise, "aside from" music, that denies the harmony of song.[49]

Unmusical music: the idea runs through Lyssa's attack on Heracles.[50]
Madness is a writhing in the mind, and a writhing performed by daemonic
aggressors attacking the mind and body.[51] It combines therefore the resonances of good, true music with its opposite: "fluteless" dances like those
of Ares, "lyreless" song like that of Erinyes, or "most unmusical" riddles
from Sphinx the "singer."[52] Daemonic music drives the human. It is contrary to the very idea, the nature, of music. It is music that is not music.

NONHUMAN PASSION

Daemonic music negates the nature of music. It is apt, therefore, for madness, which negates the humanity of a human being. Tragedy's musical
form contains, controls the wild disorder of passion and madness. As a
human form it also contains and controls the essential nonhumanity of
passion and madness.

Tragedy, I have argued, speaks of passion as the nonhuman in the self.[53]
Madness, supremely, is the nonhuman in the human. Madness-daemons
are mainly compound, female-*cum*-animal figures, human and nonhuman.
Snake hair, snake bracelets, vulture wings.[54] Orestes' Erinyes are "hounds"
of his murdered mother. "Go, hounds of Lyssa," cry the Asian maenads, as
Pentheus walks off to be torn apart by *his* mother; just as his cousin Actaeon was torn by his own hounds. The word "Actaeon" prepares a parallel
between Pentheus's impiety and Actaeon's. Pentheus's death-by-maenads
(egged on by hounds of Lyssa), Actaeon's death-by-dogs. Lyssa appears on
one Greek vase with a dog's head above her own, maddenings Actaeon's
hounds to kill their master. Lyssa is dog-madness, wolf's rage.[55]

[49] *Phoen.* 791, 808, 784–91.
[50] *HF* 871, 897; above, pp. 18–19.
[51] Padel 1992:66–68, 117–19, 129.
[52] See *OT* 36; *Phoen.* 1507.
[53] Padel 1992:152, 161.
[54] Padel 1992:158–60, 173, 180.
[55] *Cho.* 1054; *Ba.* 337–40 (cf. 230, which should probably be kept: see Dodds *ad loc.*);
Padel 1992:125, 163.

Lyssa's verb, *lussaō*, used of people means "I rave in madness." Used of dogs it means "I have rabies." The top Greek archer can hit every Trojan except Hector. "Only this mad (*lussētēra*) dog I cannot hit." Hector in killing rage is mad and (like) mad-dog.[56] When Athene deflects Ajax's murderousness from men to cattle, she "throws into" him a *lussōdē noson*, "mad-dog disease." He "bloods his hands on these beasts." Lyssa is also like Erinyes, or "Gorgon with hundred-headed hissings of serpents."[57]

Daemon, mad wolf-dog, snake: Lyssa and Erinyes incarnate nonhuman violence.[58] Human beings are their prey. The Erinyes feed on Orestes: he is their "appointed" beast, their quarry. Dreaming of hunting, they dog-whimper, "Grab grab grab grab!" This is their first word in the play.[59] Like Actaeon's hounds, these multiple, nonhuman causes and incarnations of madness tear you apart.[60] It is madness, above all, that brings into the open the possibility that human is also nonhuman.[61]

Madness has a nonhuman cause, and nonhuman effects. Both the maddening daemon and the maddened person are nonhuman. Daemonic causes of madness may be part animal. And, like Dionysus, mad (see Chapter 3). So is their victim. When you go mad, you are (like) animal. Io becomes cow when her madness starts. Orestes, who has suffered repeated bursts of madness, flashes lightnings from his eye like a snake.[62] He becomes like the Erinyes. The effect they have on him (repugnant horror, terror), mirrors the effect he has on other people. He is "sick from *phantasmata* [appearances, visions]." His *lussa* began in the night as he gathered the corpse's bones. But he himself looks like "one of the *nerteroi* [lower people, the dead]." His hair is wild: like snake locks of Erinyes. Like them, he "glares terribly."[63]

A mad person incorporated a daemonic bestiality that Greek society attributed to madness and crystallized in the body of madness-daemons. Lyssa and Erinyes embody the human form's invasion by the nonhuman. They have a human form and outline, marred by nonhuman attributes:

---

[56] Hector, "mad dog": *Il.* 8.299. *Lussaō*, of people: *OT* 1258; *Ant.* 492; Pl. *Rep.* 329C, cf. *erōtes luttōntes*, 586C. Of dogs: Ar. *Lys.* 298; Arist. *HA* 604A6. Of wolves: Theoc. 4.11. See above, Chapter 3, n. 24. Animal code for human behavior: Padel 1992:147–52.

[57] *Aj.* 452–53; *HF* 883–84; see Lincoln 1975.

[58] Dog/snake resonances: Padel 1992:123–25, 145.

[59] *Eum.* 328, 130–32, 147, 264–65; cf. Padel 1992:138–44, 173–74.

[60] Cf. Vickers 1982:98–105, with connections between loss of control and corruption of the body's visible form (see Parker 1983:326).

[61] Gender is another resonance here. Causers of madness are female, and female belongs with nonhuman, in Greek as other cultures: Ortner 1974; Just 1989:217, 262–63. Compare Renaissance "gendering of melancholy": Schiesari 1992.

[62] *PV* 673–74; *Or.* 480.

[63] *Or.* 407, 401–402, 385, 387.

wings, snakes, dog heads, talons, claws. So does their victim: human in-vaded, damaged by nonhuman.

After tragedy, this notion that the mad are animal or animal-like feeds another: that human beings have animal in them. The animal takes over in madness or passion. For Plato, failure to control desire is failure to control "the beasts within."[64]

In Western fantasy about madness since, this notion has been expressed differently in different religious and social contexts. The nonhumanity of madness is important through Renaissance thought. Montaigne finds it obvious that genius can edge over into the bestial. The Church pointed to "the guilty innocence of the animal in man," using this to explain how madness is a sign of crime, sin, and divine punishment. In some societies, the caged mad have been put on show like animals. Madness has been seen as inversion of the human form and spirit, into animal.[65]

Madness spoils human shape, figure, and face as well as mind.[66] It spoils the eye, channel of communication between the inside and outside, the individual and the outside social world. Here is a spoiling of the human that stands for all others: madness bloodies and twists the two-way chan-nel between how self sees, and how other sees self. Mad eyes are rolling, bloodshot, twisted.[67] Inverted vision is central to tragic ideas of madness.

Its prime example is the inversion of animal and human. Madness mud-dles civilization's basic knowledge of what is animal, and what human. Ajax sees animals as men. Other mad figures see people as animals.[68] The invasion of human by animal is implicated in the damage madness does, not only to the human form, but to human ways of seeing and understanding.

This damage goes both ways. Mad people and their eyes look animal. Orestes' gaze glints like a snake's. But they see animal too. Their eyes con-fuse animal and human. Ajax sees cattle as his human enemies, Agave sees Pentheus as a lion. In Aeschylus's lost play *Athamas*, Hera maddens Ino and Athamas because they reared Zeus's son Dionysus. She makes Ath-amas kill his son as a deer.[69] Like divinity, like passion, but even more so, madness threatens the boundaries of the human. It damages the human form and human ways of reading the world. It cancels distinctions be-tween human and nonhuman, both in human behavior and in human seeing.[70]

[64] Pl. *Rep.* 590C.
[65] Foucault 1971:72–78, 20; Screech 1991:23–29 (see Chapter 6, n. 9).
[66] Cf. *ephtharmenos*, HF 932; *amorphia*, *Or.* 39; *morphē*, PV 673; see Chapter 12, n. 62.
[67] E.g., PV 673; OT 528; above, Chapter 7, nn. 37–39; Padel 1992:59–63.
[68] See Chapter 7, nn. 36–37.
[69] Apollod. 3.4.3, 3.5.1; see Chapter 7, nn. 48–49.
[70] Padel 1992:150.

Madness is a stepping out from the social norm, the "safe house" of the *phrēn*. The nonhuman belongs to the unsafe outside. "It is mad to walk out, there is an abyss there, there are wild beasts."[71] Yet the nonhuman is inside too. The inside and outside, human and daemonic causality of tragic passion is ambiguous.[72] Madness's violence is human and nonhuman. Its nonhumanity comes from outside, yet is also, already, within.

[71] Laing 1971:42.
[72] Even what seems to grow from inside may have been planted from outside: see Padel 1992:134–37.

Chapter 14

SKIN: POLLUTION AND SHAME

BOUNDARIES

Deborah pulled her arm away from the doctor's hand because of some obscure fear of touching. She was right, for the place where the hand had paused on her arm began to smoke and the flesh under the sweater sleeve seared and bubbled with the burning.

"I'm sorry," said the doctor, seeing Deborah's face go pale. "I didn't mean to touch you before you were ready." "Lightning rods," Deborah answered, looking through the sweater arm to the charred flesh, and seeing how terrible it must be when one was the grounding path for such power.

—Hannah Green, *I Never Promised You a Rose Garden*

RUNNING THROUGH Greek images of madness is a sense of strongly defended boundaries between diseased and healthy, human and nonhuman. Boundaries that the sane perceive, between themselves and the mad. They are on one side. They put the mad on the other.

Ancient Greece was a culture of intense boundaries monitored by fear of pollution. In your home were boundaries protected by divinities whose powers overlapped each other. And other boundaries, also monitored by divinities: at your door, crisscrossing the city, threading agricultural lands and plantations outside.[1]

In Part 3 I have been focussing on madness seen from outside, on perceptions of madness, rather than fantasy about what it is like inside. I began (see Chapter 10) with stone: society's material, which can keep the mad, like the polluted, out. City walls, like domestic house walls (though these were often mud brick) were an ever present boundary, symbolically vital to an Athenian sense of self. I close this section with two chapters on what the sane actually see: the body. And start with another boundary: the outside of the self. The skin.

Another person's skin contains things you cannot see, which deeply affect you. Someone else's sickness or pollution is hidden in their body. It

---

[1] Protection and defilement of sacred land: Parker 1983:76, 160–74. Gods of boundaries, boundary crossing, domestic boundaries: Padel 1992:3, 6–8.

may threaten you from within, and you not know. You are endangered by association with a polluted person,[2] even by meeting their gaze. Menelaus is afraid of the mad polluted matricide; Orestes' eyes flash infectious lightnings like the poisonous eyes of a snake. This idea lodges in a web of fears about the eyes' powers to poison and hurt.[3] Eyes, channel between you and another person's inside, can hurt and pollute you.

So does touch. In the fifth century, out of this quarry of images about the body's relations with the outside world, the idea of *poroi*, "channels" (our "pores"), was born.[4] Explanations of perception assumed channels between inside and outside in which *poroi* played a central role. Skin too is site of two-way traffic between another person's inside and yourself.[5]

Greek doctors faced the outside of a sick body. They had not yet learned to know its insides through dissection, observation, and textbook diagrams. They wrote in military terms about their enemy, disease, but did not see it at work within. They fantasize endlessly, and lay down many unverifiable laws, about what goes on in their skin-hidden invisible battleground. Their strategy was putting things in and making things come out. Diet, emetics, purging, bloodletting. Invasion, and eviction.[6]

Skin-Sores

Skin, covering this unseen site of theory, was a place for signs: "These are signs: smell of the skin, mouth, ear, stools, farts, urine, sores, sweat, sputum, nose; saltness of skin, sputum, nose, tears, or of the humors generally." Skin-sores were a common such sign: "If there was a sore before the illness, or if one arises during it, pay great attention. If the patient is going to die, before death it will be either livid and dry or pale and hard." Certain skin colors and textures are dangerous signs: "skin about the face hard, stretched and dry; the general color yellow or black." So are some swellings: "Swellings that are hard painful and big indicate death in the near future."[7]

By contrast, external signs of inner danger in other people are lacking in the social world. "I wish there was some outside mark to distinguish bad people from good" is a cry expressed increasingly through the last half of the fifth century, in tragedy and outside it. You want to know if someone endangers you. Tragedy—genre of covering, costume, mask—first uses *charaktēr* (a word with a great future) for the outside of human beings: a word for the sign scratched on a coin to mark if the coin was genuine or

---

[2] See below, nn. 24–35.
[3] *Or.* 480; Padel 1992:60–62.
[4] Padel 1992:40–44.
[5] Padel 1992:59–64.
[6] See Chapter 5 n. 11; Padel 1992:49–58.
[7] Hp. *Hum.* 4.12 (Loeb 4:68), *Progn.* 3.30, 2.20, 7.30 (Loeb 2:14, 8, 18).

counterfeit, how much it was worth, and where it came from.[8] All you wanted to know about people.

Outside should give some sign about inside. Skin is where this could be put. In mourning, a common tragic motif is nail marking the cheeks. Red on white cheeks is sign of grief within:

> My skin shows bright in bloody furrows
> fresh-cut by my nails.[9]

All this wish for signing affects how the sane see mad people's bodies. In perceptions of the time, madness did have external signs. In the urban West, madness may seem to be about mental things only. But our world has for centuries been a place where mad bodies are mostly hidden away. Some writing about madness has mirrored this, in its abstract, speculative tone. This may change now, in Britain and the United States anyway. The closure of mental hospitals and wards has put patients back on the streets, often homeless, physically infectious, at risk, ill. As in the Middle Ages and Renaissance, they are now *seen*.[10] Both in popular perceptions and in fact, they bodily threaten the sane.

So, though we may think of madness generally as mental and unseen, in fifth-century Athens, as in seventeenth-century Europe, you expected to know someone was mad from physical signs: what their body did, how it looked.[11] Madness was physical and concrete, had the body as its base, and carried resonances of other bodily conditions like pollution and disease. It could apparently be caused by concrete things: for example, by blood on hands. When the Nurse sees Phaedra delirious she asks, "Is there blood on your hands?" That is how the chorus explains the first signs of Orestes' madness too: wet blood on his hands.[12]

The mad endanger other people's bodies. Their changed eyes, hair, and limbs are signs of madness.[13] Sometimes skin shows it too. Greek myth and medicine point to close connections between skin disease and madness. For doctors, skin-sores are associated with excess black bile. In *Problem* 30, the skin-sores of Heracles and Lysander the Spartan prove they were melancholics. Skin-sores tell of "hot black bile."[14] In life and myth, medicine and magic, cleansing treatments for skin disease and madness were very similar. In some myths skin disease has the same structural role—punishment for angering a god—as madness does in others.[15]

---

[8] A. *Supp.* 282; Padel 1992:14.
[9] *Cho.* 24–25; cf. *Or.* 960.
[10] See Gilman 1982.
[11] See Chapter 3, n. 34; Chapter 13, nn. 41, 44, 62–63.
[12] *Hipp.* 316; *Cho.* 1055; see Parker 1983:129.
[13] See above, pp. 74, 132, 140–43; Padel 1992:60 n. 31.
[14] *Problem* 30.1: see Chapter 5, n. 23; Chapter 6, n. 6.
[15] Parker 1983:208, 214–15, 218–20.

Skin was the outside. Boundary between outside and inside a person, dividing one person from another, sane from mad. Madness is mainly *done to* you. Lyssa sinks *into* Heracles's breast. Madness enters body, mind,[16] changing someone, making them dangerous inside, unseen. But the skin is visible. Skin-sores go the opposite way from madness coming in. They erupt. Madness or black bile is ex-pressed: on the outside.

Skin disease could be, then, an externally visible sign. Of divine anger or pollution, for example. Like madness, it may be punishment for breaking divine rules. The Delians, who did not stop a burial on their holy island, were punished with skin disease.[17] But skin disease might work *with* madness. The daughters of Proetus are punished for insulting god by madness *and* leprous skin.[18]

Gods threaten to inflict skin disease if you ignore them. After he kills his mother, Orestes goes mad, with his body wasted, his blood drunk by filthy Erinyes. But if he failed to kill her he would be punished with madness and

> ulcers that ride on the flesh, and cling,
> and gnaw away the tissue with savage teeth:
> on this disease, a leprous fur shall grow.[19]

Part of the disgusting surface physicality surrounding Orestes (foul rheum from Erinyes' eyes, their smelly breath), this idea of skin-sores gets over the untouchableness of his necessary act: of piercing his mother's skin.[20] All set him physically apart.

Athenians were used to the parallel between a stone building and a human body. You purged mad bodies with hellebore. According to Theophrastus, you also used hellebore to purify a house.[21] Stone walls were the city's skin. The sane kept the mad out by stone:[22] a hard boundary protecting them from the madness a soft skin boundary contained and expressed. The sane see madness according to relationships and boundaries incarnate in skin, a person's boundary, and in the house's or city's boundary of stone.

We might compare Foucault's argument that the treatment of leprosy in Europe after the end of the Crusades was the model for future treatment of madness. As leprosy withdrew from northern Europe it left the lazar houses, plus "the values and images allotted to the figure of the leper, as well as the meaning of his exclusion." The associations with which Europe

---

[16] See Chapter 2, nn. 13–14, 19; Chapter 3, nn. 41–43; Chapter 13.
[17] Parker 1983:218; [Aeschines] *Epistle* 1.2.
[18] Parker 1983:213–20.
[19] *Cho.* 280–300; cf. threat of madness, 287.
[20] See Padel 1992:102–105.
[21] Thphr. *HP* 9.10.4. Hellebore: see Chapter 5, nn. 6–8.
[22] See Chapter 10, nn. 6–13.

reacted to leprosy colored understanding of and response to "vagabonds, criminals, and 'deranged minds.'" These "took the part played by the leper."[23] The fifth century does not offer the same possibility: no dramatic chronological relationship here between responses to skin disease and madness. Instead, it seems, the resonance of each is the keynote of the other.

MIASMA AND DIVINE HOSTILITY

Madness and skin disease: either might be due to divine hostility or pollution. *Miasma*, pollution, was one of the most important aspects of Greek life. It was a stated cause of many wars. It made you ritually impure and unfit to enter a temple. It was contagious, dangerous, and "expressed a sense of disorder." It was connected with gods.[24]

In Greek as other cultures there were similarities between sacred and impure things. Both were surrounded with restrictions, but the two were quite distinct. One sacred law distinguishes three categories of thing: sacred, profane, and polluted. The sacred is not impure in itself. What happens if you touch it wrongly is cause and effect. Break divine rules by unsafe contact and pollution comes.[25] You are polluted if you enter a sacred precinct at the wrong time or in the wrong way, or defile it with bodily activity like sex, death, birth, or defecation.[26] Tragedy, so full of gods and their attacks, is full of pollution too.[27] Curses pollute you; and crime, especially murder.[28]

One factor in the relation of madness to pollution is how accidentally, involuntarily, pollution arrives. It operates, in Dodds's words, "with the same ruthless indifference to motive as a typhoid germ."[29] Something suddenly goes bad. Like good blood spilt on the ground. Or food dropped from table, that turned bad, and belonged to chthonic divinities, the *heróes*. Greek culture had an intensely concrete notion of good turning bad.[30]

It is hard to distinguish between pollution and results of divine anger or

---

[23] Foucault 1971:6–7. If true (it has been challenged), this follow-on may have been encouraged by preexisting Western (originally Greek) connections between madness and skin disease.

[24] Parker 1983:1, 4–9, 124.

[25] Parker 1983:11–12; Sokolowski 1962: no. 115 A9.

[26] Parker 1983:162.

[27] Parker 1983:15–16 argues tragedy does not overrepresent Athenian pollution worries: Athens's concern with pollution is shown by producing this genre that explored family violence, and its pollution consequences, so intensely. See also Padel 1992:4–6.

[28] On curses: Parker 1983:191–200. On crime: Parker 1983:104–43, 275–92. There was less pollution if your act of murder was considered appropriate (124).

[29] Dodds 1951:35.

[30] Padel 1992:103, 175.

enmity.[31] Both were catching. In the *Odyssey*, Aeolus gives Odysseus devastating violence hidden in skin: the winds, gathered and bound in a bag. He leaves the West Wind out to blow Odysseus home. The companions think the skin contains treasure, open it, and the freed winds blast them back to Aeolus. When he hears what happened, Aeolus tells Odysseus:

> Go from our island, quickly, you most disgraced
> of living creatures! It is not right for me to escort
> nor send back home a man hated by blessed gods. Go!
> For you come here hated by gods!

In Sophocles, Odysseus says they marooned Philoctetes on his island, because his yells of pain disturbed their libations and sacrifices. No word of not being able to sleep, or to bear his noise the rest of the time. They could not sacrifice. His *nosos*, due to divine anger, endangered the Greek army's relation to gods.[32] You must drive someone hated by gods from your own "island," from contact with you. Divine hostility threatens you. You see the mark of it on the skin, or in the story, of the other.

Madness in tragedy is often a sign of divine hatred. "It's clear I'm hated by gods," says Ajax. He is right, as the audience knows and the prophet later says. Iris asks Lyssa to madden Heracles "that he may learn what sort of anger Hera has against him."[33] Madness signs the anger of gods.

The sane are physically afraid of the mad. In Ajax's presence, Tecmessa is afraid for their little son (even though Ajax is now sane). Odysseus is afraid of Ajax mad as he would not be of Ajax sane. Bystanders flee in panic from mad murderous Heracles.[34] But there are other grounds for fear. Madness is sign of destructive divine attention, which is itself contagious. It may attract further destruction, like (to use an anachronistic image) a lightning rod. Heraclitus makes a play between *miainomenoi*, being polluted, and *mainesthai*, to rave, be mad. As if to be mad is itself to be defiled.[35]

"IN THE CONJUNCTION"

> I've got the pox! At last! the real thing! . . . which Francis
> I died of. The majestic pox, pure and simple! the elegant
> syphilis! . . . I'm proud of it, by thunder, and to hell with

---

[31] Parker 1983:10.

[32] *Od.* 10.20–25, 72–75 (see Chapter 11, n. 9). *Phil.* 8: fears of pollution are sharper when people are more at risk, e.g., in seafaring (Parker 1987:17), and this project of war *and* ships is endangered by spoilt sacrifices. Also Philoctetes' *nosos* is *theia*, "sent by god": see Chapter 15, n. 6.

[33] *Aj.* 457–58, also 757, 777; *HF* 840; above, p. 44.

[34] *Aj.* 531–33, 82; *HF* 1009.

[35] Heraclitus fr. 5DK (KRS 241, p. 209); see Chapter 19, n. 17.

the bourgeoisie. Allelujah, I've got the pox, and don't
have to worry any more about catching it. I screw the
street whores and trollops and afterwards say "I've got
the pox." They're afraid, and I just laugh.
      —Maupassant, letter to Robert Pinchon, 1877

Greek perceptions of mad bodies are bound up with fears of pollution.
Civilization rests on contact with other people. But good contact can turn
bad: can destroy you.

In approaching this notion at work in Greek tragedies, we must try to
think away our sense of medical contagion. It is not clear that the Greeks
had a notion of infectious disease, except for some awareness that contact
was dangerous during plague.[36] We should keep infection out of it, except
as a parallel: an unrelated bit of our own minds, something we understand
from.

We must think away also our inheritance of something else that deeply
underlies Western notions of contagious contact, and is absent from Greek
culture: awareness of sexually transmitted disease. Yet this is useful as a
parallel. It helps make vivid to us how Greek society felt about pollution.

Since 1500, fears of polluting contact have been bound up in the West
with the erotic. The act on which human life, if not civilization, depends,
has been a way of passing on a foul and finally lethal disease, which was
also intermittently associated with madness. (Though the causality was
not scientifically established till the late nineteenth century, random connections between syphilis and madness were made much earlier.)[37]

As Greek madness was said to do, syphilis put signs on the skin. "The
most remarkable symptoms of syphilis," wrote Auzias-Turenne, promoter
in the 1850s of a syphilizing vaccine, "appear on the skin. They are like the
label on a vase, or the signature of the pox written in large characters." In
Rome occupied by French soldiers, Théophile Gautier said he saw "del-
toids of staff officers spangled with constellations of pustules. Lieutenants
walking in the streets look like leopards, they are so dotted and speckled
with roseola, freckles, coffee-colored marks, warty excrescences, horny and
cryptogamic veruccae and other secondary and tertiary manifes-
tations. . . ."[38]

Syphilis made Western imagination invest erotic contact with special
risk. The poison showed on the skin and spread through populations. One
eighteenth-century author described syphilis hitting Canada, for instance,
at appalling speed: "We have seen a new sort of venereal disease here to
which the name of *Mal de la baie de Saint-Paul* has been given. Within just

---

[36] Parker 1983:219.
[37] Quétel 1990:162; cf. Chapter 3, n. 35, and Chapter 6, n. 40.
[38] Quétel 1990:113; Gautier, *Lettres à la presidente*, quoted in Quétel 1990:122.

a few years this disease has made rapid and substantial progress. . . . Fathers transmit it to their children. . . . When it breaks out in a family it is rare for even one individual to be spared. . . ."[39]

The parallel with pollution is very strong. Here is a contagion with overtones of moral and even divine punishment, visited on the children. As divine punishment is a persistent motif in some writing about AIDS, so was syphilis called divine punishment for sin. The sixteenth-century writer who invented the name syphilis gave this motif a Greek form: divine punishment for offense. The shepherd Syphilis offended the Sun by overturning his altars and replacing them with altars to King Alcithous. To punish him, the sun god sent him venereal disease. Local inhabitants around called it syphilis, in memory of the first person to have it.[40]

Furthermore, syphilis often meant that literature (especially Anglophone) was comparatively silent about a deep, intimate threat to society. Comparative, that is, to its pervasiveness. You would never guess from Fielding or Dickens that syphilis was increasing wildly in the eighteenth century, or that middle-class Victorian fathers caught it from family servants and infected their wives. Literature sometimes mentions the physical facts of syphilis, but does not (before the very late nineteenth century) go into it deeply. Again, this is like the physicality of pollution in most Greek tragedy.

Oskar Panizza, a Bavarian-born doctor who worked in a mental hospital from 1882 to 1884, contracted syphilis as a student, and wrote a play that explained the beginning of syphilis in Naples, in 1495. God (plus Mary and Jesus), angry with the sex-obsessed Neapolitans, asks the devil how to punish them. The devil suggests poisoning the site of their sin:

DEVIL: We should put this thorn, this poison—hmmmm—in . . . in the thing itself, in the . . . hmmmmm! in the . . . conjunction?
MARY: Delightful! Oh—delightful.[41]

Satan's phrase, "in the conjunction," pinpoints the horror in Greek pollution too: a powerful parallel for *miasma* in ancient Greece. Like syphilis, pollution destroys through the conjunction—in this case social rather than erotic—on which civilization depended. (Before the First World War, syphilis itself was called "the social disease.")[42] Contact with other people was the most needed thing; was what a city ran on. Yet physical and social contact with someone polluted held danger as physical and ruthless as

[39] F. Swediaur, *Practical Observations on Venereal Complaints* (1801) 4th ed., quoted in Quétel 1990:116.
[40] Girolamo Frascatoro, *Syphilis sive morbus gallicus* (1530).
[41] Panizza, *The Council of Love* (1895), quoted in Quétel 1990:45–47.
[42] Quétel 1990:145.

syphilis.[43] Orestes' visit to Athens, as he comes trailing Erinyes behind him, was commemorated in the Athenian calendar's "most polluted day." Aeschylus's Orestes argues he *must* be clean, he *has* been purified, by saying he has associated with many households and there's no sign of harm on them.[44] In this case, the Erinyes are there to prove otherwise. Faced with them, his "proof" is shaky as a British agriculture minister "proving" British cows do not have a disease (transmission unknowable, with an eight-year incubation period) by making his baby daughter eat a hamburger on television.

Contact with the polluted can destroy even a whole population: as Coronis did, who provoked Apollo's anger. She was his lover, but made love with a mortal too. When she was struck down, "many neighbors perished with her."[45]

In the Greek world, with different nosological as well as religious and social associations from ours, the "works of Aphrodite" were of course obsessing and important. But they did not resonate with fears of transmitted pollution as they have done traditionally (and now do again) in the West. Where pollution was concerned, sex was a bodily function along with others.[46] Where contact was intensely important and also potentially contagious and damaging was not in sex but hospitality.

Letting someone in, not to your body but your house, had a body charge with emotional implications that, for the modern Western world, is only comparable in intensity to sex. There were many divinely monitored rules governing relations between host and guest. In our vaccinated age, when researchers through four centuries have worked so long and often dangerously to understand bacilli, and yet we now face another sexually transmitted epidemic we cannot control, we should not underrate the physicality, and pervasiveness, of Greek pollution. Like syphilis or AIDS, it was physical, mysterious, and no respecter of motive.

PURIFYING

> My sister Eléonore . . . insisted on wearing gloves to read
> *Bubu de Montparnasse* because this novel . . . is about
> syphilis. On learning that someone had got "the great
> disease" she would immediately say, "That's what comes
> of eating in restaurants: spoons and forks are
> contaminated."
> —Julien Green, *Jeunesse*

[43] Antiphon 5.82; above, nn. 24–35; Parker 1983.
[44] *Eum.* 285; Padel 1992:182–85.
[45] Pi. *P.* 3.36; see Chapter 17, n. 3.
[46] Parker 1983:160–65.

Physical pollution from unknown causes was everywhere in the Greek world. So, therefore, were remedies: like the thousand useless cures for syphilis sold through the centuries. At Athens, purifications were needed. Purifiers treated disease, and disease was often caused by pollution.[47] Some purifying was done in temples; some on the streets, by magicians. The doctor-author of *The Sacred Disease*, opposed to popular magic, pious in his own strict way, attacks epilepsy's popular name of "sacred disease." "It is not more divine or more sacred than any other." Diseases are "all divine and all human." "I think," he growls, "that those who first called this disease sacred were men like the lot we have around today: magicians, purifiers, witch doctors, charlatans."[48] The way these witch doctors purify epileptics infuriates him: "In using purifications and incantations they do what I think is unholy and irreligious: they purify sufferers . . . with blood and so on, as though they had a *miasma*, or *alastoras* [avenging daemons] or were poisoned by someone, or had done something unholy. They should treat them the opposite way, and take them into sanctuaries with sacrifices and prayers." Proper prayers and rituals are better: "Divinity purifies, sanctifies, and cleanses us from the biggest and most impious of our errors [*hamartēmata*]. We put boundaries to gods' sanctuaries and precincts, so no one may cross them unless they are pure. When we enter we sprinkle ourselves: not as if we are polluted, but in case we have some earlier defilement, to wash that away."[49]

For charlatans and precincts alike, purifying is physical. Blood. Water. Its concreteness matches that of pollution and disease.

SHAME

> But there was so much that one must never mention.
> —James Fenton, *Nest of Vampires*

As pollution is in the body and can be passed on by contact, shame too is felt concretely, in the body. Boys who lose the wrestling slink home by back paths. Their shame is felt physically. They avoid the touch of other eyes on their bodies that have failed.[50]

Medical texts describe poignantly the shame felt by epileptics who "hide their heads" from people when they feel an attack coming: "They flee away from other people, to their home if it is near, if not to the most deserted place possible." These are the adults. Children "run to their mothers or

---

[47] Parker 1983:217–18.

[48] Hp. *DMS* 1.1, 21.8 (Loeb 2:138, 182); 2.1 (Loeb 2:140).

[49] Hp. *DMS* 4.35, 50–60 (Loeb 2:148–50). *Hamartēmata*: cf. *hamartei* in Phoenix's prayer to Achilles: see Chapter 16, n. 34.

[50] *Sōmatessin*): Pi. *P.* 8.82–87.

someone they know well, through terror at what they are suffering, since they don't yet know how to be ashamed."[51] Epileptics expect to feel ashamed. Children "don't yet know how to." Adults do not want other people to see what their bodies do.

Bodily shame engenders bodily isolation. We have seen how images of the isolation of the mad are complicated by other people's horror, fear, and anger. Greek texts suggest that the isolation in madness comes from the mad side too. The mad isolate themselves, for shame. In the *Phaedrus*, Plato implies that people in his day feel *mania* is shameful in itself.[52] The fact that gods cause madness does not mean you cannot be ashamed of it. (Even we in some contexts feel shame for what is not our fault: children are ashamed of parental behavior for which they are not responsible.)

But the shame of madness itself is inseparable from shame about what you did when mad. The madness is in the mad act. Lyssa makes Heracles kill his children. Lyssa is inseparable from the murders. Afterwards, he feels his touch, gaze, and presence may pollute others. "Flee my unholy pollution," he tells Theseus.[53]

Shame is felt, it seems, about both the madness and the act. You cannot separate them. Ajax is ashamed and dishonored by having been mad, having failed to do what he meant, and having let his enemies live; and he is ashamed at killing cattle. He feels "no longer worthy to look on any benefit of gods or mortals," caught up "in wild stupidities."[54] All these are elements in his shame. Io is "ashamed to tell of the god-swept storm and destruction of my shape": to tell of Zeus's approach to her and the distortion of her body and mind.[55] Phaedra is ashamed at her mind and language apparent in her delirium. When she recovers, she asks,

> Where did I wander from a virtuous opinion?
> I was mad. . . .
>
> . . . .
>
> I'm ashamed at what I said.[56]

The ex-mad are expected to feel shame: at how their mind, body, tongue behaved in madness.

Madness, therefore, is a wandering and shameful houselessness of mind and body.[57] It deviates, and that is shameful. It separates you from society, and that too aligns it with shame. Shame separates. The mad and ex-mad

---

[51] Hp. *DMS* 15 (Loeb 2:170).
[52] Pl. *Phdr.* 244B. See Dodds 1951:82–83 n. 2; above, Chapter 11, n. 30.
[53] *HF* 1233, 1229–31.
[54] *Aj.* 364–68, 373–82, 398–400, 408.
[55] *PV* 642–43, 673.
[56] *Hipp.* 240–44.
[57] See Chapter 11.

are seen as self-outcast, self-isolated in their madness, in their perceptions,[58] and also afterwards. For they have to live with the fact of that mad episode and the shameful things—bad, grotesque, dangerous, or polluting—they said and did in it.

[58] See Chapter 7, nn. 36–37, 40; Mattes 1970:96.

Chapter 15

DISEASE, PASSION

DISEASE AS *DAIMŌN*

Nosos, DISEASE, is *daimōn* in Homer. Children watching their sick father are watching fierce *daimōn* at work. Plague is the arrows of angry Apollo, clattering on his shoulders: the first sound and sight of divinity in Western literature.[1]

In all cultures, images of disease interact with other available images of how you feel hurt. In Greece, the core of these is invasion: a central image also in the experience of divinity. Disease, like pollution and passion, is part of the "coming-in things" by which Hippocratics explain how people sicken. Intrusion, armed attack, is also how *daimōn* gets to work on you, in you.[2]

In the plague that opens *Oedipus Rex*, the Priest sees the country sick with god-sent *nosos*:

> A blight on buds, on plants in the earth;
> a blight on herds in the fields; and on our women.
> No children are born. A fire-carrier god,
> a deadly plague, has swept down, driving our city.

The chorus hopes gods will ward off this invasion:

> No women feel the hurt of birth. You may see them
> one after another, quick birds on the wing,
> swifter than uncontrolled fire, flicking away
> to the western god's shore. The city dies
> in its citizens' unnumbered deaths. Corpses lie
> unpitied on naked earth, spreading death. . . .

Both Priest and chorus know this is caused by a god. Delphi explains it by "pollution ingrained in the land."[3]

In life, as well as tragedy, disease was treated as if god caused it. Despite white-collar medical complaints, the magicians' purification practices overlapped methods not only of recognized temples, but also of doctors.

---

[1] *Od.* 5.395–96; *Il.* 1.48–52.
[2] Padel 1992:50, 54–59, 125–35, 159–78.
[3] *OT* 25–29, 172–80, 97.

This net of Greek links between religious and magical healing continued into the Middle Ages (which inherited Greek medicine through Rome): in cults of "medical saints," in "incubation" near sacred wells, in water cults. All had parallels in the classical period, as a type of healing practiced by both medical and religious centers.[4] You had to purify, wash away, expel. Cities were purified as people were.[5]

In tragedy, one of the sharpest models of *theia nosos*, *nosos* caused by divinity and how it impinges on others, is Philoctetes' festering foot. A "raw-minded" nymph sent it because he trod on her snake in her cave shrine. For that sin, he suffered years of disgusting pain and loneliness.[6] No one who lands on his island will take him home. He is too foul. They give him alms, not passage. The sailors say, "Take him aboard." Do they really want to? Neoptolemus warns. "Maybe afterwards, when you are nearer the *nosos*, living with it, you'll change your minds." This *nosos*-stench (with its resonances of integrity corrupting) runs through the play:

> Raise me yourself, don't let the men
> get fed up with the terrible smell before they have to.
> It'll be bad enough living with me when I'm on board.

When Neoptolemus's scruples (he is taking Philoctetes to Troy, not home as he pretends) overpower him, Philoctetes is terrified his foulness has stopped the young captain "taking me aboard."[7]

MADNESS AS DISEASE

Nosos, "plague," "disease," could mean anything bad. It is also used for madness.

We speak of mental disease. We do not think it is infectious; maybe hereditary. But we do think it belongs in medicine. Yet in most societies (less so in ours, now) notions of illness and cure, of making disease comprehensible, are also tied irrevocably to religion. Fifth-century Athens did not distinguish literal from metaphorical meaning, or not in the ways that we do.[8] So when illness is an image for madness, each contributes real resonances of daemonic cause and cure to the other. Disease, like passion, is due mainly to outside things coming in.[9] Madness, disease, pollution, divine anger, all reinforce each other's fields of meaning. The images inter-

---

[4] Clarke 1975:16, 127–30; Lloyd 1979:30–45; Parker 1983:207–454. Purifiers: see Chapter 14, nn. 48–49. Incubation: Padel 1992:72.
[5] Parker 1983:235–56, 257–80, 219.
[6] *Phil.* 192, 1326–28.
[7] *Phil.* 310, 519–21, 890–92, 900.
[8] Padel 1992:34.
[9] Padel 1992:51–59, 118–33; cf. Clarke 1975:23.

play. We may see them as separate fountain jets. But in Greece they make one stream.

Tragedy shows interest in the developing medical terminology and treatment of its day.[10] Both tragedy and medicine are seriously concerned with the causes of human hurt. Like medicine, tragedy operates a causality of hurt in which two different types of cause, daemonic on the one hand, and organic, or the materially human, on the other, shift against each other.[11] The two collide most deeply in the word *nosos* and its resonances.

Ajax's madness is *lussōdēs nosos*, "frenzied disease," "god-sent *nosos*." Athene "threw it in" him. It swooped down on him. He is "sick in a dark-muddy storm." As *nosos*, madness attacks the body: especially *phrenes*. When Darius's ghost hears his son bridged the Hellespont and invaded Greece, he cries

> A *nosos* of *phrenes* seized my son.
> How could it not be so?

God makes you mad, but the reason may not be knowable by us. When a total stranger tries to embrace him, Ion asks, "Are you in your right mind? Or has some harm of god made you mad, stranger?" He thinks the man is "raving."[12] No question of divine vengeance: just something that happens.

Nosos attacks like a spear. Aphrodite's *erōs* "wounded" Phaedra. She is "broken down" in her *phrenes* by "terrible *nosos* of Aphrodite." Broken down: a word Homer uses for the heart "breaking down" in grief and fear, and which Hippocratics use for the body "reduced," or "broken," by fever.[13]

In the fifth century and later, madness and epilepsy were purified by ritual. Most of the gods specified by professional purifiers had special associations with disease, especially skin disease, and madness. In Aristophanes, the son of a mad father has him "washed and purified."[14] Of gods connected with madness, Hecate was particularly associated with very physically impure "stuff" and bad dreams or hallucinations. When Menelaus meets Helen in Egypt, having left a phantom of Helen on board ship, he thinks she is a hallucination sent by Hecate.[15]

The concreteness of madness fits the concrete Greek imagery of mind. Disease spoils the human body, inside and out. So does madness, which

[10] Collinge 1962.

[11] Padel 1992:57: see Vernant and Vidal-Naquet 1981:13; Williams 1993:33.

[12] *Aj.* 452, 282, 206, 185; *Pers.* 750–51; *Ion* 520, 526.

[13] *Hipp.* 392, 765 (*phrenas* is "accusative of respect" to *kateklasthē*); *Od.* 4.538, 9.256; Hp. *Coac.* 510 (Littré).

[14] Parker 1983:245, 208, 215–16; Ar. *V.* 118.

[15] See Padel 1992:102–106. *Ion* 1047–48; *Hel.* 569–70; O'Brien-Moore 1924:102–103.

twists and changes the human, inside and out. But the late fifth century, with the rise of medicine, was an age of speculating about physical *as well as* divine causes. Madness could be caused by fresh blood on the hands.[16] Discussing the Spartan king Cleomenes, who died chopping himself to pieces, Herodotus collects different opinions on the cause of his madness. Most Greeks say it began because Cleomenes made the Delphic priestess lie to the king he wanted to depose. Athenians say, because he invaded Eleusis; Argives, because he burnt a sacred grove in Argos. Spartans "say Cleomenes was mad from no daemonic cause, but because he kept company with Scythians and drank strong drink [i.e., unwatered wine] and went mad from that." Four explanations: three daemonic, one physical. Herodotus chooses a daemonic cause: "It seems to me he was paying for what he did to Demaratus."[17] But the physical possibility is in there too.

The author of *De morbo sacro* denies that god pollutes. He is not denying god can cause disease. But he objects to magical treatment of epileptics on two counts. First, if god is entirely responsible, epileptics should be taken to proper shrines. Second, he hates talk of god polluting: "If a god is really the cause, take the patients to sanctuaries. . . . But I don't think a human body can be polluted by a god. One's corrupt, the other holy. No: even if the body is polluted or hurt by some other agency, divinity is more likely to purify and make it holy than pollute it." His argument shows how close pollution was, in popular talk, to divinely caused disease, especially madness.[18]

This author wants all diseases to be thought of equally, in terms of humanly comprehensible physical cause *and* divinity. The disease called sacred

> comes from the same causes as others. From things that come into and go out of the body: cold, sun, and the changing restlessness of winds. These things are divine. No need to make this a special case, and say this is more divine than others. They are all divine, and all human. . . . Most are cured by the same things as caused them. . . . Whoever understands how to cause things in patients by a regime of moist, dry, hot, or cold, can cure this disease too—if he diagnoses the right seasons for treatment—without purifications and magic.

[16] Concrete Greek imagery of mind: Padel 1992:40–44. Of madness: see Chapter 14. Madness changing the human form: see Chapter 13, pp. 140–43. Madness caused by blood on hands: see Chapter 14, n. 12.

[17] Hdt. 6.66, 75, 84. Cf. the story of Cambyses, 3.29–33. Already part mad, he kills the god-calf Apis, and "because of this crime" went mad. Herodotus considers "sacred disease," and divine revenge for offending a god, among possible causes of madness. See Dodds 1951:65, Parker 1983:243 (with n. 44).

[18] Hp. *DMS* 4.50 (Loeb 2:148); cf. Chapter 14, nn. 48–49.

"Without magic": the last words of this powerful, angry plea for rational medicine.[19] But his very vehemence shows how popular were magic cures and talk of divine causality.

To some extent, therefore, physical causes of madness were considered side by side with daemonic ones. In *Bacchae*, a play that starts with god and is god-driven all through, Teiresias seems to suggest that Pentheus has been maddened by chemical means. "No drug can cure your sickness, but some drug has caused it." A form of chemical cause already in the *Iliad*: snakes feed on evil *pharmaka*, "drugs," which cause their *cholos*, "anger" (a word that has resonances of black bitter liquid). And there are a few tragic examples of murderous rage or folly supposedly caused by swallowing something "bad."[20]

But a *pharmakon* not mentioned in tragedy, hellebore, is the prime example. In the late fifth century, it can cure and cause madness. The idea of a madness-inducing, madness-curing plant lingers on into the Renaissance. After seeing the Witches, Banquo asks, "Have we eaten on the insane root / That takes the reason prisoner?"[21] Aristophanes' characters mention hellebore and black bile, nudging sometimes at physical explanations of madness. The emergence of *melan-cholia* as cause of madness and delirium itself points to increasing interest in physical sources of madness.[22] But in tragedy, the physical cause that invokes daemonic sanction against pollution— madness caused by blood on your hands, for instance—is far more powerful.[23]

Some scholars have stressed physical causality of madness. Others find it reductive.[24] But the daemonic acts through and interacts with the physical: it is not a separate category. Hippocratics, dedicated to physical cause and cure, use naturalism as a deliberate rhetorical technique, to deglamorize symptoms popularly thought to be daemonic.[25] But even for them, daemonic cause is still a reality. They invoke divine patronage for their

[19] *DMS* 21 (Loeb 2:182); see also 5.1, 16.40 (Loeb 2:150, 172). He uses a familiar homeopathic (see Chapter 17, n. 16) backwards (*DMS* 3.1 [Loeb 2:145]): "He who removes this suffering by purifications and magic can induce it by similar means." This argument sets aside the action of divinity (though two manuscripts here read *apoluetai*, "washed away").

[20] *Ba.* 327 (see Dodds *ad loc.*); *Il.* 22.94; *Ag.* 1407–408; *Hipp.* 318 (with scholion, "lest some enemy *se epharmaxe*"); cf. Ar. *Thesm.* 534.

[21] Roots, hellebore: Padel 1992:69–71, 101; above, Chapter 5. *Macbeth* 1.3.84–85. Homeopathy: see Chapter 17, nn. 15–16.

[22] Ar. *Nub.* 1275, 832–33, *Pax* 65–66. See Dover 1974:127; above, Chapter 5, nn. 3–4. Cf. brain injury: Ar. *Nub.* 1726; Padel 1992:13 n. 3.

[23] See above, Chapter 14, n. 12.

[24] Pigeaud 1981:376, 435–39 and passim. He finds Starobinsky 1960 too mechanistic in reducing Ajax's madness to "necessities of the body" (Pigeaud 1981:385), arguing that a concrete, physiological dimension to psychological and moral discourse complicates tragic motivation, rather than reducing it. See Williams 1993:18–49.

[25] Lloyd 1979:27–29.

human art. The Hippocratic Oath begins by calling on Apollo the healer, Asclepius, Hygieia, and Panacea as witnesses.[26] Aristophanes raises a laugh by isolating the physiological. That does not mean everyone did. Rather the opposite: Aristophanes takes things into the absurd where no one else goes.

In ages with a different outlook on "disease," madness as disease becomes differently concrete. In the eighteenth century, when most of the educated abandon purely divine causality of mental disease, doctors seeking secrets of disease in liquids and solids use mechanistic metaphors to explain mania or melancholy.[27] But in the fifth century, physiology is inseparable from daemonology. By the fourth century, a few authors write in terms of a solely physical cause for madness.[28] But physical cure and explanation went on interacting with ritual cure, divine causality.[29]

In our day, the fact that chemicals can control schizophrenic or depressive states makes many want to feel chemicals are also their sole cause. There is a willed confusion: if schizophrenia can be chemically described, contained, even understood, it must be (only) chemically caused. But this is too thin. Any complete account of a culture's understanding of madness must invoke the religious (or spiritual, or psychological) along with the physiological. Even Hippocratics operate with more than one level of causality. Chemical description and causality interlock with many others. A poodle can be chemically described and explained: but that does not explain how the one on your knee came into being.

From the twelfth century A.D. onwards, under the influence of the newly absorbed Graeco-Arabic tradition of medicine and philosophy, the West has been conscious that there are real, painful relationships between physical and mental illness; and also between physical and mental illness on the one hand, and social or spiritual deviation on the other.[30] Madness and religion interact with madness and medicine.

PHAEDRA: A "DISEASED LYING-DOWN"

Medico-organic explanation and magic are at work in the female response to Phaedra in the first half of *Hippolytus*. She suffers from "diseased *koita*."[31] An ambiguous word, *koita* means "lying down" in sex or sickness. The chorus consider divine cause in a spread of divinities specializing in

---

[26] See Lloyd 1979:41 (with nn. 162–64).

[27] According to Foucault 1971:87–88, 125–35, 150.

[28] Fifth century: Padel 1992:14, 114, 137, 138–47. Fourth century: Xen. *Mem.* 3.12.6; Parker 1983:243–45 (with nn. 44–45). Pl. *Legg.* 934C–D, *Ti.* 86B.

[29] Parker 1983:215–16; Lloyd 1979:10–58.

[30] See Ladner 1967:253 (with n. 113); Clarke 1975:114–17, 140.

[31] *Hipp.* 132.

possession. Or is this sexual jealousy? Has a woman got Phaedra's husband in secret *koita*?[32] That word, image for her disease, turns up in diagnosis of its cause. Has "hidden *koita*" caused "diseased *koita*"? Is this some specifically female sickness? They compare their own experience of childbed when they asked Artemis for help in pain.[33]

They have wound up, in Euripidean irony, with the totally wrong deity. Artemis presides over chastity and childbirth. Aphrodite, balanced against her in this play, is worshipped in sex, which joins and separates these. It is sexual longing that diseases Phaedra. A divine disease. Phaedra trusts the Nurse's promise of an organic magical cure for it, a drug. Aphrodite is responsible for Phaedra's "diseased lying-down," as she is for the physically broken figure of Hippolytus who also ends up "lying down": stretchered onto stage, his prone figure parallel to that of Phaedra at the beginning.[34] His commands to be lifted, carried, put down gently, parallel those of Phaedra to be lifted and held.[35] The play keeps them apart in their lyings-down. One at the beginning, one at the end. Aphrodite forced Phaedra to want them to lie down together. Both painful *koitai* come from *nosos* sent by Aphrodite, specialist in *koita*, in *nosos* that can be cured only by *koita*.[36]

"Eros Doubled": Madness as Passion

Wondering what's wrong with Phaedra, the chorus mixes madness, disease, and passion. In an age generating new images and explanations for disease itself, "disease" used of madness collides with language describing extreme, god-sent passion as madness. In later Greek centuries (maybe before), you could get yourself purified from obsessing love. Love as disease: a long-historied Western image that starts in Greece.[37] Outside tragedy, fifth-century rhetoricians and philosophers can speak of madness as a far point along a line of passion. "Eros is desire doubled: Eros doubled is *mania*." In the fourth century, Plato talks of taking pleasure "to the point of madness."[38]

In this language, madness is the far end of a continuum, the most intense degree of pleasure or pain. We have already heard Aristotle: "Outbursts of anger, sexual appetites, and other such passions change our bodily condition and in some produce fits of madness."[39] Madness is non-

---

32 *Hipp.* 140–50, 154.
33 *Hipp.* 165.
34 *Hipp.* 1400, 1361, 1445. Phaedra: *Hipp.* 180; see Padel 1992:133.
35 *Hipp.* 1361, 1445, 198–201.
36 *Hipp.* 765; see 283, 765.
37 Parker 1983:221; cf. Padel 1992:53.
38 See Prodicus fr. 7DK; Pl. *Phlb.* 45E; Dover 1974:126–29.
39 Arist. *EN* 1147A15. See Chapter 4, n. 1; Chapter 5, n. 29.

human passion: divine invasion, inner storm, bestial pursuit.[40] "Too sharp are the *maniai* of unattainable desires," says Pindar at the end of an ode about human longings that have "no clear proof" of success.[41]

It is crucial to tragedy that emotion changes *phrenes*. Theseus's anger distorts his mind, makes him act "badly." The gods think him "bad" because he would not wait for proof or divination, but acted "quicker than he should." He says gods made him "fall from good judgment."[42] "Terrible anger" attacked his *phrenes*. His "pride" destroyed his son.[43] Greed for money "changes" *phrenes*, "turns good *phrenes* to shameful deeds," says Creon: his own thin version of *Antigone*'s theme that "bad seems good" to the person "whose *phrenes* god leads to *atē*."[44]

Passion, like divinity, changes things, inside and outside. And in tragedy as in medicine, change is seen as cause of suffering, and a sign of something wrong.[45] And madness is the extreme of tragic passion. Oedipus's curse against his sons is uttered in pain and anger with "a raving heart." Antigone's *phrēn* "is mad with grieving" at her brothers' deaths. Clytemnestra is suspected of being "mad with pleasure" to hear of Orestes' death. Hippolytus's horses are mad with fear; Medea went off with Jason mad with love, "with a raving heart." In Greek tragedy, as in other eras of tragedy, "the possibility of madness is . . . implicit in the very phenomenon of passion."[46]

There are several conditions or experiences, therefore, to which madness is assimilated. Excessive passion, divine hatred, pollution, skin disease. Madness, passion, pollution, and disease are deeply bound to each other. Madness is seen in terms of them. But they are also seen in terms of it.

[40] Padel 1992:49–99, 114–34; above, Chapter 13, nn. 53, 64, 72.

[41] Pi. *N.* 11.43, 48.

[42] *Hipp.* 1320–24, 1414.

[43] Anger: *Hipp.* 892, 1334, 1434 (*amplakōn, hamartia, exhamartanein*). See his *deinē xustasis phrenōn* (and *menos phrenōn*) 983, 1123. Pride: *Hipp.* 1123.

[44] *Ant.* 294, 621–23. See Chapter 1, n. 3; Appendix, nn. 44–46.

[45] Padel 1992:68; Hp. *Anc. Med.* 10 (Loeb 1:30).

[46] *Sept.* 781; 967; S. *El.* 1153 (extreme pleasure and pain are the mind's worst diseases, Pl. *Ti.* 86B); *Hipp.* 1229; *Med.* 432; Foucault 1971:88; cf. 30, and ch. 4 passim. Cf. Elizabethan assumptions that extreme passion can lead to madness: Campbell 1961:79–83; Kinsman 1974c:273–320.

PART 4

Damage

Chapter 16

MIND DAMAGE BEFORE TRAGEDY

FROM MADNESS as imagined inner darkness, twisting the way you see (Part 2), and madness as deviance (Part 3), we move to mad behavior. Madness explained and judged.

I have brought out areas where Greek tragedy's ideas of madness differ from ours. From Plato to the Renaissance, interpretation of ancient images changed (see Chapters 6, 9, 11). But it is in *explanations* of madness that these differences really matter. Madness weighed up in action: its theological and ethical presence.

To reckon and respect this, maybe learn from it, we must start, again, with the linguistic background, because the words carry the explanations. Our own words and categories are different. We have to look at Greek madness from our own standpoint and in our words: but we must try to understand theirs in context. That context includes the prehistory of tragic madness and *its* words.

I have to plunge back to Homer and the alien net of Greek language again here. But I hope the conclusions will give us depth of field. For it was Homer (where madness is mainly absent) who laid out the blueprint for thinking morally about madness. His words are the vehicles for his, and tragedy's, explanation of damage. Watching these words in action might help us see where modern operations like psychoanalysis are useful in tackling madness represented by such a different world, and where not.

ATĒ AS "HARM"

Greek tragedy deals in harm: the multiple causes of harm, and its chain of consequences. At the bottom of the pile of many harms is harm to *phrenes*, "the mind." This harm causes acts that damage lives. It happens through passion and, more spectacularly, madness. In madness, Heracles kills his wife and children. In madness, Agave kills her son, and Athamas hunts his son as a deer and kills him. How did Athenian tragedy evolve this chain of harm, enacting the damage a damaged mind can do?

Behind tragedy's picture of the mind and what happens in human beings is Homeric understanding of inner and outer harm.[1] One Homeric

---

[1] *Phrenes* as "mind," Homeric background to tragic "mind": Padel 1992:20–23.

word, *atē*, points to the central role of madness and mind-damage in tragedy.[2] *Atē* has two main areas of meaning.[3] Damage to mind, and damage
to life or fortune.[4]

The common denominator is "harm," "damage": *blabē*.[5] This is the first
explanation of *atē* in the ancient lexicon, the *Suda*. The question modern
commentators have asked is, What sort of harm, essentially, is *atē*?

To answer, we must get rid of any hankering for "original" or "primary"
meanings. "Priority" of meaning is a big motif of *atē*'s critical literature,[6]
but in fact we cannot get back to "original" meanings before Homer. The
yearning to believe that a Homeric word "originally" meant one thing,
"and then" developed a metaphorical, abstract meaning, is a nineteenth-
century passion: part of the Romantic "search for origins" and faith that
the origin of something, like a word or an institution, explains its current
function, in a text or in a culture.[7]

This yearning has cultural and historical importance itself. It was part of
the nineteenth-century thought-world but is a hangover now. It does not
illumine Greek thought. It expresses personal fantasy[8]—which may be evidence for many things, but not for what an ancient word means, in someone else's language.

What we *can* do is watch, as objectively as we can, how a word behaves
in use. As foreign observers of Greek words in their ancient habitat, we
learn more if we study their behavior (like that of some leopardlike animal), without wishing on them prior categories of our own. The word *atē*
fed into Greek tragic madness, and so on into the broth of Roman, mediaeval, Renaissance, and later fantasies, and perceptions, of madness. Over
and over, medical writers return to Greek tragedy's madness. We must not

---

[2] Stallmach 1968 is the most sophisticated *atē*-study I know. Vos 1971 adds to its bibliography. Dawe 1968 and Bremer 1969:99–134 (the best I know in English) agree with its
general approach.

[3] Useful discussions: Dodds 1951:2–8, 18; Barrett *ad Hipp.* 241; Vlastos 1975:13–19.
See Padel 1992:162–63. Doyle 1984 lists mentions of *atē*.

[4] Barrett *ad Hipp.* 241 calls *atē* a disastrous "deterioration," in one case of wits, in the
other of fortunes. Stallmach 1968 goes first, like the *Suda*, for "harm." He avoids deciding
between *Schaden* ("injury") or *Verblendung* ("damage to understanding").

[5] See Latte 1920–21:271–78; Dodds 1951:32–38 (on *theoblabeia*); Dawe 1968:104–
105; Stallmach 1968:20, 46–49, 60, 80. *Blaptein* of *phrenes*: below, pp. 166–67; cf. Padel
1992:132–33.

[6] Dawe 1968:97 documents arguments over whether concrete *blabē* or mental "infatua-
tion" is *atē*'s first meaning. On priority of meaning: e.g., Müller 1956; J. Gruber 1963:56.
Dawe 1968 wants us to "make up our minds" about it.

[7] Padel 1992:37–39.

[8] E.g., Doyle 1984 opts without support for physical blindness as his "original meaning."
Once he nearly finds it: in a line where *atē* "seems almost to be used in [this] original meaning." He calls other passages "evidence for a metaphorical blindness," not asking what this
might mean.

muddle *atē*'s behavior, in its first context, with the overspill of these later fantasies onto our own imagination. If we connect Homeric *atē* with the later stuff we must do so knowing that what we bring to the connection, from our side, is ours.

INNER AND OUTER, CONCRETE AND ABSTRACT, MENTAL AND PHYSICAL

Above all, we cannot heave onto Homer's *atē* distinctions deriving from our own world: between mental and physical, active and passive, "concrete" and metaphorical. These distinctions, product of a line of cultures later than Homer and tragedy, get in the way. Homer and tragedy represent "the mind" as a collection of "innards," sited in the guts not the head. The way they speak of these suggests these are thought of as concrete *and* mental, literal and metaphorical, both at once. Before the fourth century, Greeks have no separate category, "metaphorical." We cannot speak of a relationship, or slippage, between literal and metaphorical, concrete and abstract meanings, in pre-fourth-century Greek. These are not two meanings "fused" together, for they have not yet been seen as distinct from each other. There are no two separate things to slip between.[9]

This means we cannot ask if an early Greek mind-word is concrete *or* abstract, literal *or* metaphorical. These questions miss the point. Mental, you might say, *is* physical. To understand an early Greek word for mental and emotional equipment—like, say, *phrenes*, "mind"—we have to watch what behavior the mind-word goes in for. What images it attracts to its neighborhood.[10] Equally, when we approach the way these "innards" suffer, the harms that happen to them, we cannot assume there is a "prime" concrete, physical meaning to their damage. Their damage, like themselves, will be (to use our distinctions and our terms) both physical *and* mental, simultaneously.

"I WAS DAMAGED"

> With him along is come the mother-queen,
> An Atē, stirring him to blood and strife.
> —Shakespeare, *King John* 2.1.

All the same, there seems *to us* to be an important difference between mind damage and damage to life, and it is we who are doing the understanding. "We" (whatever range of outlooks that word covers)[11] cannot leave our

[9] Padel 1992:33–44, especially 39.
[10] See Padel 1992:18–33. Stallmach 1968 insists on *atē*'s multiplicity of meanings.
[11] Cf. Padel 1992:10.

own distinctions behind. They are what we understand with. A Greek word's meanings will not walk over to meet us by themselves without effort from us.

"We" feel there are two distinct areas of meaning here. I want to get at the way they work, by watching the word's Homeric behavior in detail. It seems an odd way to approach tragic madness, that profound disturbance of soul that has shadowed so many central Western texts and so much thought. But some basic word-watching should set tragic madness in its Greek, rather than its later Western, moral context.

Atē is "related," in the mysterious, uninformative relation Greek nouns have with Greek verbs, to the verb *aaō*, "I harm."[12] When this verb is used in the active voice, its grammatical objects are usually *phrenes* or other organs of mind, but sometimes a person, life, or self. Wine "damaged" the *phrenes* of the centaur, Eurytion, making him rampage disastrously at the Lapith wedding.[13] "An evil fate from *daimōn* and wine 'damaged' me," explains the ghost of Elpenor, who died when he slipped off the roof in a drunken sleep.[14]

There is a luxuriant range of related words. *Ateō* seems to mean "I defy [the gods]."[15] *Atēros* is "blinded by *atē*," or "harmful."[16] *Atasthaliai* is "self-destructive reckless aggression." The first besiegers of Thebes died "through their own *atasthaliai*." Penelope thinks god killed her suitors because of their *atasthaliai*. Hesychius, the ancient lexicographer, relates *atasthaliai* to *atē*. He explains it as *atas thallōn*, "burgeoning with *atē*."[17]

Apatē[18] and *auata* (an alternative form of *atē*),[19] are "deception" and "blindness." *Aasiphrōn* or *aesiphrōn* is "*atē*-minded."[20] Some adjectives combine *atē* with the *a* of negation (the "alpha-privative"): *anatos*, *apatos*, "unpunished," "not exposed to penalty."[21]

All these have that essential *at*-root. But *nēpios*, "foolish, blind," a core Homeric word unrelated linguistically to *atē*, is also drawn into *atē*'s orbit:

---

[12] Seiler 1954; Müller 1956; *Lexicon des frühgriechischen Epos* (Göttingen 1955), and Chantraine 1968, s.vv. *atē*, *aaō*.

[13] *Od.* 21.297.

[14] *Od.* 11.61.

[15] *Il.* 20.322: "one of the gods" made Aeneas so "mad," *ateona*, that he squares up to Achilles, "a greater man, dearer to gods."

[16] *PV* 746; *Ag.* 1483; *Andr.* 1007; *Theog.* 433, 634. S. fr. 264 applies it to *phrēn*.

[17] *Il.* 4.409; *Od.* 23.67. Its *a* is short. *Atē*'s is normally long. But sometimes *atē* may have a short *a* (e.g., Archil. 73, Call. fr. 537). If you accept *atē* with short *a*, Hesychius's etymology is sound (Chantraine 1968 s.v.).

[18] Dawe 1968:100–101. Hera *apatēsen* Zeus, he was greatly *aasthē*, therefore angry with Atē herself (*Il.* 19.97, 113, 126): see Chapter 17, nn. 5–6.

[19] Coronis made love with someone other than Apollo, *megalan auatan*, Pi. *P.* 3.35.

[20] Hesychius explains it as *blabēn pherōn*, "carrying damage."

[21] Chantraine 1968 s.vv.; Stallmach 1968:64.

into the same nexus of Homeric explanation for harm.[22] Most of these words look to some central meaning, "damage," and imply that whatever else is damaged (a self, a life) there is also somewhere a damaged mind. Odysseus's companions died *nēpioi*, "fools': they ate the forbidden cattle of the Sun. This is the *Odyssey*'s first criticism of anybody. Homeric narrative, which knows much more, both morally and about the gods, than the characters do, will often use *nēpios* in this way. "He did X. *Nēpios*. For he did not know that Y."[23]

Damaging agents (the subjects of "to damage") are more varied than what gets damaged (the verb's objects). Subjects are things that impair judgment, like Elpenor's sleep, or wine. They include *atē*, and gods using *atē* as an instrument. Zeus uses *atē* to "damage" someone's mind.

The verb appears often in the middle and the passive voice. It is used most often in the *Iliad* (but not the *Odyssey*) in the passive ("I was acted upon"), especially passive aorist: the past tense denoting a single, instantaneous act. "I was damaged, I don't deny it," says Agamemnon of his role in the quarrel with Achilles.[24]

One scholar wants "a clear sign that *atē* must originally have described something *done to* someone, not something of which he is himself the originator." Believing that *atē* expresses divine rather than human responsibility for folly, he highlit the aorist passive in the *Iliad*'s use of the damage verb.[25] But he exaggerated the "done to" element in *atē*.[26] He ignored the role, in *atē*-related words and in verbs (like *mainomai*) central to the area of mental blindness and damage, of the characteristically Greek middle voice, which crops up often with *atē*.

Middle denotes "what you *get done for* yourself." But in many tenses it is formally the same as the passive: "what I *have done to* me." So *aaomai*, present tense, could be middle ("I get myself damaged," "damage myself"), or passive ("I am damaged"—by something outside me).[27]

The importance of this double possibility is vital. We have seen it at work already, with *mainomai*, "I am mad." The formal identity of middle and passive, in the present tense of both, means that the verb's form may reflect deep ambiguity about who is responsible for the activity: the person going mad (being damaged) or an outside agent. This formal ambiguity

[22] Bremer 1969:101–106; see, e.g., *Il*. 16.46, *Od*. 9.44; Pi. *P*. 3.82.

[23] *Od*. 1.8, 16. 686.

[24] *Il*. 19.95 (*atē* as subject in aorist middle), cf. 8.237 (Zeus "damaged" us [active] with *atē*). "Agamemnon's apology": Dodds 1951:1–27; Bremer 1969:105–109. Passive, aorist: cf. Chapter 3.

[25] Dawe 1968:98, arguing for total divine responsibility for *atē*. He attacks Seiler 1954 for saying middle is the "primary" use of *aaomai*, and active and passive uses are "later."

[26] See Bremer 1969:105 n. 19.

[27] See above, pp. 23–24.

corresponds wonderfully to the causality for folly and madness—divine *and* human—that drives Homer and tragedy.

We ourselves, reading in a mainly godless world, tend to assume responsibility is either divine or human. In Homer and tragedy, this "either/or" makes no sense. Cause and motivation are double. Divine *and* human, both.[28]

SOMETHING LOST, SOMETHING ADDED

"I was damaged." Agamemnon means he acted foolishly, without judgment:

> I could not forget *atē*, by which first
> I was damaged [aorist passive].
> But, since I got myself damaged [aorist middle]
> and Zeus took away my *phrenes*,
> I want to make amends. . . .[29]

As Agamemnon describes it, two things happen in this "damage." One: his *phrenes* are "taken away" or "led aside." Two: something comes on his mind from outside.

The first, also involving *atē*, happens elsewhere. Dolon was persuaded into a self-destructive act: to raid the Greek camp. "Hector led aside my *noos* [mind] with many *atēs* [*atēisi*]."[30] Characters tend to attribute this *atē*-act, "leading aside the mind," to other people. Like Dolon, they claim it was *done to* them. No one claims actually to have done it, or boasts, "I led his mind aside with *atē*."[31] The sequence of events as Dolon, the *atē*-victim, sees it, enacts the archaic and classical proverb *Engua, para d'ata*: "Give a pledge, and disaster is near." It expresses the involvement of *atē*-ideas, and Erinyes ("Furies") also, with contract and betrayal.[32]

For understanding tragic use of Homer, it does not matter that Dolon's book, *Iliad* 10, may be later than the rest of the *Iliad*. If we want to receive *atē* as the fifth century received it, we should be democratic about its Homeric appearances, not dismiss one as later, atypical. The "pledge" to

---

[28] Lesky 1961; Dodds 1951: ch. 1.

[29] *Il.* 19.136–38.

[30] *Il.* 16.808 (*phrenes* taken away), 10.391. *Nous, noos*: Padel 1992:32–33.

[31] Dodds 1951:19 n. 20 thinks *Il.* 10.391 refers to Hector's divinely inspired *atē*. He wants to fit *Il.* 10 to the *atē* of *Il.* 9.115. Agamemnon calls his part in the quarrel "my *atē*." I think it enough that Dolon's explanation invokes the *atē*-sequence.

[32] Pl. *Charm.* 165A. Erinyes and oaths: Padel 1992:165–66. Zeus was deceived into swearing his oath to Hera, *Il.* 19.113. "Oaths" and *atē* in archaic legal Greek: see Chapter 17, n. 48. Cf. *atē*'s *apatē* aspect, above, n. 18, see also Chapter 17, nn. 39–42. Unwittingly, Hector deceived Dolon.

Dolon, Hector's promise of horses, elicits the fatal act: *atai* are the tool by which Hector persuades him (or are the "promises" themselves).[33]

Agamemnon too says something got added to his mind. Zeus, Fate, and Erinys sent "savage *atē*" to his *phrenes*.

Atē is "sent," or "given." "I wept afterwards," says Helen, "for the *atē* Aphrodite gave me, when she led me to Troy." Atē takes hold on the mind. You are "grasped" by "dense *atē*."[34] The model could be Zeus's eagle, assaulting Prometheus's liver.[35] Something "sent," which takes brute hold of innards.

Atē's damaging effect on the mind, then, is twofold. It is a subtraction, but also a greedy addition. *Phrenes* are removed, led "aside." Here *ek* and *para*, "out of," "aside," mark the "deviance" of passion and madness (see Chapter 12). But *atē* also fastens on: "seizes" you, like passion.[36] Something is removed: something we ourselves might identify as judgment or self-preservation. And something horrific, some wild destructive force, is added.

[33] *Il.* 10.393. Cf. Epich. 268; Solon 13.13; Chapter 17, nn. 27, 47.
[34] *Il.* 19.88; *Od.* 4.261; *Il.* 24.480.
[35] Padel 1992:19, 120.
[36] Padel 1992:117–32, 138–61.

HOMER'S DAMAGE-CHAIN

THE *ATĒ*-SEQUENCE

All I had gotten I deserved, I now saw this,

And though I had contempt for my own deep pain
I lay drained in bed, like the same dry carapace
I had made of others, till my turn came again.

It could not lift the heavy agonies I felt
for the fatherless wanderings of my own sons,
but some sorrows are like stones, and they never melt.
—Derek Walcott, *Omeros*

THE MODERN lexicon, Liddell-Scott-Jones, has a confused entry for *atē*. Its confusion is illuminating. "Category 1" is "bewilderment caused by blindness or delusion sent by gods, mostly the punishment of guilty rashness": a Chinese box of cause and effect that hardly counts as explanation but shows how alien a concept *atē* is to us. Category 2 calls *atē* "the consequences of such visitation," subdividing examples arbitrarily into "Active" and "Passive." The only example of "Active" consequence is three words, "because of the *atē* of Paris."[1] *Atē* could mean anything here: for instance, the "bewilderment" of Category 1.

The entry shows how *atē* mingles the cause and consequence of harm. *Atē* is damage that is doubly spoken of. Mental *and* physical, inner *and* outer, *atē* dovetails into that Greek impulse to see inner and outer happening simultaneously. You infer inner movement—in this case, inner harm— you cannot see, from outer harm, which you do see. This simultaneity has a causal twist. The inner unseen harm may cause the outward, visible harm.[2]

In most but not all Homeric contexts, *atē* and *aaō* seem to mark inner, prior "damage" done to a mind, which then *causes* a terrible outward act. Call it the X-act. It is a mistake, a crime, with consequences: further outward "damage." Damage in the world. *Atē* belongs in a causal chain. Damage, X-act, damage. This chain is the word's main point.

Usually the first damage is inward, done to innards (see Chapter 15),

---

[1] *Il.* 6.356. *Archē* has been read here instead (as at *Il.* 3.100) but seems unlikely. It looks like a gloss. Helen has just said Paris's *phrenes* are not *empedoi* (6.352); *atē* fits this better.
[2] Cf. Padel 1992:67; above, pp. 100, 120, 148–50.

the second outward: damage to body and life. *Atē* from Aphrodite made Helen run to Troy. Consequence: widespread war. Helen regrets Hector's pain. It is caused by her and (that ambiguous phrase) "the *atē* of Paris." Paris's *atē*, when he insulted Hera and Athene, awarding the gold apple to Aphrodite, made these goddesses hate Troy: hence Troy's suffering. Paris's X-act hurt others as well as himself.[3] So did Helen's. From *atē*, to X-act. From X-act to war and (says Helen) the pain this causes Hector. Any mention of *atē* in connection with these lovers fits the chain: mind damage, X-act, outward damage. Whatever it means in a passage, *atē* also points to a whole sequence of suffering.

ATĒ, WINE, AND SLEEP

It is not always *atē* that "damages." Sleep and wine do it too. They often work *with atē*. Odysseus, explaining why he was blown off course in sight of home, says

> bad companions, and also a wretched sleep:
> these damaged [*aasan*] me.

Sleep visited him. Looking back, he calls it "wretched" though it was "sweet" at the time. It fooled him: like his later sleep, when the companions again disobey him, and eat the Sun's cattle. The gods sent him sleep "towards *atē*." The companions open the wind bag, the ship is blown back. *Aasan* slides into the idea of damaged *fortune* the idea of a *mind* not functioning in sleep. Odysseus loses consciousness, then Ithaca.[4] Inner and outer damage coalesce.

In the *Iliad*'s *Dios Apatē*, "Deception of Zeus," Hera gets Sleep to lull Zeus while Poseidon helps the Greeks. *Ap-atē*, "Deception," has *atē* in it.[5] In the core sexual relationship whose tension governs the world and the war, this episode has much in common with the oath Hera made Zeus swear, which resulted in Heracles' labors. Here Hera asks Sleep to work on Zeus after sex. Sleep reminds her of yet a third episode, when he put Zeus to sleep for Hera to stop Heracles sacking Troy. Heracles was blown off course to Cos. Zeus, furious, would have thrown Sleep from heaven to the bottom of the sea, if Night had not intervened.

Sleep's speech links the *Dios Apatē* to damage (like the damage sleep does to Odysseus, blown "away from his dear ones" as Heracles is blown away from Troy) and to Zeus's anger with Ate, whom he throws from

---

[3] *Il.* 24.28; cf. Coronis in Pi. *P.* 3.35. In both cases, one person's *atē* makes many others suffer.

[4] *Od.* 10.68–69, 10.31, 12.372, 10.47–48.

[5] See Chapter 16, n. 18.

heaven in punishment for the damage Ate enabled Hera do to Heracles.[6] Ate and Sleep are parallel. Both damage Zeus's mind.

Hera bribes Sleep to help her. Zeus makes love, sleeps, and only wakes when Hector lies spitting blood on the battlefield. Furious, Zeus tells Hera to stop "deceptions." She "beguiled" him.[7] *Atē*-language— beguilement, deception, damage—connects divine loss of consciousness with human damage.

Wine does too. Wine "damaged" that centaur's *phrenes*. The damage he then caused, caused damage to his *thumos* when he is mutilated in punishment. Wine and "evil *daimōn*" damage Elpenor. Together they explain his death, as bad companions and sleep together explain Odysseus's wind-bag disaster.[8] Wine and sleep join *atē*'s verb. The sleep or wounding of *phrenes* *is* the damage. *Atē* is like, and is at work in, sleep or drunkenness.

"I'll Hate You as Deeply as I've Loved You"

In this world run by gods, violent foolishness provokes violent response. Inner damage, inner violence, calls out world violence, incarnate in divinity.

Achilles tells Patroclus, "Don't fight the Trojans without me, nor lead the fighting to Troy, lest a god enter the battle against you." Zeus, wanting Patroclus's death, rouses *thumos* in his breast. He presses on to Troy. *Meg' aasthē*: "he was greatly damaged," and *nēpios*, a "fool." His error is met by divine *atē*. Apollo hits him and undoes his armor. *Atē* grips his *phrenes*. His limbs dissolve. He stands stunned. Someone wounds him. Then Hector kills him.[9] Mind damage leads to body damage, *atē*, and death.

There is a morality behind the answering violence. Zeus hates violent *aphradiē*, "in-sanity," "un-thinkingness," and punishes its unjust acts. Hesiod advises listeners (presumably on private incomes) to turn their *thumos*, "spirit," away from *aesiphrona*, "damage-minded" acts. You must inherit riches:

> Money shouldn't be grabbed. God-given wealth
> is better. If someone seizes riches violently,
> with his hands, or talks his way into it as often happens
> when profit deceives (*exapatēsei*) the mind . . . ,
> gods weaken him. They shrink his house. He's not rich
> for long. Like someone who harms a suppliant or stranger,
> seduces his brother's wife . . . , harms orphaned children—

[6] *Il.* 14.236, 255–61, 19.130.
[7] *Il.* 15.10, 75; *apatai, Il.* 15.31; *ēpatēsas,* 15.33.
[8] *Aase: Od.* 21.296, 297; cf. 21.201. *Blaptei: Od.* 21.294, 11.61.
[9] *Il.* 16.688, 691, 87–96, 90, 100, 252, 685–87, 791, 804, 805–21.

madness [*aphradiē*]!—or, with rude, bad-tempered insults,
hurts his own father at the threshold of old age.
Zeus is furious with men like that. At the end, he sends
a harsh response [*amoibē*] for all these wicked deeds.
Turn your heart completely from such damage-minded acts.

Mad violence to others—stealing, intrafamily cruelty, or adultery—are
aphradiē, mad recklessness. *Aesiphrona erga*, damage-minded acts. They call
out an equally violent *amoibē*: a word for "punishment" that also means
"answer."[10]

Gods have a heavy stake in the human mind, as in all human feelings and
relationships.[11] They are also deeply concerned with damage. They are the
environment's violence. They are, and are in, wind, storm, and fire. In the
human world, they send, are, and are in damaging passions: sexual passion, murderous fury.[12] In all this, *atē* points to a bitter paradox. The same
divinity that stimulates a fatal act demands "penalty" for it.[13] This paradox
explains Erinyes as well as *atē*. They demand murder; and they punish it.[14]

"The one who gave the blow can heal it" is an important principle in
archaic Greek imagination, as in some other cultures. (Compare the Do-
lorous Stroke in Arthurian legend.) It is homeopathic, like much Greek
medicine and magic,[15] and reversible. *Atē* and Erinyes may incarnate this
principle, but every god, however large their persona, can operate according to it. All gods punish as well as promote human beings within their
own, jealously policed, spheres of action.[16] Aphrodite, for example, favors
Helen (and men who desire her), yet she is the god most likely to hurt her.
Careful! she says (when Helen refuses sex with Paris in the most bravely
insulting words anyone in Homer offers to a god): if you don't obey me,
"I'll hate you as deeply as I've loved you."[17]

This principle underlies tragedy as well as Homer. Divinity punishes in
the same area in which it helps. "Good" divine attention can turn "as
deeply" bad. That which god commands, god also punishes. This is at
work in tragic madness and its "double bind" (see Chapter 19). In
Homer's *atē*-sequence, it means divinity may cause the mind damage that
causes the X-act. But divinity may also punish that act with life damage,
afterwards.

---

[10] *Erg.* 320–36. *Aesiphrona*: cf. *Od.* 15.470.
[11] See Chapter 13, n. 15; Padel 1992:16–17, 139–40.
[12] Padel 1992:114–116, 152–57, 125–33.
[13] Stallmach 1968:4.
[14] Padel 1992:166.
[15] See Chapter 5, n. 10; Padel 1992:69.
[16] Dodds 1951:98 n. 100; Vernant 1980:103; Padel 1990b:104, 166; above, Chapter
15, n. 16.
[17] *Il.* 3.412–17. Padel 1992:103; above, Chapter 14, n. 30.

Helen says Aphrodite "sent" her *atē*. In the *Odyssey* a woman damaged by Helen's act spells out divine agency behind damaged *phrenes* that damage lives. Penelope says god "stirred" Helen:

> before that, she did not place in her *thumos*
> bitter *atē*, by which sorrow first came also to us.

Divine "stirrings," plus Helen's self-"placing" of *atē* in her *thumos*, explain the "shameful" act and "suffering to us."[18] We have already heard what Penelope says to Eurycleia's claim that Odysseus has arrived. Penelope says Eurycleia is crazy:

> The gods have made you mad.
> They can make even the wisest people
> *aphrōn* [mad] and turn an idiot to wisdom.
> They have damaged you. Before this
> you were wise in your *phrenes*.[19]

Gods are responsible for *atē* and madness. But so, somehow, are human beings. Penelope's verb for Helen, "place in," is middle voice like *aaomai*.[20] Getting *atē* into *phrenes* was something Helen did "for" herself. But Penelope puts gods first, implying that gods are *more* responsible for Helen's responsibility.

Crime caused by *atē* offends humans *and* gods. Either may punish it.[21] Men mutilate the centaur. But when Odysseus yields to sleep sent by gods and his companions eat the Sun's cattle, divine anger kills them. Divinity caused the crime. "I knew *daimōn* was planning something bad" says Odysseus, who cannot stop them landing on the Sun's isle. Yet divinity punishes them too.[22]

"AND THEN": *ATĒ* AS CONSEQUENCE

As divine favor can become hatred, so *atē* as cause can become *atē* as "answer": as consequence, punishment. This is *atē*'s other main Homeric role.

Zeus is "deceived" by Hera and Ate into swearing that the hero born next (who should be his son Heracles) will be a great king. "Zeus didn't notice the fraud, but swore a great oath, *and then* was greatly *aasthē*." Hera delayed Heracles' birth, and another hero was born first, whom Heracles was bound to serve. Sharp *achos*, sorrow, "hit Zeus in his deep *phrēn*":

[18] *Od.* 23.11–16.
[19] *Od.* 23.222–24; cf. Chapter 2, n. 32.
[20] See Chapter 3, n. 2.
[21] Divine options at both stages of *atē*: below, nn. 39–43.
[22] *Od.* 12.297–420, especially 295, 337–38, 372.

"mental" pain, concretely expressed. This is the consequence of damage Ate caused.[23]

The consequential force of *atē* is not so clear, or so common, as the causal. There are not many Homeric passages where *atē* or *aaō* unambiguously refer to terrible consequences. Most wrap it up, leaving the word like a time bomb in the sequence. They do not spell out what *atē* did. To say precisely what *atē* means in them, interpretation has to dance a bit, or bluster. For instance, a murderer suffers *atē*: but is it cause here, or consequence?

> As when dense *atē* grasps a man
> who, having killed someone in his own country,
> arrives in a land of foreigners. . . .[24]

If you think of *atē* only as prior mind damage, causal harm, you say *atē* made the murderer do his crime. But the word order is odd. If you prefer *atē* as consequence, you say the murderer's *atē* is life damage: exile, the result of his crime. Either way, you have to argue it. There's no way to know objectively. It is no good category spotting Homer's uses of the word.[25]

One scholar, wanting a concrete, original meaning—*atē* as "something *done to* you"—thinks it was originally consequence. He weights interpretation of unspelled-out lines, like these, in favor of *atē* as physical consequence, and equates this with the purely external: with physical damage. He thinks any mental angle is "secondary," and stresses the penalty-like aspect of *atē*.[26] He assumes emotion comes from within, and is not "done to" you. But "done to you" is exactly how Homeric and tragic Greek describes emotion. *We* think of emotion coming from inside. Greek does not. If "mind" is thought of concretely, as it is in Homer and tragedy, then harm done to it is also concrete.[27] *Atē* may be as concrete in "mental" damage as in "physical" consequences.

This scholar also equates "nonmental," that is, physical, only with consequences. But if we do not make this equation, as Homer does not, *atē* does not have to be "primarily" a consequence. Consequences do not have

---

[23] *Il.* 19.113 (see Dawe 1968:98 on *epeita* here), 125.

[24] *Il.* 24.480–81.

[25] Dawe 1968:95–100, looking for a single meaning in each usage, finds seven: misfortune, forced error, unforced error, wrongdoing (perhaps part of unforced error), "stupefaction," penalty, and allegory (by which he means personification; see below, n. 35). Stallmach 1968 keeps multiple meanings in play simultaneously.

[26] Dawe 1968:98–99; cf. Bremer 1969:105 n. 19. The penalty side is vital *after* Homer (below, nn. 46–47).

[27] See Padel 1992:114–61, 40–44.

to be purely nonmental to be *atē*, either. The mutilated centaur is (among other things) in pain, the punishment for his fatal act. But he goes off "carrying his *atē*" in his *aesiphrōn thumos*: his "mind-damaged spirit."[28] Zeus's sorrow at Heracles' labors is mental pain but, as we have seen, physically expressed. It "hit his deep *phrēn*." *Phrēn* or *thumos* is involved even when the pain is physical, and when the damage is consequential.

Atē as consequence comes at the point in the sequence where we ourselves would locate guilt. But cross-cultural readings of guilt are a complicated affair.[29] We, from our thought-world, might read the pain which the centaur carries in his spirit after punishment as guilt. I doubt the Homeric line means that. But when guilt does get going, *atē* can absorb it. When guilt becomes an accepted part of crime's consequence, *atē* will be able to mean the pain of guilt. Guilt becomes part of the "and then" pain.[30]

With Zeus's mental agony over Heracles, which offers the clearest Homeric linkage between mind-damage *atē* as cause and mind-damage *atē* as consequence (where "and then" qualifies "was damaged" and clearly refers to the consequence), there is no guilt. We may call Zeus sad or angry, watching Heracles laboring when he should be a king.[31] But Homer says Zeus is wounded. There is no sign of guilt (or the modern worry, "It's worse that it's my fault . . .").

Atē is nomadic, in fact, in the damage sequence. Any mention of it gestures to the whole causal chain. We cannot separate penalty and consequence from the misjudgment and mind-damage that provoke it. Across the individual passages, *atē*'s reference shifts: between damaged mind, agonizing consequences of the X-act, and possibly on occasion the X-act itself.[32]

The centaur departs, "damaged in his *phrenes*, bearing *atē* in his mind-damaged *thumos*." His *phrenes* were "damaged" by wine before he went berserk: does this *atē* refer to that mind-damage? Or is he now mind-damaged differently, as a *result of* his punishment? Or is *atē* here the physical consequence, the punishment, the mutilation and its pain? But he is "bearing" it "in his *thumos*," his "spirit."

This passage alone shouts at us that we can rarely fix an English word as guaranteed meaning to *atē*. Rather, it *exactly* means something both su-

---

[28] *Od.* 21.302; see below, nn. 8, 10.

[29] Bremer 1969, chs. 3–6, discusses Homeric in relation to tragic guilt, and analyzes centuries of guilt's interpretation as *hamartia*. See below, Chapter 19.

[30] Dodds 1951:5–6 denies that *atē* had "originally" any connection with guilt, but arguments about origins do not help: above, p. 168; Padel 1992:37–39. Arrival of "guilt-culture," in Dodds's still compelling story: Dodds 1951:28–63. Cf. body-felt shame: above, Chapter 14, nn. 50–51.

[31] *Il.* 19.125, 132–33.

[32] See perhaps *Il.* 6.356. This is concrete *atē* in a different sense; cf. Appendix, nn. 30, 42, 52.

premely important and rather vaguely edged: the presence of the sequence. Wine damages *phrenes*. The centaur does "bad things." Heroes punish him. The centaur leaves, again "damaged in *phrenes*," "carrying *atē* in his spirit," which is itself "mind-damaged."[33] It is all a muddle of damage. *Atē* is the medium through which the story works.

PERSONIFYING THE DAMAGE-CHAIN

Inter atē *et Atē non semper distingui potest.*
—Italie, *Index Aeschyleus*

Homer personifies *atē* twice. Here, according to conventions of scholarship and poetry that imitates Greek, we start calling her Ate. But orthography makes no difference to how she operates.

Personification, the externalizing and divinizing of states of body and mind, is a vital part of Greek imagination. Ate, like most states of being, especially mind-damaging ones, is female. Lyssa, Mania, Erinyes—and Ate.[34] But unlike tragic Lyssa, Homeric Ate has a varying role in the damage-chain.

She appears first in a speech to Achilles. The *atē*-sequence often calls the X-act "error," like Zeus's oath to Hera, or Odysseus's falling asleep in sight of Ithaca. Phoenix is apologizing for Agamemnon, whose wrong toward Achilles is the *Iliad*'s prime image of *atē*. (Ten books and many deaths further on, Agamemnon himself will say *atē* harmed him.) Trying to soften Achilles, Phoenix says that if someone *hamartei*, "goes wrong," "errs," prayers can help to get that wrong forgiven. "Prayers" run after Ate to repair her damage.

Ate, "harming human beings," "strong and fleet footed over the whole earth," outruns Prayers. But if someone refuses them, refuses (like Achilles) apologies for *atē*-caused injury, Prayers complain to Zeus. They ask that Ate "follow" that man. Anyone who refuses them will, "being harmed, pay the penalty." Prayers aim to heal Ate's damage, but they loose her, like a boomerang, against anyone who blocks their reparation.[35] Ate causes damage, goes "in front of" Prayers. But she also "follows," the consequence of refused apology. She is at the front, and at the back: a dramatization of the *atē*-sequence.

The other personified image is Agamemnon's *atē*: the *atē* that drives the plot of the whole *Iliad*. Agamemnon narrates the *atē* of his divine parallel: Zeus (along with Erinys and Fate) sent him *atē*, but even Zeus once suf-

---

[33] *Od.* 21.301–302, 21.297–98, 301–302. *Thumos*: Padel 1992:27–30.

[34] Padel 1992:157–63. Mania, Lyssa: Padel 1992:79–81; above, Chapter 2.

[35] *Il.* 9.499–500, 504, 507, 512; cf. 19.136. "Error": see Chapter 19, nn. 10–15. (*Il.* 9 with its personifications is thought to be late, like *Il.* 10; but see Chapter 16, n. 33.)

fered *atē*, too. Agamemnon personifies Zeus's *atē* as he personifies the sources of his own. "Harmed," Zeus threw Ate out of heaven:

> Angry in his *phrenes*, he took Ate by her head
> with its shining locks, and swore a strong oath
> she should never come again to Olympus
> and the starry sky: Ate, who damages all.
> So he spoke, and flung her from the starry sky,
> whirling her in his hand. And soon she came
> to the fields of human beings.[36]

What happens to Ate is the *atē*-sequence: a fatal act, a punishment. It explains why *atē* is so near human beings. She is a refugee, walking "on the heads of mortals, harming them." She was a first product of Zeus, his "eldest daughter," but he is protected from "error" now. Her business is with us.

All this emphasizes priority. Ate is Zeus's *first* daughter, who runs *in front* of Prayers. She *causes* Zeus's oath, *causes* crimes for which the lame Prayers beg forgiveness afterwards. Yet Ate as "and then" penalty is here too. Anyone refusing Prayers is punished by *atē* following. Zeus "is greatly *aasthē*." Afterwards.

Homeric personifications are not a separate category. They fit *atē*-meanings and resonances throughout Homer: mainly cause, partly consequence. Personification does not divide off "a meaning" of a word. "Love" does not "mean" anything different, as a feeling, if its daemonic cause is personified. It is one richness of Greek that it can personify (or daemonify) emotion, while treating it simultaneously as an inwardly felt force.[37]

These elaborate personifications of *atē* are unique; no one else personifies *atē* like this. Later archaic poets use genealogical imagery for her, but only in brief images: one or two words, no more. Nowhere again does *atē* have such lavish iconography: swift feet, shining hair. When we explore tragic madness as divine (Chapter 20) we may see why.[38]

THE TWO "STAGES" AND THEIR DIVINE OPTIONS

Personified or straight, *atē*'s core function in Homer is to invoke, but not spell out, the whole damage-chain. Harm happens, first, inside an individual: stage 1—prior damage, mind damage. That harm *then* is expressed in action, *then* felt outside in the world: stage 2—"calamity" following the X-act, "Harm" to life, body, fortune.

---

[36] *Il.* 19.126–31.
[37] *Pace* Dawe 1968; above, n. 25. Personification: see Buxton 1982; Burkert 1985:183–86; Padel 1992:157–59.
[38] See Chapter 19, nn. 39–40, Appendix; Padel 1992:162–64.

Each stage has a divine interpretive option. Achilles sees Agamemnon's behavior as stark stage 1: a damaged human mind. But Agamemnon later sees his *atē* with a divine spin on it: Zeus, Erinys, and Fate sent it.[39] The notion that god inflicted it is very close to *apatē*, "deception."

The issue of *atē* in the *Iliad* (as we have it) is interwoven with the role of *apatē*. Both are diffused through the relationships of and between Zeus and Agamemnon. Agamemnon is *nēpios* to credit the dream Zeus sends him. He "did not know what deeds Zeus planned." When the truce is broken, Agamemnon says Zeus will be angry at this *apatē*. In a sense he is right, for his vision (that Zeus will destroy Troy) will come true. Yet this breaking of the truce is initiated by Zeus himself. The dream he sent was false. He makes sure the Trojans break their oath and tricks Agamemnon into thinking that victory is near, and divinely ensured. Divine trickery interlocks with that of human beings. But the deceived human leader is mirrored in the deceived Zeus of the *Dios Apatē*.[40]

The Zeus-Agamemnon parallel is vital to the *Iliad*'s *atē*-stories. Some relation between *apatē* and *atē* is intrinsic to the *Iliad*'s plot. Achilles must accept Agamemnon's apology. He can accept it, because it draws the parallel between Zeus and Agamemnon. Even Zeus suffered *atē*. *Therefore* Achilles can relent towards Agamemnon, and Zeus has fulfilled his promise to help the Trojans, temporarily. The oath Zeus swore to Thetis (to honor her son by helping Troy) is unmade by human rhetorical use of the oath he swore to Hera under the deceiving stress of *atē*.[41]

It was the *apatē* dimension of *atē*, perhaps, that made Spenser give Ate's name to the lying hag, companion to Duessa. "Mother of debate / And all dissention," she lives "Hard by the gates of hell,"

> There whereas all the plagues and harmes abound,
> Which punish wicked men, that walke amisse.

She incarnates strife, caused the fall of Babylon, Thebes, Rome, and Troy. She caused the centaur's havoc among the Lapiths, and treachery among friends and brothers. Round her house are "wicked weedes" which she grew from "little seedes." Spenser brings Ate's doubleness—cause *and* consequence—into play by describing Apate's hands: "That one did reach, the other pusht away."[42]

"Deception" has to be deception by someone. Dolon is "beguiled" into folly by a man. But usually *atē* as *apatē* involves deception by god: stage 1, with divine option.

---

[39] See *Il.* 1.412, 9.115–16, 19.88. *Apatē* dimension of *atē*: Stallmach 1968:64; above, Chapter 16 nn. 5, 18.

[40] *Il.* 2.38, 4.163–68, 72, above, p. 178. Trickery: see Detienne and Vernant 1978.

[41] *Il.* 1.528; 19.112–13.

[42] *Faerie Queene* 4.1.19–30, especially stanzas 20, 23–25, 29. Seed imagery: cf. below, nn. 57–58.

It is the same with stage 2. *Ate* can be simply stark calamity, like the war that follows Helen's elopement. But there is often the extra thought: calamity is punishment. Punishment must be imposed *by* someone. Usually (not invariably) a god. Men punish the centaur. But when someone refuses to reverence Prayers, Ate "harms" them, makes them atone. Zeus backs this up. Stage 2, backed by god: divine punishment.[43] Both stage 1 and stage 2 may be seen in human terms. But when they are evaluated, seen in depth, they are explained, if at all, by divinity.

HOMERIC VERSUS ARCHAIC WEIGHT

All Homeric mentions of *atē* imply the whole sequence. Individually, any Homeric *atē* may be stage 1 (alone, or with divine option), or stage 2 (alone, or with divine option). But Homer invokes stage 1 more often than 2. And inward damage is sometimes present even when *atē* refers to stage 2. Stage 1 is *atē*'s main Homeric weight.

Words and their weight change with time. In archaic Greek, between Homer and the tragedies, *atē*'s weight shifts. In the legal code set up at Gortyn, Crete, in the sixth century B.C., *atē* means "penalty," "fine." It is the misfortune you "pay" for your crime: in cash. *Ate* is the "cost" of crime.[44]

This code is Doric, not Ionian like Homer and Athens. Doric Greek used *atē* in its sense of legal penalty or retribution.[45] How does this fit *atē*'s Homeric weight? Was *atē* as "penalty" a late development in Ionia? Or a late importation from outside?

It is impossible to say. Most likely the word brought with it, wherever it went, the whole *atē*-structure, of which "penalty" was always one element.[46] Though Homeric weight is on stage 1, *atē* as "punishment" *can* appear in Homer. In archaic times, especially in Doric areas, *atē* tips that way.

And she turns austerely economic. "Ate is daughter of pledge making, pledge making is [daughter] of loss." If you incur financial loss you get into debt. If you get into debt, you meet ruin: *atē*. "[Give] a pledge, and *atē*'s near at hand" was a proverb ascribed to the sixth-century philosopher

---

[43] Barrett *ad Hipp.* 241, missing *atē*'s link of cause and consequence, thinks punishment "secondary"; but the dominance of this meaning after Homer does not make it "secondary" *in* Homer.

[44] *Leg. Gort.* 11.34.

[45] See Latte 1920–21; Chantraine 1968 s.vv. *aaō*, *atē*. Stallmach 1968:64 collects more Cretan inscriptions.

[46] See Dodds 1951:6. Stallmach 1968:3–4 reviews the arguments, insisting on the "*atē*-phenomenon" as a whole.

Thales. The Athenian lawmaker Solon uses *atē* often; sometimes ambiguously, sometimes clearly meaning "penalty."[47]

Archaic Greek, newly obsessed with law, stresses *atē*'s relation with contract and promise that it is criminal to break. In Hesiod, Ate and Horkos, "Oath," were siblings. In the *Iliad*, Zeus's own X-act is a promise. Archaic involvement in promises brings this out, and brings out Ate's closeness to Homeric and Hesiodic Erinyes, who punish false–oath makers in Hades, and were present when Conflict bore Oath.[48]

It is now human penalty that matters, more than divine. There are few divine options for stage 2. Solon does say Zeus sends *atē* "in payment," *teisomenē*. But the would-be-good who fails to use foresight "falls into huge, difficult *atē*." This does not seem god-sent: it is human, material. What matters is problems with arrears. Theognis thinks you responsible for your own *atē*, and your own "gain." If your *noos*, "intellect," fails to conquer your *thumos*, "spirit" or "impulse," you'll always be in *ataisi*, "troubles," and great *amēchaniais*, "difficulties." This is stage 2 *atē* talking economics in tough times.[49]

But archaic authors can still invoke the whole *atē*-sequence. *Atē* does not change its meaning, merely shifts in weight. Stage 1 still appears. Theognis says doctors would get rich if they could heal *atēras phrenas*, "minds affected by *atē*": presumably crime's inward cause, not its outward result. (Punished minds do not need curing. Reckless minds do, when they head for disaster.)[50] *Atē* just refers more often now to stage 2: punishment, damage to fortune, the cost of crime or folly, deserved according to a perceived system of human justice.

PENALTY, HARVEST, DAUGHTER

Archaic Greek personifies *atē* in two images, daughters and harvest, that express the causal link of stages 1 and 2. Homeric Ate is Zeus's eldest daughter; Hesiod's Ate is Conflict's daughter, one of Night's grandchildren.[51] Ate's mother, Conflict, is Night's daughter. So are Fate, Death,

---

[47] Thales: Epich. fr. 268; Pl. *Charm.* 165A (with Kollmann 1941:18); above, Chapter 16, n. 32. Dawe 1968:98–99 collects passages where *atē*, "loss," is opposed to *kerdos*, "gain." See Stallmach 1968:82–83; Solon 13.75, cf. 13.67; Müller 1956.

[48] Atē and Oath: *Theog.* 230–32. Erinyes and Oath: *Erg.* 804; *Il.* 19.418; Padel 1992:165.

[49] Solon 13.75; Thgn. frr. 133, 631.

[50] Thgn. fr. 433 (cf. *atēros phrēn*, S. fr. 264). Cf. *ateōn* (see Chapter 16, n. 15). Both words have a stage 1 weight, but *atēros* can also invoke stage 2. At *Ag.* 1483 and *PV* 746 (of "pain," *tuchē*), *atēros* is something like "crushingly terrible."

[51] *Il.* 19.91, 130; *Theog.* 211–25, 226–30. Lonely fertile Night: *Theog.* 213; Padel 1992:101.

Sleep, Dreams, Apate, and Friendship. Conflict herself is mother to Pains, Forgetfulness, Famine, Murder, Sufferings, and Oath, as well as Ate: horrors we see nightly on our news screens in the 1990s. *We* cannot explain them except, despairingly, at some specific historical level. They are explained in 700 B.C. by genealogy. Appalling things that human beings do to each other, and suffer, come from Night and her daughter, Conflict. Hesiod's explanation seems viable as any.

Ate and some of her siblings and aunts are forces that inhabit the dark of night and Hades. They also inhabit the inner world when it darkens in passion. "Night" and underworld can stand for the inner world, the mind.[52] Ate and her siblings are "fauna of the Night."[53] They live in darkness, enter the mind like Dreams and Sleep. They are forces of damage in the outer world like Famine, Murder, and "Pains." All derive, according to Hesiod's persuasive genealogy, from "black Night." From this lonely fertile blackness, the absence of light in the world outside, but also the hidden shadows within our minds, come War, Death, Dreams—and Ate.

That is the Hesiodic background. In the sixth and early fifth centuries, Ate is "daughter" of other things too. (Of "making a pledge," in the proverb quoted above.) In Empedocles' portrait of the results of sin, her companions are forces resembling her Hesiodic siblings: Murder, False Oaths. Human beings are primally sinful, fallen *daimones*: fallen because they trusted "in raving [*mainomenōi*] conflict." "One of whom," says Empedocles, "I am now: an exile from god and a wanderer."[54] He too links *atē* with oaths, conflict, and punished crime. Elsewhere, he calls this world we inhabit the world of *Kotos* (a word for "wrath" people feel with each other, which has undertones of daemonic fury):

> a joyless place, where Murder, Anger,
> tribes of other Fates, Withering Diseases,
> Corruptions, Flood, all wander
> over Ate's meadow in the dark.[55]

Our world is in the dark. (Compare Hesiod's "Night.") It is Ate's "meadow": a field filled with, sown with, *atē*. (Or, a field belonging to Ate, her territory? Maybe both.) A field of grim harvest. We are here because of our sin, because we trusted in "mad conflict." "Ate's meadow" is the flowering of our prison sentence, our punishment for sin; combined with madness.[56]

---

[52] Padel 1992:75–81, 99–102.
[53] Auden, "In Memory of Sigmund Freud": quoted (in this context) Padel 1992:76.
[54] Emp. fr. 115.3–4, 13–14DK. *Daimōn*: Padel 1992:114, 138, 141.
[55] Emp. fr. 121DK. *Kotos*: cf. *Eum.* 840; it is daemon's "grudge" at *Ag.* 635, 1211.
[56] Cf. Emp. fr. 122DK, a world of opposites: our crime was trusting to conflict; our punishment is living in a world run by the conflict of opposites.

This "meadow" links Ate as daughter with another *atē* image, "crop." Good law "withers Ate's flowers." Ate is the "crop" of *hubris*, insolence of mind or deed.[57] These are interdependent images, for Greek often describes begetting children, or emotion "growing" in the mind, in words of ploughing and sowing.[58] Given the X-act, "penalty" is as inevitable as a baby or a harvest. Results are engendered by their act. Conception and planting: inward acts with outward visible fruit. The *atē*-sequence begins in inward harm and flowers out to world damage. Ate is seen growth, sprung from an unseen act.

In the late archaic world, images explain relationships. Day is not really a "result" of Night, but part of the same cycle. Yet fifth-century imagery speaks of Sun as "brought to birth" by Night, drawing on Hesiod's genealogical explanation.[59] Archaic *atē* images express and explain the inevitability of the *atē*-sequence. Punishment is seen consequence of secret crime. If you lodge an IOU, overmortgage yourself, swear a false oath, murder a fellow countryman or your kinsman, you *must* go bankrupt, get exiled, get attacked by Erinyes. The punishment is your "harvest," your action's "daughter."[60]

Harvest images can be used for stage 1: "*atē's* ploughfield yields death as its harvest." *Ate* as field is a place of *punishment* in Empedocles. But they may also imply a soil that *pre*exists a fatal crop.[61] "Daughter" mainly personifies stage 2. Daughters are secondary. They embody financial "penalty" in a dowry system. But the *Iliad* personified stage 1 *atē* as Zeus's daughter, and linked her to his other daughters, Prayers. Even "daughters" can occasionally embody something prior.

[57] Solon fr. 4.38; *Pers.* 153. Harvest and plant-growth imagery, things flowering in the mind: Padel 1992:134–37.

[58] Begetting: Padel 1992:107–109, 136–37. Emotion: 134–37.

[59] E.g., *Trach.* 95, *Theog.* 124; see Padel 1992:34.

[60] Cf. Pl. *Charm.* 165A; *Il.* 24.480, 19.259. See Padel 1992:165–66.

[61] *Sept.* 601. The *spartoi* were "sown" from dragon's teeth by Cadmus (Pi. *I.* 1.30, 7.10; *HF* 5): a concretely lethal harvest. Aeschylus uses imagery associated with stage 2 *atē* (penalty) for stage 1 (fatal mind damage, vital to the action of this play).

Chapter 18

THE TWO ROLES OF MADNESS

ATĒ'S REPLACEMENTS: DECEPTION, ERINYS, MADNESS—AND TRAGEDY

TRAGIC POETS had to thin the meaning of *atē* down till it meant simple "disaster" or "death," had to ditch interplay between its two meanings—because the whole genre enacted *atē's* sequence. This sequence lasted the play. Most tragedies are built round one momentous act, performed in a disastrous state of mind or terrible error, which radiates destructive consequences. The *atē*-sequence offered a shape for tragic narrative, plus shared associations for choral reflections on the cause and effect of harm. *Atē's* Homeric semantics would get in the way. (See below, Appendix.)

The links between inward and outward violence are tragedy's whole business. To keep the word's epic range in a tragic play would overload things. It would sing too loud: a Wagnerian soprano in a madrigal choir. A tragedy explores the process and minutiae of the *atē*-sequence: puts the sequence under the microscope, to use an anachronistic image. In Homer, it is all over in one or two lines. You cannot have one word for the link between a harmed mind and harm in the world in a genre that exists to explore that very link. Dionysus's development as "god of" madness, the proliferation of roles of madness in his cults, helped too. His persona fostered the alchemy of the *atē*-chain into an entire art form.[1]

Within its own body, tragedy replaced *atē* more precisely with madness. Madness slipped into the pre-prepared *atē* apparatus of relating cause of crime to consequence and punishment. Tragic madness is inseparable from Homeric *atē*. Madness is mostly absent from Homer.[2] He uses *atē* where tragedy puts madness. "Madness" lay round Homer in the myths, and tragedy seized on it: but Homer had the *atē*-sequence. No one needs both. As *atē's* meanings thinned, tragedy highlit madness as the ultimate damage to *phrenes*, which has disastrous effects on the world outside. Or tragedy's bent to madness helps explain why it thinned the word.[3]

---

[1] See Padel 1990b:336; above, Chapter 3 (with n. 19), and below, Chapter 22, nn. 2–12.
[2] See Chapter 3, nn. 11–12; Simon 1978:67.
[3] See Appendix, n. 61. Dawe 1968:101 says Euripides replaced *atē* with "other words and processes concerning the derangement of the mind." But all tragedy, not just Euripides, replaces *atē* with other things. Xerxes seized by *nosos phrenōn*, Ajax captured by *mania*, recklessly insulting Athene (*Pers.* 750, *Aj.* 216, 766): Homer could call them all *atē* (see Dawe 1968:115).

Tragedy explores the damage a damaged mind can do. Tragedy, like Athenian society, inherited a sequence of damage and punishment in one word. Tragedy and society together pared this word's meanings to simple "disaster" (see Appendix). No classical poets personify *atē*. No painter represents her, though they personify other mental and physical states, endlessly. There have been many comments on this, but not many real explanations.[4] One reason is the evolution and obsessions of tragedy.

Two forces early associated with *atē* are Apate (Deception) and Erinys. Hesiod's Ate is Apate's niece. They seem related etymologically. *Atē* "damaged" Zeus when Hera "deceived" him. "Cunning" is important to *atē*:[5]

> What mortal escapes god's cunning *apatē*?
>
> . . . .
>
> *Atē*, fawning-friendly, decoys mortals aside
> to nets impossible to escape.[6]

This echoes a Homeric line: Telemachus trapping treacherous servants in a "narrow place, from which it was not possible to escape," and hanging them there as punishment.[7] Aeschylus describes an impulse to crime, by echoing a punishment for crime. Both are situations you "cannot escape."

Atē as decoy "aside" belongs with the aside imagery of tragic madness.[8] Stage 1 *atē* works like *apatē*: an impulse that knocks your mind askew, out of its right place. There is "deception" by some daemonic deceiver. The second explanation of Atē in the *Suda* (the ancient lexicon), is *ho diabolos*, the devil.[9]

Erinys too is *atē*'s daemonic associate. In Homer, she helps "send" *atē*. Melampus suffers

> because of Neleus's daughter and the heavy *atē*
> which the goddess, terrible Erinys, laid on his *phrenes*.[10]

Aeschylus often stresses the Erinys link in *atē*'s archaic weight. In *Agamemnon*, Clytemnestra swears,

> by my daughter's justice, by Ate and Erinys,
> with [or "by," or "for"] whom I killed this man,

---

[4] See Appendix, n. 64.

[5] *Theog.* 224–30; *Il.* 19.95–97: see Chapter 16, nn. 18, 32; Chapter 17, nn. 5–7, 39–42; Dawe 1968:99–100 (category 1); Bremer 1969:105 n. 19. *Atē*'s *dolios* dimension: Stallmach 1968:23, 43–45. Etymology: Chantraine 1968 s.v. *aaō*; Dawe 1968:100.

[6] *Pers.* 93–100: cf. A. *Supp.* 110; *Ant.* 617–23.

[7] *Od.* 22.460; *Pers.* 93–100.

[8] See *parasainei*, *Pers.* 97; see also Chapter 12, nn. 6–19.

[9] *Suda*, s.v. *atē*.

[10] *Od.* 15.232–34; cf. *Il.* 9.512. See Padel 1992:164; Dodds 1951:7–8; Dawe 1968:100–101.

that she was right to murder Agamemnon. In the next play, *atē* is *hustero-poinos*, "punishing later": like Erinys. Erinys' weight on a murderer is "*atē* hard to bear." Ate and Erinys, both involved in oaths, are retributive. They "follow" and punish crime.[11] The Erinys-figure, like the *atē*-sequence, depends on the paradox that the force which made you commit a crime may punish it.[12] If stage 1 *atē* belongs with *apatē*, stage 2 belongs with Erinys.

The fifth century seems to have replaced *atē* with several different things: most immediately with Apate and Erinys, *atē*'s old associates. The *atē*-sequence embodies their connection. One South Italian vase, portraying a lost Sophocles tragedy, represents Apate (labelled Apa) *dressed as Erinys*.[13] Apate, like stage 1 *atē*, is inner, prior. But outside, what the world sees, is Erinys: a punisher, inflicting stage 2 *atē*. The *atē*-sequence: Apate in Erinys' dress.

But there is also a newer figure. On some vases, Erinys herself is sometimes interchangeable with Lyssa. Erinys and Lyssa play similar roles in scenarios where Ate might have appeared.[14] The personifications and imagery of Homeric and archaic *atē* stand behind classical iconography: not of *atē* but of *apatē*, Erinys, and Lyssa. Tragedy itself (Lyssa's biggest promoter) became *atē*'s most far-reaching fifth-century replacement.

Painters express some links between all these. They represent "Tragedy" herself as a maenad in Dionysus's train,[15] and draw maenads that look like Erinyes. They use Lyssa and Erinys, it seems, as emblems of tragedy.[16] Maenads are also linked to tragedy through Dionysus. *Atē* fed all these, and all these connections, conceptually. She got knocked out of visual iconography partly because of them, but mainly, I think, because tragedy itself, in which Erinys and madness were also centrally important, became the ultimate vehicle of the *atē*-sequence.

It has been argued that the contradictoriness of *atē* emerged increasingly as the culture developed.[17] I would put it differently. Successive Greek societies expressed these contradictions in their changing literature differently, and with increasing complexity, through shifts in words, concepts, and genres. The fifth century articulates an established insight into the ambiguities of cause and effect through *atē* and her spin-offs, but, increasingly, through other divine forces too.[18]

[11] *Ag.*1432–33; *Cho.* 382–83; *Eum.* 372; *Il.* 19.87; see Chapter 17, n. 48.
[12] See Chapter 17, nn. 11–14.
[13] See Dawe 1968:101 (with n. 23).
[14] Körte 1874:8. Lyssa: see Chapter 2.
[15] See Burkert 1985:185. Lyssa on vases: see Chapter 2, n. 21; Chapter 19, n. 56. Erinys: Padel 1992:172.
[16] See, e.g., Bierl 1991:90 n. 146, 120–22 (with n. 30); Henrichs 1993:14 n. 1.
[17] Stallmach 1968.
[18] Cf. Padel 1992:159–60, 171–71.

TRAGEDY AS *ATĒ*-SEQUENCE

Tragedy bases its whole structure on the *atē*-sequence. In different ways, Aeschylus's *Seven against Thebes* and *Persians*, Sophocles' *Electra* and *Antigone*, and Euripides' *Hippolytus*, *Bacchae*, and *Medea* explore the world-damage damaged minds do. The *atē*-sequence is background to tragedy's uses of madness. Tragic madness too has two possible stages: it may cause crime, or punish it.

From the beginning, Greek poetry presents violence as generative. It ripples out, begetting more of itself:[19] it moves from violent mind to violent act, and on to larger destruction. The *atē*-sequence carried that vision in the Homeric and archaic worlds. Tragedy articulated it for the Athenian fifth century.

Violence was also the core of *mainomai*, "I rage, rave, am mad." Madness is violent damage: to mind, to outward appearance, to behavior. When Heracles goes mad,

> he was himself no longer, but destroyed;
> his rolling eyes
> bulging their bloodshot roots.[20]

"Destroyed." This verb, *phtheirō*, can mean "I ruin" (cattle, virtue, people, or wealth—by spoiling precious tapestries), or "I pervert," "seduce." It figures in curses. In medical writing, your patients will not survive if their guts are "ruined."[21] It can also imply "wander," "drift off course" on sea or land: such wandering itself suggests madness.[22]

In "damaging" mind and body, madness is *atē*'s heir. *Atē* is *blabē*, "harm": harm to *phrenes* and to relationships or people in the outside world. From the beginning of tragedy, such "harming" is a tragic theme. "Sickness of *phrenes* seized my son," says Darius's ghost.[23] Madness incarnates this harm. Sanity is being "in": in home, in mind. Having *phrenes* "safe" in you.[24] Madness is their movement away, displacement, wandering, destruction.

MADNESS AS INSTRUMENT AND PUNISHMENT OF CRIME

The *atē* legacy highlights a vital aspect of madness in tragedy: that madness has two distinct roles.

[19] Girard 1977:29–32, 81–86, 93–96, 108.

[20] *HF* 931–33. *Mainomai*: see Chapter 3, nn. 4–5, 9–10.

[21] *Phtheirō*: *Od.* 17.246; Arist. *EN* 1103B8; Thuc. 3.13; *Trag. adesp.* 484; E. fr. 1024; *Ag.* 949; Ar. *Ach.* 460, cf. *Andr.* 715, "'stand off' from her"; Hp. *Anc. Med.* 13 (Loeb 1:34).

[22] *Hel.* 774; *IT* 276; *Cyc.* 300, cf. *Pers.* 451; E. *El.* 234. *Phthora* is destruction, ruin, death. Cf. *phtheirō* for a ship "drifting off course": *Hel.* 766; *IT* 276. See Chapters 10, 12.

[23] *Pers.* 750: see Chapter 16, nn. 4–5; Padel 1992:132–34.

[24] "Safe" *phrenes*: see Chapter 12, nn. 58–59; Padel 1992:23 nn. 43–44, 113.

There are two roles for punitive wandering in Greek myth, centripetal and centrifugal.[25] There are likewise two prime roles for madness in tragedy: as instrument and as punishment of crime. Madness to make you err, and madness to punish error. Gods make Ajax, Heracles, Agave (and others, in lost plays) mad for an extra purpose: to make them do something that triggers pollution and destroys their lives. As a whole package, this is punishment: gods are offended and angry. But the madness is not the punishment. It is an instrument of it. By contrast, for Orestes and Io, the punishment and pain *are* the madness.

Like Homer's stage 1 *atē*, tragic madness appears only once in a story: to cause some terrible act, or to punish it. Yet as with Homer's *atē*-sequence, there is a bond between the two roles of madness: madness as prior damage, madness as subsequent damage. In both stage 1 *atē* and tragic madness, you suffer temporary inward harm that causes permanent damage.[26]

It has been suggested that Greek culture distinguished madness as punishment "for ritual or moral offence" from madness "as seizure by capricious amoral spirits," as if they were "different sorts" of madness.[27] I do not believe this. The *atē*-sequence ensured that stage 1 and stage 2 were seen as part of a whole damage-chain. Mad cause of crime; mad punishment of it. Tragic madness inherited this. Something that can either cause or punish crime is at the heart of Greek tradition. It is part of a whole structure of understanding. *Atē* expresses early archaic insight into the relation of cause and consequence.[28] Tragedy's madness, I think, is a potent fifth-century use of the same insight. Homeric stage 1 *atē* and tragic madness offer their respective thought-worlds an explanation: *why* you did that terrible thing. As with pollution, you came up against some outside force; yet you are responsible for the evil, and enduring, consequences.[29]

Later Europe found a potent formulation for tragic madness as stage 1 *atē*, in "Whom god wants to destroy, he *first* makes mad" (see Chapter 1). But what about stage 2: madness as punishment?

Madness as divine punishment is a force in many myths.[30] The madness may be the punishment itself, as with Orestes, or the instrument of punishment, as with Heracles: stage 2 operating as stage 1.[31] Like Homeric *atē*,

---

[25] See Chapter 11, nn. 22–30.

[26] Cf. the aorist passive of *mainomai* and *aaō*: see Chapter 3, nn. 1–4; Chapter 16, nn. 24–25. Madness as temporary: see Chapter 4.

[27] Parker 1983:246.

[28] Stallmach 1968:5.

[29] Pollution: see Chapter 14, nn. 24, 29. Madness: Chapter 19, nn. 17, 57–58. *Atē*: Latte 1920–21:261–71; Stallmach 1968:27, 74. Responsibility within a framework of daemonic compulsion: Williams 1993:16–20, 31–37.

[30] Punitive madness imposed by divinity: Mattes 1970:36–38, 42–45, 47. Cf. Corneille's reworking of madness as just punishment: Foucault 1971:30.

[31] *Eum.* 328–39; *IT* 931–35; *HF* 831.

punitive madness can be associated with Erinyes.[32] Gods sometimes punish one person through another's madness: Dionysus punishes Pentheus through Agave's; Aphrodite punishes Hippolytus through Phaedra's.[33] At the core of all this is the principle dominating divine relation with human beings. Divinity punishes in the area where it helps, punishes acts prompted by divinity. Punishment may come from the same force that inspired the crime: god, or madness.[34]

The interplay and inevitable ambiguity of madness's two roles underlies many mentions of madness in tragedy. Instrument or punishment? When we hear of something happening "in" or "with" fits of madness, we often cannot know if the fits of madness caused the offence, or constituted the punishment. The grammatical case of the noun is the same in each case. Sophocles mentions Lycurgus who insulted Dionysus in "coarse boastful words": *maniais*, "*in* fits of madness." Or did he "come to know the god" *by* fits of madness: as punishment *for* the insult? Either is possible.[35] The grammatical point is tiny. The interpretive impasse demonstrates the double role of tragic madness.

In *Bacchae*, Teiresias says Pentheus is mad now, but "even before, *exestēs phrenōn* [you stood outside your wits]." Does this mean "Your first speech was bad enough and this is worse"?[36] No. This is language of madness used to describe behavior (insults to Dionysus) that will be punished through madness. First, by Pentheus's madness when seized by Dionysus's maddening power. Dionysus intends "first" to "send him out of his mind" (*ekstēson phrenōn*), then "put *lussa* in him." Pentheus will not dress up as a maenad *phronōn*, "thinking sanely" but when "driven *exō tou phronein*," "outside thought."[37] Second, he will be punished by his mother's madness, whose hallucinations parallel his.[38] "Madness" that caused insults to Dionysus becomes madness through which these are punished. Tragedy goes in for doubleness. Double meanings. Double causality. And a double role for madness.[39]

---

[32] *Atē*: Dawe 1968:108–109. Madness: *Eum.* 328–29; *IT* 931–35; *Or.* 36–37.

[33] *Ba.* 1079–128; *Hipp.* 22–28.

[34] See Chapter 17, n. 13–17.

[35] *Ant.* 960–61. Stinton 1990 supports Jebb that "in coarse boastful words" goes with *psauōn*. ("*Psauō* takes a genitive; *ton theon* must be governed by *epegnō*".) *Maniais* "makes the meaning of *psauōn* clear." Eventually Lycurgus recognized the (power of the) god, *because* he had (madly) insulted him: an interpretation rooted, as it should be, in grammar. But we can also respect the ambiguity that the odd word order (acknowledged by Stinton and Jebb) brings out. Lycurgus was later punished *with* madness. Listening, you could catch the echo of punitive as well as causal madness.

[36] *Ba.* 359; see Dodds *ad loc.*

[37] *Ba.* 850–53; cf. 810–38, 918–62.

[38] *Ba.* 32, 1122–23, 918, 1175.

[39] Cf. Vernant and Vidal-Naquet 1981:13.

"Hyperbolic" and "Real" Madness

The *idea* of madness is commoner in tragedy than its occurrence. Sometimes the stage 1 madness is not real, but hyperbolic. This is behavior, or a way of seeing, *said to be* mad but not mad: not as tragedy presents real madness. Tragic characters often accuse each other of madness in a sane context. "You're mad" is a common judgment on people the play does not present as mad.

We do it in English. It happens all the time. "You must be mad . . ." The only explanation of your reckless behavior would be that you are mad: yet I know you are not. This is a hyperbolic use of "mad" (like saying, "You're a saint"). In the dock, I would admit I did not mean you were technically mad (or a saint). I meant "very unwise" (or "very good"). My use of "mad" or "saint" comes from my *idea* of real madness or saints. I stretched that idea, applying it to you. Hyperbolic madness, the exaggerating application of "mad," runs throughout tragedy, and depends on tragedy's images of true madness.

Of course, with any interpretation across cultures, it is risky to think we know when "mad" is hyperbolic, and when not. But the tragedians (especially Sophocles) often use formulations like, "If you do [or think] X you are mad."[40] Or, "I am not so mad as to X"; "You would not X if you were sane.[41] Or again, "Whoever X is mad"; "I would be mad if I X"; "No one is so mad as to X"; or, "Who is so mad as to X?"[42] In these patterns, the "is mad" part varies.[43] But they all suggest common ground with real madness: showing where the perceived boundaries of normal behavior lie.

As in the *atē*-sequence, the "X-act" is often a fatal miscalculation. Clytemnestra says she thought Agamemnon mad to sacrifice his daughter. Haemon says if Creon were not his father, he would call Creon mad for entombing Antigone. Deianeira says she would be mad to blame her husband for being in love, since love is omnipotent, and rules even gods.[44] Statements like these condemn error or stupidities that boomerang on the agent, who suffers for them, eventually. Not to foresee that suffering is, hyperbolically, mad: for madness is self-destructive (see Chapter 19).

Hyperbolic accusations of madness in sane contexts, like real madness, imply that failing to see your situation as others see it—what is wrong in

---

[40] *OT* 550, 552.

[41] S. *El.* 941, 365, 529.

[42] *Trach.* 442; *Ant.* 67; *Trach.* 445; *Ant.* 220; *Ag.* 479.

[43] It is conveyed in images, or parts of *mainesthai*, phrases like "lacks *nous*," "does not think," "does not think straight": e.g., *mōros* (*Ant.* 220); *ouk orthōs* (or *eu*) *phroneis* (*OT* 550, 552); *planktos* (*Ag.* 593); cf. (endlessly) *aphrōn, anous, ou phronōn, ouk emphrōn, kekommenos phrena, paraphrōn, kenos phrenōn.*

[44] *Ag.* 802; *Ant.* 755; *Trach.* 446.

it, what will damage you—is wrong seeing, and therefore evidence of madness.[45] People "prove" sanity by their reasoning; logic comes from minds that "see" properly. "Listen, and see if I am sane or not."[46] At the core of hyperbolic accusations, as of real madness, is a flash of self-neglect, which shows your *phrenes* not working properly.[47]

This self-neglect has two main elements: breaking rules and ignoring your own interests. Behavior that violates rules is mad, whether they are divine rules (Xerxes is "mad" to have tried, blasphemously, to chain the sea) or human social conventions (Ion wonders if the stranger who suddenly hugs him "is mad"). This holds outside tragedy, in cases of real madness. Herodotus says Cleomenes went mad on returning to Sparta: "at once a *maniē nousos* [a 'madness sickness'] seized him; he had been a bit mad even before. Now he would hit any Spartan he met in the face with his staff. . . . He was doing this, and had gone mad. . . ."[48] Breaking rules, human or divine, is self-destructive; and self-destruction is mad. You are *aphrōn* (mindless), rather than *sōphrōn* (prudent, self-controlled). As in stage 1 *atē*, destruction of *phrenes* is answered by destruction in the world.

"Hyperbolic" madness in which someone self-damagingly offends divinity or breaks human rules is not "real" madness. There are no body signs, no violence. Yet underlying it, binding it to real madness that punishes, is madness's twofold role, derived from the Homeric bond between stage 1 and stage 2 *atē*. Madness can cause as well as punish disastrous acts.

Is hyperbolic madness inward, a human mistaking? And is real, punitive madness externally derived, god-sent? Remember the double operation of Homeric *atē*: something taken away *and* something added (see Chapter 16). Does hyperbolic madness, a loss of judgment, correspond to one, and real madness, a daemonic savage thing sent to the mind, correspond to the other? Or try this: through its images, tragedy implies a double model of mind. Mind as passive vessel, enterable and woundable from outside, and, less often, mind as an active organ.[49] Can we say that in hyperbolic madness the mind is active, a human organ going wrong, whereas in real madness the mind is passive, wounded and invaded by god?

No. Too simple. Tragic causality does not just mean divine outside, human in. Tidiness is artificial here. Divine is outside and inside, the mind is

---

[45] Cf. S. *El.* 213–15; *Aj.* 387; *Phil.* 1164–69; *Ba.* 506; maybe *OT* 413 (a special case: the plot's point is that Oedipus cannot know who he is). Twisted seeing: see Chapter 7.

[46] S. *El.* 890.

[47] Self-damage: see Chapter 19, nn. 43–58. *Bacchae* presents this through paradox: in its world, one deep need is to be *out* of control, mad under Dionysus's control. Dionysus's presence in the outside world may be mad, but the human psyche must accommodate it. Human beings did not generate this presence: it is due to Zeus.

[48] *Pers.* 750; *Ion* 520–26; Hdt. 6.75.

[49] Padel 1992:106, 110–13.

passive and active, all at once. The fifth century operated external *and* internal explanations of disease, suffering, perception, and passion, simultaneously.[50]

We might turn instead to Plato's insight into Greek language of madness. Madness is one thing that can be seen two ways: as human and divine.[51]

---

[50] Padel 1992:49–58, 106–13, 132–38, 159–61.

[51] Madness classifiable according to divinity *and* to human activity: see Chapter 8 (with n. 47).

Chapter 19

"HAYWIRE CITY"

"Some Big *Hamartia*"

There was a certain amount of sorrowing for Gazza—but
not much. . . . Gascoigne had "brought it on himself." It
was . . . "Haywire City. Yeah, '*course* I knew he was capa-
ble of such acts of stupidity. But it was freaking me out to
the point of total insanity. I still wanted to love him! But
for the Gaz to plummet from such a towering high? No. I
could no longer defend the man. I had to expel him from
my soul. Paul Gascoigne. You are a Bastard. Get out of
my life."
—Ian Hamilton, *Gazza Agonistes* (quoting *The Spur*)

LIKE MOST things in tragedy, tragic madness is both human and divine.
Prayer is a good idea, but when you call on gods you should weigh in
yourself as well, All through the classical age, divine explanations operate
alongside human ones. Aristotle's account of tragedy concentrates on the
human, and finds the most dramatically effective pain in the image of a
good man suffering: a man of high reputation and fortune, yet "not pre-
eminent in virtue and justice." Why does he suffer? Not because of basic
badness but "through some *hamartia*." "The change is from good to bad,
not vice versa. Not through wickedness, but through some big *hamartia*."
"Some big *hamartia*" echoes the "greatly" that often qualifies Homer's
verb *aaomai*. In the *Iliad*, Patroclus and Zeus are both "greatly *aasthē*
[blinded by *atē*]."[1] Aristotle's words resonate with Homer. In the second
half of the fourth century (long after our tragedies were written), they
began centuries of debate in tragic criticism. *Hamartia* means, roughly,
"fault," "error," "mistake." What did Aristotle mean by it here: a word
explaining how and why people suffer, in a genre built to explore
suffering?[2]

His words used to be taken to mean suffering caused by personality

---

[1] Arist. *Poet.* 1452B34–53B5, 1453A10–16; *Il.* 16.685, 19.113; above, Chapter 17, nn.
9, 23. Divine *and* human: Vernant and Vidal-Naquet 1981:12–13; Williams 1993:18–19,
33; Lloyd 1979 passim; below, Chapter 21, n. 21.

[2] History of interpretation of *hamartia*: Bremer 1969:65–98; Halliwell 1986:215–30.
Details: Lucas *ad loc.* and app. 4; Dawe 1968:89–90; Bremer 1969:4–65; Stinton
1990:144–69.

"flaw." No one thinks that now.[3] In the mid-twentieth century, interpreters reacted, rightly, against conceptions of tragic flaws and character anachronistic to fifth-century Athens. They swung away from the moral, and stressed the factual element of "mistake" in *hamartia*. But they overcompensated. Aristotle's *hamartia* cannot be simply "mistake of fact," with the narrow English connotations of "mistake." Moral blame does hang about it in Greek. *Hamartia* operates in an area of explanation that does not separate error from misdeed, madness from badness, unintended mishap from responsibility for pollution. It comprehended many things we separate: crime, misdeed, shameful deeds, and intellectual mistaking.[4] From this range of meanings came, much later, its basic Christian meaning, "sin."

Before Aristotle, Plato had already made some famous statements about "mistaking." Towards the end of the fifth century, Socrates said, "No one willingly *hamartanei* [mistakes]." That's fine as far as it goes. We might agree. But if you marry this to Socrates' other claim, that "virtue is knowledge," you get the paradoxical statement that "no one *is bad* on purpose": because if they understood, if they truly *knew*, an action was bad, they would not do it. If virtue is knowledge (a paradox), it is correct (and not a paradox) to say that wrongdoing is a mistake, an intellectual error. The unparadoxical "no one willingly errs" becomes paradoxical (no one is bad on purpose). Part of the issue raised by Socrates is: where is the paradox? In Plato's *Euthydemus*, wisdom by definition cannot err; otherwise, it would not be wisdom. These statements do not drain moral meaning from mistaking. Socrates' dictum would not be striking, if the verb *hamartanein* did *not* normally have a moral dimension.[5]

In Plato, and later in Aristotle, *hamartēma* is at the center of a spectrum between misdeed and misfortune.[6] It looks both ways: to morality and to failure. What Aristotle himself means by *hamartia*, in the *Poetics*, seems most plausibly to cover acts of unintended badness, mistake and moral error: acts committed maybe in passion, maybe in ignorance. Bad acts, but with extenuating circumstances.[7] It represents his understanding of tragic

---

[3] See, e.g., House 1961:94; Jones 1971:12–20, 39, 46–50; Stinton 1990:143.

[4] Cf. Bremer 1969: ch. 3; above, Chapter 17, n. 29; Stinton 1990:143.

[5] See Pl. *Euthyd.* 280A, *Protagoras* 345D-E (though Dodds 1951:17, 26 [n. 105] follows Nestle in the claim that this was not a paradoxical novelty but a formulation of an ingrained, *echt griechisch*, habit of thought). Cf. Pl. *Hipp. Min.* 376B and Arist. *EN* 1148A3, where lack of bodily restraint is *kakia*, not only *hamartia*.

[6] *Hamartēma* midway between *adikēma* and *atuchēma*: Arist. *EN* 1135B18, *Rh.* 1374B7. At Pl. *Rep.* 551C1, *hamartēmata* must mean "faults of character" in a *politeia* (here parallel to *ēthē*; cf. 557D).

[7] Stinton 1990:158.

human "instability" and should be "located" (according to a recent critic) in "a space between guilt and vulnerability to arbitrary misfortune."[8]

Hamartia is part of Aristotle's *interpretation* of tragedy: the insight of a critic writing and thinking after Plato, in and for the fourth century. If it represents a truth about tragedy, it does so in fourth-century terms, which are in many ways quite different from those of the fifth century. "A serious critique of Greek tragedy," writes one scholar, "can never be achieved by a piecemeal adjustment of Aristotelian insights. It should start by a complete rejection of his terms of reference." Aristotle's insights are profound. The terms in which he expressed them may truly reflect something in tragedy or Homer.[9] But they do so in a way characteristic of their time and culture.

Tragic "Mistaking"

How does tragedy itself use *hamartia* and cognate words? It is shameful," says the chorus to Prometheus, "for a wise [or clever] man *examartanein* [to err]." Shameful *to make a mistake*? In our world, in popular imagination at least, mistake exonerates. But watch what happens to Prometheus. *Hamartanō*, "I err," tracks him throughout the play. "Do you not see you erred [*hēmartes*]?" asks the chorus early on. I did so "willingly," says Prometheus:

> willingly, willingly I erred [*hēmarton*].
> I'll not deny it.[10]

You cannot do this in English. It is a daft thing to say, a contradiction in terms. In our world and language, "mistake" is involuntary. But *hamartanō* covers more than "I mistake." In Homer, it is "I miss the mark."[11] In tragedy, this mistaking, missing, failing—this "error"—can be both voluntary and shameful. It has a recognized role in moral discourse.[12]

The noun *hamartia* appears in a mad context. Pentheus implores Agave,

> Pity me, mother! Don't kill your son
> in *hamartiai* [errors].

These "errors" are madness. Agave is raging, horrific:

---

[8] Halliwell 1986:229, 220.

[9] Stinton 1990:169, 167.

[10] *PV* 1039; 261, 266.

[11] E.g., *Il.* 5.287: see Bremer 1969:24–64; Dawe 1968:91–93; 102–105. *Hamartia* and *atē*: Dawe 1968:102–105; Bremer 1969:99–172; Stinton 1990:173.

[12] If *PV* is fourth-century, Socratic paradox and other rhetorical/philosophical play (above, n. 5) on "error" may well affect it.

> spewing out foam,
> rolling her whirligig eyes,
> possessed by Bacchus,
> not thinking as she ought to think.

She is tearing Pentheus to pieces. *"Mistakings"*? But in a sane context of the same play, the same word means simply a sexual misdeed. Agave herself used it. Her sister Semele claimed she was pregnant by Zeus. By some man, say her sisters, including Agave. They insisted that,

> pregnant by a mortal man, Semele projected onto Zeus
> the *hamartia* of going to bed with him.[13]

Agave's *hamartiai* are involuntary. She sees her son as a lion, and kills him. Semele's supposed *hamartia* was voluntary, a run-of-the-mill crime: an un-married princess going to bed with someone. The same word covers both. Behind *hamartia*, as tragedians use the word, seems to be the basic insight that "mistaking" where your own interests lie may be bad and mad. "Er-ror" shades into madness.

This relation comes over in the Latin meaning of *error*, wandering," veering off course: as *delirium* is veering *de lira*, *out of* the furrow.[14] Even our word "error" contains (historically, if not in popular imagination) these resonances of mad wandering, which carried in Greece a charge of shame. "Wandering" and displacement are bad. People do not like wan-derers; nor madness, of which wandering, *error*, is an image. Both are unwelcome, dangerous. Shameful.[15] So is a wandering mind, which makes mistakes of judgment. Madness is "de-viation," de-viance aside: with moral and religious as well as geographical or intellectual dimensions. To leave the path is mad.

Madness does not diminish responsibility. You "pay for" what you do. Aegisthus warns the chorus they'll pay for their *moria*, "folly," in defying him.[16] *Mainomai*, "I am mad," is often close in Greek imagination (as Heraclitus pointed out) to *miainomai*, "I am polluted." Madness, pollu-tion, divine hostility, and disease are related. Like error and folly, all pro-voke automatic bad consequences.[17] You pay for madness inflicted on you. Wrongdoing and madness are not divisible. Error is part of both: and gets punished.

---

[13] *Ba.* 1121–24, 28–29.

[14] See Chapter 12, nn. 20–24.

[15] See Chapter 11, nn. 4–12; Chapter 14, nn. 50–58.

[16] *Ag.* 1670. See Dover 1974:148.

[17] Heraclitus: see Chapter 14, n. 35. Dodds 1951:66–67; Parker 1983:235–56; above, Chapter 14, nn. 24–34.

IGNORING GODS, FIGHTING GODS

In one vital area of life, error has especially sharp moral weight. This is in relations with gods. In tragedy as in Homer, ignoring gods is among the worst things you can do: a maybe involuntary, but dreadful, mistake. Meleager's father failed to offer Artemis her share of his harvest:

> either he forgot or he did not notice.
> He was greatly blinded in his *thumos*.

Enraged, Artemis brought "evil" on his people, which ended in his son's death. You suffer for an involuntary mistake, just as you can incur pollution involuntarily. In *Philoctetes*, Neoptolemus, voice of eventually uncorruptible integrity, is spokesman for the thought that Philoctetes' agony (the play does not let up on his foulness and pain) is god-sent, deserved. Deserved? Because he trod on a snake in a nymph's sacred cave.[18] Gods punish humans for "not noticing," "forgetting"; and treading on sacred snakes.

But gods also punish another mistake: deliberate insult. They punish, for instance, Hippolytus, Ajax, and Pentheus.

Hippolytus deliberately cuts Aphrodite from his menu of worship. "Each man cares for different men or gods"; he does not care for Aphrodite. She is "holy and glorious among mortals" but he'll "greet her from afar," having nothing to do with her. His servant prays for him. "May you fare well, and have as much *nous* as you should." Hippolytus "speaks emptily." He has lost *nous*.[19]

Ajax tells Athene he'll fight without her. His father told him to acknowledge gods' help in battle, but he does not think "mortal thoughts." He does not "think as men ought to think":

> Extreme, senseless men, any human creature
> who doesn't think in human ways: gods make them fall
> with heavy misfortunes. So the prophet said.
> When Ajax left home, his father called him mad [*anous*].
> "Son," he said, "try to conquer with your spear,
> but always do it with the help of god!" Proudly,
> stupidly, Ajax replied, "Father, even a nobody
> conquers with gods' help. I'll get fame without them."

Ajax later told Athene herself,

---

[18] *Il.* 9.533–37; *Phil.* 192; above, p. 158.
[19] *Hipp.* 102–104, 119.

"Lady, be near to help the other Greeks.
Where I am, the battle will never break."
With these words, not thinking as human beings
ought to think, he got her hating anger.[20]

Ajax's approach to divinity reflects the way he treats all relationships. He
refuses help or pleas, insisting on self-sufficiency.[21] This is self-destructive:
not thinking within the limits gods set to mortal thought, limits whose
infringement they punish. Human beings are, must be, related. Gods'
"honors" are at stake in all human relationships. Ajax refuses relatedness all
the time. Hence his punishment. There is irony in the madness Athene
sends. When mad, he accepts her help. His punishment involves delusion,
believing her his ally: the ally he denied her to be, when sane.[22]

Pentheus goes further. He refuses to acknowledge Dionysus a god. "He
theomachei [fights god] against me," says Dionysus:

he pushes me from libations, and in his prayers
has no memory of me at all.[23]

Theomachia, "fighting god," is an implicit story pattern in many myths and
tragic scenarios. That rare verb *ateō*, related to *atē*, seems to mean "I defy
the gods." Euripides explored *theomachia* themes in several lost plays.[24] We
meet a version of it in Aeschylus's first extant play. Bridging the Hellespont, Xerxes was trying to "overcome all gods including Poseidon." He
did so "being mortal." "How was this not a *nosos phrenōn* [sickness of
mind]?"[25] Yoking the sea is trying to master gods. In Plato's pictures of the
evolution of tyrannical soul and tyrannical city, powerful erotic love "tyran-
nizes the soul": "Its bodyguards are *mania* and *oistros*. . . . A man who is
mad and deranged tries to rule not only over men but over gods: and
expects to succeed."[26] Trying *theomachein*, "to fight against god," is impossible, mad.

This verb first appears in late Euripides.[27] It is the talismanic word for
Pentheus in *Bacchae*. He cannot persuade Teiresias "to fight god." Mad

[20] *Aj.* 758–70, 774–77.
[21] *Aj.* 369, 592, 840; cf. Chapter 7, nn. 5–13, 20–21. One scholiast says Sophocles
"makes clear that the man who was sane and practical has not stepped out of himself *dia to
theomachēnai*" (Radt, *Scholia on Sophocles* 118.4; cf. 666.3)
[22] He accepts Athene's word *summachos*, but refuses her one onstage command "Don't.
. . ." (90, 117, 111), as if he could control her and pick what he wants of her help.
[23] *Ba.* 45–46.
[24] *Atēo*: see Chapter 16, n. 15.
[25] *Pers.* 749–51.
[26] Pl. *Rep.* 573B–C.
[27] *Ba.* 45; *IA* 1408.

Agave hopes he will be a great hunter like her, though "he can do nothing but *theomachein*."[28] His *theomachia* lives in his images of imprisoning and destroying holy things: in which, like a "wild-eyed monster, not a human man," like "a murderous *gigas* [giant] that fought against gods," he reveals his monstrous, earth-born descent.[29] In myth, the first time the gods used their weapons in war was in the "Battle with Giants" and "Battle with Titans." These huge, violent, quasi-human figures are a prime model for *theomachia*. Pentheus fighting Dionysus (both in the outside world and in himself) is like a (doomed) giant "fighting god."[30]

In human form, Dionysus warns Pentheus "not to bear arms against a god":

> I'd rather sacrifice to him
> than kick against *kentra* [goads] in anger,
> a mortal against god.

"To kick against the *kentra*" was a proverb. It surfaces in several fifth-century poems. The New Testament author of Acts probably knew *Bacchae*, and twice uses the phrase as a warning to his own *theomachos*. "Saul, Saul, why do you persecute me? It is hard for you to kick against the *kentra*."[31] This characteristically tragic image filters down to Christian Greek. God drives the mind, and masters it, with *kentra*. Human resistance is futile. But in tragedy, unlike Christianity, the very passions you feel within you are daemonic, divine. Passion and madness, like divinity, are an adversary you cannot fight.[32]

Ignoring *ta theia*, things belonging to gods, insults them. It has many forms.

> To speak ill of gods is hateful wisdom.
> Untimely boasting is attuned to *maniai* [madnesses].[33]

Since mortals have to give in to gods, it is mad to blame someone for doing so. Love is a god. Deianeira cannot blame her husband for loving another woman:

[28] *Ba.* 45, 325, 1255. The opposition between *thnētos*, mortal, and *theos* or *daimōn*, god, accumulates through Dionysus's prologue (28, 42, 45, 47, 53, 54—he has changed to *eidos thnētōn*) and on through the play itself.

[29] *Ba.* 226–32, 239, 348–51, 355, 451, 493–94, 497, 505, 508, 538–41, 542, 544.

[30] See Padel 1992:153. Cf. Lycurgus, another *theomachos*, who expelled Dionysus from Thrace, "injuring the god in insulting words." He too went mad: *Ant.* 96–61; see Chapter 3, nn. 6–9; below, n. 56.

[31] *Ba.* 789, 794–95; Acts 26.14, cf. 9.5 (see Dodds *ad Ba.* 795, 45). See Pi. *P.* 2.88; *Ag.* 1624; *PV* 323; Kamerbeek 1948:278–79 n. 30; above, n. 21.

[32] Padel 1992:117 19, 152–57, 125–32.

[33] Pi. *O.* 9.37–39.

> whoever stands up against Eros,
> coming to blows like a boxer,
> is not thinking sanely. Eros rules
> even the gods as he pleases. And me. . . .
> If I blamed my husband for being captured
> by this disease, I'd be really mad [*mainomai*].[34]

In real life, separate gods' honors were invested in all you did: fighting, lovemaking, promising; talking, falling silent; making pots, entertaining friends, giving birth, running a race. You lived your physical and social life in a jungle of overlapping divine territories. All gods demanded recognition in all this, all the time. If you refused, you were trying to control gods, rather than accepting their control of you. "Mistakes" of ignoring and resisting divinity get punished. To think you can ignore divinity's power in your activities and relationships is an insult. "Not thinking properly." Hyperbolic madness. An appalling mistake.[35]

"Mortal against god" is the core of these images of "mad" behavior. Refusing gods their recognition is opposing, fighting them. Mortal opposition to divinity is mad—and also the worst mistake in the book. Madness both is, and is a punishment for, human transgression of divine law. It both incarnates, and punishes, offence to gods:

> The gods keep watch. Carefully, though late.
> They notice when someone leaves divine things
> and turns to madness.

Leaving "divine things" is turning to *mainesthai*, "madness."[36]

ATĒ, MADNESS, HAMARTIA

> He saw human veins as the gods' net
> where they trap us like animals. He tried
> to pierce it. . . . Dogs tore him to bits.
> —Seferis, "Euripides the Athenian"

Though the word *hamartia* occurs in tragedy, it is not that big a deal there, not that common.[37] It is not, as it became for Aristotle and his readers since, a linchpin in tragic explanation of why people suffer. As used by Aristotle, *hamartia* interprets some other element, or elements, in tragedy. It is not a tragic idea per se.

Two scholars have suggested that where Aristotle puts *hamartia*, tragedy

---

[34] *Trach.* 441–46; see Padel 1992:128.
[35] Padel 1992:139–40, cf. 6–9.
[36] *OC* 1536–38.
[37] See Bremer 1969:31–36.

itself puts *atē*: that *hamartia* translates and interprets *atē* in tragedy. This was a very important insight.[38] In principle. But, as I argued, and others have shown, *atē* is not that big a deal in tragedy either. Overall, tragedy replaced *atē*: on one hand, it offered its own body, its structure and shape, as an enactment of *atē*. On the other, it replaced *atē* with the personifications, or the experience, of madness.[39]

In that case, Aristotle's *hamartia* cannot translate or interpret *atē* in tragedy, because tragedy has already practically abandoned it. Only exceptionally does tragedy use it in any way resembling Homer's. *Hamartia* cannot stand for *atē* in tragedy. Rather, it replaces the things tragedy put in as Homeric *atē*'s replacements. Aristotle's *hamartia* is basically, I think, a response to tragedy's madness. Not a response to real madness, but rather the more widely prevalent hyperbolic madness.

Both real and hyperbolic madness are heirs, so I argued, to Homeric *atē*. Tragedy alchemized the *atē*-sequence into a double role for madness. Aristotle alchemizes in his turn. He uses the word and concept *hamartia* for the matrix of interpretive possibilities that madness, both real and hyperbolic, offered to tragedy and its listeners.

In real madness, divine causality is unambiguous. Theseus, seeing his friend, that wonderful "savior of Greece," sitting among the corpses of his children, says

> this is the conflict of no other *daimōn*
> but the wife of Zeus.[40]

Of course. Hera hates him. So much destruction must be her fault: she maddened Heracles.

But in hyperbolic madness, or the recklessness in which Pentheus insults Dionysus, both *daimōn* and human agency are present.[41] This is the legacy of Homeric *atē* to tragic causality. Daemonic interference with your mind and judgment is also human. Patroclus's *atē* in the *Iliad* exemplifies the rash madness that tragedy uses and *hamartia* interprets. Achilles gave Patroclus a limit. He must not go beyond it. Yet he does. He was pushed by gods, but the act was his. He was *nēpios*, foolish.

---

[38] Dawe 1968; Bremer 1969. Bremer and Dawe met while working this out ("I was glad his views confirmed mine"; Bremer 1969:99 n. 1). The insight needs work now but was a vital contribution (made separately by each) to understanding Aristotle's relation with tragedy. Girard 1977:203, 219 replaces the image of tragic "flaw" with "violence": another way of interpreting *harmartia* as being, itself, an interpretation of *atē*-derived violent tragic madness. See Stinton 1990:173, evaluating the insight of Dawe and Bremer.

[39] See Chapter 18, Appendix. I wish Tom Stinton were around to meet this objection to his claim that *atē* is central to, e.g., Heracles' downfall (Stinton 1990:179). In a way he is right, of course. But the play does not use the word. What we see instead is Lyssa.

[40] *HF* 1311–12.

[41] *Ba.* 359; see Chapter 18, n. 36.

You could recode his rashness as hyperbolic madness. If he'd followed instructions, he would have survived.[42] You can also recode it as *hamartia*, a good man suffering not through wickedness but by "big error." As Homer says, "greatly *aasthē*." *Hamartia* stands, you might say, for the human face of madness: tragedy's use of madness, both the real thing and the idea, as the worst possible mistake.

SELF-NEGLECT, SELF-DAMAGE

One of the defining features of madness is its self-damage. Someone mad is "destroyer of his own things."[43] Mad people neglect their bodies. Orestes does not eat or wash. When the chorus hears Phaedra does not eat, they ask if this is "from *atē*," which here means (most likely) "madness."[44]

The absence of normal self-ministration means madness. The extreme end of this is self-mutilation. Mad Cleomenes hacks himself to death in the stocks. In "mad raving," Evadne throws herself to her death. Philoctetes "wanders in a tempest of grief, uttering words *para noun* [astray from his mind]," demanding a sword "to hack my flesh and limbs."[45]

What corresponds to all this in hyperbolic madness is neglecting, or damaging, self-interest.[46] At the end of *Prometheus Bound*, Prometheus is told to give Zeus information that only he knows. He refuses. He knows Zeus will torture him further; he foresees it all. But he hates all the gods

> who repay my benefits to them
> unjustly, wronging me.

Hermes, Zeus's spokeman, replies: "I hear you raving with a terrible sickness." "May I be sick," returns Prometheus, "if it's sick to hate one's enemies."[47]

Hermes tells him to do what Zeus wants. The chorus thinks this good advice, and talks about shameful error:

> he tells you to leave stubbornness
> and seek good, wise counsel. Obey him!
> It's shameful for a wise man to err.[48]

Hermes says Prometheus is sick, because it is self-damaging to oppose Zeus. But popular morality thought it right to "harm one's enemies and

---

[42] See Chapter 17, n. 9.
[43] Ar. *Pl.* 242.
[44] *Or.* 40–42; *Hipp.* 276.
[45] Hdt. 6.75; E. *Supp.* 1000–1001 (*ekbaccheusamena*); *Phil.* 1193–95, 1206.
[46] See below, n. 51.
[47] *PV* 935, 975–78.
[48] *PV* 1036–39.

help one's friends"—and to help oneself. It is reasonable, even right, to hate one's enemies.[49] Prometheus wishes to *be* mad if the ordinary, accepted stance towards enemies is mad. According to Gorgias, the fifth-century rhetorician, "Madness [*mania*] is trying impossible, shameful deeds, deeds that harm yourself [*asumphora*], that harm your friends and benefit your enemies, cover your own life in shame and make it liable to fall [*sphaleron*]."[50] Madness is doing things that are against your own interest as the world perceives it; turning your life into something "liable to fall"; inverting normal attitudes to friends and enemies. It is mad not to hate your enemies. Prometheus, therefore, is claiming madness in order to say he is not mad.

This play generates friction between different bits of conventional morality partly through its contradictory vision of Zeus and Prometheus's relation with him. Zeus rules the world. Prometheus sees him as one of the "younger gods" whom he helped, who repaid him with ingratitude and injury.[51] This exchange presses on the play's key issue: can you apply conventional morality to the divine ruler? It puts the self-injury of hyperbolic madness at the center of interpreting moral behavior.

Hyperbolically, it is mad to neglect self-interest. "If you think you can wrong a kinsman and not pay the penalty," Oedipus tells Creon, "you're not in your right mind." Oedipus is "not thinking well" when he will not trust *his* kinsman. Haemon is "empty witted" to threaten his father, Creon, who is "full of sickness of not-thinking" in his impious, self-damaging stubbornness. Yet another Creon is "empty of *nous*" to kidnap Athens's suppliants. Mistaking where your interest lies, as Hermes thinks Prometheus is doing, is evidence, hyperbolically, of madness.[52]

CHILD-MURDER

Is this the promised end?
Or image of that horror?
—Shakespeare, *King Lear* 5.3

Real and hyperbolic madness both involve self-damage. You damage your body, your family, your self-interest, your future. The worst image of this self-damage is the most unimaginable act of all: killing your own child, a murder that is the prototype of horror in Greek imagination. It is typically associated with tragic madness but appears outside tragedy too.

[49] See Dover 1974:182–83; Vlastos 1991: ch. 7; Blundell 1989.
[50] Gorgias DK82B 11A25.
[51] *PV* 960, 221–25.
[52] *OT* 550–53, cf. 626; *Ant.* 754, 1052; *OC* 931; see Chapter 18, nn. 40–44. Cf. Chapter 7, nn. 7, 42, 46, 49.

It is sometimes given an extra macabre gloss:

> The father lifts his own son . . . and slaughters him
> with a prayer. Blind fool [*mega nēpios*]. The son screams,
> imploring his father as he sacrifices. But he doesn't listen
> and kills him, preparing an evil feast in his halls.[53]

Eating your children. In Plato's vision of souls choosing future lives, one picks a life of "greatest tyranny" without checking it, then discovers he will eat his own children. The motif was in many myths used in tragedy, like the story of Thyestes.[54] Killing children is bad enough. Eating them underlines the self-annihilation of the act. You are consuming your own future, your way of surviving death. Your child is your "hope." As a heartbreaking, real-life epitaph on a child's grave says:

> His father Philip put away here
> *tēn pollēn elpida* [all his hope]
> Nikoteles. A child, twelve years old.

In poetry, father-to-small-son scenes often use comparative adjectives. Ajax wants Eurysaces to be happier than his father. Hector hopes they'll call Astyanax "far better than his father."[55] The son must enlarge his father's qualities, take the adjectives further. To kill and, worse, consume this small growing future self, this "great hope," is the worst of self-destructions. It can happen through error or a trick, as with Thyestes. But mostly it happens in madness. Madness makes Lycurgus kill his son, Dryas; makes Heracles kill his children and family; makes Agave kill Pentheus.[56] It is mad to destroy your hope, your future.

Killing your children is self-damaging in another way. Killing your kin, you break divine law. Heracles is polluted by murdering his children.[57] Error and polluting punishment come together in killing your own child. The worst, strangest thing about Medea is that she is *not* mad. And apparently she does not incur pollution.

What do the mad do? What is tragic madness, behaviorally? Error. Self-damage. Why does it happen? To answer that, we can look back to the action of Homeric *atē* on the mind, which entails two operations at once.

---

[53] Emp. fr. 137DK. Stressing connections between Homeric *atē* and tragic madness, Girard 1977:164 translates *mega nēpios* here as "in a fit of madness" (see above, Chapter 16, n. 22). See further Parker 1983:376, app. 7; Burkert 1983:78, 282. Cf. "eating" your own *thumos*: above, Chapter 3, n. 11. Both are mad images, images of self destruction.

[54] Pl. *Rep.* 619B–C; see Burkert 1983:170, 174, 177–85. Thyestes: *Ag.* 1095–96.

[55] *AP* 7.453; *Aj.* 550; *Il.* 6.479.

[56] Lycurgus, A. *Edoni*: above, n. 30. Illustrations of Lycurgus in drama: Sechan 1926:63–79. Cf. *HF* 835–36; *Ba.* 1122–24; Chapter 2, n. 21.

[57] *HF* 1233; Parker 1983:104–37.

There is the loss of something valuable—judgment, self-preservative care—plus a destructive violent addition: the incursion of an alien force.[58] *Atē* was the prehistoric model for tragic madness. Both connect damage done to others with damage done to self. The most satisfying tragic explanation for appalling damage, done simultaneously to others and to self, is madness. The incursion into self of something savage and daemonic, plus the simultaneous loss of some human core.

[58] See Chapter 16, nn. 29–30, 35–36.

Chapter 20

DIVINE DOUBLE BIND

DAEMONIC SELF-CONFLICT

> The tragic emotion, in fact, is a face looking two ways.
> —James Joyce, *Portrait of the Artist as a Young Man*

TRAGIC MADNESS has an important human dimension to which Aristotle's concept of *hamartia* corresponds. But it is mainly divinity at work. This self-damage and murder of self-hope must (mustn't it?) come from gods. "Whom gods want to destroy, they first make mad."[1] The present tense form of *aaomai* and *mainomai* is both middle *and* passive, but in the aorist, the instantaneous past that pronounces on things after they happen, their dominant grammatical voice is passive. "I *was done harm to*."[2] "I was a victim." Madness is mainly daemonic persecution.

But tragedy, always facing "two ways," does not leave it there. Its language plays between passive and active models of mind but stresses the passive.[3] "Coming from god" does not have to mean "from outside": daemons are in us as well as outside us.[4]

One factor here is division among gods themselves. The language has two main words for "god." As a general rule, *theos* and *daimōn* seem to suggest two different ways of regarding gods. *Theos* denotes something separate from human beings, something out there, in itself. It may watch you closely but anything it does is done from afar. *Daimōn*, it has been argued, is divinity that moves in: the nonhuman in the human. It is divinity getting its hands dirty, wading into human lives. Close, active, involved. The same god, therefore, may be called *theos* and *daimōn* at different moments.[5]

One etymology of *daimōn* is *daiō*, "I divide."[6] Does this express a sense

---

[1] See Chapter 1, nn. 1–4; Appendix, nn. 44–48. Cf. Theodorou 1993:32 (with n. 6).

[2] See Chapter 3, nn. 1–4, 30; Chapter 16, nn. 24–25, 27.

[3] Padel 1992:111 (cf. 137).

[4] Padel 1992:114, 128.

[5] E.g., *Il.* 4.420; see Brunius-Nilsson 1955:7–8, 118–26, 138. See, with different perspectives on this, Padel 1992:159–61; Vernant and Vidal-Naquet 1981:54; Williams 1993:16–19.

[6] See Basset 1919; Porzig 1923; Untersteiner 1939; Brunius-Nilsson 1955:140. Cf. the derivation from *daēmōn*, "knowing": Pl. *Crat.* 397C–98C.

that divinity *makes divisions in* human lives and minds? Or an insight that *daimōn* itself is essentially divided? We cannot tell. There is plenty of room for both senses. All gods are "many-named." All activities are governed overlappingly by several gods. The multiplicity and divisions of divinity are an essential aspect of tragic, as they were of real, life.

Tragedy's picture of inner life reflects this. Feelings are other in self, the moves of *daimōn* in you. Like the society of gods, consciousness is a multiplicity.[7] Inevitably, therefore, madness, upsetting and darkening consciousness, is a multiplicity too. The diversity of daemons matches the diversity of tragic madness. Madness as self-injuring error, darkness, twisted perception, alienation, and the rest are many aspects of one thing.

Plato divides madness according to what human beings do, and according to which god makes them do it.[8] The daemonic agents of tragic madness—Erinys, Dionysus, Aphrodite, Ares, Eros, Lyssa, Hera, even Athene—reflect its multiplicity, which comes over at a linguistic level in multiple words for madness. *Oistros, lyssa, mania*; adjectives, verbs, participles; the works of *ek, para*, and *en*.[9]

Tragedy proliferated the words and daemonic embodiments of madness, as well as its images: of darkness, twisted mind and eyes, self-damage, child murder, and the rest. Faced with this diversity in tragedy's use of madness, we might come up with the word "fragmentation" here. But this word comes too easily, now, into late-twentieth-century talk about consciousness and madness.[10] Linguistically, imagistically, and daemonically, Greek tragic madness is a bouillabaisse: one thing, with many aspects.

DIVINITY IS CONFLICT

Division is key to Greek divinity in another way too. The gods incarnate conflict. The idea that human conflict has daemonic force—is, in fact, *daimōn*—is central to the archaic thought-world. Eris, Conflict, is "elder daughter of Night." Zeus set her "in the roots of earth." In one of Hesiod's poems, Night bears Oath, with Erinyes as midwives. In the other, Night bears *Ponos* [Pain], Battles, Murders, *Neikea* [Quarrels], and Ate as well as Oath.[11] Hesiod makes the dark "roots" of conflict endemic in this world, whose schism and multiple conflict his two self-divided poems each enact.

---

[7] Padel 1992:ix, 157 (with n. 51). See above, Chapter 2, nn. 1–3.

[8] See Chapter 8, nn. 30, 34, 47.

[9] See respectively Chapter 2, nn. 9, 14, 15–23, 27–28; Chapter 2, nn. 30–34, and Chapter 3, nn. 1–5, 20–26, 28–30; Chapter 12, nn. 5–24, 47–57.

[10] See Padel 1992:46.

[11] *Erg*. 17–19, 804 (see Padel 1992:165); *Theog*. 226–31; Theodorou 1993:32 n. 6; Emp. fr. 17, 30DK (Arist. *Met*. B4, 1000B12).

In the *Iliad*, human nature and human lives are the locus of gods' conflict with each other. "The gods went into battle, divided in their *thumos*. . . . Gods against gods." Zeus's policy is to preserve divine harmony. Hera stops him acting "beyond fate" on the grounds that "all we other gods do not approve." If he were to go beyond fate, he would "put terrible anger" among the gods. But there is schism even within Zeus. He yields to Hera, who is "raging" to destroy the town he loves. But he yields reluctantly (that "this quarrel may not be a cause to conflict between you and me"): "willingly but with an unwilling *thumos*."[12] To keep harmony between him and Hera, he endures division within himself. Self-conflict touches even the soul of the divine ruler.

The narrative is self-conflicted about him. He wants divine peace, yet laughs at the noise gods make battling with each other, when "the *thumos* in their *phrenes* blew dividedly":

> The wide earth groaned. The great sky trumpeted.
> Zeus, sitting on Olympus, heard and laughed:
> delighted when he saw gods come together in conflict.[13]

Tragedy inherited this sense that conflict is *daimōn*, that the world is run by conflicted divinity whose disunity fatally affects human lives. With its special interest in inward events and their effect on the outer world, tragedy sees divine disunity as both reflected in and causing disunity and self-conflict in human minds.[14] Tragedians use the self-conflict of divinity in different ways. On the whole they avoid direct confrontation between deities. In *Eumenides*, Apollo tries to expel Erinyes from his temple. It is not clear that they leave because of him. They acknowledge his greatness according to "the throne of Zeus," but leave because they want to track Orestes, who has already left. Later, Apollo confronts them again in a human court.[15]

In tragedy, god normally meets god in conflict not face to face but through human beings and their relationships. Human relations are *daimōn*'s battleground or courtroom. Aphrodite punishes Artemis's favorite, Hippolytus, because his intense relation with Artemis excluded her. Artemis promises Hippolytus as he dies that she will hit back at Aphrodite through *her* favorite. Revenge killing: this is what she does for him.[16] The gods go on. Hippolytus (and later Adonis) are ammunition in gods' conflict with each other. Tragic understanding of daemonic splitting draws on

---

[12] *Il.* 20.32, 75; 16.443, 449; 4.32, 46, 38, 43.

[13] *Il.* 20.386–90; see Williams 1993:51.

[14] See Padel 1992:48.

[15] *Eum.* 181–97, 229–31, 547–48.

[16] *Hipp.* 1420–22. She reconciles his father to him too, but this is not represented as a gift.

earlier poetry, and on local imagination of divinity as divided. But it made this domain peculiarly its own.

The *daimōnes* of your life, and the human relationships in which they inhere, define you. In tragedy, the gods are divinities of, above all, relationship. Of joining (Aphrodite, Eros). Or fighting (like Ares). Of entertaining, making and breaking promises, signing contracts, competing in games.[17] You could read *Antigone* as conflict between gods of family versus civic relationships. The relationships you sustain in your living define you. But these gods are also centers of individual identity, hauling their own concerns and resonances with them into a human self. Medea has altars of Hecate in her *muchoi*, inner chambers: an image of the darkness and murderousness within her self.[18] In narrative terms, divinity comes across as aid and persecution. In the *Odyssey*, Odysseus is defined by Athene's love and Poseidon's hatred. Euripides' Heracles is defined by Zeus's pride in him, and Hera's hatred.

The spectrum of divinity is the spectrum of human relationships. Gods jealously inhabit our contact with others, our social nerve endings, infusing each individual's web of family, social, and business relationships with daemonic energy and sudden violence. Yet no god protects you from the demands made upon you by another, or cares that *their* stake in you—their jealous protection of their rights (in a relationship with, for example, your father, daughter, business partner, guest)—means you may offend another god. They do not shield you from the result of honoring them. Apollo defends Orestes, but his conflict with the Erinyes, even when Athene has cast her own vote for Orestes, ends in a tie. Apollo is "great"; but not great enough to save Orestes from the Erinyes. Another god ends the conflict by making them see their role differently: as beneficial to human ground.[19]

Scission in the divine world entails self-scission: impulses and loyalties acting against each other in the self. Madness in tragedy is often the result (though not the only result) of the way divinity fights out its conflicts on the battle site of individual lives. *Daimōn* is in conflict with itself.

In our terms, we can read this (as long as we remember the cultural translation we are doing) as different forces within a self, battling with each other. Madness is one outcome of conflicting divinities (maybe different ones, maybe different aspects of the same), forcing you to do things for which it punishes you.[20] Human beings live and think their lives in a divine trap. One result of this is madness.

[17] E.g., Erinyes: Padel 1992:168, 173; Hermes: 6 9.
[18] *Med.* 397; cf. Moll 1976:552–80.
[19] *Eum.* 735, 753, 229; cf. Padel 1992:165–72.
[20] Cf. Chapter 17, nn. 13–14, and Chapter 18, nn. 28–34.

Double Bind

A modern parallel here is the childhood scenario identified, in mid-twentieth-century theory, as a factor in the genesis of schizophrenia. The double bind is a concept first formulated by Gregory Bateson, and refined in use since.[21] It had enormous impact on psychoanalytic thought,[22] and goes something like this. In expressing emotions, or issuing commands, a "schizophrenogenic" parent sends conflicting messages. The message of the emotion conflicts with the message of words that convey it. "Of course I love you," through clenched teeth which imply, unspoken, "You little bastard." A spoken order ("Don't dirty the floor"), subverted by the unspoken message with which it comes: "Go on, make the floor dirty, I'll love you if you do." Praise ("What a lovely picture") spoken in a tone that says the opposite: "Oh God! More rubbish!"

Children of such parents get punished whichever order they obey. If they obey the spoken command, the parent punishes them with lessening interest and love. If they obey the unspoken one, they are punished according to the parent's explicit rules.[23]

In this scenario, the same authority figure issues contradictory messages and commands. The child, trying to mitigate the desolating pain this causes, responds in kind. Divided messages elicit division. You have to divide either self, or "reality" (that is, the parent), or both.[24] It is intolerably painful to blame the parent for inconsistency. So, instead of seeing reality at fault, you generate a "split" within the self. "Schizophrenia" is "division of *phrēn*." The resulting madness, fought out in the self, expresses the clash of conflicting demands that originated outside.

Double-bind theory also expresses a more general modern psychological insight, that people "go mad" to escape pain. If the world is abnormally painful, the mind abandons normal ways of coping with it. It would be mad not to.

True or not, double-bind theory helps us respond to the two roles of tragic madness. Tragic humanity's god-trapped state matches that of a child faced with a schizophrenogenic parent. Divinity guards and enforces human morality, but is not bound by the rules it imposes. Divinity is a

[21] "Towards a Theory of Schizophrenia" (1958), "Double Bind" (1969), collected in Bateson 1973 (see 167ff., 215ff., 242ff.). Developments: Berger 1978.

[22] Though the concept has been resisted by some practitioners of psychiatry, especially those who explain "schizophrenia" as due only to (as distinct from being describable in terms of) neurological events or a developmental defect in the brain.

[23] This is a much-simplified account of the scenario. Early versions of it: see Bateson 1973 (above, n. 21).

[24] Laing 1965:162 and 1971:88 underline the difference between "splitting" reality and "splitting" self.

source of contradictory orders, punishing you for obeying one according to the logic of another. Divinity issues prohibitions (do not kill your mother), forces you to break them, then punishes you for breaking them.

To relate the double bind to tragic images of madness is not, of course, the same as saying that fifth-century Athenians were schizophrenic in relation to their gods. That would be coarsely thought, a muddle. To compare the problems of Orestes to double-bind theory is simply to say that this is what *we*—since the concepts of schizophrenia and double bind exist (however controversially) in our world—can relate them to, in our effort to imagine what *it was like* to inhabit that earlier imaginative world:[25] a world in which real people, as well as literary characters, lived subject to daemonic split. In the fourth century, Xenophon, one of the sanest, most conventionally honest minds we contact in antiquity, is advised by Delphi to sacrifice to Zeus Basileus, Zeus the King, when he begins an expedition.[26] When things go wrong, he learns from another source, a seer, that Zeus Meilichios, Zeus Merciful, is angry and "in his way," because he has not sacrificed to *him*.[27]

Xenophon is not schizophrenic. It is another person, a seer, who tells him Zeus Meilichios is angry. Zeus, as the Greek world sanely perceives him, has many roles and personae. These can, all too easily, have conflicting relations with one and the same individual. Reality—daemonic reality—is endlessly split. Fifth-century Athenians could cope more successfully, it seems, with the multiple and conflicting demands of the world upon them than can the child of a schizophrenogenic parent today.

For one thing, they were supported by the shared perceptions of their society. They did not have to split themselves or how they saw reality. Conflict was part of the human world as run by gods. Reality itself was divided. One god says do something, another punishes you for it. That is how the world really is.

CAUGHT IN THE CROSS-FIRE: ORESTES AND IO

Orestes and Io crop up together again, at this point.[28] They are tragedy's examples of long-term madness. They are also the prime examples of madness caused by cross-fire between contradictory divine wills: when one god interferes in a human life, bringing that individual into collision with another god's interests. Often there is only one god behind the madness. Ajax, Pentheus, Cassandra, Phaedra, Heracles: their madness is not the result of daemonic cross-fire. It comes from the difficulties of relationship

[25] See Padel 1992:141.
[26] Xen. *An.* 6.1.21 (cf. 3.1.5); 7.6.44.
[27] *Xen. An.* 7.8.4 (see Burkert 1985:201).
[28] Cf. Chapter 4, nn. 8–18.

with one particular god. They go mad once, and after that are trapped by the consequences.

Orestes and Io, however, go on suffering bursts of madness. I think this is because they are caught in divine conflict. Translated into our terms (the demands of relationships bleached of divinity), they keep going mad because there are demands on them from conflicting sources that are not resolved in the real world, so cannot be resolved in the individual either.

These are human beings trapped in crazy dictator's logic, as in Koestler's *Darkness at Noon*, where the hero is imprisoned for being the sort of person who will have the thoughts he does have when imprisoned. They are punished whichever command they obey. Out of that trap comes their madness, expressing the clash of divine interests in an individual human being.

> Apollo's oracle, pressuring Orestes to murder his mother,
> described angers out of the ground
> from powers ill-disposed to mortals.[29]

It threatened "ulcers that ride on flesh with savage jaws": sufferings await Orestes if he fails to avenge his father. As he says, "Mustn't I trust oracles like these?"[30] Yet Erinyes punish him for murdering his mother. Their angers too, are "out of the ground." "Daughters of Earth," they "hold a position below earth and in sunless dark."[31]

Madness is the result of Orestes' relation to all these powers simultaneously. He goes mad "out of the ground" of the play, because the universe is as it is. His dilemma parallels that of his father earlier. Zeus sent Agamemnon an omen to show he would capture Troy. But the omen's enactment involved the destruction of a pregnant hare and this angered Artemis, as the goddess who cares for birth and its issue. Artemis is

> angry at her father's winged hounds
> who sacrifice before its birth
> a young frightened thing
> with its mother.[32]

---

[29] Or, "describing propitiations for the angry ones: propitiations from out of the ground": *Cho.* 278–80. See, e.g., Paley *ad loc.* Lobeck conjectured *mēnimata* for *meiligmata.* (*Mēnimata* might support the idea that Plato is thinking of tragic madness at *Phdr.* 244D: see Chapter 8, nn. 16–17, 21, 46.) Page stressed the *men/de* distinction: "*describing*" propitiations, but "mentioning" diseases. Conington thought the first limb (with *meiligmata*) stated a general law: the two parts refer to different aspects of Orestes' choice. Either he kills his mother (the propitiation required) or (*de*) he suffers. With *mēnimata*, the things distinguished are, on one hand, angers "out of the ground"; on the other, afflictions these angers will send if he does not do what they want. Murray, hesitantly, read *mēnimata.*

[30] *Cho.* 297. Cf. Padel 1992:186–89.

[31] *Eum.* 395–96; Padel 1992:103–10, 172–76.

[32] *Ag.* 135–37. See Denniston/Page ed., intro. and *ad Ag.* 135; Fraenkel *ad loc.*

Artemis demands in return the "sacrifice" of another young frightened creature. Iphigeneia.[33]

Long before we see Orestes, therefore, we hear of his father caught between the conflicting demands of *daimōn*. These demands were deeply personalized, in divine relationships that seem irrelevant to human concerns: Artemis angry with her father's eagles. But as with terrorism, conflict that lands randomly in human lives has a disastrous and lasting effect. Orestes' dilemma comes from the long-prepared ground of his father's. Both dilemmas express universal and divine conflicts. Young against old; female against male; domestic against civic.

This ancient conflictedness of the world is made explicit in Apollo's confrontation with the Erinyes. They say, "We drive matricides from their home." What about a wife who kills her husband? asks Apollo. Not the same, they reply. None of our business. Not murder of kin. Then, says Apollo,

> on this argument you make the promises
> of Hera, Marriage-Fulfiller, and Zeus,
> dishonored and invalid. Aphrodite too,
> from whom come mortals' dearest things.
> She too is dishonored.[34]

They do not care. Like some crazy bureaucrat, they pursue only their own function, regardless.

Orestes' entrapped condition results from, and crystallizes, the trilogy's whole vision of daemonic split, split expressed intermittently as sexual or generational conflict,[35] but which also points to the divisiveness of divinity, and its divisive effect on human minds. The Erinyes' music is

> striking aside, carrying aside,
> crazing the *phrēn* . . . binding the *phrenes*.[36]

The accident of our image, double "bind," answers to the bondage in which tragedy (enacting the conflict of divinely monitored human relationships) pins its human figures. It uses madness in both roles, both means and an end, to do so.

Io suffers from daemonic split too. Zeus tells her in her dreams that he desires her. Her father asks advice. Delphi says cast her out, or a thunderbolt will shatter the house.

> Obeying these words of Loxias, my father drove me out
> and barred the door. It was against his will. And mine.

[33] *Ag.* 241.
[34] *Eum.* 210–16.
[35] See Goldhill 1986.
[36] *Eum.* 329–32.

Her sufferings, her wandering and madness, are a "god-swept storm," caused not just by Zeus's desire but by Hera's anger with her for arousing that desire.[37]

The plays eventually end the dilemmas of Orestes and Io. But these resolutions are local, particular. They do not undo the perennial possibility, endemic to the tragic world, of double bind. Madness remains one outcome of daemonic scission.[38]

There is a further dimension to the double bind in which tragic divinity holds humanity. Destructive passion is sent by gods, incarnate in gods. You have to fight it. Yet it is impious, ultimately impossible, to fight gods. *Theomachia* is both doomed and wrong.[39] These are contradictory imperatives. You must fight your own deepest feelings and yet you cannot, must not. If you do, you come to grief. If you do not, they destroy you anyway.

[37] *PV* 669–70, 643, 590–92, 704. You might ask why Heracles, also caught between Zeus and Hera, does not suffer long-term madness like Io. But there is nothing Zeus wants from him. His life is one long persecution by Hera, of which his madness is the culmination.

[38] See Chapter 4, n. 34.

[39] Padel 1992:128; see Chapter 19, nn. 23–24.

PART 5

Madness: A Rough Tragic Grammar

This is where I came from.
I passed this way.
This should not be shameful
Or hard to say.

A self is a self.
It is not a screen.
A person should respect
What he has been.
    —James Fenton, "The Ideal"

Chapter 21

MAD IN ANOTHER WORLD

"To Feel for Bearings": Other People's Madness

IDEAS OF madness do not operate in a vacuum. They are given meaning by, and give meaning to, local activities and perceptions, they belong in a specific society's understanding:[1] of people and relationships between them, of relations between emotion and the self. They are closely bound to local ways of perceiving other experiences. In ancient Greece, associations to (among other things) wandering, pollution, root-magic, black bile, and dance affect the local picture of madness. One vital further dimension (left out of this book), which differs from one society to another, is the gendering of madness.[2]

As far as ancient Greece goes, we are foreign observers who think we own the place. To try and do something enormous and immodest, like talk about its ideas of madness, we must set these as deeply as we can in the texture of the culture. We must never do violence to that culture's own representations: the expressed causalities, scientific, religious, and popular; the available patterns of explanation for what happens in and to people, normally. The one nonvariable is that "mad" everywhere depends on the locally agreed judgment "normal." If there is enough evidence, the historian or anthropologist can relate beliefs and images of madness to local representations of normal inner life. Each will illuminate the other.[3]

All this is taken as read by social historians and anthropologists. To them, "normal" and "mad" are local judgments, constructed by a specific time, place, and culture. Other writers do not think so. One motif of British thrillers after both World Wars was the brave man, cherished in war, who turned out to be a disturbed, dangerous misfit in peacetime. Peace is the norm: judgments made in peace are the true ones.[4]

But Britain has a privileged history in this respect. For many societies, war has always been and still is the norm. As it was at Athens for over half

---

[1] Cf. Chapter 4, n. 36.

[2] Cf. Schiesari 1992; Showalter 1987; Padel 1981.

[3] MacDonald 1981 uses ideas of madness to illuminate ideas of normal inner life in the society he studies. See his intro., xii–xiii.

[4] See e.g., Agatha Christie, *The 4.50 From Paddington* (cf. Buchan, *The Three Hostages*). Cf. Showalter 1987:190.

the fifth century, and at Rome and in many other ancient societies. The top political job at Athens, "General," was a military appointment.

A fiction genre that explores and orders chaos, like a thriller, can choose its own standpoint. But historians and anthropologists have a responsibility to the alien perspective. Assuming that terms local to your own are the norm won't do.

This is where the aims of anthropology diverge from those of psychoanalysis. The central gift from both these disciplines to other interpretive projects has been the same: the knowledge that self mixes itself with other while describing it. But in the Anglo-American world, at least, the two have an oddly competitive relationship now. One puts cultural difference center stage. The other claims universal insight into the psyche.[5] Good writers in both make self-awareness crucial to interpretation but do not let it take over. Like all good readers, they know the magnifying glass is the same fabric as the mirror, but does not have to reflect. You need complete darkness behind the lens to make it reflect your eye only.[6]

But ignoring the history and language of the culture whose works you are talking about does put black behind the glass through which you look. It is fine to use the Greek tragedies, with no reference to the society which produced them, to think with. To reflect your insight into, for instance, modern psyches. What are the plays for, now, if not also for that? But it is *not* fine to claim that what you see in that operation is thereby "in" the plays. If you see yourself reflected in a flake of burnished obsidian, this does not mean the person who polished it two thousand years ago, for an unknown purpose, put you there.

Psychoanalysts all too easily turn a blind eye to the ethnocentrism of their project. One, for instance, thinks Oedipus in *Oedipus at Colonus* enacts a "retreat from truth to omnipotence"; a "retreat" whose madness "is more evident as a social problem in times of crisis such as war, when its psychotic nature may be more difficult to recognize. At these times, omnipotence is so much sought after by all of us that we are ready to accept an individual as a hero who, in normal circumstances, we would recognize as a madman."[7] But peace is not "normal circumstances." According to the research group World Priorities, twenty-nine major wars were being fought around the world at the end of 1993. Ten million were killed 1914–18, in "the war to end all wars." Conservative estimates say fifty-five million died 1939–45. No accurate figures exist, but one report estimates twenty-three million have died in conflicts since: at least two million in

---

[5] Padel 1990a:198.

[6] The word *glas* (as in *Glasnost*) is the old Slavonic for "voice." But as used by Derrida, it blends (literary) "gloss" with the "knell" of secure reading, and also with *glace* (both "ice" and "looking glass"): G. Steiner 1981:214.

[7] J. Steiner 1990:235.

Korea, at least one in the Iran-Iraq war.[8] A lot of death in war, for normality. For peace. And our age is not unique in this.

"*Recognize* as" implies that this judgment "mad," derived from peace-time values, is universally valid. It is a peace-centric assumption. In war, the mechanism labelled "retreat from truth" may be not a problem but a necessity—may *be* the norm, for societies permanently at war. It may be mad not to do it. How snugly you smooth such labels to Greek tragic figures depends on definitions of, and differences between, heroes and madness in fifth-century Athens, Renaissance Europe, and modern imagination.[9]

Though there are many honorable and subtle exceptions, psychoanalysis encourages in its writers the idea that "psychoses" are the same everywhere, that its own explanations are universal.[10] But most anthropologically focussed studies of non-Western or past cultures dismiss the assumption that there are universal categories of madness. If you want to spot "formations and treatment of psychological disorders" in someone else's society, you need empirical depth, tact, and a responsibly gentle way of "feeling for bearings" within a foreign culture. All the time you come up against a self-validating vicious circle. If you apply your own categories without questioning them, of course self finds them validated in other.[11]

One 1963 psychiatric study of the Yoruba, for instance, tried to "avoid classification of conditions as far as possible, record symptoms descriptively with few assumptions," hold back from imposing its own categories, and "elicit local notions of the range of mental disorders and the concepts used." The team found parallels between Yoruba conceptualization of mental disorders and diagnostic categories standard in American psychiatry. But these may well have arisen from "the researchers' training in thinking in the usual psychiatric categories."[12]

---

[8] Quoted in *The Observer*, 14 November 1993:1.

[9] See Padel 1981:118–23; below, Chapter 22, nn. 18–28.

[10] E.g., Spiro 1993 argues against Malinowsky's "relativistic" idea that the Trobriand Islanders did not have an Oedipus complex because the psychological constellation of their matrilineal society did not fit it. Spiro did no original research but looked at Malinowsky's data and decided he was wrong for, differently analyzed, his data suggest Trobrianders could have an Oedipus complex. But many analysts are of course far more flexible. One Argentinian therapist in conversation said that a father murdering the mother for adultery would not traumatize her patients *as much as* it would traumatise British children, since *crime passionel* is an accepted part of their culture.

[11] Clarke 1975:11. His alien culture is early Britain. See below, nn. 61–62.

[12] Reported by Clarke 1975:4–5 (with n. 12), 23. Clarke 1975: ch. 1 is a fair, succinct account of methodological problems here. Ten years later, Bynum, Porter, and Shepherd 1985b further developed problems of method and classification involved in studying madness in earlier societies. MacDonald 1981:114–15, discussing seventeenth-century mental disorders, avoids modern terms. All this is basic methodological work, which anyone now

Psychoanalytic divergence from the critical standards of anthropology or history is inevitable. Psychoanalysis has an extra responsibility. It is a way of reading people that also tries to change them (or help them discover whether and how they hope to change themselves). It draws material and conclusions from people who ask it for help. But the last thing *anthropologists* want is to change people they study. Their different professional dependence on the people from whom they draw insight affects the way psychoanalysts and anthropologists write.[13]

The narratives of psychoanalysis may be heuristic fictions, but if they help heal, this does not matter. Good analysts put what happens between themselves and their patient above the truth-or-fiction status of the narratives (like the Oedipus complex) that direct their relationship. It may help *patients*, at some point, to think these narratives more or less true. But to back some late-nineteenth-century constructs as universal truths against criteria of empirical anthropological research is oddly narrowing for the analyst.

For an analyst, theoretical as well as historical truth can, maybe should, be a disregardable therapeutic tool. Helping is the first priority. But for anthropologists and historians, getting as near historical truth as you can, while keeping a cold eye on implications of method and theory, is an end in itself.

The idea that "psychoses" are universal implies a biological or medical model. Within psychoanalysis, it grew, complicatedly, from Freud's grounding in neurology. But disease models for madness are very ancient.[14] There is no need to consider cultural difference if mental disease works *like* physical disease.

Arguments against it doing so, however, are rather strong. Medical facts are against it: even physical illnesses vary symptoms and behavior in different times and places. So are sociological facts. Every society perceives and structures illness according to beliefs and values of its time.[15] If this is the case with physical illness, how much the more for mental. Furthermore, medical images of madness depend on available local models of disease. I have suggested there is little fifth-century medical interest in chronic disease. This is reflected in tragic images of madness as a temporary event, known by external appearances, with no nineteenth-century sense of something hidden, lurking long-term "in" a personality.[16]

---

tackling madness in past or other cultures responsibly, or claiming that behavior represented in alien texts "is mad" when the text says it is not, has to absorb or seriously confront.

[13] See Padel 1991:210. Of course there are exceptions (see, e.g., Clément 1983, 1987, 1989) and a genre of psychoanalytic anthropology is developing; see, e.g., Vitebsky 1993:238–50.

[14] See Chapter 4, n. 31.

[15] See Herzlich and Pierrot 1987; above, pp. 32, 42, 158–62.

[16] See Chapter 3, nn. 24, 33, 37.

I have reached the methodological question, how to think about madness in alien cultures, via Greek images of mad *behavior* (see Part 4). What do the mad do? How are they judged? Madness is embedded in a culture's ethical as well as medical specifics. It may be there is no natural subject, "madness," at all. Perhaps the historian of madness, "like the student of religious heresy," explores only "essentially relativistic cultural constructs." Historians of what gets called madness ask how people were "labelled" mad. In worlds like late modern Europe, where institutions developed that operated the label, historians explore social factors that created these institutions, and the assumptions on which they were founded.[17]

A historian or anthropologist is gunning for a local currency of madness: its meanings in, meanings to, a specific society. But you go into an alien thought-world lugging your own categories along. You cannot leave them behind. But you can make a checklist: and, as far as possible, be aware of what you have brought with you.

There are two things to respect as we learn the local currency. One is cultural difference. Unless we are open to the idea that the foreign system is really different, in ways we cannot foresee before we enter, much of its meaning will elude us.[18] We cannot responsibly evaluate Andalusian views on childrearing, for instance, without going there. And learning Spanish.

The other thing to respect is the constructed, history-bound nature of our own culture's categories, and the processes by which they came into being.[19] As I have tried to show, many of our images derive in some way from the Greek, and often specifically the tragic, tradition, but were changed radically by the centuries that tossed them to us. This means Greek images of madness are even more likely than those of the Yoruba to look "the same" as ours, when they are not.[20]

DIVINITY VERSUS MORAL MISMANAGEMENT

As with all evaluations of tragic action and responsibility, the most fundamental difference between our ideas of madness and those of Greek tragedy is in relation to divinity.[21] Faced with schizophrenia, we invoke chemi-

---

[17] See Clarke 1975:4–7, 23, ch. 1 passim. See also MacDonald 1981; Porter 1987; Showalter 1987; Salkeld 1993.

[18] Cf Padel 1990a:204–206.

[19] E.g., see Chapter 3, nn. 38, 43; Chapter 5, n. 34; Chapter 6, nn. 25, 37, 43, 50; Chapter 9, nn. 18–24.

[20] Cf. similar problems over verbal images of emotion: Padel 1992:34, 75–77.

[21] See Chapters 3, 13, 20. What is true generally of Greek tragedy's portrait of action, that it "involved beliefs about the human and the daimonic which we could not possibly accept, which are no part of our world," but yet are comprehensible in our terms (Williams 1993:17 and passim), and its portrait of tragic responsibility, where "the human and divine planes are distinct enough from one another to be opposed but nevertheless appear as inseparable"

cal, neurological, psychiatric, genetic, and sociopolitical explanations. For fifth-century Athenians, what mattered was *daimōn* causing the madness. This is true even in medical writers. Although they concentrated, unlike most of the rest of their society, almost entirely on the human, they too assumed divinity affected illness and madness.[22]

It is worth bringing up some background to our own perspective here, as a reminder that our ideas of madness in relation to divinity are also historically constructed.

Early in the Christian era, depression and sadness are "sin" as well as "disease." John Cassian (who died c. A.D. 433), writes on "the eight principal sins." He lumps together six sins and two *morbi* (diseases), which he calls *tristitia* (sadness) and *acedia*. *Acedia*, Greek *akēdeia*, means literally "not-caring." Cassian defines it as *anxietas sive taedium cordis*, "anxiety or boredom of the heart."[23] It attacks body and mind.

People associated *acedia, accidie*, with the element of earth. By the twelfth century, there are cosmological and humoral psychosomatic explanations for it. But it is still a "capital vice," a sin often aligned with sloth. Analysis of it is moral, psychological, *and* biological.[24] By the fourteenth century, *accidie* has snowballed. It gathers endless layers and resonances. Popular handbooks align it with grief or depression. But they still think of it in physiological and theological terms, like melancholia. All these types of explanation contribute to the understanding of mental suffering and madness.

In 1482, a monk, Gaspar Ofhuys, tells a story about a painter, Hugo van der Goes. Gaspar's explanations, like those of Herodotus on Cleomenes in a different socioreligious context, assume interaction between physiological and divine aetiology. Hugo, stricken by mental illness, would have hurt himself "corporeally and lethally," if not restrained. A prior tried music therapy. It failed. Hugo said he was "a son of perdition," and died. Gasper ponders the causes and nature of this illness. Frenzy? Possession? Distress caused by melancholy, brought on by strong wine at banquets? Perturbation of the mind? Worry about work (Hugo had more commissions than he could have fulfilled in nine years)? Or affliction by God? Gaspar opts for God. God sent mental disease to make Hugo meet his end by eschewing pride. Or God meant Hugo to be an example to monks, to restrain their passions.[25]

(Vernant and Vidal-Naquet 1981:21–22, retranslated in Williams 1993:16), is also true of madness. But tragedy loads madness more deeply, and specifically, to the divine side of things: see above, pp. 9–16, 24–29, 40–42, 114, 210–13.

[22] See, e.g., Hp. *De victu 4* 1. See Chapter 14, nn. 48–49; Chapter 15, nn. 1–5; Chapter 19, n. 1.

[23] Kinsman 1974b:11–18. Cf. Snyder 1965; Chadwick 1968:46, 148.

[24] Wenzel 1968:8; Kinsman 1974b:14.

[25] Destree 1914:214–18; Kinsman 1974b:16–17.

In Elizabethan and Stuart England, a religio-demonic view of madness permeates the culture.[26] By the seventeenth century, medical explanations for insanity are winning out over religious ones, but only among the educated. Popular explanations still lean on demonological cause and effect. Here is the beginning of a split within society, in attitudes to madness and divinity: a split made complete in the eighteenth century. Richard Napier, the seventeenth-century astrological physician whose records include more than two thousand insane or troubled patients, healed (as his patients suffered) "on the cusp between two eras, dominated by the antagonistic forces of magic and science."[27]

The question of responsibility for what you do while mad, responsibility for your own madness, is now an acute muddle. Jeremy Collier attacks Shakespeare in 1698 for making public Ophelia's unseemly mad fantasies. He should not have blackened her: "Since Shakespeare was resolved to drown the lady like a kitten he should have set her swimming a little sooner. To keep her alive only to sully her Reputation . . . was very cruel. It may be said the Freedoms of Distraction go for nothing, a Fever has no Faults, and a Man non Compos may kill without Murther. It may be so: but then such people ought to be kept in dark rooms and without Company."[28] A fever *may* "have no Faults." It *may* not be murder if "a Man non Compos" kills. But there is something wrong and dangerous about mad people that is like sin. Keep them dark (see Part 1). Keep them isolated (see Part 2). Exorcise them. Maybe there is "fault." Perceptions of madness have always been tied to moral questions (see Part 4). An old name for the devil is *alienus*: the wanderer, stranger. (Until very recently a psychiatrist, especially someone specializing in legal aspects of madness, was called an "alienist.") What is "alien"—madness, mad sickness—may be wrong and evil.[29] Preachers based sermons on the correspondence between madness and sin. Thomas Adams's "Mystical Bedlam, or The World of Mad Men" conducts readers through a theological Bedlam, observing twenty men suffering different types of moral madness.[30]

Eighteenth-century medical thought gives new prominence to the role of the nervous system. Excess sensibility maddens the mind. But just at the time when God is kicked out of madness, its *moral* implications get a new boost. Madness acquires "a new content of guilt." "Moral sanction, just punishment" are now the issues. Madness is the "psychological effect of a moral fault."[31]

[26] MacDonald 1981:172.
[27] MacDonald 1981:9, 16–71.
[28] Jeremy Collier, "A Short View of the Immorality and Profaneness of the English Stage"; quoted in Salkeld 1993:11.
[29] Salkeld 1993:11, 16 n. 11; see above, Chapter 11, n. 4.
[30] MacDonald 1981:168–69.
[31] Bynum 1985; cf. Foucault 1971:158.

Hence the "scientific psychiatry" of the nineteenth century, when madness is believed to result from "moral weakness":

> He who has given a proper direction to the intellectual force, and thus ob-
> tained an early command over the bodily organ [the brain] by habituating it
> to the processes of calm reasoning, remains sane amid all the vagaries of
> sense; while he who has been the slave rather than the master of his animal
> nature, listens to its dictates without question even when distorted by
> disease—and is mad.[32]

Moral mismanagement needs "management." Restraint and fear *cure* madness. Patients confess (to their doctor, who reports these gratifying confes-
sions) that "when they found themselves effectually restrained from fulfill-
ing the dictates of their will, they became enlightened by a gleam of
reflection, and ceased to obey the impulse which prompted them."[33] This
has the paper worth of a confession from H-Block, but the proponents of
the theory, who wielded the power, and the manacles, believed it. Restraint
brought "reflection." Madness can be mastered by thought, by will.
"Moral management" was crucial in the nineteenth-century "making of
psychiatry."[34]

From early Greece onwards, madness is *ek*, *de*. "Out of, away" (see
Chapters 10, 11, and 12). Madness "wanders." *Error*, Latin for wandering,
points to moral implications buried in English resonances of madness.
Madness is "error" of thought, departure "from" right judgment. It is
"loss of" moral will.

Up to the late nineteenth century, each age reacted to madness in Greek
tragedy in terms of divinity and/or morality, equating intellectual and
moral, intellectual and theological, disorder and mistake. Divinity is implicated in madness. Whom gods destroy . . . The thought is reflected in
Irish, which has two expressions for a "mad person." One word (*gealt*)
relates madness to the moon (*gealach*), like "lunatic." The other is a phrase
relating madness to God: a mad person is a "person with God" (*Duine le
Dia*).[35]

All this boosted "moral flaw" readings of *hamartia* in the *Poetics*. Religion and morality hover round the word from early on. In the fourth
century, divinity "purifies us from the worst, most impious of our *hamartēmata*." *Hamartia* in the New Testament is "sin." For Gregory of Nyssa,
hamartia is *allotriōsis*, "alienation": from God.[36]

By the mid–eighteenth century, the prevailing educated view in Europe

---

[32] John Barlow, *Man's Power over Himself to Prevent or Control Insanity* (1843). See Skultans 1975:135–56, 157–203; Berrios 1985; Showalter 1987:30–32; Porter 1987:206–28.
[33] Haslam 1817:30–32.
[34] Porter 1987:169, 206.
[35] Thanks to Sean Dunne for this information.
[36] *DMS* 4.53: see Chapter 14, n. 49. Gregory: see Chapter 11, n. 4.

is that anyone claiming divine or demonic visions is mad. The gulf between views held by the elite and the less educated, among whom a religious psychology and religious stereotypes of mental abnormality prevailed, continued into the nineteenth century. Revelations reported by John Wesley show how widely the populace accepted demonic explanations. "The political pressures that prompted the governing classes to adopt a more secular attitude toward apparently supernatural phenomena were not felt by the poor."[37] This split underlies the jumble of twentieth-century attitudes to madness. You could argue (optimistically) that the educated in the West today accept sociopolitical and intrafamilial pressures as mad-making factors.[38] Simpler ways of making sense of madness stress the moral, daemonic, or magically chemical.

The assumption that all earlier views (of madness, for example) lead naturally to the one transparently true perspective where we stand is naive "progressivism."[39] For all our command of chemistry, our own chaotic approaches to madness and its relation to divinity are as anthropologically local, as historically constructed, as those of fifth-century Athens.

SELF-VALIDATION: PSYCHOANALYSIS AND ANACHRONISM

Now for a few psychoanalytic approaches to tragedy and its madness. Do they fit my two principles of respect: for the realities of cultural difference, and for the constructed nature of modern views?

I have to disagree here with lines of approach I think wrong. Much psychoanalytic writing today seems to me to betray the wide reading and intellectual generosity of its early days, by closing itself against other disciplines that study people:[40] especially anthropology and social history. When you tackle texts from another culture and the past, these disciplines should be the touchstone, for they do it all the time. Their own debates test the limits and possibilities of this kind of reading. To be taken seriously, as something that illuminates not their own theories but the tragedies or the Greeks themselves, psychoanalytic approaches to Greek tragedy must take these disciplines on board.

Here are some examples of not doing so, from professional psychoanalysts, or classical scholars playing the analyst. Agave is a neurotic who has, and recovers from, a psychotic seizure. Hippolytus's psychopathology is due to his Amazon mother. Iolaus's reported rejuvenation in Euripides'

---

[37] MacDonald 1981:171–72, 284 n. 227.

[38] Cf. Williams 1993:150–66.

[39] Williams 1993:4–9.

[40] Dodds 1951 in his preface says he used "recent anthropological and psychological observations and theories," believing "we must work with what light we can get, and an uncertain light is better than none," and trusting a "promising recent alliance between social anthropology and social psychology" (viii–ix). If this promise has been lost, we all lose out.

Children of Heracles is a recovery from psychosomatic rheumatoid arthritis. Tragic heroes are interpretable according to a dialectic between the schizoid-paranoid position and the depressive position.[41] Orestes' illness is "rooted" in his experience of aggressive, persecuting women. His paranoid psychosis is expressed in acute phases, when he attacks real females and has delusions of persecuting ones, and in quiescent phases of apparent sanity, which reveal his disturbed pattern of interaction with other people. When not deluded he is depressed, as psychotics in real life (that is, in our culture) often are.[42] Ajax is another psychotic in different phases of a permanent condition: a delusional state and a "lucid state of despair and shame, culminating in suicide." He has a breakdown, but his psychosis, unlike Agave's, does not stop.[43] He is mad all the time, even when Sophocles says he is sane. Yet for another critic, he "is never mad, in any strict sense, at all."[44]

There have been many similar claims, of course, in Shakespearian criticism. If we go back to A. C. Bradley, before psychoanalysis hit literary criticism, we find other moments when the observer's psychology takes precedence over the play's own words. The Fool in *Lear* must be "slightly touched in the brain," because the storm scene "would be more effective" (to Bradley) with three characters "each having a different kind of insanity": the king really mad, the Fool "slightly touched," and Edgar pretending madness. Kent is lying when he says, "I have years on my back forty-eight": "It is clear he is much older. Not so old as his master but, one may suppose, three-score and upward." Bradley interprets Kent entirely from that. "If his age is not remembered, we fail to realize the full beauty of his thoughtlessness of himself."

This is wonderful, in its way. But it ushers in a near century of putting flawless black—that casual "one may suppose"—uncritically *behind* the lens. This is criticism moving nakedly into fiction, reflecting and privileging the supposing psyche.[45]

One critic, discussing the madness of Heracles and Orestes, thinks one "externally caused," the other "innerly caused." Orestes "never seems" to get better, was mad before he started. *Orestes* "seems to suggest" that Or-

---

[41] Agave: Devereux 1970:44 (with n. 62). Hippolytus: Rankin 1974. Iolaus: *Heraclid.* 843–66; Devereux 1971. Symptoms and personality suggest Iolaus is not old but psychosomatically ill. The "rejuvenation" is the illness's remission. Psychopathological dialectic: Klein 1963:37; see A. Green 1979:84.

[42] Simon 1978:102–13, 302 n. 44. Cf. Theodorou 1993:35–36: "although he recovers from individual attacks of madness, Orestes *never seems* to recover fully from the disease itself" (see below, n. 46). For anachronism in the metaphor "rooted," which does not fit Greek images of madness in relation to the self, see above, pp. 8, 31–32, 44; Padel 1992:134–37.

[43] Simon 1978:101–102, 126–30; cf. Goldhill 1986:180–98.

[44] Vandvik 1942; Adams 1955.

[45] Bradley 1911:311–12, 308–809. For early reactions against Bradley, see Campbell 1961:267–87.

estes' murder is "the manifestation of a permanent psychopathological state."[46]

"*Seems* to suggest?" Who to? We are back with Kent lying about his age. How can we know what would "seem" to that alien audience driven by such different assumptions about persons, madness, and divinity: except by studying in depth their ways of evaluating normal people?

The procedure is semicircular. Psychoanalytic use of Greek myth proves the "richness" of Greek tragic psychology. It rests on an appeal to "seeming" made in loaded language: "As Electra indulges her hatred of Helen and her mother something seems to go wrong in Orestes' mind. He abruptly admonishes Electra to be different from these evil women." "Indulges." "Abruptly." "Seems to go wrong."[47]

Orestes' madness is caused by his human relationships (as this particular critic reads relationships), and by "unacknowledged" guilt and grief, which he "blocks" except "when he loses control": "Orestes would be sane only if he admitted consciously his guilt and faced his shame—which he never does. All his repressed feelings find their only outlet in attacks of madness. Immediately after the attack, when Orestes is still in an extremely vulnerable state, they surface and prevail." Sometimes Orestes "seems" to want to admit this guilt: "Although probably not entirely conscious of it, what Orestes seems to be saying here is that his grief must have been curable if he were able to bring his emotions to the surface, admit and accept them. His mania consists of the refusal of his self to do this. . . . That is why he went mad."[48]

This is inadequate. The new assumption, a recent, maybe transient, local ideal, that "acknowledging your emotions" puts everything right, in fact puts black behind the lens, and ultimately forces the critic to deny Greek words mean what they say: a sure sign of darkness. "Orestes is not completely sane at any point in the play." *Emphrōn* ("in your right mind") "does not seem to mean 'in his *right* mind.'" Ajax recovers from delusion, becomes *emphrōn*, "but this does not necessarily mean he is in his right mind." It is all rather like an earlier critic's claim that *mainesthai* does not have to mean "to be mad."[49]

This writer does not think Orestes, Ajax, or Pentheus are ever in "a *healthy* state of mind." The word *nosos* "seems to imply a permanence in the

---

[46] Theodorou 1993:35–36 (with n. 18). He thinks Orestes' symptoms are more like delirium, while Heracles suffers something more like an epileptic seizure (cf. above, pp. 32, 192), because Heracles' madness causes his bad deed, while Orestes' results from guilt at his bad deed. But see above, pp. 192–96.

[47] Theodorou 1993:32 n. 2. (He conflates the "poets' original material" with the texts themselves, which muddles questions about whose psychology we are talking about and begs general questions about madness in literature.) *Or.* 251: see Chapter 7, n. 45.

[48] Theodorou 1993:37.

[49] Linforth 1946a:147.

disturbance of their *phrenes*." Seems? Again, who to? Not to an audience whose image of madness is temporary, whose doctors often ignore long-term physical illness, and who are used to hearing *nosos* applied to divine things like Poseidon's trident, or momentary states like lust or recklessness.[50]

If you take this position, you have to discount what poets say about divine motivation. It is "only the ostensible excuse." Orestes' madness is "not godsent, but inside him." Erinyes are not real, but "only one of the symptoms, his persecutory hallucinations which result from his guilty conscience." Failure of "emotional responsibility" is the real issue. At the end of *Choephoroe*, "there is no explicit mention of madness" (though *before* he sees the Furies Orestes says he is still *emphrōn*, which suggests he is not sane when he does). Seeing Erinyes is "not the result of insanity but an understandable response to his situation." They are "a self-created vision." "Even if they exist, it is ambiguous what they represent."[51]

But if you talk of ambiguous representation, you have to consider the local horizons: to consider *whom it was ambiguous to* in its original performance. For its Athenian audience, Erinyes were already quivering with multiple significances in cult, poetry, and visual images. But this particular modern perspective has no room for figures whom everyone agrees exist, who mean several different things. It assumes that the Athenian poet, by representing Erinyes with what looks now like ambiguity, implies they do not exist. "Are they the avengers of Clytemnestra, or Orestes' guilty conscience? Or are they one sign of his madness, itself the result of his guilty conscience?"[52] You might as well say the Empire State Building does not exist because for some people it is a phallic symbol.

This mess comes from imagining that fifth-century Athenians, whose homes and city crackled with gods, who spoke of emotion as the nonhuman within, as something that comes from outside, may look different from us but actually had *exactly* the same ideas of passion, divinity, and the self as—well, as the boy next door. Euripides' method of "portraying" emotion is "similar to one psychologists use to *detect* emotion." The argument is circular, if you use modern "psychologists" to argue that Euripides *is* working in this way.[53]

Retreat from Truth

This is unsophisticated stuff, in a classical, not analytical journal. But some analysts are not much better. Oedipus, Jocasta, and Creon "chose not to

---

[50] Theodorou 1993:37. *Nosos*: above, Chapter 15; cf. *PV* 924.
[51] Theodorou 1993:39–41, 44.
[52] Theodorou 1993:41.
[53] Theodorou 1993:32.

pursue inquiries" about where Oedipus had come from when he turned up at Thebes, because of "their reluctance to know the truth." They "dealt with unwelcome reality by turning a blind eye." Oedipus is already "in retreat from the truth" when he blinds himself in *Oedipus Rex* (produced perhaps around 425 B.C.). He hates Jocasta because she tried to kill him as a baby. After his self-blinding, he begins to deny his guilt and hate "by introducing a split between his hands and eyes." (The evidence for this is that Oedipus, like many characters in tragedy, addresses both.) This kind of approach generally ignores literary conventions of specific genres.[54]

When a figure called Oedipus appears in a separate play, written some twenty years later, this is the same personality, whose psychopathology has "developed." "His" retreat from the truth of his guilt is now shown by "a new trend in his psychic processes which will come to dominate his character": self-justification. "If we compare the character of Oedipus as we see it in *Oedipus at Colonus* with that portrayed in *Oedipus Rex* we cannot but be impressed with the change in him."[55]

As if many other plays on Oedipus (seventy-odd is one estimate) had not been produced in that theater in the intervening years. As if all the previous audience were still there checking, Filofax in hand. As if "Oedipus" were a soap opera character, talking through a scriptwriter; or Paul Newman in films twenty years apart but still the same face and voice: "We no longer see a man who could acknowledge his guilt and who was subsequently shattered by the discovery of and the true nature of the oedipal crime, but an arrogant man who makes self-excuses, adopts superior grandeur, and relates to others including his sons with coldness and cruelty and also in taking on divine characteristics sheds the very humanity he fought so hard to achieve." "Fighting to achieve humanity" is not what Oedipus did in *Oedipus Rex*. Fifth-century Athenians did not think you achieved humanity. You had it. Gods penetrated and manipulated it. In *Oedipus at Colonus*, divine characteristics are thrust on Oedipus by gods who, the play says, organized the scenario of his life and now do the same for his death. For the late-fifth-century Athenian audience, Oedipus is becoming a *hērōs*, a cult "hero," with all the valid, recognizable marks of that status.[56]

---

[54] J. Steiner 1990:228–30 (referring to J. Steiner 1985, where he follows the argument of Vellacott 1971 that Sophocles means his audience to see that Oedipus knew it was his mother all along; cf. the cogent attack on an another expression of the same thesis, Vernant 1981:83).

[55] J. Steiner 1990:229–33 (citing the idea, put forward by Rudnytsky 1987, that Oedipus hates Jocasta): "The change in Oedipus, between the integrity when he faced the truth in *OT* and the arrogant denial of it in *OC*, is perhaps the most impressive feature of the play." Odd to identify a difference in characterization, from a play twenty years old, as "the most impressive feature" of another that deals poignantly with war, age, death, betrayal, the mysteries of nationalism, and divine territory in human space.

[56] J. Steiner 1990:231; cf. Knox 1964.

This approach makes Oedipus go mad by denying his guilt. "The claim that he was victimized is a loss of respect for reality," a defence against disintegration. It shows "paranoid grandiosity." Oedipus misrepresents "the truth": a common mechanism, "when reality is unbearable."[57] There is no sense here of a play giving its "truth" to its audience through its words; that part of the truth in this play, which its audience would respect, is that Oedipus *is* set apart. By gods who truly exist.

This analyst might say, "The play *says* gods are calling Oedipus to death, but indicates to me no such thing is happening. *I* see a paranoid retreat from reality to grandiosity. Therefore this retreat must really (unlike Sophocles' gods) be there in the play. Why should I believe *you* that this strategy—saying something about gods while meaning another thing that denies gods—was impossible for a fifth-century Athenian dramatist?"

Because the fullest possible historical picture tells us so. This approach is itself a retreat into omnipotence. It retreats from the only truth we can hang onto: as-close-as-we-can-get historical truth, responsibly evaluated, which tells us Athenians did think gods bossed human lives about, did worship at hero shrines of the kind Oedipus is heading for. It retreats also from a basic anthropological principle, that unless observers take as their basis for response what the alien text actually says (about madness, emotion, the past, people), *in relation to* available evidence for how that particular society understood these things, they will not learn much about it.

Such attempts to "pathologize" texts in a sociological vacuum, to analyze fictitious characters through anachronistic ideas of self, are debunked by more sophisticated work within psychoanalysis itself. André Green, in the most demanding psychoanalytic approach to Greek tragedy I know, thinks "nosographical diagnosis" of fictitious heroes is "sterile." He underwrites Aristotle: "It is not the poet's business to tell what has happened or the kind of things that would happen." Analysts face a text "communicated through written speech, no more analyzable than its author would be through it." They cannot "say anything they like about it" and risk "shaping the work into a lock . . . to fit [their] own particular key."

Green concentrates not on tragedy's characters, but its use of myth. Tragedy is "one way of decanting" myths. You look for "traces of the conflict of the unconscious," but never attribute this to nonexistent literary characters.[58] But he does make Freudian theory the basis of everything. "Every text springs from a murder (of the father) carried out with the intention of obtaining pleasure, sexual possession (of the mother)." All sought-for "conflicts of the unconscious" are oedipal. The Oedipus com-

[57] J. Steiner 1990:234–35. He is quoting an unpublished paper (Vellacott 1978) that I happen also to have read. I did not share his valuation of it. See above, n. 12.

[58] A. Green 1979:xi, 1, 22, 25, 36, 84, 89. By contrast, Caldwell 1989 and Greenstadt 1982 concentrate on myth itself.

plex, universal to every culture, informs every artifact. (Does every Hep-plewhite chair "spring from a murder of the father carried out with the intention of obtaining sexual possession of the mother?") When the chips are down, Green too assumes that what analysts see in the text must really be in it. "A work only allows itself to take the form of a lock [i.e., open to a key] if it can so be taken."[59]

Yet analysts expect resistance. They are trained to war with it, like Hip-pocratics for war with disease.[60] *Oedipus Rex* cannot walk out of the room when analysts in battle gear retreat to omnipotence, master key (or electric drill) in hand. Asking the Oedipus complex to illuminate the tragedies, rather than asking tragedies to illuminate or amplify the complex, Green too is vulnerable to a charge of self-validating psychoanalytic imperialism.

Another refreshing corrective to the "Ajax is mad all the time," "Oedipus knew all along" camp, is C. Fred Alford. Alford begins by sup-posing "insights into the human psyche contained in Greek tragedy [are] more profound than psychoanalytic theories often used to explain them." His study, grounded not in clinical experience but psychoanalytic and aes-thetic theory, has many acute things to say. Like Green, he is clear what he is doing: not "psychoanalyzing Euripides" or his characters but looking for conflicts a dramatist might be "holding" for his culture.

Alford tackles self-validation head-on. "The problem is we shall all learn nothing new from the Greeks but how well they conform to Freud." If you want to find tragedy compatible with Freudian theory, you will. He knows he is vulnerable here: "Like Freud, I find in the tragedies themes I have already identified as important in my readings in psychoanalysis and phi-losophy."[61] He confronts the challenge as articulated by Jean-Pierre Ver-nant.

Vernant backed a sociohistorical approach against self-validating Freud-ian accounts and laid his own method out carefully: "Take as your starting-point the work itself as it comes to us . . . studied from every point of view possible, in an analysis appropriate to the particular type of creation." Then progress to "the historical, social, and mental context which gives the meaning of the text full force."[62]

To this Alford, amazingly, says "Hogwash!" For "Who could know," he says, as if proving Vernant unviable, the "texts as they truly are?" "All interpretation is the imposition of concepts. The alternative to the imposi-tion of Freudian concepts is the imposition of better concepts." But "texts as they truly are" is not how Vernant put it. And who is to decide what

[59] A. Green 1979:22, 25, 32.
[60] Hippocratic "battle" with disease: see Chapter 5, n. 11.
[61] Alford 1992:ix, 4, 8.
[62] Vernant 1981:64, 70–86.

"better" is, in "better concepts"? What would "better" mean here, anyway?[63]

In representing Vernant, Alford blanks out Vernant's historical ideal of getting to know the society in the densest possible context through the maximum number of appropriate perspectives, and letting that, rather than theory, lead your response.[64] Alford's own interpretation of Vernant's text "imposes" a concept ("texts as they truly are") that is not present as Vernant's original text comes to us: which is itself a recognized genre, namely, a work of historical scholarship.

MAKING THE SMOKE A DOOR: RESPECTING TRAGEDY'S TERMS

You cannot say "hogwash" to Vernant without looking silly. It is like denying the Louvre: a construction that houses real things, collected over years with discipline of thought, and a depth and vivacity of "knowing" on a scale Alford does not envisage. Things organized and displayed with care (in every sense); with firsthand knowledge, arduously acquired. Rubbishing this means saying history, sociology, anthropology, archaeology, and philology ("every point of view possible," as Vernant puts it) are worth less than bits of psychoanalytic theory eclectically imposed.

When Vernant says "the texts," or "full meaning," he means texts as they have been received, collated, and painstakingly related to cultural evidence in a way psychoanalysis has yet to catch up with. He does not mean texts in a vacuum (or a mirror); nor that chimaera, "texts as they know themselves." He means, as he says, the texts "as they have come to us."

If you do not know how the Paris Metro works and want to get somewhere on it, it is dotty not to consult a map or ask someone who does know. Ignorance helps you blank out things you may not wish to consider, but it cannot stop other people knowing them. Vernant's route offers bearings—on tragic texts in their time and place—that are the closest we can get to true.

Alford is excellent on the limitations of psychoanalytic critics who "reduce something important to something less important." But he does not think they are wrong to apply unrelated categories, like ointment from a state-of-the-art vinyl cabinet, to the tragedies. Their mistake is applying

---

[63] Alford implicitly contrasts "imposing concepts" with "texts as they truly are." In effect, he is saying: "All interpretation imposes concepts, and therefore cannot know Greeks as they are; so all interpretation falsifies, but some falsifications are better than others. Like mine." (How "better"? Pragmatically? They *feel* nicer to you?) The rhetoric collapses if you change "all interpretation is imposition of concepts" to "all interpretation involves the use of concepts."

[64] Vernant 1981:65; Alford 1992:4. Alford's solution is eclectic. He takes bits of several theories from Lacan, Klein, and Robert Lifton. Cf. Padel 1990a:205.

the *wrong* ointment: "To correct this, it is neither necessary nor possible to go to 'the texts themselves.' Rather, we must find better psychoanalytic categories." Yet he himself feels the call of "texts themselves." By "drawing on" *several* theories, he feels he has given texts priority over theory: "One must make a choice . . . between fidelity to a particular theory and fidelity to the truths of the poets. I have chosen the latter."[65] Many of his responses to individual texts *are* alert and acute. But what he means by "truths of poets," or "texts," is hopelessly thin and subjective compared to the informed response Vernant desires.

Alford might say, What's wrong with how *I feel* the "truths of poets"? Why take Vernant's historicist principles against my unfettered instincts?

> Why not see Helen
> as the sun saw her, with no Homeric shadow,
> swinging her plastic sandals on that beach alone,
> as fresh as the sea-wind? Why make the smoke a door?[66]

But no reader of tragedy has unfettered instincts. No one sees as the sun sees. Not being aware of "Homeric shadow" at work within your own ways of seeing does not make your seeing the less constructed. There are many wonderful things you can do with Greek tragedy. Using it for what you want, in your own work, is fine. But if what you want is to "make the smoke a door"—to find out about past, alien people (and, in this case, their ideas of madness)—you have to learn from those trained professionally in how to think about past, and other, people: historians, anthropologists, classical scholars. The best of whom are testing, refining, and sharing methods and possibilities in this area all the time.

In reading ancient madness, you need not make the historical the only perspective, but you must take it into account.[67] This means respecting the poets' terms. Believing them when they say people are mad, sane, or about to become divine.

---

[65] Alford 1992:4–6.
[66] Walcott 1990:271 (*Omeros* bk. 6, ch. 54, 2.24–27).
[67] Clarke 1975; MacDonald 1981; above, n. 12.

Chapter 22

KNOWLEDGE THAT IS SAD TO HAVE TO KNOW

TERRORS OF THE EARTH

To SUM UP. Greek tragedy represents madness as something temporary, come from outside. It darkens within like a storm, twists how you see. It is inner writhing, expressed externally in dancelike jerkiness. People know you are mad by how you look and move. Madness is associated with "black earth" (a deep Greek image for the mind itself), with what comes out of it (Erinyes, black roots), and with the emotion that does most outside damage: anger. (The West's first sentence asks the Muse to sing of Achilles' anger, that brought pain to the Greeks.)

Madness is an overdetermined black: color of anger, storm, earth, and tragedy itself. In this black, you see differently. You may see true things—but not things it is safe or comfortable to see. Madness isolates. The mad do not look or see like other people. They are dangerous. Self–set apart, walled out by others, madness wanders. It resembles other isolating marks of divine hostility: disease, skin disease, pollution. Madness is mistake, damage, and ultimately self-damage whose cruellest examples are *theomachia* (battle against god) and killing your own children.

This, very roughly, is Greek tragedy's grammar of madness. We inherit it. Its elements have patterned tragedy through centuries. They are at work, for instance, in Shakespeare and our response to him as Lear faces madness:

> I will have such revenge upon you both
> That all the world shall—I will do such things—
> What they are yet I know not; but they shall be
> The terrors of the earth. You think I'll weep.
> No, I'll not weep. [*Storm and tempest.*]
> I have full cause of weeping; but this heart
> Shall break into a hundred thousand flaws
> Or ere I'll weep. O fool, I shall go mad!![1]

But why was it tragedy that gave us this? You can see many of these elements in other classical writers, but tragedy is the body of work that estab-

---

[1] *King Lear* 2.4.278–85. Earth and underworld as image of mind: Padel 1992:99–102; above, Chapter 5, n. 26, and Chapter 17, n. 52.

lished the whole Western grammar of madness. Why? What has madness to do with tragedy, and tragedy to do with madness, that brought this about?

In the Mad God's Theater: Taking Illusion for Reality

GLOUSTER: Come, cousin, canst thou quake and change thy colour,
              Murder thy breath in middle of a word,
              And then begin again, and stop again,
              As if thou were distraught and mad with terror?
BUCKINGHAM: Tut, I can counterfeit the deep tragedian. . . .
                                        —Shakespeare, *Richard III* 3.5

Tragedy structured itself, I have suggested, round an initially Homeric insight into the world-damage a damaged mind can do. Within that structure, madness has two roles. It is both human—a permanent possibility, a hyperbolic presence against which tragic acts are judged—and divine: a sudden incursion, daemonic destruction of mind or life. Madness takes up this position in a genre which evolved, specifically, in a "mad" god's theater.

Mainomenos Dionusos.[2] Out of all the features of this god's impacted persona, and the relation each of them bears to his madness, tragedy's madness most sharply, I think, mirrors three.

First, his violence. The violence both of madness and of Dionysus mirrors that of tragedy: the reported violence of Greek tragedy, the performed violence of tragedy in other ages. This is particularly clear in the Renaissance, which received the tragic tradition through the prism of Roman violence, especially Seneca, and responded to its violence in a way the nineteenth century did not.[3] Dionysus connects interior violence, hurt mind, mad thought, with violence performed: on stage, in the world. In cult and in tragedy Dionysus is a link between madness and murder.[4]

Greek tragedy's interest in a connection between violence and madness comes over also in its use of Delphi. In many lost tragedies, Delphi purifies madness caused by bloodguilt. Orestes was not the only one. Alcmaeon, Telephus, Athamas: their madness was there in the myths but tragedy kept choosing to stage it; to explore the link between madness and spilled blood.[5]

[2] Taplin 1978:162 approved the ancient saying that tragedy is "nothing to do with Dionysus," and got a many-voiced indignant response: see, e.g., Seaford 1981; Goldhill 1986:74–78; Zeitlin and Winkler 1990; Padel 1994:132 nn. 28–29; above, Chapter 3.

[3] Spencer 1962; Howard 1974:74.

[4] Padel 1990:336.

[5] See Parke and Wormell 1956 1:305–307. Murder as link between blood and madness: Padel 1992:172–89.

Second, the relation between Dionysus's madness and his interest in illusion, disguise. Madness involves taking illusion for reality (see Chapter 7). This is what any audience does. "Actors are madmen, playgoers are fools," says an ancient Chinese proverb. In context, this speaks to a traditional Chinese image of the theater's votaries: to an insiderism that has nothing to do with Athenian theater. But the words reflect a strange remove in the bond any theater creates between those who watch and those who play. Athenians sat in the precinct of a "mad" god, with whom it was normal to "be mad." They did so to share illusion as truth, for a while. The theater's truth is illusion, which you treat as reality: doing that is madness.[6]

Feigned madness is another feature of tragedy. The story that Odysseus pretended madness, to duck the Trojan war draft, went back to a Homeric epic, the *Cypria*. The fifth century loved it and Cicero implies he thinks tragedy invented it. Lost plays that used it include Sophocles' *Odysseus Mainomenos*.[7]

Feigning madness became big business in Renaissance tragedy. Asked to seem "mad for grief," Buckingham "can counterfeit the deep tragedian." Madness and feigning belong automatically in "deep" tragedy. Hamlet's madness, interpreted as proving him "mad for love," is tested. What he told Ophelia "was not like madness." Once it is seen through, Hamlet is in danger. Like Edgar's, his madness is disguise. Both fake madnesses have enormous power in their plays, mirroring the genuine madness of other characters.[8]

This is madness as mask. Pretend madness, with imagined sanity behind it: as the Greek audience knows the real actor is behind and in the mask.[9] "Real" madness on stage is the drama itself feigning madness. Illusion, taken for reality, is presented by the illusion of a person, a mask that hides the actor. Madness and feigned madness alike belong with the strangeness of tragic performance: masses of people, collectively taking illusion for reality. Dionysus presides over disguise.[10]

Third, the relation between Dionysus's own madness and his outsider status. Tragic madness evokes images of darkness and nonhumanity, of

<hr>

[6] See Padel 1981:126–29; Scott 1982; Foucault 1971:35; Segal 1982.

[7] Apollod. 3.7; Hyginus *Fabulae* 95. Lucian *De saltatione* 46 follows the story with the typically tragic Philoctetes. Aeschylus probably mentioned it in *Palamedes* (Jebb/Pearson *ad.* S. frr. 462–67). Arist. *Poet.* 1451A26 says Homer avoids it. See Cic. *De officiis* 3.97: *ut quidem poetae tragici prodiderunt*.

[8] *Hamlet* 2.1.77–85, 103, 109; 2.2.5, 9, 165–222, 234–306; 3.1.86–172. *Richard III* 3.5.1. *King Lear* 3.4, 3.6. Cf. the flute test for possession, in Men. *Theophoroumenē*: Handley 1969.

[9] Cf. Padel 1990b:358–59.

[10] See, e.g., Burkert 1985:162, 166; Schlesier 1993.

being "outside," alienated. In several cults and myths, Dionysus's persona had this "outside" status too.[11]

These, I think, are some background reasons for the importance of madness in fifth-century tragedy. Vase-painters reflect this importance, and give tragic madness a high profile. Their market too valued tragedy's madness and its daemons.[12] For the Athenian imagination, Dionysus connected violence, wild madwomen on mountains, death, illusion—and the theater. The fact that this is his theater itself makes madness important for tragedy.

"TRAGIC FALL"

The ship, the black freighter. . . .
—Brecht, *The Threepenny Opera*

Madness is also the perfect image of tragic "fall." In mediaeval Christian Europe, when tragedy is simply the narrative of disaster, laying bare "the universal drama of the fall of man," "fall" resonates with images of Adam, and tragedy is "harm" of the "fallen":

> The harm of hem that stode in heigh degree
> And fillen so that ther nas no remedie.

From the first European account, criticism takes the damage-fall as tragedy's characteristic movement: "Tragedie is noon other maner thing."[13] Even earlier, in Greek tragedy itself, "fall" is an image through which tragedy can see itself. The chorus, faced with Oedipus's "fall" from king to moral outcast, sings

> Mortals, I count you as nothing.
> As dead generations. No one has more
> than this much luck with life and gods: just
> to seem happy. Then, having had that seeming,
> fall away. Oedipus, you, and your *daimōn*,
> I cannot call happy.[14]

---

[11] See, e.g., Burkert 1985:163; Segal 1982; Seaford 1993; Cole 1993.

[12] See above, pp. 18–20. Lyssa in vase-paintings: Padel 1992:118, 125, 131, 156, 163.

[13] Chaucer *The Monk's Tale*, 2–3, 3951. "Fall" is the point of the string of exempla throughout the *Tale*. See G. Steiner 1961:11–16.

[14] *OT* 1187–95; cf. Winnington-Ingram 1980: ch. 8. Cf., from an anonymous English tragedy, c. 1591 (quoted in Barton 1962:136):

> O fickle fortune, O unstable world . .
> Wherein as in a glasse we plainly see
> That all our life is but a Tragedie.
> Since mightie kings are subject to mishap.

In Greek tragedy, vulnerability to "fall" is double. Daemonic agents of harm rush above in the air and "fall" on human heads. "With a great leap from above," say the Furies,

> I bring down my foot's heavy-falling force.
> My limbs make even fast runners fall:
> a terrible disaster. And as he falls,
> he knows nothing, in mad folly.

"Fall" has daemonic resonance. Unseen agents ambush human lives:

> It creeps up on
> the man who knows nothing
> before he approaches his foot
> to the hot fire.[15]

This Greek awareness of chaotic vulnerability to daemons that "fall at" you out of the air, making *you* "fall," became the tragic sense. Conrad, according to Bertrand Russell, thought of "civilized and morally tolerable human life as a dangerous walk on a thin crust of barely cooled lava, which might break at any moment and let the unwary sink into fiery depths."[16] From outer to inner. Daemonic fall in tragedy is answered by, and also explains, fall within. Madness is central to this image: that we live on the edge of chasm. It gives tragic "fall" its inner echo chamber. Greek daemons operate inside as well as outside. Sophocles' image of approaching fire unawares comes from his "*atē*-song."[17] Madness is the inward correlative of external "fall": reason "topples." "What a noble mind is here o'erthrown."

"DISEASE OF HEROES"

In many respects, all tragic heroes are *like* the mad. Or (the other way round) a mad person is image of a tragic hero. There are important similarities between heroes and the mad, as tragedy represents both. What madness does, heroes also do. Even sane, Greek tragic heroes are a destructive and self-destructive lot. They kill others and themselves, blind others and themselves.[18] In tragedy as in cult, a near-animal capacity for violence can make someone a "hero." Tragic madness is violent. It upsets distinctions between human and animal, often violently.[19] Sometimes one violent

---

[15] *Eum.* 372–78: see Padel 1992:131; *Ant.* 618–19.

[16] Russell 1956:82; cf. above, Chapter 6, n. 47. Daemons "falling at" you out of air: Padel 1992:129–31.

[17] Padel 1992:125–29, 138–40, 158–61. *Atē*: below, Appendix.

[18] *Hec.* 1120–21; *OT* 1276.

[19] Mattes 1970:60–63; Girard 1977:40, 128, 164; above, Chapter 3, nn. 4–5, and Chapter 13.

act was enough to turn a historical figure into a worshipped "hero."[20] Tragic heroes are isolated in their unshareable vision. Antigone the hero rejects, even "hates," the nonheroic sister who loves her but cannot see things her way. Tecmessa begs Ajax to soften, not endanger himself by rebelling. He shakes off her loving plea: "You're a fool if you want to educate my nature now."[21]

If heroes are *like* the mad, they are also the people likely to go mad. From late antiquity madness can be called *to pathos hērōikon*: "the disease of heroes." The thought could be reported ironically, but it was there all along, getting a boost in the Renaissance from the reevaluation of *Problem* 30. Heroes go mad. Not just tragedy's heroes, but those of Arthurian and Irish myth like Lancelot, Tristan, Sweeney.[22] In this relation of tragic heroes and madness, here is another turn of the crystal. Heroes are specially *prone to* madness.[23]

You might say, *Of course* the elements of tragic madness are manifest in tragic heroes. It is they who go mad. The features they demonstrate as heroes match features of madness you found *in them*. Circular, isn't it?

No. On the one hand, tragic heroes display many of the qualities of madness, like aggression or self-destruction, when they are sane. And on the other hand, tragedy does not sign its interest in madness only in its heroes. Madness is everywhere. Lyssa and Erinyes are characters on the stage of some tragedies, and are painted in scenes from other tragedies by vase-painters *as if* they were around, even though the plays themselves had not put them on the stage. Madness is often spoken of, rather than brought on stage. Its hyperbolic presence contributes to a continual sense of madness. In *Antigone*, the chorus hints that Haemon is mad with love. His father calls him "empty of mind," and expects him not to "rave against his sire." *He* says his father is "not in his right mind." The chorus later sings of someone else's madness: Lycurgus opposed Dionysus and maenads, and madly killed his son. As one commentator says, "madness on the one side, madness on the other." Madness is a presence *around* the figures and songs. In one comedy, two characters try to guess the identity of a strange figure. "Perhaps it's an Erinys from tragedy," says one. "She has a mad and tragic look." It is from choral references, hyperbolic accusations of madness, and the identification of Erinyes with tragedy, as well as heroes themselves going mad, that we know madness matters to tragedy.[24]

---

[20] Knox 1964:42, 56.

[21] *Ant.* 1–93; *Aj.* 596; Knox 1964:32–35.

[22] Aulus Gellius 18.7.4. See Padel 1981:122–23; Klibansky, Panofsky, and Saxl 1964:42 n. 100; Kinsman 1974b:20. *Problem* 30. above, Chapter 6.

[23] Foucault 1971:108–11 claims the opposite: "The tragic hero can never be mad." But his model of "classic" is seventeenth-century France, not Greece.

[24] Ar. *Pl.* 422. See Winnington-Ingram 1980:102–104 on *Ant.* 754, 756, cf. *Ant.* 791–92, 633. Lycurgus: *Ant.* 954–63. "Hyperbolic" madness: above, pp. 194–95. Erinyes iden-

Madness visits Greek tragic heroes. It is not "in" them as firmly and clearly as it is in later heroes. For the Renaissance, madness is something wrong within. You must get it out: purge the black bile, exorcise the demons. Horrific sixteenth-century drawings and paintings show doctors cutting the "stone of folly" from the forehead of the mad, who queue up for the operation.[25] Greek tragic heroes are marked rather by a *relation* to madness, which is out there in the world: an external possibility that permanently threatens the human interior in its pain.

Maybe being apt for madness, and being *like* the mad, makes them heroes. Maybe tragedy uses madness as a metaphor for a hero. In a sense, the ultimate "hero" of tragedy is its image of consciousness, divided and ambiguous, active and passive in its suffering: something that gets destroyed and yet survives. The "place where the terrible is good," which lives catastrophe, suffers divine damage, and endures.[26] It goes mad, and survives.

Tragedy is about something that goes suddenly wrong—in a house, family, city, and in the inner correlate of this, the mind. One thing wrong in the tragic universe is the permanent possibility of sudden madness, of mind damage leading to outside damage. Madness, the nonhuman inside the human, shatters "human" in outer and inner worlds.[27] It is reversal at every level: reason's polluted shadow; being suddenly hated as much as you were loved by gods; being outside society instead of safe within. It twists and damages seeing, feeling, relating. It is the permanent shadow to ordinary ways of being. Tragedy's compound image of madness belongs with this sense of damage and survival. Madness is the epitome of tragic harm: outer and inner, savage, temporary, daemonic, miraculously survivable, but with enduring terrible results. Apt metaphor for a tragic hero.[28]

TRUTH FROM ILLUSION, TRUTH FROM PAIN

Heroes resemble the mad in one more thing. Both produce truth out of pain. Sometimes the truth is a prophecy; the pain is physical agony, grief, or simply being on the point of death. Polymestor sees his children murdered in front of him, then gets blinded. Then he prophesies the deaths of Agamemnon and Cassandra, and the metamorphosis of his tormentor Hecuba. Oedipus hears gods "herald" his death and sends for Theseus,

---

tified with tragedy: Wilson and Taplin 1993:176. Elizabethan and Jacobean tragedies also make constant side reference to madness, outside madness-scenes: e.g., *Duchess of Malfi* 1.1.505, 4.2.5, 4.2.17, 5.2.8–26, 5.4.15.

[25] E.g., a Hieronymous Bosch painting of 1480: see Gilman 1982:38–42, plates 47–53. Purging bile: see Chapter 5, nn. 7–8, 12.

[26] *Eum.* 517: see Padel 1992:132–34, 192; above, Chapter 4, n. 49.

[27] See Chapter 7, n. 45; Chapter 13 nn. 53–72.

[28] In a modern sense of metaphor; cf. Padel 1992:9, 33–34.

that Theseus may find him still "straight in his *phrēn*." Before dying, he tells Theseus secret truths, important for Athens.[29]

Truth coming out of pain, or at the edge of death, underpins Athenian torture of slave witnesses. A slave's testimony was not believed unless he was tortured. Physical pain also accompanied prophetic possession.[30] The *splanchna*, innards, were prophetic: animal *splanchna* were consulted in entrail divination, and tragedy often speaks of human *splanchna* as "knowing" and "prophesying." It is as if the gods had a special line to innards, particularly apparent at the moment of death.[31]

Prophecy at the point of death was connected, anciently, with Pythagoras.[32] It had deep appeal throughout the classical period and caught fire in mediaeval and Renaissance imagination:

HOTSPUR:	O! I could prophesy,
	But that the earthy and cold hand of death
	Lies on my tongue. No, Percy, thou art dust,
	And food for—
PRINCE:	For worms, brave Percy.
	Fare thee well great heart![33]

The truth produced in agony before death may be prophecy about a particular future (as for Theseus and Hecuba). Mental or moral agony, at the edge of madness, also produces prophecy and true utterance: maybe a moral truth from the brink, like that uttered by Orestes as he feels madness approaching, which embodies a specific view of the past.[34] Truth comes from the edge of the normal, where people do not usually go. Like prophecy *from* madness: the historical truths sung by mad Cassandra.[35]

We have met before the thought that truth may come from madness. Madness is darkness; but Greek thought expects illumination through the dark. Madness takes illusion for truth, yet some of its illusions *are* truth.[36] Some mad illusions are wrong. Agave and Heracles see their children wrongly. But sometimes the mad see more truely. The Erinyes Orestes sees are really there, for the audience sees them in the next play.[37]

Madness has something deeply to do with the illusions of drama itself:

[29] *Hec.* 1261–80; *OC* 1511, 1456–518.
[30] DuBois 1991:37–38; Padel 1983:14.
[31] Padel 1992:14–18, 68–75.
[32] See Bolton 1962:154, 202 (with n. 16); Brenk 1977:125–26.
[33] See Pl. *Apol.* 39C3; Plu. *Mor.* 432C; Shakespeare *Henry IV Part One*, 5.4.83–86.
[34] *Cho.* 1026–27.
[35] See Chapter 4, nn. 19–29.
[36] Padel 1992:112–13; above, Chapters 8, 9.
[37] *Ba.* 1107, 1171, *HF* 970–1000; *Cho.* 1048; Padel 1981:126–29; above, Chapter 8, nn. 1, 5–7.

masked actors pretending a story, conveying truth to an audience. An important possibility of madness for other people, the not-mad, is that somewhere in the damage and illusion it may get a truth across. This, perhaps, is the tragic value of madness. It was, I guess, at the heart of Plato's response to tragedy's madness and tragedy's mad god. It made possible his alchemy of the tragic tradition: his revolutionary revaluing of madness as a source of goods, of seeing truth.[38]

A tragic hero produces truth out of pain most deeply and simply by embodying it. In the Greek tradition, what is destructive, like Sirens, also illumines.[39] Spectators do come away from tragedy with new insight: even though it is knowledge that is "sad to have to know."[40]

Like the mad, heroes are *outside* normal ways of being human.[41] From that outsideness, they convey something about what lies within human limits. Heroes are ec-centric: from *ek*, "out," and *kentron*, a "sharp point," the fixed "pin" of compasses, the "center" of the circle. Heroes are extravagant: from *extra-vagare*, "to wander outside." From extra-vagance and eccentricity come truth about pain and desolation within the human circuit. Throughout Western literature, especially on stage, insights about men have been communicated through representations of women. Equally, insight into the normal self has been got across by representing what is outside and other. By madness.

Madness stages the possibility that out of ec-centric pain, out of taking illusion for reality, may—for the onlookers—come insight into reality, as tragedy presents it.

MADNESS AND THE TRAGEDY-PRODUCING SOCIETY

In the twenty-five centuries since the Greeks, tragedy has emerged quite rarely, in a handful of different times, languages, and societies. In many ways, it is not a continuous tradition. Tragedy expressed itself at specific moments: fifth-century Athens, Elizabethan and Jacobean England, seventeenth-century Spain and France. Some periods tried it and failed. For the Romantics, tragedy was the supreme goal they never reached (except, for a while, in Germany).[42]

[38] See Chapter 8, nn. 28, 46–47.
[39] See Padel 1992:113.
[40] Howard 1974:70. Cf. *pathei mathos*: *Ag.* 177.
[41] See Chapter 10; cf. Knox 1964:42–43.
[42] See G. Steiner 1961:106–107, 123, 126–29. Steiner attributes the Romantics' failure in tragedy to revolutionary ideals fading after the French Revolution, and to optimism about human nature. They put responsibility for crime and evil outside: "Evil cannot be wholly native to the soul." In tragedy, it must be: as well as being abroad in the world. True tragedy, Steiner argues, is anti-Romantic. "Redeeming insight comes too late to mend . . . or is purchased at the price of irremediable suffering." There is no "compensating Heaven" like that of which Romanticism dreamed.

Why should madness resurface in tragedy in these different epochs? Maybe one thing these societies share in common is this: that they were all, in different ways, poised on some momentary cusp between theological, or daemonological, and innovative scientific explanations for human pain.[43] Maybe tragedy lives best through a particular interplay or confrontation between these types of explanation in general, and in particular as this confrontation affects ideas of madness, its most poignant example.

In Britain, for example, in the late sixteenth and seventeenth centuries, there is a tension between theological and scientific perspectives on pain and insanity, which might evoke parallels from fifth-century Greece: another society where vibrant religious life rubbed against developing scientific theories of human hurts.[44] Maybe a medical and theological tug-of-war between religious and scientific explanation encourages an attention to madness as illustration of human suffering that is best expressed in tragedy.

It certainly seemed so in the Renaissance, when madness, perceived in real life as shameful and dangerous, had enormous literary value. Robert Burton was born in 1577 and his formative years were those of *Hamlet*, *Othello*, *Lear*, and *Anthony and Cleopatra*. Burton calls the "melancholy" man "the cream of human adversity, the quintessence and upshot."[45] The cult of melancholy had an impetus of its own, but I suspect Burton's image illustrates a general point: that a time of intense making of tragedy is a time of intense interest in madness.[46] Madness belongs to, and is valued by, tragic literature in some special way.

Violent physical hurt resonates through tragedy wherever it appears. This hurt reflects tragic verbal imagery, in which passion wounds the innards. What tragedy says happens to mind and spirit reflects what happens to its bodies.[47] Tragedy has many forms of extreme pain. You could read its madness as the supreme example of tragic obsession with mutilating hurt, both physical and spiritual. In the early Renaissance, madness is a *speculum*, "mirror," where human nature sees its own self-hurt.[48]

In or out of tragedy, madness is not the only "disaster." Tragedy, staging many disasters, turned *atē* (its model for madness) into a general word for disaster.[49] It is madness's totality, I think, as result and cause of damage—

[43] I first put forward this suggestion in Padel 1981:123–25. It would of course need detailed support, by historians of madness, religion, and science in the societies involved, to make it stick.

[44] See Lloyd 1979:37–58; Padel 1992:44, 49–68, 73–75.

[45] See Burton, *Anatomy of Melancholy* 1.4.1; Fox 1976:17. MacDonald 1981:147 warns against idealizing Renaissance idealization of madness, or assuming that what they liked in literature they liked in life.

[46] This seems to fit Racine's France; does it fit Racine? Cf. above, n. 23.

[47] Padel 1992: ch. 6.

[48] See, e.g., *The Mirrour of Madness*, translated by J. Fan[ford], (1576).

[49] See Appendix.

itself damage both inside and outside, damage to the values and perceptions on which human society frailly rests—which makes it so useful to tragedy.

"THE SCREAM"

Though it is noon, the helmet screams against the light;
Scratches the eye; so violent it can be seen
Across three thousand years.
—Christopher Logue, *War Music*

The West's images of madness always come back to tragedy and are, essentially, tragic. Madness may be "subversive,"[50] in that it provides *other* people, writers, with ways of challenging safe ways of seeing. But it *is* a tragedy: in our sense, the modern sense, of disastrous pain. These tragic elements of madness are not just a literary construct but part of a syntax that helped to define Europe's images of suffering.

They are ours too. We think of them as (loaded word) "natural." You see them in Munch's *The Scream*. Isolation, distance from people, a single figure set against black freighters in the harbor, against blood-colored sky and a black god-shaped menace in the landscape. Black on the body and in the world; black centered on the open eyes and mouth of a tragic mask.

Grammars change. Modern Greek demotic lost the infinitive. People use the same grammar to say different things. Psychoanalysts use Greek elements of thought to express ideas about madness very different from those of Greek tragedy. But different as modern perceptions are, they rest on a grammar stamped "made in Greece," and put together for the first time, for better or worse, by Athenian tragedy.

[50] Felman 1985.

ATĒ IN TRAGEDY: THE THINNING OF THE WORD

IN TRAGEDY, the word *atē* loses most of its Homeric meaning. Scholars disagree about how.[1] I think the genre, from Aeschylus onwards, thinned it for two main reasons. First, because each entire play exemplified the sequence (see Chapter 18). Second, because tragedy used madness instead of *atē* (see Chapter 19). Each tragedian contributed his bit. Here I document the thinning process.

AESCHYLUS: FROM "RECKLESSNESS" AND ITS PUNISHMENT TO "DOOM," OR INSTRUMENT OF DOOM

Aeschylus counts partly as archaic. His choral work expresses thoughts similar to those of lyric poets in similar language; for example, by using genealogical and harvest imagery (see Chapter 17). He sometimes uses *atē*'s archaic weight associated with retributive Erinys: divine punishment.[2] The result of folly is being caught in a "net of *atē*." His *atē* can seem a *post eventum* judgment of responsibility for crime, almost like guilt. Or it can appear as the continuing presence of appalling deeds: the polluting consequence of crime.[3]

In Homer, the connection between stage 1 and stage 2 *atē* is not guilt.[4] The *atē*-sequence is a way of *not saying* "guilty or not guilty?" Aeschylus can push the punishment element very near guilt. The *Oresteia*, especially *Choephoroe*, plays between *atē* and *aitios*, "responsible." External rites are supposed to drive *atē* out, but *dialgēs atē* (*atē* that hurts right through) fills the *aitios* man with *nosos*, "sickness." The chorus pray to Zeus to put "inside" (in the house? in the person?) a "murderous *atē*," destroying the man "who deserves [is *aitios* for] death." Orestes would suffer "stormy *atai*" if he did not avenge his father.[5] *Atē*'s relation to guilt acquires a new intensity.

---

[1] Does *atē* have a "rise and fall" in tragedy, with a crest of meaning and cutoff point at *Ant.* 610–26 (Stallmach 1969:4–5)? Or did *Euripides* "replace it with other words" (Dawe 1969:101)?

[2] E.g., at *Ag.* 1433, *Cho.* 402–403, *Eum.* 374–76, 982, *atē* could be interpreted as stage 2.

[3] *PV* 1078–79. Guilt and *atē*: see Chapter 19.

[4] Bremer 1969:111; cf. Stallmach 1968:53–63.

[5] *Cho.* 968, 70, 273, 836–37.

Aeschylus uses archaic genealogical images typical of stage 2 *atē. Hubris*, arrogant pride, begets more *hubris*, and also *thrasos* [reckless boldness]— which is an *amachos* (unfightable) *daimōn*. These become "black Atai to the halls, resembling their parents." Ate is the consequence of *hubris*. Like Thrasos, she resembles her parents. The punishment fits the crime because it is its child.[6]

Like archaic poets, he can invoke the *atē*-sequence with one mention of *atē*: especially in the *Oresteia*, which incarnates a chain of murder for murder, where he uses the word more often than in any other play. Fifteen times in *Agamamnon*, twelve in *Choephoroe*, two in *Eumenides* (much fewer: *Eumenides* brings on Erinyes, *atē*'s replacements; see Chapter 18). Yet it is not always clear what the word actually means. Orestes will put the copingstone on "these *atai*." An ambiguous image: he both adds to and ends the growing structure of *atai*. The last word of *Choephoroe* is *menos atēs*, "force of *atē*": when will it die down? *Atē* is the connecting word between the second and third play. The trilogy deals with a *genos*, race, "bound to *atē*."[7] But what is this *atē* exactly? If you want, you can see the *atē*-sequence in many of these passages. But in each it is hard to identify a precise meaning.

Aeschylus also uses *atē*'s Homeric weight: prior damage to judgment. His contemporary, Pindar, uses *atē* (he calls it *auata*) in this way too: for a mental state in which a mortal fatally offends a god, and is subsequently punished.[8] When Aeschylus's Eteocles decides to fight his brother, the chorus asks, "Why are you madly raging [*memonas*]?" They use a word related both to *menos*, force, and to *mainomai*. ("Why so eager?" plus "what do you intend?" plus "why are you mad"?: with resonances of mad martial violence, familiar from Homeric *mainomai* onwards.) The chorus continues:

> Don't let a *thumos*-filled *atē*, mad for the spear,
> carry you away. Throw out the onset of evil desire.

Atē here is mad beginning: of evil "desire," of damaged understanding.[9] The tragedy shows its consequence.

Atē as *apatē* is treacherous, prior: "foreplanning," "cunning," "secret."

[6] *Ag.* 763–71; cf. Peitho, Ate's child, *Ag.* 385.

[7] *Ag.* 1283; *Cho.* 1076; *Ag.* 1566. See Bremer 1969:124 (n. 12 here is mystifying: its numbers do not support the point he makes).

[8] Ixion's *hubris* "drove" him to *auata*. He was afterwards "bound" to the wheel, his "doom": Pi. *P.* 2.28, 41. Coronis, Apollo's lover, had sex with a stranger: "great *auata*" (later called *daimōn heteros*: it "turned her to bad and overcame her"; *P.* 3.24, 34–35). She burnt to death. "Many suffered and died with her: on a mountain much fire from one seed destroys a huge forest" (3.39, 36–38). A mad impulse is a spark that ends in jungle fire.

[9] *Sept.* 686–88. Cf. *Supp.* 110–11, whose ambiguous text suggests a "frenzied understanding": *apatē* turns the suitors to *atē*.

The lion cub is "priest of *atē*, from god." Agamemnon does not know what evil the "treacherous hound" prepares "whose tongue licked him like a secret Atē." Peitho (Persuasion), "child of *proboulou atas*," "forces" forward men who despise Justice's altar. In sacrificing Iphigeneia, Agamemnon "laid *dolian atēn*" on the house. For Clytemnestra, *atē* began with this wicked sacrifice.[10]

In these passages, the language is often ornately ambiguous, the text sometimes corrupt. Even elsewhere, *atē*'s precise grammatical function (let alone what it means) can be unclear. When Io is carried off by *lussa*'s breath, and her words "strike against" the "waves of *atē*," is this madness-implicated *atē* a prior mind damage, or punitive consequence? Or is *atē* here coming to mean, as it will sometimes in Sophocles and Euripides, simply "disaster"?[11]

Often *atē* cannot be fully translated by one English word. It seems to work as a sign of madness, and mad misjudgment or desire; a sign that *daimōn* is at work disastrously; a warning that the immediate damage in front of you has a long, complex explanation. When Eteocles dies in battle with his brother, the chorus sings:

> *Atē*'s trophy stands on the gates
> where they were killed. *Daimōn*
> conquered the pair, and stopped.

We cannot say what Atē "means" here. Maybe there is no one meaning and, as often in Homer, the word summons the *atē*-sequence.[12] Translators have to choose. Sometimes they stress the prior, inward state, sometimes the later calamity. Both choices misrepresent, because they narrow, the Greek.

Aeschylus fits *atē* to the resonance of each plot. In *Seven against Thebes*, a play "full of Ares," *atē* is associated with battle, and death in battle.[13] In *Prometheus Bound*, and even more in *The Persians*, *atē* comes across through images of hunting, binding, and nets, apt for acts that defy divinity: for a protagonist "bound" to a rock, or another who blasphemously "bound" the sea. Xerxes' friends suffer "sea *atai*," deaths at sea, because of his behavior to the sea.[14] *Atē* is there at the beginning, when Xerxes "did not *phronein* [think] well" and yoked the sea, and at the end, when his friends die in it.[15] *Atē* is a hunting, imprisoning net in one play, a cable or yoke in the other.[16] In *Suppliant Maidens*, whose pulse is the chorus's ter-

---

[10] *Ag.* 735, 1230, 385–86, 1522.
[11] *PV* 883–86, cf. Bremer 1969:131 n. 27.
[12] *Sept.* 956–60; see Bremer 1969:131–32.
[13] *Sept.* 687, 315; cf. 601.
[14] *PV* 883–86, 1072, 1078; *Pers.* 99 (cf. genealogical imagery at 822).
[15] *Pers.* 1037, 725, 722.
[16] *PV* 6, 20, 52–77 and passim; *Pers.* 67–72, 114, 722–25.

ror of pursuit, *atē* is either felt by, or embodied by, people whom the chorus face, who become antagonists because of them: the suitors who hunt them, the king who protects them.[17]

In the *Oresteia*, *atē* is often a divine "stroke" hitting the house: apt for a trilogy that presents the "blows" of two murders.[18] The "stroke of *atē*" is exemplified in the blow Orestes will strike to kill Clytemnestra. Appropriately for a trilogy that begins with ambiguities of divine and human causality,[19] *atē* images the beginning, middle, and end of the continuum of violence: inner damage and its answering punishment. *Atē* is all-catching, preplanning, a twin-speared murderous destruction.[20] The lion cub feasted "in sheep-killing *atai*" and was "priest of *atē*." Hybris and Thrasos are "black *Atai*."[21] "Whirlwinds of *atē*" live at Troy now. "Swift *atē*" comes after a mortal wound. These references mount up, presaging *atē*'s application to the house of Atreus, which is articulated in Cassandra's vision of Erinyes. They sing "the first-beginning *atē*."[22] Clytemnestra is a treacherous hound "like a hidden Ate." Cassandra tells the priestess's insignia, as she strips them off her, to "enrich another woman with *atē*."[23] Clytemnestra says she killed Agamemnon by, or with, Ate and Erinys. It was he who "laid *dolian atēn*" on the house.[24]

This family "is bound to *atē*." *Atē* pains the guilty man. *Atai* will attack Orestes' liver, if he fails in revenge. Electra thinks *atē* impossible to fight. Orestes hopes Zeus will send *atē* on their enemies. Murder brings one *atē* after another.[25] The family's pain is constantly entwined with the "bloodstained blow of Ate." Do women destroy men in passion? This is passion conspiring "with the *atai* of human beings." The chorus hope *atē* will keep off those they love, and tell Orestes to kill his mother in a "blameless *atē*." Zeus must "put bloody *atē* within." After the murder, purifying rites will drive out *atē*: yet *atē* ends this play. Will its "force" cease?[26] The Erinyes kick down at the guilty, bringing *atē*. But they eventually pray blood will not flow "through anger," in *antiphonous atas*: murder responding to murder.[27]

[17] A. *Supp.* 110–11, 470 (the king facing a "sea of *atē*"), 444–45 (there is no painless outcome, but one choice may mean "greater *atē*"). The Danaids call their suitors' ship an *atē*, 530.
[18] E.g., *Cho.* 467, 830, 836. Dawe 1968:97 documents the argument that *atē*'s central idea is a blow.
[19] *Ag.* 218–21; cf. Padel 1992:92–95.
[20] *Ag.* 361, 386, 643.
[21] *Ag.* 730, 735, 770.
[22] *Ag.* 819, 1123–24, 1192.
[23] *Ag.* 1230, 1268.
[24] *Ag.* 1192, 1433, 1522.
[25] *Ag.* 1566; *Cho.* 68, 272, 339, 383, 403.
[26] *Cho.* 467, 598, 826, 830, 836, 968, 1076.
[27] *Eum.* 376, 982.

Though Aeschylus summons the *atē*-sequence when he wants, he thins what the actual word means. You might say, grandly, that he thins *atē*'s semantics while exploiting its semiotics, heightens its value as signifier but lets precise meaning fall away. Hence the difficulties of translation. You could argue that "disaster" or "death" is *atē*'s true center now. Especially outside the *Oresteia*. The "sea *atai*" of Xerxes' friends are simply "deaths."[28] "Death" or "doom" is often the simplest translation.[29]

By itself, this usage might not be so significant. In Homer too you can sometimes translate *atē* (especially stage 2) as "death, destruction, disaster." But Aeschylus also starts a new trend. In one passage, he uses *atē* of a physical object: something that brings disaster. The ship, carrying the chorus's hated suitors, is a "black-yoked *atē*."[30] This begins *atē*'s slide into a new meaning: not just concrete "destruction," but also the concrete instrument of such destruction.

SOPHOCLES: "CALAMITY," "DISASTER," "GRIEF"

Sophocles follows suit. In most of his work the best translation for *atē* is "misery, plight, calamity." Or (in plural) "disasters." There is little sense of punishment. In many of these passages, *atē* refers to an *un*merited painful situation, calamity, plague, death: or grief at these things. The word's range, binding inner damage to consequential deserved destruction, has shrunk.

For instance, the chorus (who "brought *atē* on Troy" by beseiging it) tells Ajax not to make "*atē*'s bitterness" worse.[31] Who could fight a strong enemy and escape *alupos atēs*: "without the grief of disaster?" asks Chrysothemis. She was "unaware where we were in *atē*," what a mess they were in.[32] Apollo saved Thebes from "former *atē*," an earlier "plague." Creon will not keep quiet if he sees *atē* approaching the Thebans.[33] "Disaster" or "destruction" fits all these. Even in the choral ode of *Antigone* focussing on *atē* (which I shall discuss presently), "disaster" is a possible translation when the song claims nothing comes to human life "without *atē*." Without, that is, "calamity."[34]

In Aeschylus, *atē*'s images differ in each play. In Sophocles, too, *atē* as "disaster" is nuanced differently in each play. Sometimes it is an instan-

---

[28] *Pers.* 1037; cf. 653: Darius "never destroyed men in war-destroying *atai*," i.e., in "disasters" like this.

[29] E.g., *Ag.* 1124, 1268; *Cho.* 339, 403, 598, 826, 830; cf. *Sept.* 315.

[30] A. *Supp.* 530.

[31] *Aj.* 363, 1189; cf. 848.

[32] S. *El.* 1002, 936.

[33] *OT* 165; *Ant.* 185.

[34] *Ant.* 615. See below, nn. 44–45.

taneous destruction against which you struggle; even physical anguish. Heracles feels a "spasm of *atē*" in the robe burning with acid.[35] Sometimes it is the physical results of that damage. Ajax sees the house "full of *atē*": full of the animals he tortured and killed, the concrete result of his madness.[36] You could, if you wished, interpret some of these as stage 1 or stage 2 *atē*. But you would have to argue each case against the simplest meaning, "destruction."[37]

Another new note: some of Sophocles' *atē* is mental pain *at* disaster. Electra, grieving overmuch for her father, must not beget *atē* (misery) in addition to *atai* (existing disasters).[38] The word can mean "expression of grief" and "misfortune," the thing about which you feel pain. You groan at *atē*, "sing *atē*'s melody." Heracles "suffered *atē* worse than all men."[39] This is "misfortune," something to feel grieved at: but close to grief you feel at it.

Ajax makes *atē* "flame to heaven." In the *Iliad*, the clang of battle goes up to heaven as Greeks die.[40] Fire's brightness flashes to the sky, the battle plain flashes with bronze.[41] This *atē* combines Homeric battle noise and battle flash, a shout and a shine: the din of disastrous conflict, and the sheen of its image, reaching the sky.

Disaster: and grief at it. Sophocles mingles "disaster" with feelings about it, and the expression of those feelings.

Occasionally Sophocles' *atē* is concretely embodied disaster. Not, as with Aeschylus's ship, a physical object, but an institution or person. The context is always Theban, the institution, marriage: specifically, that of Jocasta and Oedipus. Twice this marriage appears in the genitive case (conventionally understood as a "genitive of definition") after *atē* (or plural *atai*): the "disaster of" (i.e., constituted by) "the marriage." And the

[35] *Trach.* 1082; *Phil.* 705; cf. *Ant.* 1097.

[36] *Aj.* 307. Cf. *Trach.* 1002 and *OT* 1283, where groaning, *atē*, death, and shame, "the names of all evils," touch Oedipus' house.

[37] E.g., the chorus might mean "Alas for my blindness" at *Aj.* 911–12, but is more likely to mean "Alas for my disaster." Creon's fate is "not an *allotria atē*: he himself erred" (*Ant.* 1260). Despite intricacies of possible relationship (in a post-Aristotelian reader's mind) between *atē* and *hamartanō* in tragedy (Bremer 1969:99–172), *atē* here could simply mean "disaster." The disaster is due only to Creon: he was "wrong." So they may be saying. On the other hand, this is *Antigone*, which does seem to summon the specter of the *atē*-sequence.

[38] *El.* 235, which we should read in the context also of *El.* 224: she will not contain "these *atai*" in her *deina* (her wretched sufferings). Here *atai* seems to mean "expressions of grief." The feeling and its expression are both *atai*. The complexities of Sophocles' usage of singular and plural come into play here: the chorus warns her not to beget *atē* in addition to *atai*. But throughout 220–33, *atē* (in both sing. and pl.) could be translated "grief."

[39] *El.* 1298; *Aj.* 976; *Trach.* 1274.

[40] *Aj.* 146; *Il.* 12.338, 17.424–25, 14.60.

[41] *Il.* 8.509, 20.156.

daughters of that marriage, Ismene and Antigone, part of its disastrous results, are "two *atē*'s," "twin disasters," to their father or uncle.[42] A person, or relationship, can embody "disaster" to others.

Especially at Thebes. Of Sophocles' extant plays, the exceptional use of *atē* is *Antigone*'s third choral song,[43] Sophocles' so-called "*atē*-lied," or "*atē*-hymn": the play's spiritual heart.[44] In this song, "god" (*theos*) "drives *phrenes* to *atē*." Nothing comes to mortal life "without *atē*." *Atē* is divinely inflicted, but humanly generative, the cumulatively harmful consequence of wrongdoing.[45] When god drives your mind towards it, "bad seems good" to you. In this play alone Sophocles uses *atē* to press fiercely upon the play's central issue, questioning where "god" is in human acts and feelings. It is true both that god drives your mind to *atē* and that your *atē* is "your own, no one else's."[46] The ode radiates the *atē*-sequence out through its play: coloring, explaining, its disasters.

Is this song *atē*'s climax, in its semantic history? Or its Indian summer, a later, archaizing flowering of its earlier significances, Homeric and archaic?[47]

I do not think we need to ask. The *atē*-sequence was not dead but sleeping: and was also enshrined in the form of tragedy itself. It could be woken. Aeschylus began a trend toward thinning the meaning of the word *atē*. Sophocles continues this. But here, at need, he invokes the *atē*-sequence in its complexity and ambiguity.[48]

Antigone apart, *atē*'s core meaning in Sophocles is simple, concrete "disaster." Plus, sometimes, its physical results or human embodiment: your resultant anguish, or your expression of pain.

---

[42] *Atē*, a "disaster that is marriage": from Jocasta's (and Antigone's) viewpoint at *Ant.* 862; from Oedipus's viewpoint at *OC* 526. The daughters are "two *ata*" to Oedipus because of the incest, to Creon because they upset his house: *OC* 532, *Ant.* 533.

[43] *Ant.* 582–626.

[44] So Dawe 1968:118–23. Important discussions of it include Müller ed. *ad loc.*; Lloyd-Jones 1957:16–23; Segal 1964; Stallmach 1968:23, 50; Bremer 1969:141–43; Easterling 1978; Winnington-Ingram 1980:165–72.

[45] *Ant.* 623, 614, 624, 584.

[46] *Ant.* 623, 1259.

[47] Vos 1971, documenting approaches to tragic *atē*, stresses that *atē* is a poetic word. Dawe 1968:95 says the ode is abnormal in *atē*'s "decline of vigour"; see Winnington-Ingram 1980:161 n. 25.

[48] Sophocles' need for *atē* in this play is aesthetic as well as moral. *Erōs* in the 4th stasimon parallels *elpis* in the 3rd (cf. *Ant.* 788, 616; Stallmach 1968:23): both drag *phrenes* aside. Cf. *atē* in the 3rd stasimon vs. outrage (*lōbē*) in the 4th. The use of *atē* is interdependent with that of other daemonic agents. The play gives us the family misery in *atē* terms in line 4, Antigone's pronouncement on her family: "What is there in the fate we suffer that is not painful, shameful, or without *atē*?"

EURIPIDES: "DOOM," "DEATH," AND AGENT
OR INSTRUMENT OF DESTRUCTION

Euripides too heads for a simple core meaning: "calamity," "doom," "death."[49] The kind of thing colloquial English calls "a tragedy." Sometimes this has a human cause. Medea ensures her rival shall not escape *atē*; Helen causes Hecuba's *atē*; Hippolytus was not *aitos atēs*, responsible for Phaedra's tragedy.[50] Sometimes the cause is divine: *daimōn* hands out greater *atai* when angry.[51]

He too uses *atē* for a physical instrument or agent of destruction. The wooden horse, Helen, a poisoned coronet, are all *atē*. Like Sophocles, Euripides uses *atē* once of a Theban marriage: not of Oedipus, this time, but of his son Polyneices.[52] The use underlines tragedy's perception that human beings embody each other's destruction.

But, like Sophocles, Euripides can archaize when he wants, and revitalize *atē*'s Homeric and archaic weight. He too is writing against the edge of Aeschylus. Though his use of *atē* demonstrates his vision that human beings are each other's tragedy, he can also make *daimones* responsible for *atē*, especially when it involves inward or mental damage. The chorus, hearing what a bad state Phaedra is in, think this may be daemonic possession. But when they see her, interrogate the Nurse, hear how she refuses food, they ask if she is acting "from *atē* or in an attempt to die?" The most convincing translation of *atē* here would be "madness." It fits what Phaedra says of her earlier delirium: "I was mad, I fell by a daemon's *atē*."[53] Cadmus began the sequence of Theban crimes, but divinity egged him on. So a chorus says, in odd lyrics that embody a prayer to the very divinity they think responsible for the original crime:

> May we, may we be mothers happy in children!
> We pray to you, dear lady Pallas
> who conquered dragonblood
> with one stone thrown, and roused
> Cadmus's mind towards that act

[49] E.g., *Med.* 279; *IT* 148, 114; *HF* 1284. It is a motif of *Tro.*: e.g., 137, 163, 535, 1314. You "fall into" *atē* (*IA* 134). "Murder, death": *HF* 918, *Hec.* 688, *Ion* 1240, *IT* 226. "Mutilation, destruction": *Or.* 962.

[50] *Med.* 988; *Tro.* 137; *Hipp.* 1150.

[51] *Med.* 129–30.

[52] *Tro.* 535; *Andr.* 103; *Med.* 979 (cf. A. *Supp.* 530); *Phoen.* 343 (cf. *OC* 526, *Ant.* 862).

[53] *Hipp.* 241, 276. Castor attributes Orestes' murder to Apollo: Apollo ordained that the children become their mother's murderers (E. *El.* 1269, 1303–307). They are both grazed by ancestral *atē*. Electra shared her brother's deed and motive, so must share his punishment. *Atē* may be shorthand for the *atē*-sequence (cf. *dolion atan, Tro.* 530): inward cause of deserved punishment.

from which there rushed on this land
some *atē* of *daimones*, captures, seizings.[54]

Euripides underlines divine responsibility for past events that led to present *atē*. The Sphinx. The civil war. And Cadmus's crime. The singers, praying for personal happiness in their children (unlike unhappy Jocasta), suddenly address Athene "who" (the pivot) moved Cadmus's mind "towards that deed" from which the present disasters sprang (including those of Jocasta's children), represented by that final list of wild vague nouns. The goddess they petition for security is ultimate cause of the crime for which the land is punished. The poet calls up the *atē*-sequence (full daemonic baggage, stage 1, stage 2) as a revenant from past poetry. God caused the inward damage. God inflicts outward subsequent damage as punishment.

In another late play, Euripides connects *atai*, Aeschylus-like, with another "first crime."[55] Pelops murdered Myrtilus: hence the "groaning curse" on the house of Pelops. The *atai* "looked at" by successive generations are connected with human murderousness. Yet the citizens' current impulse to kill Orestes is also due to divine *phthonos* (angry envy).[56] This song interweaves divine jealousy and necessity with human murderousness. The family "look at" *atai*. *Atai* are both what this family "sees" and what other people, including the audience, "see" when they "look at" the family.

DISASTER: THE TRAGIC WEIGHT OF *ATĒ*

From what they inherited, Sophocles and Euripides concentrated on a thinned meaning: *atē* as "disaster." Sometimes they use *atē* in contexts redolent with *atē*-sequence. But even then, they usually use the actual word for the consequence: awful punishment for crime (though the context may also suggest a damaged mental state that caused it).

They sometimes use Aeschylus's *atē* images of yoking, striking, nets, sea waves, but not so fully, or explicitly. In Aeschylus, *atē* is conjured up by, or has association with, nets, hunting, yokes; bondage, a striking blow, a goad, a storm.[57] Sophocles implies yokes, nets, sea wave, or shipwreck, in his verbs or adjectives. We find a possibly daemonic *atē* in a complex song.[58] But archaic genealogical and harvest imagery, Homer's sense of

---

[54] *Phoen.* 1060–66.
[55] Cf. *prōtarchon atēn*, *Ag.* 1192.
[56] *Or.* 988, 997, 973.
[57] Nets: *PV* 1078, *Pers.* 110–11; hunting: *PV* 1072, *Pers.* 110; yokes: perhaps *Supp.* 530. Bondage: *Ag.* 1566–67; a striking blow: *Cho.* 467, perhaps *Ag.* 131; a goal: *Supp.* 110; a storm: *Ag.* 819, *Supp.* 470, *PV* 886.
[58] *Aj.* 123; E. fr. 285.10; *Med.* 988; *Tro.* 137; *Alc.* 91; *Ant.* 582–624.

"unconquered" *atē*, a *daimōn* in relation to other *daimones*, a countenance that glares at you, or Aeschylus's "swift," "inescapable" hound that fawns upon you: all these have disappeared.[59] At the same time, Sophocles and especially Euripides develop a concrete use of *atē* as agent or physical instrument of destruction. All this prunes *atē*'s resonances of generative harm in which gods are involved.

So we might call "disaster" the tragic weight of *atē*.[60] It has increasingly little daemonic resonance, becoming an etiolated word compared to the *atē* of Homer and lyric poets. It was not Euripides' fault the word lost its Homeric riches. It was nobody's fault. Or it was the fault of the genre.[61] But turn things the other way round: the richness of Homeric *atē* gave tragedy its structure (see Chapter 18) and, I think, its interest in madness.

It has been argued that *atē*'s shifts in accent mirror changes in Greek religious consciousness: away from attributing evil desire and consequent punishment to divinity.[62] Is *atē*'s tragic weight in fact the weight of the age, rather than the genre? Is "disaster" the general fifth-century understanding of *atē*?

We cannot tell. The evidence of fifth-century prose is practically useless. *Atē* appears mainly in poetry. In extant prose, Herodotus speaks of Solon (who often uses *atē* in his poems) on a theme relevant to tragic issues, "Call no one happy until his life ends." He compares "the great" to the lucky. The great "fall." The lucky man "may not be as strong as others at dealing with *atē* and desire, but luck keeps these away." Herodotus, recalling a lyric poet, uses *atē* in Homeric weight: evil desire, precipitating disastrous consequences. But Democritus uses it to mean "disaster": "bravery makes *atai* small," that is, mitigates disasters.[63]

Then there are the vases. Vase-painters contemporary with tragedy

---

[59] "Harvest" and genealogical imagery: *Pers.* 822; *Sept.* 601; *Ag.* 386, 770. "Hound": e.g., *Pers.* 110–11; *Ag.* 1230. "Swift": *Ag.* 1124; "glaring"; *Pers.* 1007; "inescapable": cf. *Supp.* 110, *Cho.* 339; related to other *daimones*: *Ag.* 1433, *Cho.* 383.

[60] Doyle 1984: chs. 5–7 divides "objective" from "subjective" *atē*. He tends to work from tragedy backwards, claiming that tragic *atē* has mainly his "objective" meaning, i.e., "disaster."

[61] Bremer 1969 thinks *atē* "a central category" in Aeschylus because it fits the theology, denoting "both the demonic constellation in which man is trapped and the evil brought about by man." He thinks *atē* present in Sophocles as a "comprehensive notion" against which *hamartia* is to be understood. Creon's *atē* both causes and is his "fall" (Bremer 1969:132, 139, 145). One of Bremer's quests is to map the relation between tragic *atē* (as he conceives it) and *hamartia* as Aristotle conceives it: see above, Chapter 18. But he invokes the concept *atē* when the word is often absent or used only in a concrete vague all-embracing sense ("death," "disaster"). He often omits other related images: e.g., madness, Erinyes. The Sophoclean lexicon offers more examples of the "death, disaster, ruin, calamity" meaning than any other.

[62] Stallmach 1969:4–8.

[63] Hdt. 1.32: see Müller 1956; Dem. fr. 213DK.

avoid picturing *atē* (see Chapter 18), though they represent all kinds of other personified inner states. Why?[64] Do they reflect tragedy's thinning of *atē*'s moral, daemonic resonance? Or does tragedy reflect an *age* bleaching *atē* of daemonic presence?

I cannot believe the poets' thinning and the painters' avoidance were caused by changes in religious sensibility. Vase-painters personify plenty of other daemonic forces. There are lashings of daemonic guilt, pollution, and terror, divinized and personified, in tragedy and outside it in society. I think *atē*'s falling-off, in the language, was due to the influence of tragedy. You cannot go on deploying *atē*-sequences in a genre that incarnates the thing. Especially when tragedy was also offering, in *atē*'s place, something more exotically, behaviorally specific. Madness.

[64] See Körte 1874:14–19, 46 (on S. fr. 592: human life is beset by *poikilomētides atai pēmatōn*, a "half-personification" according to Jebb/Pearson *ad loc.*); Dawe 1968:96 n. 10.

WORKS CITED

Adams, S. 1955. "The *Ajax* of Sophocles." *Phoenix* 9:93–110.

Alford, C. F. 1992. *The Psychoanalytic Theory of Greek Tragedy.* New Haven and London.

Allderidge, P. 1985. "Bedlam: Fact or Fantasy?" In Bynum, Porter, and Shepherd 1981a 2:17–33.

Anderson, J. 1970. *Military Theory and Practice in the Age of Xenophon.* Berkeley and Los Angeles.

Anderson, W. D. 1966. *Ethos and Education in Greek Music,* Cambridge, Mass.

Arendt, H. 1958. *The Human Condition.* Chicago.

Babb, L. 1951. *The Elizabethan Malady.* Michigan.

Barton, A. 1962. *Shakespeare and the Idea of the Play.* London.

Basset, S. E. 1919. "*DAIMŌN.*" *Classical Review* 33:134–38.

Bateson, G. 1973. *Steps to an Ecology of Mind.* St. Albans.

Becker, O. 1937. "Das Bild des Weges." *Hermes Einzelschriften* 4. Berlin.

Beier, A. L. 1985. *Masterless Men: The Vagrancy Problem in England 1560–1640.* London.

Berger, M. M., ed. 1978. *Beyond the Double Bind.* New York.

Berger, P., B. Berger, and H. Kellner. 1974. *The Homeless Mind.* Harmondsworth.

Berrios, G. E. 1985. "Obsessional Disorders during the Nineteenth Century: Terminological and Classificatory Issues." In Bynum, Porter, and Shepherd 1985a 1:166–87.

Bierl, A. F. 1991. "Dionysos und die griechische Tragödie: Politische und 'metatheatralische' Aspekte im Text." *Classica Monacensia* 1. Tübingen.

Birkbeck Hill, G., ed. 1888. *Boswell's Life of Johnson.* 6 vols. Oxford.

Birrell, A., ed. 1906. *Boswell's Life of Johnson.* 6 vols. London.

Blundell, M. W. 1989. *Helping Friends and Harming Enemies.* Cambridge.

Bolton, J.P.D. 1962. *Aristeas of Proconnesus.* Oxford.

Boorde, A. 1567. *A Compendyous Regimente or a Dyetary of Health.* London.

Borgeaud, P. 1988. *The Cult of Pan in Ancient Greece* [1979]. Trans. K. Atlass and J. Redfield. Chicago and London.

Borthwick, E. 1967. "Trojan Leap and Pyrrhic Dance in Euripides' *Andromache* 1129–41." *Journal of Hellenic Studies* 87:18–23.

Boyne, R. 1990. *Foucault and Derrida: The Other Side of Reason.* London.

Bradbrook, M. C. 1979. *Shakespeare the Craftsman* [1969]. Cambridge.

Bradley, A. C. 1911. *Shakespearian Tragedy* [1904]. London.

Bremer, J. M. 1969. *Hamartia.* Amsterdam.

Bremmer, J. 1983. *The Early Greek Concept of the Soul.* Princeton.

Brenk, F. 1977. "In Mist Apparelled: Religious Themes in Plutarch's *Moralia* and *Lives.*" *Mnemosyne* supp. 48. Leiden.

Brunius-Nilsson, E. 1955. *DAIMONIE: An Inquiry into a Mode of Apostrophe.* Uppsala.

Buffière, F. 1973. *Les mythes d' Homère*. Paris.

Burkert, W. 1972. *Lore and Science in Ancient Pythagoreanism*. Trans. E. Minar. Cambridge, Mass.

———. 1983. *Homo Necans* [1972]. Trans. P. Bing. Berkeley.

———. 1985. *Greek Religion* [1977]. Trans. J. Raffan. Oxford.

———. 1987. *Ancient Mystery Cults*. Cambridge, Mass., and London.

Buxton, R. 1982. *Persuasion in Greek Tragedy: A Study of "Peitho."* Cambridge.

Bynum, W. F. 1985. "The Nervous Patient in Eighteenth- and Nineteenth-Century Britain: The Psychiatric Origins of British Neurology." In Bynum, Porter, and Shepherd 1985a 1:89–102.

Bynum, W. F., R. Porter, and M. Shepherd, eds. 1985a. *The Anatomy of Madness: Essays in the History of Psychiatry*. 3 vols. London.

———. 1985b. Introduction to Bynum, Porter, and Shepherd 1985a 1:1–24.

Caldwell, R. S. 1989. *The Origin of the Gods: A Psycho-Analytic Study of Greek Theogonic Myth*. New York.

Campbell, L. 1961. *Shakespeare's Tragic Heroes* [1930]. Cambridge.

Carcopino, J. 1956. *De Pythagore aux Apôtres*. Paris.

Carpenter, T., and C. Faraone, eds. 1993. *Masks of Dionysus*. Ithaca and London.

Chadwick, O. 1968. *John Cassian*. 2d ed. Cambridge.

Chantraine, P. 1968. *Dictionnaire étymologique de la langue grèque*. Paris.

Clarke, B. 1975. *Mental Disorder in Earlier Britain*. Cardiff.

Claus, D. B. 1981. *Towards the Soul*. Yale.

Clément, C. 1983. *The Lives and Legends of Jacques Lacan*. Trans. A. Goldhammer. New York.

———. 1987. *The Weary Sons of Freud*. Tr. N. Ball. London.

———. 1989. *Opera or the Undoing of Women*. Tr. B. Wing. London.

Cole, S. G. 1993. "Voices from beyond the Grave: Dionysus and the Dead." In Carpenter and Faraone 1993: 276–95.

Coles, R. A. 1974. "A New Oxyrhynchus Papyrus: The Hypothesis of Euripides' *Alexandros*." *BICS* supp. 32.

Collinge, N. 1962. "Medical Terms and Clinical Attitudes in the Tragedians." *BICS* 9:43–55.

Conacher D. 1980. *Aeschylus' "Prometheus Bound": A Literary Commentary*. Toronto.

Dawe, R. 1968. "Some Reflections on Atē and Hamartia." *HSCP* 72:89–124.

Deacon, J., and J. Walker. 1601. *A summary answere to al the material points in any of Master Darel his bookes. More especiallie to that one booke of his, intitled, The doctrine of the possession and dispossession of demoniaks out of the word of God*. London.

Delatte, A. 1934. *Les conceptions de l'enthousiasme chez les philosophes présocratiques*. Paris.

Derrida, J. 1978. "*Cogito* and the Writing of Madness." Trans. A. Bass. In *Writing and Difference*, pp. 31–63. London.

Destree, J. 1914. *Hugo van der Goes*. Brussels and Paris.

Detienne, M. 1979. *Dionysus Slain*. Trans. M. and L. Muellner. Baltimore.

———. 1989. *Dionysus at Large* [1986]. Trans. A. Goldhammer. Cambridge, Mass., and London.

Detienne, M., and J-P. Vernant. 1978. *Cunning Intelligence in Greek Culture and Society*. Trans. J. Lloyd. Hassocks, Sussex.

Devereux, G. 1970. "The Psychotherapy Scene in Euripides' *Bacchae*." *Journal of Hellenic Studies* 90:35–48.

———. 1971. "The Psychosomatic Miracle of Iolaus: A Hypothesis." *La parola del passato* 138:167–94.

Devoto, G. 1940. *Storia della lingua di Roma*. Bologna.

Dodds, E. R. 1951. *The Greeks and the Irrational*. Berkeley.

———. 1965. *Pagan and Christian in an Age of Anxiety*. Cambridge.

Dover, Sir K. 1974. *Greek Popular Morality in the Time of Plato and Aristotle*. Oxford.

Dowden, K. 1989. *Death and the Maiden: Girls' Initiation Rites in Greek Mythology*. London and New York.

Doyle, R. E. 1984. *ATĒ: Its Use and Meaning*. New York.

Drury, N. 1989. *The Elements of Shamanism*. Dorset.

DuBois, P. 1991. *Torture and Truth*. New York and London.

Duport, J. 1660. *Homeric Gnomologia*. Cambridge.

Easterling, P. E. 1978. "The Second Stasimon of *Antigone*." In R. D. Dawe, J. Diggle, and P. E. Easterling, eds., *Dionysiaca*, pp. 144–58. Cambridge.

Eigen, J. P. 1985. "Intentionality and Insanity: What the 18th-Century Juror Heard." In Bynum, Shepherd, and Porter 1985 2:34–51.

Eliade, M. 1964. *Shamanism and Ancient Techniques of Ecstasy* [1951]. Trans. W. Trask. London.

Faraone, C. A. 1992. *Talismans and Trojan Horses: Guardian Statues in Ancient Greek Myth and Ritual*. Oxford.

Farnell, L. 1896–1909. *Cults of the Greek States*. 5 vols. Cambridge.

Felman, S. 1985. *Writing and Madness*. Cornell.

Ferrari, G. F. 1987. *Listening to the Cicadas*. Cambridge.

Flashar, H., ed. and trans. 1962. *Aristoteles*. Band 19, *Problemata Physica*. Berlin.

———. 1966. *Melancholie und Melancholiker in den medizinischen Theorien der Antike*. Berlin.

Foucault, M. 1971. *Madness and Civilization* [1961]. Trans. R. Howard. London.

———. 1979. "My Body, This Paper, This Fire." *Oxford Literary Review* 4, no. 7:9–28.

Fox, R. A. 1976. *The Tangled Chain: The Structure of Disorder in "The Anatomy of Melancholy."* Berkeley, Los Angeles, London.

Frame, D. 1978. *The Myth of Return in Early Greek Epic*. New Haven.

Gascoyne, D. 1938. *Hölderlin's Madness*. London.

Gilman, S. L. 1982. *Seeing the Insane*. New York.

Girard, R. 1977. *Violence and the Sacred* [1972]. Trans. P. Gregory. Baltimore and London.

Gokey, F. 1961. *The Terminology for the Devil and Evil Spirits in the Apostolic Fathers*. Washington, D.C.

Goldhill, S. 1986. *Reading Greek Tragedy*. Cambridge.

Goodwin, W. W. 1902. *A Greek Grammar*. Rev. ed. Boston.

Green, A. 1979. *The Tragic Effect: The Oedipus Complex in Tragedy* [1969]. Trans. A. Sheridan. Cambridge.

Green, H. 1964. *I Never Promised You a Rose Garden*. London.

Greenstadt, W. M. 1982. "Heracles: A Heroic Figure of the Rapprochement Crisis." *International Review of Psycho-Analysis* 9:1–24.

Groningen, B. van. 1960. *Pindare au banquet*. Leiden.

Grmek, M. D. 1989. *Diseases in the Ancient Greek World*. Trans. M. and L. Muellner. Baltimore and London.

Gruber, G. 1952. *Einführung in Geschichte und Geist der Medizin*. 4th ed. Stuttgart.

Gruber, J. 1963. "Über einige abstrakte Begriffe des frühen Griechischen." *Beiträge sur klassischen Philologie* 9. Meisenheim.

Hall, E. 1989. *Inventing the Barbarian: Greek Self-Definition through Tragedy*. Oxford.

Halliwell, S. 1986. *Aristotle's "Poetics."* London.

Handley, E. 1969. "Notes on the *Theophoroumene* of Menander." *BICS* 16:88–101.

Harriott, R. 1969. *Poetry and Criticism before Plato*. London.

Harrison, A.R.W. 1968. *The Law of Athens*. Vol. 1. Oxford.

Haslam, J. 1817. *Considerations on the Moral Management of the Insane*. Ed. R. Hunter. London.

Hawkes, C.F.C. 1977. "Pytheas: Europe and the Greek Explorers." J. L. Myres Memorial Lecture, New College, Oxford. Oxford.

Heaney, S. 1984. *Sweeney Astray*. London.

Henrichs, A. 1978. "Greek Maenadism from Olympias to Messalina." *HSCP* 82:121–60.

———. 1984. "Loss of self, Suffering, Violence: The Modern View of Dionysus from Nietzsche to Girard." *HSCP* 88: 205–40.

———. 1993. "He Has a God in Him: Human and Divine in the Modern Perception of Dionysus." In Carpenter and Faraone 1993:13–43.

Herzlich, C., and J. Pierrot. 1987. *Illness and Self in Society* [1984]. Trans. E. Forster. Baltimore and London.

Heusch, L. de. 1981. "Possession and Shamanism." In *Why Marry Her? Society and Symbolic Structures*, pp. 151–64. Trans. J. Lloyd. Cambridge.

Holmes, R. 1986. *Footsteps: Adventures of a Romantic Biographer* [1985]. Harmondsworth.

House, H. 1961. *Aristotle's "Poetics."* London.

Howard, D. R. 1974. "Renaissance World-Alienation." In Kinsman 1974a:47–76.

Ibsen, H. 1957. *Ghosts*. Trans. W. Archer. In S. Barnet, M. Berman, and W. Burto, eds., *Eight Great Tragedies*. New York.

Ingram, A. 1991. *The Madhouse of Language*. London.

Jarman, A.O.H. 1960. *The Legend of Merlin*. Cardiff.

Jones, J. 1971 [1962]. *On Aristotle and Greek Tragedy*. London.

Jung, C. G. 1967. "Alchemical Studies." *Collected Works*. Vol. 13. Trans. R.F.C. Hall. London and New York.

Jung, E., and M-L. von Kranz. 1971. *The Grail Legend*. Trans. A. Dykes. London.

Just, R. 1989. *Women in Athenian Law and Life*. London.

Kagarov, E. V. 1934. "Shamanstvo i proyavlenie ekstaza v grecheskoi i rimskoi religii." *Proceedings of the Soviet Academy of Sciences, Social Sciences Division* 5:387–401.

Kaiser, W. 1963. *Praisers of Folly*. Harvard.

Kamerbeek, J. 1948. "On the Conception of *Theomachos* in Relation with Greek Tragedy." *Mnemosyne* 4, no. 1:271–83.

Kerenyi, C. 1976. *Dionysus*. Trans. R. Mannheim. London.

King, W.F.H. 1904. *A Dictionary of Classical and Foreign Quotations*. London.

Kinsman, R., ed., 1974. *The Darker Vision of the Renaissance*. Berkeley, Los Angeles, London.

————. 1974b. Introduction to Kinsman 1974a:1–23.

————. 1974c. "Folly, Melancholy, and Madness: A Study in Shifting Styles of Medical Analysis and Treatment, 1450–1675." In Kinsman 1974a:273–320.

Kirk, G., J. Raven, and M. Schofield. 1983. *The Presocratic Philosophers*. 2d ed. Cambridge.

Klauser, T. 1963. "Das Sirenenabenteuer des Odysseus—ein Motiv der christlichen Grabkunst?" *Jahrbuch für Antike und Christentum* 6:71–100.

Klein, M. 1963. *Our Adult World and Other Essays*. London.

Klibansky, R., E. Panofsky, and F. Saxl. 1964. *Saturn and Melancholy*. London.

Knox, B. 1964. *The Heroic Temper*. Berkeley and London.

Kollmann, A. 1941. "Sophrosyne." *Wiener Studien* 59:12–94.

Körte, G. 1874. *Über Personificationen psychologischer Affekte in der späteren Vasenmalerei*. Berlin.

Kristeva, J. 1989. *Black Sun: Depression and Melancholia* [1987]. Trans. L. S. Roudiez. New York.

Kudlien, F. 1973. "Schwärzliche Organe im frühgriechischen Denken." *Medizin historisches Journal* 8:53–58.

Ladner, G. 1967. "Homo Viator." *Speculum* 42:233–59.

Laing. R. D. 1965. *The Divided Self* [1959]. Harmondsworth.

————. 1971. *Self and Others* [1961]. Harmondsworth.

Latte, K. 1920–21. "Schuld und Sünde in der griechischen Religion." *Archiv für Religionswissenchaft* 20:254–98.

Lefkowitz, M. 1981. *Heroines and Hysterics*. London.

Leibrand, W., and A. Wettley. 1961. *Der Wahnsinn*. Freiburg.

Lesky, A. 1961. *Göttliche und menschliche Motivation im homerischen Epos*. Heidelberg.

Leumann, M. 1950. *Homerische Wörter*. Basel.

Lewis, I. M. 1986. *Religion in Cult and Context*. Cambridge.

————. 1989. *Ecstatic Religions: A Study of Shamanism and Spirit Possession* [1971]. 2d ed. London and New York.

Lincoln, B. 1975. "Homeric *Lussa*: Wolfish Rage." *Indogermanische Forschungen* 80:98–105.

Linforth, I. M. 1946a. "The Corybantic Rites in Plato." *University of California Publications in Classical Philology* 13, no. 5:121–62.

————. 1946b. "Telestic Madness in Plato, *Phaedrus* 244D–E." *University of California Publications in Classical Philology* 13, no. 6:163–72.

Lippman, E. 1964. *Musical Thought in Ancient Greece*. New York.

Lloyd, G.E.R. 1979. *Magic, Reason, and Experience*. Cambridge.

Lloyd-Jones, H. 1957. "Notes on Sophocles' *Antigone*." *Classical Quarterly* 7:12–27.

Löffler, I. 1963. "Die Melampodie." *Beiträge zur klassischen Philologie* 7. Meisenheim.

Lonsdale, S. 1993. *Dance and Ritual Play in Greek Religion*. Baltimore and London.

MacDonald, M. 1981. *Mystical Bedlam: Madness, Anxiety and Healing in Seventeenth-Century England*. Cambridge.

Majno, G. 1975. *The Healing Hand*. Harvard.

Mandelshtam, O. 1991. *Selected Poems*. Trans. J. Greene. London.

Mani, N. 1959. *Die Vorstellungen über Anatomie, Physiologie und Pathologie der Leber in der Antike*. Basel.

Martin Clarke, D., ed. and trans. 1923. *The Hávamál*. Cambridge.

Mattes, J. 1970. *Der Wahnsinn im griechischen Mythos und in der Dichtung bis zum Drama des fünften Jahrhunderts*. Heidelberg.

Meillier, C. 1980. "Un cas médical dans une inscription funéraire." *ZPE* 38:98.

Meuli, K. 1935. "Scythica." *Hermes* 70:121–76.

Moll, H. 1976. *Identity and the Sacred*. Oxford.

Mourelatos, A. 1970. *The Route of Parmenides*. New Haven and London.

Müller, G. 1956. "Der homerische Ate-Begriff und Solons Musenelegie." *Navicula Chiloniensis: Studia Philologica F. Jacoby*, pp. 1–15. Leiden.

Müri, W. 1953. "Melancholie und Schwarze Galle." *Museum Helveticum* 10:21–38.

Murray, P. 1981. "Poetic Inspiration in Early Greece." *Journal of Hellenic Studies* 101:87–100.

Nisbet, R. 1966. *The Sociological Tradition*. New York.

O'Brien-Moore, A. 1924. *Madness in Ancient Literature*. Weimar.

O'Keefe, J. G., trans. and ed. 1952. *Buile Suibhne* [1913]. Irish Texts Society. London.

Ortner, S. B. 1974. "Is Female to Male as Nature Is to Culture." In Rosaldo and Lamphere 1974:67–87.

Otto, W. 1965. *Dionysus, Myth and Cult* [1933]. Trans. R. B. Palmer. Bloomington and London.

Padel, R. 1981. "Madness in Fifth-Century Athenian Tragedy." In P. Heelas and A. Lock, eds., *Indigenous Psychologies: The Anthropology of the Self*, pp. 105–31. London.

———. 1983. "Women: Model for Possession by Greek Daemons." In A. Cameron and A. Kuhrt, eds., *Images of Women in Antiquity*, pp. 3–19. London.

———. 1985. "Homer's Reader: A Reading of George Seferis," *PCPS* 211 (n.s. 31):74–132.

———. 1990a. "Between Theory and Fiction: Reflections on Feminism and Classical Scholarship." *Gender and History*, 2, no. 2:198–211.

———. 1990b. "Making Space Speak." In Zeitlin and Winkler 1990:336–65.

———. 1992. *In and Out of the Mind: Greek Images of the Tragic Self*. Princeton.

———. 1994. "George Steiner and the Greekness of Tragedy." In N. Scott and R. Sharp, eds., *Reading George Steiner*, pp. 99–133. Baltimore.

———. (Forthcoming). *Mad, Possessed, and Female*.

Parke, H. W., and D.E.W. Wormell. 1956. *The Delphic Oracle*. 2 vols. Oxford.

Parker, R. 1983. *Miasma*. Oxford.

Pigeaud, J. 1981. *La maladie de l'âme*. Paris.

Poliakoff, M. 1992. "Vergil and the Heart of Darkness." *Arion* 3d ser. 2, no. 1:73–97.

Porter, R. 1983. "In the Eighteenth Century, Were English Lunatic Asylums Total Institutions?" *Ego* 4:12–34.

———. 1985. "'The Hunger of Imagination': Approaching Samuel Johnson's Melancholy." In Bynum, Porter, and Shepherd 1985a 1:63–88.

———. 1987. *Mind-Forg'd Manacles*. London.

———. 1988. Introduction to *Illustrations of Madness* [1810]. By J. Haslam. London.

Porzig, W. 1923. "DAIMŌN." *Indogermanische Forschungen* 41:169–80.

Quétel, C. 1990. *The History of Syphilis*. Trans. J. Braddock and B. Pike. New Brunswick and London.

Rankin, A. V. 1974. "Euripides' Hippolytus: A Psychopathological Hero." *Arethusa* 7:71–94.

Rayfield, D. 1991. Introduction to Mandelshtam 1991:xxv–xlii.

Ribbert, M. 1899. *Die Lehre von Wesen der Krankheiten in ihrer geschichtlichen Entwicklung*. Bonn.

Rohde, E. 1925. *Psyche*. Trans. W. B. Hillis. London.

Rosaldo, M. Z., and L. Lamphere, eds. 1974. *Women, Culture, and Society*. Stanford.

Rudnytsky, P. L. 1987. *Freud and Oedipus*. New York.

Russell, B. 1956. *Portraits from Memory*. London.

Rütten, T. 1992. "Demokrit: Lachender Philosoph und Sanguinischer Melancholiker." *Mnemosyne* supp. 118. Leiden.

Rycroft, C. 1968a. *Anxiety and Neurosis*. London.

———. 1968b. *A Critical Dictionary of Psychoanalysis*. London.

Salkeld, D. 1993. *Madness and Drama in the Age of Shakespeare*. Manchester.

Schiesari, J. 1992. *The Gendering of Melancholia*. Ithaca, N.Y.

Schleiner, W. 1991. *Melancholy, Genius, and Utopia in the Renaissance*. Wolfenbütteler Abhandlungen zur Renaissanceforschung, Band 10. Wiesbaden.

Schlesier, R. 1993. "Mixtures of Masks: Maenads as Tragic Models." In Carpenter and Faraone 1993:89–114.

Schoener, E. 1964. Das Viererschema in der Antiken Humoralpathologie. *Sudhoffs Arch. Gesch. Med. Naturw.*, sp. 4. Wiesbaden.

Schwyzer, E. 1923. *Dialectorum Graecarum exempla epigraphica potiora*. Leipzig.

Scodel, R. 1980. "The Trojan Trilogy of Euripides." *Hypomnemata* 60. Göttingen.

Scott, A. C. 1982. *Actors are Madmen: Notebook of a Theatergoer in China*. Wisconsin.

Screech, M. A. 1980. *Erasmus and the "Praise of Folly."* London.

———. 1985. "Good Madness in Christendom." In Bynum, Porter, and Shepherd 1985a 1:25–39.

———. 1991. *Montaigne and Melancholy* [1983]. Harmondsworth.

Seaford, R. 1981. "Dionysiac Drama and the Dionysiac Mysteries." *Classical Quarterly* 31:252–75.

———. 1993. "Dionysus as Destroyer of the Household: Homer, Tragedy, and the Polis." In Carpenter and Faraone 1993:115–46.

Séchan, L. 1926. *Etudes sur la tragédie grecque dans ses rapports avec la céramique*. Paris.

Segal, C. 1964. "Sophocles' Praise of Man and the Conflicts of the *Antigone*." *Arion* 3, no. 2:46–66.

Segal, C. 1982. *Dionysiac Poetics and Euripides' Bacchae*. Princeton.

Seiler, H. J. 1954. "Homerisch *aaomai* und *atē*." *Festschrift A. Debrunner*, pp. 409–17. Bern.

Sheridan. A. 1980. *Michel Foucault: The Will to Truth*. London.

Showalter, E. 1987. *The Female Malady: Women, Madness and English Culture, 1830–1980* [1985]. London and New York.

Silk, M. 1974. *Interaction in Poetic Imagery*. Cambridge.

Simon, B. 1978. *Mind and Madness in Ancient Greece*. Cornell.

Skultans, V. 1975. *Madness and Morals: Ideas on Insanity in the Nineteenth Century*. London.

Smith, W. D. 1965. "So-called Possession in Pre-Christian Greece." *TAPA* 96:403–26.

———, ed. and trans. 1990. *Hippocrates: Pseudepigraphic Writings*. Leiden.

Snell, B. 1978. "Der Weg zum Denken und zur Wahrheit: Studien zur frühgriechischen Sprache." *Hypomnemata* 57. Göttingen.

Snyder, S. 1965. "The Left Hand of God: Despair in the Mediaeval and Renaissance Tradition." *Studies in the Renaissance* 12:18–59.

Sokolowski, F., ed. 1962. *Lois sacrées des Cités grecques*, Supplement. Paris.

Spencer, T. 1962. "Greeks and 'Merrygreeks': A background to *Timon of Athens* and *Troilus and Cressida*." In R. Hosley, ed., *Essays on Shakespeare and Elizabethan Drama in Honor of Hardin Craig*, pp. 223–33. Columbia, Mo.

Spiro, M. E. 1993. *Oedipus in the Trobriands* [1982]. 2d ed. Chicago.

Stallmach, J. 1968. "*Atē*: zur Frage des Selbst- und Welterstandnisses des frühgriechischen Menschen." *Beiträge zur klassischen Philologie* 18. Meisenheim.

Stanford, W. B. 1954. *The Ulysses Theme*. Oxford.

———. 1983. *Greek Tragedy and the Emotions*. London.

Starobinski, J. 1960. "Geschichte der Melancholiebehandlung von den Anfängen bis 1900." Documenta Geigy, *Acta Psychosomatica* 4.

Steiner, G. 1961. *The Death of Tragedy*. London.

———. 1981. "Narcissus and Echo: A Note on Current Arts of Reading." *American Journal of Semiotics* 1, no. 2:1–14.

———. 1990. "A Note on Absolute Tragedy." *Journal of Literature and Theology* 4, no. 2:147–56.

Steiner, J. 1985. "Turning a Blind Eye: The Cover-up for Oedipus." *International Review of Psycho-Analysis* 12:161–72.

———. 1990. "The Retreat from Truth to Omnipotence in Sophocles' *Oedipus at Colonus*." *The International Review of Psycho-Analysis* 17:227–37.

Stinton, T.C.W. 1990. "*Hamartia* in Aristotle and Greek Tragedy." In *Collected Papers on Greek Tragedy*, pp. 143–85. Oxford.

Tambornino, J. 1909. *De antiquorum daemonismo*. Giessen.

Taplin, O. 1978. *Greek Tragedy in Action*. London.

Temkin, O. 1985. "Hippocrates as the Physician of Democritus." *Gesnerus* 42:455–64.

Theodorou, Z. 1993. "Subject to Emotion: Exploring Madness in *Orestes*." *Classical Quarterly* 43:32–46.

Timken-Zinkann, R. F. 1968. "Black Bile: A Review of Recent Attempts to Trace the Origin of the Teaching on Melancholia to Medical Observations." *Medical History* 12:288–92.

Tolstoy, N. 1985. *The Quest for Merlin*. London.

Tuchman, B. 1978. *A Distant Mirror*. London.

Untersteiner, M. 1939. "Il concetto di *DAIMŌN* in Omero." *Atena e Roma* 7:93–115.

Vandvik, E. 1942. "Ajax the Insane." *Symbolae Osloenses* supp. 11:169–75.

Vellacott, P. 1971. *Sophocles and Oedipus: A Study of the "Oedipus Tyrannus" of Sophocles with a New Translation*. London.

———. 1978. "Oedipus at Colonus: An Alternative View." Unpublished paper.

Vernant, J-P. 1980. *Myth and Society in Ancient Greece*. Trans. J. Lloyd. London.

———. 1981. "Oedipus without the Complex." In Vernant and Vidal-Naquet 1981:63–86.

Vernant, J.-P., and P. Vidal-Naquet. 1981. *Tragedy and Myth in Ancient Greece*. Trans. J. Lloyd. Brighton, Sussex.

Vickers, N. J. 1982. "Diana Described: Scattered Woman and Scattered Rhyme." In E. Abel, ed., *Writing and Sexual Difference*, pp. 95–104. Chicago.

Vitebsky, P. 1993. *Dialogues with the Dead: The Discussion of Mortality among the Sora of Eastern India*. Cambridge.

Vlastos, G. 1973. *Platonic Studies*. Princeton.

———. 1975. *Plato's Universe*. Seattle.

———. 1991. *Socrates, Ironist and Moral Philosopher*. Cambridge.

Vos, H. 1971. Review of Stallmach 1968. *Mnemosyne* 24:408–409.

Walcott, D. 1990. *Omeros*. New York.

Walker, N. 1968. *Crime and Insanity in England*. Vol. 1, *The Historical Perspective*. Edinburgh.

Watanabe-O'Kelly, H. 1978. *Melancholie und die melancholische Landschaft*. Basle Studien zur deutschen Sprache und Literatur, vol. 54. Bern.

Webster, T.B.L. 1970. *The Greek Chorus*. London.

Welsford, E. 1935. *The Fool: His Social and Literary History*. London.

Wenzel, S. 1968. "The Seven Deadly Sins: Some Problems of Research." *Speculum* 43:1–22.

Williams, B. 1993. *Shame and Necessity*. Berkeley.

Wilson, P., and O. Taplin. 1993. "The 'Aetiology' of Tragedy in the *Oresteia*." *PCPS* 39:169–80.

Winnington-Ingram, R. P. 1980. *Sophocles: An Interpretation*. Cambridge.

Wittkower, R. 1963. *Born under Saturn*. London.

Zeitlin, F. 1990. "Thebes: Theater of Self and Society in Athenian Drama." In Zeitlin and Winkler 1990:130–67.

———. 1992. "The Politics of Eros in the Danaid Trilogy of Aeschylus." In R. Hexter and D. Selden, eds., *Innovations of Antiquity*, pp. 204–52. New York and London.

Zeitlin, F., and J. Winkler, eds. 1990. *Nothing to Do with Dionysos?* Princeton.

Zijderveld, C. 1934. *Teletē: Bijdragen tot de kennis der religieuse terminologie in het Grieksch*. Utrecht.

INDEX

Aeschylus, Euripides, Homer, and Sophocles appear here if they are mentioned in the main text, but not their works. For individual scenes, check the names of characters.